*A *CHICAGO TRIB* F 2009*

Praise for *Masters of Sex*

"Told with patience and care . . . Maier writes well, and with humor."

—*New York Times*

"Maier's illuminating biography delves into the lives of the couple that started science's sexual revolution." —*Discover*

"Absorbing . . . *Masters of Sex* is this spring's true must-read book for those looking to revisit the heady, early days of the sexual revolution."

—*The American Prospect*

"Award-winning biographer Maier . . . delivers the first in-depth look at a complex couple who helped revolutionize the study of human sexual response. Academics and amateur sexperts alike will rejoice."

Library Journal

"A wo at an amazing coupl —*Booklist*

"Perha *sters of Sex* . . . may st graphy, but this unsettling story of sex and science in theory and practice is ultimately more cautionary than titillating." —*O, The Oprah Magazine*

"Writing a readable but serious biography of Masters and Johnson was no easy task. The natural impulse is to drain such passionate clinicality of personality and leave a hollow crusade in its place. Maier's book resists it constantly. It's about heroes and flaws and a couple of people whose lives underlay a good half of what we know *for sure* about what we all think we know so much."

—*The Buffalo News* ("Editor's Choice")

"*Masters of Sex* is a terrific book about the unlikely couple who touched off the sexual revolution. More than a biography, this is an intimate history of sex in the twentieth century."

—Debby Applegate, winner of the 2007 Pulitzer Prize in Biography for *The Most Famous Man in America: The Biography of Henry Ward Beecher*

"Thomas Maier has written the intimate, engaging biography that Masters and Johnson deserve. Critics often accused the pair of 'dehumanizing' sex with their research—of removing its mystery. But as Gini Johnson told *Playboy* in 1968, mystery is just another name for superstition and myth. The more we know about the physiology of arousal, the better we can enjoy the uniquely human experience of sex for pleasure. Masters and Johnson showed tremendous courage in their research."

—Hugh Hefner, editor in chief, *Playboy* magazine

"No novelist could come up with something as remarkable as the real life story of William Masters and Virginia Johnson, the married experts giving advice to America on sex and love. With insightful reporting and writing, Thomas Maier has captured this extraordinary relationship between these male and female sex researchers, a legacy that transformed the way couples live today."

—Dr. Ruth K. Westheimer

"The subject of this book—sex and love—should interest just about everyone. As a bonus, Thomas Maier is a very fine writer, an accomplished biographer, and an astute reporter. If you read only one biography this year, it should be this first-ever look at the secretive lives of Masters and Johnson."

—Nelson DeMille, bestselling author of *The Gold Coast* and *The Gate House*

"A well-written and insightful account of Masters and Johnson, who, in a clinical sense, probably knew more about sex and marital love than any other couple in America."

—Gay Talese, author of *Thy Neighbor's Wife* and *A Writer's Life*

"It's hard to imagine any sex researcher or serious student of sexuality who wouldn't profit from reading this book. The information revealed in *Masters of Sex* has never surfaced before—and besides being a real contribution to the history of science, it's a totally captivating read!"

—Pepper Schwartz, Ph.D., past president of the Society for the Scientific Study of Sexuality, and author of *Prime: Adventures and Advice About Sex, Love and the Sensual Years*

Masters of Sex

Also by Thomas Maier

The Kennedys: America's Emerald Kings

Dr. Spock: An American Life

Newhouse: All the Glitter, Power and Glory of America's Richest Media Empire and the Secretive Man Behind It

Masters of Sex

The Life and Times of
William Masters and Virginia Johnson,
the Couple Who Taught America
How to Love

THOMAS MAIER

BASIC BOOKS
A Member of the Perseus Books Group
New York

Hardcover first published in 2009 by Basic Books,
A Member of the Perseus Books Group
Paperback first published in 2010 by Basic Books
Updated paperback first published in 2013 by Basic Books

The photographs in this book are reproduced by permission.
Page vii: "William Masters and Virginia Johnson": courtesy of the Photographic Services Collection, University Archives, Department of Special Collections, Washington University Libraries.
Pages 169, 239: "Masters and Johnson with *Human Sexual Response*," "Masters and Johnson on *Meet the Press*": copyright © Bettmann/CORBIS.
Insert photos: "The Human Touch," "A Sex Therapy Better Than Freud," "Master Doctor," "Bill and Gini": courtesy of the Photographic Services Collection, University Archives, Department of Special Collections, Washington University Libraries. "Unmarried Researchers," "Remembrances": Leonard McCombe, Time & Life Pictures, Getty Images. "Feminist": Becker Medical Library, Washington University School of Medicine. "Couple of the Year": courtesy of the editors of TIME Magazine copyright © 2008. "Lost Loves": from the personal files of Robert C. Kolodny, M.D.

Books published by Basic Books are available at special discounts for bulk purchases in the United States by corporations, institutions, and other organizations. For more information, please contact the Special Markets Department at the Perseus Books Group, 2300 Chestnut Street, Suite 200, Philadelphia, PA 19103, or call (800) 810-4145, ext. 5000, or e-mail special.markets@perseusbooks.com.

Designed by Pauline Brown
Set in 11.5 point Garamond

The Library of Congress has catalogued the hardcover as follows:
Maier, Thomas, 1956–
Masters of sex : the life and times of William Masters and Virginia Johnson, the couple who taught America how to love / Thomas Maier.
p. cm.
Includes bibliographical references and index.
ISBN 978-0-465-00307-5 (alk. paper)
1. Masters, William H. 2. Johnson, Virginia E. 3. Sexologists—Biography.
4. Sexology—Research—History. I. Title.

HQ18.3.M35 2009
306.7092'273—dc22
[B]
2008050803

ISBN 978-0-465-07999-5 (rev. paperback)
ISBN 978-0-465-02040-9 (paperback)
ISBN 978-0-7867-4451-0 (e-book)

10 9 8 7 6 5 4 3 2 1

For my godparents,
June and William Underwood.

"The profoundest of all our sensualities is the sense of truth."

—D. H. Lawrence

William Masters and Virginia Johnson

Contents

PHASE FOUR

Preface

"What is this thing called love?"
—Cole Porter

Sex, in all its glorious expressions, has been an integral part of the American experience in my four biographies—respectively, about Si Newhouse, Benjamin Spock, the Kennedys, and now Masters and Johnson. As Dr. Spock, the best-selling expert who raised America's baby-boom generation, once told me with disarming honesty, "*Everything* is about sex!" Indeed, at its most powerful and transcendent, sex is about the progression of the species, the origin of self-identity, and the most intimate form of expression between adults.

The story of William Masters and Virginia Johnson, as perhaps none other, deals directly with the eternal mysteries of sex and love. Their public life provides an unparalleled window into America's sexual revolution and its historic cultural changes still with us today, while their private relationship mirrors many of the most basic desires, tensions, and contradictions between men and women. I first interviewed Dr. Masters when he retired in December 1994, already showing symptoms of Parkinson's disease, which would lead to his death in 2001. After several false starts, I gained the complete cooperation of Virginia Johnson in 2005, conducting many hours of interviews, including a lengthy visit to her St. Louis home. Despite worldwide fame, "we were absolutely the two most secretive people on the face of the earth," Johnson confided. "There's simply no one who knew us well. People have a lot of speculation, but they don't know."

For years, the work of Masters and Johnson remained shrouded in strict confidentiality as a result of their own desire to avoid public scrutiny. Only now—with the willingness of many to be interviewed and access to their letters, internal documents, and Masters's own unpublished memoir—can we fully consider their remarkable life and times. For all of the clinical knowledge they gained from America's biggest sex experiment—involving hundreds of women and men and more than ten thousand orgasms—their story is very much about the elusiveness and indefinable aspects of human intimacy. As many today still ask themselves, "What is this thing called love?"

—T.M.
Long Island, New York
APRIL 2009

PHASE ONE

Gini as a young girl

CHAPTER ONE

Golden Girl

"It often begins in the back seat of a parked car. It's hurry up and get the job done. The back seat of a car hardly provides an opportunity for the expression of personality."

—WILLIAM H. MASTERS

Into the dark, two beams of light showed the way. The piercing headlights from a Plymouth automobile cut a path through the unrelenting blackness of the Missouri countryside. Slowly the car carrying Mary Virginia Eshelman and her high school boyfriend, Gordon Garrett, rumbled down Route 160, a vast asphalt stretch without street lamps, where only the stars and moon lit the evening sky.

For his date with Mary Virginia, Gordon borrowed the brand-new Garrett family car—a green 1941 sedan with a shiny chrome grill, protruding hood ornament, muscular fenders, and an ample backseat. They motored past rows of homesteads and crops, carved from the tallgrass prairie. That evening, they joined friends at The Palace, the town's only theater, where the melodies and dancing of Hollywood musicals let them escape Golden City's dullness. Newsreels made them aware of another larger world outside their tiny hometown of eight hundred people. Bordering the Ozark Mountains, Golden City seemed closer to rural Oklahoma than big-city St. Louis—both in dirt miles and in Bible-thumping spirit.

Before heading home, Gordon turned the Plymouth off the road and dimmed its lights. Noise from the tires, pressing loudly against the gravel stones, suddenly came to a halt, followed by a palpable hush. Snuggled beside each other, Mary Virginia and her boyfriend parked in a secluded area where they would not be spotted.

In the front seat of the car, Gordon opened her blouse, loosened her skirt, and pressed himself against her skin. She didn't move or resist, just stared at him in wonderment. Mary Virginia never had seen a penis before except, as she later remembered it, when her mother changed her baby brother's diaper. On that night, shortly after her fifteenth birthday, Mary Virginia Eshelman—later known to the world as Virginia E. Johnson—was introduced to the mysteries of human intimacy. "I didn't know anything about anything," confessed the woman whose landmark partnership with Dr. William H. Masters would someday become synonymous with sex and love in America.

In her puritanical Midwest home, Mary Virginia learned sex was sinful, something far removed from the breathless tales of storybook romance she imbibed at the movies before World War II. Like many women of her generation, she learned that sex, at best, was a thankless chore, better left for the confines of marriage and bearing a family. Years afterward, she'd refer to Gordon Garrett anonymously as the "boy with fiery red hair." She masked his identity just as she concealed any unpleasant truth about her life, any memory of love that eluded her. As she admitted decades later, "I never married the men I really cared about." But she would never forget Gordon Garrett, or that night outside of Golden City, when the two teens lost their innocence.

Along the roadside, the young couple huddled in shadows, necking in the front seat until they slid into the back. Heavy breathing fogged the windows. Automobiles, still new to a place like Golden City, provided a relatively private place to be alone. Gordon pulled the clutch brake to make sure the family's parked car didn't roll away while their attention wandered elsewhere.

Throughout high school, Mary Virginia shared many moments growing up with Gordon. About six feet tall with a farm boy's physique, he was rugged enough to play on the school's football team but sensitive to Mary Virginia's finer interest in music. They were a steady couple during senior year, constantly seen together. Gordon was her beau.

After skipping two grades, Mary Virginia found herself considerably younger than the rest of her Golden City High School class, including the redheaded Garrett boy, already turned seventeen. Eager to please, she possessed light-brown hair bundled in corkscrew curls, empathetic gray-blue eyes, and demure, slightly pursed lips. She usually wore an enigmatic Mona Lisa–like grin, which could easily burst into an engaging smile. Like other Eshelmans, she had the distinctive bone structure of high cheekbones, an upright posture, and perfectly poised shoulders. Mary Virginia's willowy frame suggested enough of a bosom to make her seem mature, though in their assessment some boys could be downright mean. "She was a tall, slim, flat-chested girl," remembered Phil Lollar, then a slightly younger fellow who lived near her farm. "Just an average-looking girl." But most teenagers in Golden City admired Mary Virginia's sense of style in a place sorely in need of it. In this small-town world, she talked, dressed, and acted like a young lady, enough so that even friends in Golden City's class of 1941 didn't guess her true age. Her most memorable attribute was her voice—a captivating, finely nuanced instrument she developed as a singer. Gordon's older sister, Isabel, said Mary Virginia's clothes never seemed ragged or disheveled, the sorry way some farm kids appeared during the throes of the 1930s Dust Bowl. Her brother's girlfriend "always kept herself clean and neat and feminine-looking," Isabel recalled. "She was pretty."

Driving in Daddy Garrett's brand-new Plymouth seemed right and proper, as close to a royal carriage as Gordon could muster for his prairie princess. Unlike other Depression-era youth, Mary Virginia always acted confident in her tomorrows, perhaps because her mother, Edna Eshelman, wouldn't have it any other way. "I think Gordon liked her a lot," recalled his other sister, Carolyn. "Her mother was 'the best is none too good' and Mary Virginia was like that too." The Garrett sisters perceived Mary Virginia as a good girl, the kind a boy like Gordon could proudly escort to the graduation dance and might someday contemplate marrying. Certainly, they assumed, she wouldn't be found frolicking in the backseat of the Garrett family car.

At this tender age, Mary Virginia already understood the duplicities of modern life for young American girls like herself. She knew the right words to say, the customs to observe, the dishonesty among the moral zealots and fundamentalists insistent on a woman's lot in life. Yet she resolved never to lose that independent part of herself. She would embrace life on her own terms, regardless of what her mother or anyone else said. Earnestly, she played the part of a "good girl"—both in school and at home—though in her heart she knew she was not. "I always lived the facade of mother's little lady but I always did exactly what I wanted to do," she explained. "I just never let it be known."

On the night she lost her virginity, Mary Virginia's experience wasn't forced, sweaty, or profane. The simple act finished within minutes. Sex felt pleasant enough for her, though far from familiar. Any thoughts of orgasm, sexual performance, or mutual satisfaction—the stuff of her intense, lifelong scientific studies with Masters—were then the furthest thing from her mind. Instead she trusted her boyfriend to know what he was doing. Only later in life did she realize it was probably Gordon's first time too.

"It just evolved and was very natural," she said, both wistfully and amused, of their backseat encounter. "It would have shocked my mother to death."

So much of Mary Virginia's life happened by chance, even the way her family landed in Golden City. Her father, Hershel Eshelman, whom everyone called by his middle name, Harry, and his wife, Edna, lived in Springfield when their daughter came into the world on February 11, 1925. Harry's parents were Mormons from nearby Christian County, though neither he nor his wife was particularly religious. The Eshelmans came from Hessian stock, his ancestors brought over for the Revolutionary War. During World War I, Sergeant Harry Eshelman, of Battery A, 5th Field Artillery, witnessed a lifetime's worth of blood, mortality, and the eternal beyond in France, the same field of battle where his younger brother, Tom, was wounded but managed to survive. After the war, like Harry Truman from Independence, twenty-nine-year-old Eshelman returned to southwest Missouri, seeking a simple life for himself and his bride, Edna Evans. Harry's younger sister, a pupil in a class taught by twenty-year-old Edna at a neighborhood school, introduced them. In short order, though, the new Mrs. Eshelman made it clear she wouldn't settle for Harry's humble plan. "Mother wanted to marry up, and she was determined to marry him," recounted the adult Virginia.

Though he possessed the natural skills of a gentleman farmer, Harry Eshelman didn't burn with ambition. A rangy, slender man, Harry appeared satisfied with his own plot of land and lavishing attention on his only child. Photographs of Harry, with his long face and high cheekbones, show a resemblance to Ray Bolger, the affable scarecrow in *The Wizard of Oz.* Mary Virginia was pleased to be the apple of Harry's eye. "I was always considered to look more like my father and my father's family," she said proudly years later. "I was very much Daddy's girl." Harry could figure out just about anything—from building a house to solving his daughter's algebra homework. A former cavalryman, he certainly knew plenty about horses, enough to do tricks to entertain the farm hands or to let his daughter ride the broad backs of the Percheron stallions in their backyard. "Mother would come screaming at him, 'Watch that child!' and he would just smile and wave and put me on," she recalled. Inside their house, Harry taught his daughter how to iron her pleated skirt and made "wooden" shoes out of cardboard as part of her costume for a school concert. "There was nothing the man couldn't do!" she said.

By the time she was five, Mary Virginia's parents decided to leave southwest Missouri, already feeling the Depression's grip. They ventured by train to California in search of a new beginning. In Palo Alto, Harry found work overseeing the lush greenhouses and gardens of a government-run hospital that tended to wounded soldiers. "It was a good job," Virginia recalled. "We lived on the grounds, beautiful grounds with beautiful homes." Placed in a progressive school with a kindergarten, she excelled in her studies. Verbal dexterity and a quick mind enabled her to finish eighth grade by age twelve.

To those fleeing Missouri's arid flatlands, this hospital campus must have seemed like Eden, a garden to shelter them from the Depression's onslaught. Instead of seeing gray dust clouds raking the skies, they marveled at the Pacific's raw majesty and gazed along the shoreline at its misty splendor. On one festive occasion, Virginia recalled, her father went to the beach in a suit and straw hat. A photograph of him that day kept her childhood memory fresh. "I was in my little bathing suit, playing along in the surf," she described. "I walked out a bit and got caught in the rolling surf. I was a little bit of a thing." The waves toppled Mary Virginia, pulling her into the deep. Harry Eshelman, though fully dressed, didn't waste any time acting the hero in his daughter's eyes. "Daddy just walked out and saved me," she remembered.

Inevitably, Edna had her fill of California. It had been her idea in the first place to migrate to the Golden State, along with other beleaguered midwesterners. But soon she grew homesick and disenchanted by her husband's job as a glorified groundskeeper at the VA hospital. Edna's mind was made up, to both her husband's and daughter's chagrin, and Harry knew better than to argue. He deferred to his wife's wishes without much fuss. "My mother insisted that she wanted to go back home to her friends and family," Virginia explained, even though most of her mother's relatives had relocated to California. "She just longed to be back." Harry contacted his father, still in Christian County, to help them find a new farm near Springfield, which he did—about fifty miles to the west. The Eshelmans and their young daughter packed their belongings and returned in the family car to a place in Missouri even more desperate than where they had started. "We came back and the only piece of land Granddad had available was in Golden City," remembered Virginia. This accident of fate was further aggravated by Golden City's insignificance. "It was a teeny-tiny place," she recalled, "literally no one there." Golden City touted itself as "the prairie hay capital" of the nation. For young people with bigger dreams, "Golden City was a place to get out of," remembered Lowell Pugh, one of her contemporaries who grew up to be the town's funeral home director. Girls like Mary Virginia had two options in life, he said, "getting married or getting out of town—that would have been the goal of any girl if she weren't already married and pregnant."

The Eshelman exodus from California to Missouri underlined another glaring fact: though Mary Virginia venerated her father,

Mother ruled the family. Their struggle of wills proved to be the central drama of Mary Virginia's young life. Edna's ideas about womanhood provided the gold standard. Her daughter obediently accepted these rules—at least when within Mother's gaze—and rebelled against them when out of reach. Appearances remained all-important in the Eshelman household. "She had a pretty clear concept of what a wife and mother should be—she playacted!" explained Virginia. "She really thought she was superior to the world or wanted to be."

Edna Evans had been raised as a middle child in a family more humble than the Eshelmans. An attractive woman, she was thin and lithe, with cropped brown hair. If her husband looked out at the world with a friendly, naive stare, Edna's eyes revealed a more skeptical and socially ambitious mien. She always seemed to be in some unspoken competition. Not much in Edna's married life had turned out as she had hoped. Mired in Golden City, she seemed determined to master as much of her world as possible and to convey those lessons to her daughter. "Everyone doted on me and I grew up with the sense that accomplishment and talent were marvelous, but that marriage was the primary goal," Virginia recalled. Mrs. Eshelman insisted the townsfolk refer to her daughter by both her first and middle names—Mary Virginia. "She wanted to call me by my double-name, in that era when everyone was 'Judy Ann' and 'Donna Marie,'" Virginia remembered. Naturally, in a fit of teenage resistance, she instructed friends at Golden City High to call her only Virginia.

Mother aspired to the finer things, arranging for piano and singing lessons for her daughter, and teaching her how to be an expert seamstress and to cook. When her husband wasn't available, Edna showed she could assume a man's role too. "One summer during harvest time, Mother—little tiny Mother—got out and went into the harvest fields, running a tractor and that sort of thing," Virginia recalled. "If she had to, she could do most anything."

Living in a farmhouse five miles out from the center of this dusty misnamed town left Edna desperate for attention and a social life. Once a month, Mrs. Eshelman joined Mrs. Garrett and the other Golden City matriarchs in a monthly get-together, held in rotation at one another's house, where they chatted, shared gossip, and enjoyed female companionship so often absent on the plain. "Edna was a more lively person [than Harry], an ambitious person for her family and herself," said Isabel Garrett Smith. "She was very proud of Mary Virginia. She taught her well." Although her husband emerged a New Deal Democrat in reaction to the Hoovervilles across the nation, Edna saw her own opportunity in the state's Republican Party. "Her whole life was trying to differentiate herself," explained Virginia. Politics provided a rare moment of excitement in the otherwise lackluster life on the Eshelman farm. No one felt this isolation more than Mary Virginia. A pear tree in the back of their farm became her reading room, where on pleasant afternoons she would leaf through the Bible or novels hidden from her mother, dreaming about the world beyond her view. "I didn't have playmates," she recalled. "I just used to read people. I always wanted to know what their lives were like. My grandparents and relatives and adults used to visit us, and I spent all of my time asking, 'Tell me about when you were little.' I loved hearing about other people's lives because, I guess, of being alone as an only child."

One summer, Mary Virginia visited for a week with Edna's older sister, who permitted her niece to roam about her spacious apartment. Tucked into a drawer, she found her aunt's private possessions, including a stack of letters written by a man who was the head of a small private boy's school in the Missouri foothills. According to family lore, her aunt, then in her forties, had nearly married him. Mary Virginia discovered why she hadn't. "I found these wonderful love letters, written with passion I'll never forget the rest of my life, and they were all tied with a ribbon," she explained. "What unfolded was that he had gotten a local girl pregnant, and she would not even talk to him from then on. She walked away and never married anyone. It was this wonderful drama."

Secret tales like these about the dangers of carnal love undoubtedly affected Edna's own perception of her daughter's budding sexuality and her determination to keep her from any temptation. "I was never told about menstruation or anything," Virginia said.

"There was a rigid rejection of anything sexual. You didn't talk about it." Of course, on a farm filled with horses, pigs, and other warm-blooded animals, it was difficult, if not impossible, to avoid a heated demonstration of the facts of life. Historians of the Ozarks, that rolling woodlands amidst the prairie, confirmed the bawdy nature of farm life. When not heeding the Lord's scriptures, for instance, some rural folk practiced their own bit of paganism during the 1890s, engaging in sexual intercourse out in the fields to ensure a fertile crop. "As I grew up, I learned about women's fears of pregnancy and the town prostitute," Virginia recalled. The Golden City of Mary Virginia's generation, according to mortician Lowell Pugh, who also serves as the town's ad hoc historian, produced three young women who became prosperous ladies of the evening in Kansas City.

Avoiding the subject of intimacy became more knotty when Mother wound up pregnant, giving birth to a boy, Larry, twelve years younger than Mary Virginia. Nevertheless, Edna resolved that any lessons about sex—like all important ones she imparted to her daughter—would be done on her terms. One night before bedtime, Virginia was reading a book when Mother summoned her into her bedroom. As she entered, Edna's narrow face appeared deeply concerned. Mother began muttering about sex, using obscure terms and elliptical phrases. "I was very young when she was trying to tell me about pregnancy and how one achieved it," Virginia recalled. "She made no sense at all to me." Young Mary Virginia listened silently but paid her no heed.

By the time Mary Virginia reached puberty and her body matured, her feeling of loneliness at home was unbearable. As her interest turned to boys, she noticed that she could gain their attention by flashing an approving smile, by standing a certain way, or with a flip of her hair. Vaughn Nichols, a schoolmate who lived nearby, remembered hot summer days when he would arrive in his truck at the Eshelman place. On his weekly rounds, he'd pick up two or three cases of eggs—thirty dozen to a case—and other produce to take to market. The Eshelman farm wasn't much to look at. Harry and Edna lived in a white two-story house nearly a century old, surrounded by 160 acres of wheat, corn, oats, alfalfa, and hay. Around their barn, some three hundred chickens laid their eggs, a few cows waited to be milked, and hogs and pigs rolled in the slop. But Vaughn couldn't keep his eyes off Mary Virginia. Forever seared in Vaughn's memory was the image of Mary Virginia wearing "short shorts—real short—just because she thought I was going to be there, I guess." If Virginia liked him, though, "she never did tell me," he admitted. After watching a movie at The Palace in town, Vaughn and the other boys would dance with girls from Golden City's eight-room high school, including Mary Virginia. Behind the silver screen, The Palace theater hosted a small café called The Green Lantern, where they fox-trotted and mingled. "All the girls were better dancers than we were," Vaughn said, laughing. "Mary Virginia was really an outgoing girl." But in high school, no boy mattered more to Mary Virginia than Gordon Garrett, whose family lived about two miles from the Eshelman farm. "He really had never gone with anybody that much before her," said his sister Isabel. "I think she was one of those who had the nerve to speak up to him."

Though an upstanding young man, Gordon, known by the nickname "Red" or "Flash," could sneak a beer or two with pals in the dry state of Missouri without getting caught. He similarly evaded detection during his car rides in the moonlight with Mary Virginia. Gordon never let on about his conquests like boastful boys do. Instead he intimated about his special place in her life. "He was aware that he was my first," she recalled. "He made some reference to that fact. As a male, how could you not know you were the first? It was pretty obvious." Perhaps afraid he might have hurt her, Gordon inquired tenderly whether she was all right after they had finished. "He was not a poet by nature," she recalled, "but he asked me about my own feelings about it, whether it was effective for me. I don't know how he gauged that, but he was considerate and he was concerned. I didn't know how to answer him." Mary Virginia had no intention of confirming his claim that he was her first. She didn't need to, she said, because "he just knew it."

The senior-class yearbook placed their two photos purposefully together. Its "prophecy" section, which predicted the future for classmates with tongue firmly in cheek, published what everyone in the class expected to come true:

CHICAGO: *Mr. and Mrs. Gordan [sic] Garrett announce the entrance of their daughter to Miss Virginia Townley's Select School for girls at Sunny Slope on Chicken Creek. Mrs. Garrett was formerly Miss Mary Virginia Eshelman.*

By graduation in spring 1941, the Golden City world of Mary Virginia, once so slow and dull, expanded rapidly as the threat of war neared, enveloping her entire generation. Gordon's older brother signed up with the Coast Guard and would be stationed in Nantucket throughout the war. Gordon received a year's deferment so he could stay and work on the Garrett homestead. "The only reason I didn't marry him—or didn't think about it—was that I didn't want to live on a farm," contended Virginia. "I wanted to go to college and I wanted to be out in the big wide world." Some also sensed that, in the Eshelman family's estimation, Gordon wasn't good enough. "She left Gordon," his sister Carolyn recalled. "She wouldn't have him because he's farming. She wanted to get out. No farming for her. She was real picky." The Eshelmans decided to send Mary Virginia to Drury College in Springfield, to study music. "All I ever wanted to do was sing at the Metropolitan Opera or be an international classical singer," she would say. Eventually Harry and Edna moved away from Golden City too, back to their native Springfield.

A year after graduation, Gordon decided to enlist, swept up in the patriotic fervor following Pearl Harbor. On the day he left—as Edna later heard from Mrs. Garrett—Gordon stood forlornly with his family at the train station, waiting to be taken to the county seat in LaMar with the rest of the wartime volunteers. He hoped Mary Virginia might show up to say good-bye. Looking around with disappointment, Gordon turned to his toddler niece. "You'll have to be my girlfriend," he moaned, "because I don't have a girlfriend anymore."

By the time Mother relayed that sorry tale to her daughter, Mary Virginia was long gone from Golden City. "It didn't bother me. I couldn't have cared less," she recalled of Gordon's departure. "We hadn't even been going out by then. I had gone out with many people. I look back on that and say, 'Dear heavens, was I really that insensitive?' I didn't think of what I was doing to him at all. It was known in town that he would never marry if he didn't marry me."

CHAPTER TWO

Heartland

"Don't let the stars get in your eyes.
Keep your heart for me for someday I'll return,
And you'll know you're the only one I'll ever love."
—"DON'T LET THE STARS GET IN YOUR EYES," AS SUNG BY RED ROLEY

With a deep breath, Virginia stood up straight, as if at attention, and let out an emotional rendition of the national anthem. Her face kept a constant smile as she harmonized with a Drury College quartet in 1942. "O'er the land of the free," they sang, finishing with a flourish. "And the home . . . of the . . . brave."

Everyone in the ballroom—Missouri assemblymen, state senators, clubhouse politicians, lawyers, and various staffers—clapped appreciatively for the young women at the microphone. Jefferson City was at war. The Japanese attack at Pearl Harbor, the rush into Europe against the Nazis, galvanized Missouri's state capital, with a fatefulness that suggested the world had changed and would never be the same again. Not since the Civil War, when Jefferson City split between the Unionists and Confederates, had there been such wartime fervor.

Virginia's quartet performed at political roasts, sometimes inside churches. "I sang the 'Star-Spangled Banner' at virtually every political event you could name in Jefferson City," Virginia recalled. "I loved any kind of ensemble singing. I had a voice that could do most anything." Once, they entertained at a formal affair attended by the wife of Missouri Governor Forrest C. Donnell, a Republican elected amidst a sea of Democrats beholden to the Pendergast machine, the same that helped Harry Truman become U.S. senator. Missouri was a mix of tribal rivalries and political beliefs—a microcosm of America itself. Virginia learned that men of both parties often attended roasts and other political events just to have a good time. "I met a lot of people I hadn't known before," she said. "Everybody crossed over. It was a small city and very clannish."

Virginia joined the quartet after taking vocal lessons at Drury College, a local institution once called the "Yale of the Southwest," located several miles from Jefferson City. Several biographical sketches say Virginia attended Drury for two years, but in fact she wasn't a full-time undergraduate at all. "I was a music student at Drury but I was never enrolled," she clarified. "As a music student, I went up once a week." After she left home, her life revolved around the capitol building in Jefferson City, where she made sure everyone knew her just as Virginia, dropping the double name. As the daughter of Edna Eshelman, an energetic Republican committee member from Barton County, Virginia found herself the happy recipient of a secretarial job, which provided the entree to a much bigger world beyond her family's farm. "I left home at sixteen and never returned again—I was on my own," she remembered. "My mother, for a short period of time, got to be fairly powerful in delivering her county. She decided that, before I went to college, I would have a year in the wide world. So I had a patronage job in Jefferson City, with the insurance department." Virginia later advanced to the legislature, aiding the state senator whose district included Springfield.

Mother knew Jefferson City would be the right place for Virginia to find a successful husband, rather than some rube on a godforsaken farm. Even if she felt her own dreams had been dashed, Edna Eshelman wasn't going to let her daughter's prospects get away. In this sense, more than she might admit, Virginia was like her mother rather than her father. She resented Mother's manipulations but quickly adapted to her sophisticated surroundings. In her late teens, Virginia possessed enough outward maturity and inner spunk to be perceived as a woman several years older. She made friends with the powerful as well as their secretaries and other rank-and-file state workers. "Anytime I wanted a ride home to Springfield, I would just sort of page the community for a ride—it could be anyone," she said. "I went home with the senator many times, the one from Springfield."

While singing the national anthem at another political gala in Jefferson City, Virginia met a top-ranking official in Missouri's government. This politician, elected to the state's highest law enforcement post, was a widower with children nearly Virginia's age. He seemed enraptured by her charms, her youthful good looks, and perhaps her availability, so long as their rendezvous together remained discreetly in the capitol's shadows. Within weeks, they talked of marriage. Whether wedding vows actually took place, however, depends on what factual account one chooses. "The first I was only 19 and that lasted two days," Virginia told the *Washington Post* in 1973, which counted four husbands for her. "He was a political figure and a 19-year-old bride was clearly not for him. He's now dead." This phantom first husband was a claim repeated in some official biographies, while missing from most. Legal papers from this union have never been found. Years later, Virginia insisted she married only three times and offered her own version of this affair. "I was involved with a very high-placed politician" who aspired to run for even higher office, she explained rather obliquely. Their relationship appeared doomed from the start. "We only attracted attention when we went to a March meeting [held outside Jefferson City] and we both rode with the Highway Patrol." A fetching young woman seated next to this magnetic elected official—and not carried on his staff roster—could mean only one thing in the eyes of gossips. Though his amorousness never faded, the politician's instincts for survival prevailed. "He decided to run for governor," Virginia remembered. "He hadn't declared yet as a candidate. We broke up before that, in order for him to run. The powers that be decided that he couldn't humanly be running for governor and be going out with someone his children's age. So that ended that one."

In Jefferson City, Virginia slowly learned the social realities for young, independent-minded women like herself. Although World War II brought unprecedented employment opportunities—such as the much publicized image of Rosie the Riveter and other females who took on traditionally male jobs in factories and other businesses to replace the absent GIs serving overseas—there remained many unshakable constraints, both in public and in private. "Wartime propaganda emphasized women's femininity even as it exhorted them to take nontraditional roles in industry," observed Katharine T. Corbett in her history of St. Louis women. Nowhere was this duplicity more evident than on sexual matters. The ignorance among females about their own bodies was appalling to Virginia. At an outdoor social gathering, she remembered, one of her friends approached her with a worried look.

"I've got a question I want to ask you," said the friend. "Let's go sit in the car and let me ask you it."

Virginia followed her to a nearby automobile, where they settled in the front seat and closed the door, keeping the windows shut. From her friend's description, she was obviously involved in a sexual relationship with a man she didn't intend to marry and worried about the effect on her future.

"Will I . . . ?" she asked, haltingly. "Is it possible for someone to know that I have lost my virginity?"

Though she liked being brought into other people's confidence, asking for her advice, Virginia couldn't help this friend. "I said, 'I haven't the vaguest idea,'" she remembered. "I didn't know what a hymen was, for God's sake!"

Virginia detested the hypocrisy of women who acted coy and chaste until Saturday night, only to return to the same virtuous charade the next morning. "There were a fair number of women who were sexually active, but the 'nice' girls—the ones who were so labeled, of which I was too, for that matter—a lot of them were not," explained Virginia, who never carried herself provocatively with the intent of capturing a man. "I never set out to 'get' anyone that I know of." Sex would be embraced on her terms, for reasons that she wanted, under conditions she would define. She never feigned disinterest. "I literally didn't go out with anyone, to any degree, that I didn't have a sexual relationship with. I enjoyed sex."

During the war, Virginia socialized with many enlisted men stationed at Fort Leonard Wood, the sprawling military facility in Waynesville, Missouri, about forty miles south of the capital. Her girls' quartet harmonized in the Army-post shows produced on the field house stage. They featured dance bands and local talent, and sometimes comedian Bob Hope and his traveling USO troupe. Along with popular and patriotic tunes, Virginia developed a taste for country music, listening to the ballads of Hank Williams and getting to know Red Foley, who sang of the vagaries of romantic love with his guitar and harmonica. Eventually she sang country ballads as Virginia Gibson for radio station KWTO (its call letters spelling out "Keep Watching the Ozarks"). Inspiration for her new surname came from the program's sponsor, the Gibson Coffee Company.

At Fort Leonard Wood, summer days and weekends would bring some of the most passionate moments of Virginia's young adulthood. From the men who came into her life, she learned that romantic love—celebrated in popular songs—was often elusive in real life. Inside this Army compound, young men and women like her were coming of age against the backdrop of war. Fateful life-and-death decisions loomed ahead in faraway places. During these USO entertainments, Virginia felt vitally alive, part of something bigger than herself. "I became quite caught up because I started singing on the various Army posts," she recalled. "And I always became involved with someone." Most times, Virginia satisfied her desires without any lingering emotional entanglements. The war afforded women on the home front not only men's jobs but also the freedom of casual intimacy when so moved. With one affair, Virginia remembered a divorced officer as "a bit of the Texas Ranger" who performed wonderfully in bed. Their pillow talk included discussing the custody battle with his ex-wife, a Las Vegas showgirl, over their little boy. Virginia never viewed herself as another complicating factor in this man's life; more as two friendly ships passing in the night. "He was a superb dancer and a delightful man," Virginia remembered. "It was impossible not to respond to him sexually." No pretense of love existed between Virginia and this man, none of the qualifiers to physical intimacy that Mother taught her to insist upon first. Virginia discovered the absence of devotion didn't mean she couldn't enjoy herself in the bedroom. Love wasn't necessary in reaching a physical climax, that intensity of feeling followed by a quiver of release. "I never had any difficulty," she said of orgasm. "It was just more natural with some than with others. In fact, I didn't realize how wonderful some of the men were until they weren't in the picture." Soon afterward, this divorced officer with the showgirl ex-wife and his engaging sexual prowess went off to war.

Some men beguiled Virginia's mind, more than her sense of good looks. From these experiences, she learned just how little raw sexual attraction might mean to a relationship. One boyfriend, a gifted violinist drafted into the military from the Pittsburgh Symphony, provided Virginia with valuable insights about music and her potential as a singer. Men like these appealed to her soul and the finer intellectual pursuits, though Virginia remained surprisingly vulnerable to their opinions and judgments. "He was really a prodigy," she recalled of her violinist, who reviewed the music scores she would sing with the big band orchestras at the field house. "He always felt my arrangements were quite lovely." However, for all of his penetrating musical insights, this musical wunderkind was a bust in the rhythms of the boudoir. "He was very naive and had very little experience," she remembered of her musical lover. "I think he really was [a virgin]. I remember him kind of apologizing. I just think he felt he didn't know what he was doing." Despite this sexual shortcoming, Virginia briefly considered marrying this talented man, who promised to show her the world of music. "The least effective sexual partner was this wonderful musician, but that didn't make or break it with me," she explained. What cooled their relationship most was Edna Eshelman's condescension regarding his religion. "He was Catholic and my mother made a comment," Virginia recalled. "She never preached against marrying someone who was Catholic, but at the same time I think she saw it as a potential area of difficulty. She wanted me to consider that, but that had nothing to do with me walking away." Indeed, the final arbiter was Uncle Sam, who soon transported the Pittsburgh violinist to the European conflict. Virginia never saw him again; another lover sent off to war.

With her flings and passing affairs, Virginia always managed to get away unscathed. She never suffered a broken heart, not the way Red Foley or Hank Williams crooned in their lovesick songs. Never did she feel that way until she went out with an Army captain following a show at Fort Leonard Wood. A stagehand told her of a knock at the dressing room door. There she found the handsome captain she'd met earlier at a swimming pool. The fragility of life in wartime, the passion of youth, and the intimate dancing to slow melodies at the Army base added intensity to their romance. "The love of your life always has to do with a time and place more than anything else," she later explained. "The Army captain would have been mine, I suppose." In him, Virginia found a man as smart and assertive as he was physically attractive, someone who was her contemporary but possessed a wisdom about the world that she admired, even coveted. "He was twenty-six and I wasn't much over eighteen," she said. "He was just a magician in terms of handling people."

Over that summer, the two became inseparable. Though they were brought together by physical attraction, the Army captain kept enough presence of mind to let Virginia know of another girl in his life. "When we first met, I knew he was engaged because he said, 'You remind me of my fiancée,'" she remembered. "But he continued to go out with me." Virginia ignored this telling aside, convinced her own love and passion for him would be enough. She became part of the Army captain's social circle at the base, embraced by his best soldier friends and their wives and girlfriends. The Army captain's closest pal at Fort Leonard Wood was a slightly older man of the same rank, with a wife and small child, who managed to keep a car on the base. He let the Army captain and Virginia borrow it whenever they wanted. On long drives throughout the Missouri countryside, they parked under the trees and made love to each other with abandon. Certain of her feelings, Virginia convinced him one day to drive about seventy miles to Springfield so she could introduce him to her parents and relatives. "We were together constantly—we went everywhere and did everything," she recalled. "I took him home to my grandmother's and the family met him."

After nearly a year, Virginia knew she wanted to marry the Army captain. She had forgotten their fleeting conversation about his fiancée from a wealthy family back home. But one evening, the

Army captain's demeanor, once so open and loving, turned sullen and contrite. He had trouble getting out the words he intended to say. "He could hardly tell me that he was going to be married," Virginia recalled. "When he wound up marrying his fiancée, he broke me into small pieces."

As the news spread on the Army base, their circle of friends seemed almost as crestfallen as Virginia. "They rallied around me and got so angry with him," she remembered. "They were absolutely shaken that he had done this—stayed with me all this time and then out of the blue, married." Wives and girlfriends, perhaps mindful of their own vulnerable relationships in wartime, commiserated with Virginia. The captain's best friend—the married one who lent his car to them—kept telling her, "I'll marry you, I'll marry you!" as if applying some emotional balm to remove the sting. Soon afterward, another couple in their circle married, and Virginia went to the wedding alone with a Brownie camera. After the ceremony, she stood outside the old Anglican chapel as the crowd threw rice at the happy couple. "I was taking pictures there and someone took the camera from my hand and took a picture of me. And I looked like my family had just died. In the photo, I looked so incredibly sad. I just hadn't recovered. I was just devastated." Virginia stumbled across the faded photograph of herself later in a forgotten album. "That may be why I never married anybody I really cared about," she reflected about the Army captain, "because there was an echo of being deserted, of being left and rejected. Actually I wasn't rejected. Not exactly. Because I was never in the picture, really."

Afraid of being hurt again in the same way, Virginia entered into a series of relationships over the next few years that could be intimate and sexual, but never carried the same hope of lasting love. She learned to separate her feelings of love and desire, both with the men she dated and with those she ultimately married. "I had an active interest in sex," she explained, "but never particularly to the men I was involved with."

CHAPTER THREE

Mrs. Johnson

"She wondered if there might not have been some way, through a different set of circumstances, of meeting another man; and she tried to imagine those events which had not happened, that different life, that husband whom she did not know."

—GUSTAVE FLAUBERT, *MADAME BOVARY*

At the chapel, everything appeared in white, so fresh and so pure. Virginia wore a white crepe gown and a white picture hat with a wide braided brim, as she walked down the aisle of the Central Christian Church, a few blocks from her parents' home in Springfield. In her arms, she carried a white Holy Bible topped with pale orchids and baby's breath. An accompanist in the background played sentimental favorites about eternal love and devotion.

The innocence of this Saturday-afternoon wedding in June 1947—when "the former Mary Virginia Eshelman," as the newspaper announcement called her, became the bride of Ivan L. Rinehart—belied the difference in their ages. She was twenty-two. Her betrothed, a lawyer from nearby West Plains, was forty-three. Most inside the church didn't seem disturbed by this disparity. The groom's oldest brother, Homer, vouched for him as best man. His mother, Norah, sat contentedly in a nearby pew. Virginia's cousin, Patti, wearing a soft-pink dress and a corsage of gardenias, was pleased at age thirteen to be picked as her maid of honor. But Edna and Harry Eshelman were reserved during the small, family-only ceremony. They weren't pleased that their only daughter was marrying Rinehart, a man nearly twice her age. As Virginia remembered, "My mother and father were appalled."

With World War II over, Virginia feared she might wind up on some backwater farm in Missouri. No longer would be there any USO shows, no sense of ordinary life suspended. In the national relief following V-E Day, Americans wanted to return to some kind of normalcy, to the comforting domestic life that marriage and a nest full of children offered. At age twenty-two, Virginia was far from an old maid, though many girls she knew from school were already engaged or wed. Her short time at Drury College was followed by enrollment at the University of Missouri, where she joined two sororities and the University Singers, though never earning a degree. Getting married meant escape from her mother's withering judgments and her father's indulgences. Ivan and Virginia had met a few years earlier at the state insurance department in Jefferson City, where she worked as a secretary and he as an attorney. Though undoubtedly Ivan possessed other fine qualities, he wasn't a particularly handsome man, with a high forehead, hawkish nose, and squinty eyes. Standing next to her, sporting his pin-striped double-breasted suit, Ivan looked more like her father than her fiancé. Virginia remained adamant about marrying this older man, perhaps to prove something to her doubting parents. By walking down the aisle, Virginia felt she'd be finally on her own. Even at the wedding, though, she displayed ambivalence.

Before the ceremony began, Virginia remembered, the minister noticed something was missing. Unlike most weddings, there wasn't a photographer around. "The minister said, 'Don't you want me to call one?'" she recalled.

Virginia shook her head negatively. For some reason, she didn't want a photographer. "I said, 'No, I don't want to record this.'" Intuitively, Virginia didn't want the happy, smiling faces of Ivan and herself permanently framed for posterity. "I wasn't marrying anyone of choice," she remembered. "I think I was tired of being alone."

Their modest wedding reception took place in a church parlor, followed by a week's honeymoon. Ivan planned to return to West Plains as the junior partner at the Roberts and Rinehart law firm. As a practicing attorney, Ivan offered a solid, if not exciting, foundation to Virginia's plans of building a family, though he never stipulated that was his intent. In West Plains, near the Arkansas border in the southern Ozarks, the newly renamed Virginia Rinehart quickly grew disenchanted. "I assumed we married to have a family," she recounted. "When I realized he had no intention whatsoever of taking on that responsibility, I got a divorce." To placate his young bride, Ivan agreed to move to a big city and uproot his career. This change of venue didn't change Virginia's verdict on their marriage. "We came to St. Louis and he joined a firm down here, and that firm got me the divorce from him," she said. "In retrospect, I have no clue why I married him."

Virginia found a secretarial job at the *St. Louis Daily Record*, a journal chronicling lawyers, judges, and business movers and shakers—an ideal place to find a new husband. Through a mutual friend at the *Daily Record*, Virginia met George Johnson, a man much closer to her in age. He studied engineering at Washington University and, perhaps more important, was the leader of a local nightclub band. "If you ever need a singer," the mutual friend told George, "Virginia can sing."

George Johnson came as close to Benny Goodman as was likely to be seen in the hot spots of St. Louis. He was a neatly dressed man, with a smooth fop of hair, a carefully clipped mustache, horn-rimmed glasses, and tight lips, the result of good *embouchure*. On his own, Johnson learned to play the woodwinds—clarinet, alto saxophone, and tenor sax—and absorbed enough training about music to prepare arrangements for his own orchestra, featuring the big-band sounds of the day. "He was a very fine musician and that was the attraction," recalled Virginia, who hesitated before agreeing to date him. "I just felt very much at loose ends. I had a friend who played matchmaker and she was constantly after me, 'Go out with him, go out with him.' She pushed and I guess I felt alone. I certainly didn't want to particularly."

For Virginia, George Johnson offered one irresistible allure—a microphone with a spotlight. After years of singing in church choirs, university quartets, and USO shows, Virginia finally had the prospect of making it as a professional, as the female singer in George's band. His nocturnal world of smoky voices, richly textured syncopation, and dancing in the dark seemed so far from the daily starkness of her farm-town youth. Engineering might be his backup, but George seemed completely dedicated to music. Their June 1950 wedding occurred in the outside garden of a Presbyterian church where Virginia once sang with the choir. Her groom wore a light-colored jacket with a paisley tie and matching handkerchief in his breast pocket. Virginia, never looking lovelier than on this day, walked down the aisle, again wearing a picture hat with a big brim. Once more, there wasn't a wedding photographer, only a friend who snapped their picture after the ceremony. "I had color outdoor pictures of the wedding but no formal ones," she remembered. "I never wanted pictures taken of my weddings."

At home, as much as at the nightclub, Virginia appeared happy with her bandleader husband. "When they moved into their apartment, I helped them paint," said Ken Barry, a friend and fellow musician. "It was just the three of us, drinking beer and painting. What I saw was a pretty good relationship." With a sultry, low-pitched voice, Virginia performed with her husband's band in St. Louis locales, including the Winter Garden, the Forest Park Highland, and, most famous of all, the Casa Loma Ballroom, where Frank Sinatra once performed. Traveling with a band was thrilling for Virginia. It seemed the life she'd always envisioned, her way of achieving some recognition.

After many months, the constant drain of their late-night routine lost its luster for Virginia and exacted a toll on their marriage. Before her first anniversary with George, Virginia took a secretarial job in the advertising department of KMOX radio station. Their hectic schedules were "sort of a zoo—very stressful," George later recalled, prompting his wife to see a doctor who recommended that she "take something up, something less stressful." She decided to become a dance instructor at a neighborhood studio.

As a husband, George Johnson wasn't averse to having children, not as Ivan Rinehart had been. Virginia, then twenty-six years old, seemed even more intent on the notion. "If I hadn't had children, I would have been absolutely bereft, a failure as a human being," she recalled. "I just knew that children were important to me." Shortly after their marriage, Virginia gave birth to a son named Scott, followed a few years later by a daughter, Lisa. Adding children to the Johnson entourage, however, proved too burdensome, the kind of emotional baggage their relationship couldn't handle.

"Until my children were born, it was fine," Virginia observed. "But musicians are night people and children are day people. The two just didn't mix." She found it hard to be unpleasant with George, especially when he encouraged her musical efforts. But his limitations away from the bandstand couldn't be overcome. "We didn't share the same ideas and goals," she said. "Our only commonality was music."

With George frequently out of the house—entertaining all night at clubs and at weekend weddings—Virginia found her life unbearable. She no longer sang with the band. Staying home in the St. Louis suburbs with the kids—the June Cleaver television ideal of motherhood propagated in the postwar era—never appealed to Virginia. She had left Golden City for college and opportunity, not to find herself stuck in such a rut. Her often-absent husband offered little help. She remained in constant turmoil as a working mother, caught between what she wanted out of life and what others expected of her. "I did come from that era where being a mother was an important thing," she said. "I am a little less concerned with cleaning drapes, and a little more concerned with life and sharing." Working motherhood forced her to rely on babysitters, to trust strangers with her children's care. One evening after work, Virginia found Scott, then six, at home alone. "My little girl was gone and so was the woman" hired to mind them, she recalled. Frantically, Virginia called the police to report her daughter missing. "What I didn't know—and we learned—she [the babysitter] was an alcoholic and she had run out to get anything to drink," Johnson said. "She'd taken my little girl, maybe two years old, on a bus back to her house somewhere where she could find a bottle and bring it back."

With both kids in tow, Virginia decided to leave her marriage. Ever the affable host, George didn't fight or resist. He only asked why.

"I no longer have anything to give you," she remembered telling him before walking out the door. However, she kept her married name —Virginia Johnson.

Though adamant about leaving, Virginia was disquieted by her two failed marriages and the personal shortcomings they suggested at a time when divorce in America was still relatively rare.

She had enjoyed sex and sharing affection with both men but never forged the deep bond she had always sought, the kind of true, lasting love she sang about but never found. For reasons Virginia couldn't explain, she had married two men—possibly three if some accounts are to be believed—whom she never really loved, never genuinely cared about. "I look back on that and I wonder why," she reflected. "I don't have an answer for myself."

Those who knew Virginia well during this time period said she was too ambitious and energetic to settle for a humdrum existence with a man like George Johnson. "She would tell me that she was sort of ashamed of her position as being a bandleader's wife," recalled Dr. Alfred Sherman, who would get to know her at Washington University. "She wanted to be beyond that point. She had mentioned that she was smarter than that. She wanted to become much more of a classy woman." George knew he couldn't hold on to his wife, that she longed for something more. "She had her eye on something better all the time," he would say years later. But when the divorce papers were signed in September 1956, what that "something better" might be still wasn't clear to Mrs. Johnson.

Most students had departed for the Christmas break when Virginia walked across the empty, snow-covered medical campus of Washington University in St. Louis, on her way to a job interview. At age thirty-one, she was an unemployed, twice-divorced mother with two small children, hoping for a fresh start. In December 1956, Washington University catered mostly to local students, far from the internationally known institution it would become, and reflected Missouri's conservative roots, not far from the Mason-Dixon Line. Only four years earlier, the school had desegregated its undergraduate divisions, allowing a small trickle of black students into classes with whites. Women were a rarity on Wash U's campus at that time, especially at the university's medical school.

Virginia walked through the brisk winter chill. For her interview, she wore a simple dress, yet carried enough sophistication to mask how desperately she wanted this job. Her dark hair was pulled back in a bun. A hint of rouge covered her lips. She no longer had that willowy look of a young farm girl, but a more fully formed figure of a woman in her prime, a woman who had already experienced much of life. In anticipation, she composed replies to possible questions and practiced modulating her voice in a pleasing, well-spoken way. Once inside the medical building, Virginia entered a small, discreet office and waited for her appointment with a man she had never met—Dr. William Masters.

At Washington University, Virginia planned to pursue social anthropology, examining the cultural differences between nature and nurture in human development. Because there wasn't a specific major in this field, however, a school adviser had steered Virginia toward sociology. To pay her tuition, she knew she'd have to find a job on campus. She needed to balance the demands of working with attending class. In the wake of her divorce from George Johnson, Virginia again became dependent on her parents, Edna and Harry, who were only too happy to help. But she knew their assistance would come at the expense of her freedom. She couldn't resolve this dilemma until she finished college, secured a steady job, and made enough to raise two children by herself. She couldn't depend on George, who still dreamed of hitting it big on the bandstand circuit, this same year Elvis Presley and rock-and-roll changed popular American music forever. Virginia yearned for a new beginning, to stand on her own with a college degree. "I decided that I would be leaving those two little children to others—my mother, really—and I didn't want it to happen," recalled Virginia. "So I decided to go back to school."

With nothing available in the sociology department, she was directed to the medical school, where a working assistantship might be arranged. "I was pretty naive and I had no interest at all in the medical field," she remembered. Her initial appointment, scheduled with two well-regarded psychiatrists, was canceled suddenly, so she went ahead with an appointment in obstetrics and gynecology. Virginia knew little about Dr. Masters, only tidbits from friends familiar with the medical school. Masters's recently launched study on the physiology of sex was a tightly held secret kept from everyone at the university. Virginia assumed Masters's cutting-edge research was to assist married couples desperate for a baby. "I had heard of Masters and his work with infertility," she recalled. "And that's what I thought I was being hired for when I took the job."

During that interview, Masters stared intently at Virginia, with the cold, dry detachment of a scientist peering into a petri dish. Masters's physical appearance—his dark, narrow-set eyes, his bald pate surrounded by closely cut, graying hair, his thin-lipped smile, which was almost a grimace—made him seem much older than his forty-one years. As he sat in his white lab coat with arms folded, Masters posed several perfunctory questions about the candidate's background and experience. Virginia answered with aplomb, if not much expertise. That didn't seem to matter. With each successive reply, Masters became more relaxed and amiable, until she realized she had landed the position.

In retrospect, this paradoxical beginning was characteristic of their relationship together for the next several decades. Masters's deeply intuitive manner—the sixth sense an experienced physician develops about people—told him that Mrs. Johnson would be the perfect companion for his work. Yet he revealed very little about himself or his plans. Masters would remain a lifelong enigma, leaving those closest struggling to understand him, unsure of his true intentions and what forces drove him so relentlessly. Virginia's hiring would become the first of many actions by Masters that both thrilled her and left her wondering. For it seemed Bill Masters made up his mind as soon as Virginia Johnson opened her mouth.

"Why me? I still don't quite know," she reflected many years after her initial meeting with Dr. Masters. "I just became the princess."

CHAPTER FOUR

Never Going Home

Balanced on water skis, Bill Masters glided across Rainbow Lake, holding aloft a beautiful blond girl whose hair blew in the breeze. He beamed rapturously as the two waved to admiring onlookers along the shore. Dr. Francis Baker still has a photograph of his sister and his medical school roommate frolicking along this shimmering freshwater oasis in the Adirondack Mountains of upstate New York. "Bill and Dody used to water-ski out on my mother's Chris-Craft—he'd go up and down the lake with her riding on his shoulders," recalled Fran, who watched from the boat as Bill triumphantly carried his sister like a trophy.

Rainbow Lake brought a rare sense of happiness to William Howell Masters, a young man who until this point in life hadn't known much joy. Summers spent as a camp counselor along this wooded waterfront were a welcome respite from his constant study, first at Hamilton College and then later as a medical student at the University of Rochester. Three years in a row, Bill Masters reported directly to the Adirondack camp as soon as his classes were done and returned promptly when his studies resumed. He made sure never to go home.

One August afternoon in 1938, Fran invited Bill for lunch at his family's cottage on the lake. Although both attended Hamilton, Bill and Fran didn't know each other yet very well. At this lunch, however, Fran's younger sister Geraldine—called "Dody" by everyone—made the greatest impression on Bill. He became a mainstay around the Baker summer cottage, spending as much time with Dody as possible. "I'm sure he didn't come to see me," recalled Fran with a chuckle. "Initially to see me, yes. But once he got to know her, I was just a side issue!" Hamilton was an all-male school, and Bill hadn't much experience with girls. He struggled not to appear flustered and tongue-tied when talking with Dody. "I was not very well versed in the art of courting," Bill wrote later in an unpublished memoir. "I had a sense of total commitment when I was with her, but I was with her too infrequently to be able to express my interest effectively."

Rainbow Lake offered an idyllic place for romance. On long, hot weekends, friends cruised about the lake on the sixteen-foot mahogany runabout purchased by Mrs. Baker, a widow, purely for her children's enjoyment. Fran usually steered the boat while Bill and Dody water-skied off the back. "Afterward they'd be swimming, and sometimes we'd all have cocktails on the beach," Fran recalled. Even in this relaxed setting, though, Bill Masters kept a wall around himself that he let few breach. As he learned more about Bill, Fran realized the complexity of this young man and his troubled home life. At Hamilton, Bill spent holidays with roommates whose families lived nearby. "Bill didn't go home for Christmas," Fran said. There seemed a great hurt from which Bill Masters would spend a lifetime trying to overcome. "The relationship that he had with his father made him very protective," recalled Fran. "He was really hurt by his father. This was the relationship with the closest man in his life."

Bill's father, Francis Wynne Masters, was a hard-driving man with a short temper who showed little tolerance when he came home. As a traveling agent for what became the Pitney Bowes postage meter company, Frank Masters dragged his wife and two sons, Bill and his younger brother, Francis, throughout the Midwest, opening up new branch offices. Never in one place for very long, the Masters family resided in Cleveland during Bill's birth on December 27, 1915, and soon moved on to Pittsburgh; Evanston, Illinois; a small ranch outside Houston; and twice to Kansas City, Missouri. Frank Masters's anger and frustration at the world focused particularly on his oldest son and his perceived shortcomings. As a frail youngster, Bill suffered two serious bouts of septicemia, a blood infection, leaving him bedridden for several months. The high fever from this disease caused Bill's left eye to turn slightly to the side. A dense white opacity surrounded the cornea of his eye, which gazed outward. This "walleyed" condition would last most of Bill's life. It cursed him with a harsh stare that many found unnerving. "If he didn't like you, he could look right through you as if you weren't there," remembered a school friend, Addison Wardwell. "His eyes had a trick of being very cold at times."

By age twelve, Bill possessed an intelligence that elevated him into high school, though this advancement proved a mistake. "I simply wasn't sufficiently mature to meet the social challenges that the male high school student encounters as he practices being a man," Masters later wrote. Too small and immature, he found dating girls out of the question. At home, though, Bill suffered lasting humiliations. Frank Masters's fury at his oldest son spilled over into violence, as beatings became commonplace. "My father would call me into a bedroom, lock the door, and proceed to whip me with his belt (always the buckle end)," Bill recounted. "He would whip me severely every month or six weeks to the point of blood occasionally being drawn from my skinny buttocks." These thrashings with a leather strap were also unpredictable, and Bill felt helpless against the relentless attacks. "He repeatedly told me that he intended to continue these whippings until I got down on my knees and begged for mercy," he later wrote. Defiantly, Bill refused to beg, and the beatings turned worse. As Bill screamed in pain, his mother tried to intervene. "I have vivid memories of my mother pounding on the locked-door bedroom door trying to rescue me from his wrath," he wrote. But Estabrooks Taylor Masters seemed too afraid and intimidated by her husband's violent streak to be of much help. Frank ruled their house with a clenched fist, insisting his commands be followed. As an adult, Bill remembered how his mother was treated: "He ordered his meals and told her how to vote. New clothing had to pass under his scrutiny. . . . All decisions and events had to pass my father's review."

Bill later learned his father suffered from meningioma, a swelling tumor in the brain capable of causing persistent headaches, personality changes, and hair-trigger outbursts. He wondered whether his father's violent mood swings were caused by this lingering illness. "How long he had that tumor and how it may have affected his behavior, I can only guess," he wrote. "The rejection by my father was so very hard to live with, especially during my early teenage years. . . . By this time, he had progressively rejected me not only as a member of the family, but as his son."

The last real exchange between Frank Masters and his eldest son occurred on a trip to the Lawrenceville School in New Jersey, a private boarding school between Princeton and the state capital of Trenton. As a young man himself, Frank Masters had attended this preparatory school, but the decision to send Bill was Estabrooks Masters's, as a way of getting her son out of her husband's clutches. His great-aunt, Sally Masters, paid Bill's tuition, grateful for the generosity of Bill's grandfather years earlier in lending her money to establish a private school for wealthy girls in Dobbs Ferry, New York. At age fourteen, Bill left his house in Kansas City and traveled by train with his father on the long trip to Lawrenceville. They stopped in New York City, where his father took him to famous restaurants and his first Broadway show. Bill enjoyed this weekend in the big city, surprised by his father's magnanimity. "But all the while I had an uncanny feeling that some kind of boom was about to be dropped," he later remembered.

During the train ride, halfway to Trenton, Frank Masters engaged in another fatherly duty: informing his son about sex. "You know there are certain private things that husbands and wives do together that most people do not understand and know very little about," Frank began. As his son listened attentively, Frank's face turned bright red and he started sweating. A woman sitting in the train car with her young daughter turned around and signaled her own unease with Frank's lesson. He continued on. "He could not have been more wrong about many of the details of his subject, but he was firmly and loudly convinced of his expertise, and expressed his convictions with force and feeling," remembered his adult son. "To this day, I still do not have any real grasp of what he was trying to tell me."

When they arrived at Lawrenceville, Frank Masters showed his son around his old stomping grounds. They wandered over to the office of the dean, who chatted with them for a few minutes and wished Bill well at his new school. And before heading back to Kansas City, Frank Masters treated his son to his first "jigger," a concoction of ice cream and other sweets, a familiar delight from his own youth. "I thought that buying me a jigger was an olive branch on his part," Bill later wrote. "How wrong I was." Instead, as they neared the train station, Frank Masters stopped and announced his son's banishment. With Aunt Sally paying his expenses for the next four years, he declared, "I feel that my responsibilities to you are terminated." Father would send some money so Bill could come home for Christmas, but nothing more. He warned him not to seek his mother's help or turn to other relatives. "It is about time you took care of yourself," Frank informed his young son. He walked away without a good-bye, and Bill cried himself to sleep that night.

At Lawrenceville, young Bill developed a stoic self-reliance, throwing himself into vigorous sports like football and spending endless hours in the library—a habit he continued throughout college and medical school. "I would never be accused of being a great student, so I needed extended study time in order to squeeze by," he would say. Bill grew friendly with other boys at Lawrenceville, including Carleton Pate, whose parents invited him to spend that Thanksgiving at their home in New York City. During his visit, Mrs. Pate, a sensitive soul, recognized the young man's pain. When she asked about his father, Bill later recalled, "I was completely open and honest with her, and when I had finished telling her my tale of woe, we both had tears in our eyes."

Just before Christmas, a letter from Bill's father arrived, with enough money for a round-trip train ride between Trenton and Kansas City. In his absence, though, nothing had changed. "My father more or less ignored me during my visit home for Christmas," he wrote. In this struggle of wills, Bill announced to his mother's horror that he would leave the day after Christmas—and not stay around for his fifteenth birthday on December 27. "I simply felt that I had little in the way of revenge that I could foster on my father," he explained years later, revealing his own embitterment. "I was accepting the gauntlet that he had thrown down when he said there would be no further support from my family."

Estabrooks Masters urged her son to change his mind. When Bill's father left for work, they took a long walk together. "She would try to explain away my father's feelings toward me," Bill wrote, "although she could not offer any reasonable explanation for his severe beatings and attitude toward me." Bill pitied his mother, a virtual prisoner in his father's brusque, overbearing world. "I had two different women as a mother," Bill later described. To her son, one side of Estabrooks Masters was a sympathetic mother who labored mightily to give him the best of care. The second woman, though, was "my father's wife," as Bill described it, more of an indentured servant than a freethinking individual, a woman told what to do and when. Despite her pleas, Mother's rapprochement failed.

The day after Christmas, Frank Masters drove Bill to the train station, just as his son had asked. There would be no candle-lit cake for Bill's fifteenth birthday, no singing around the dinner table. Mother slipped him an envelope containing cash—three twenties, three tens, three fives, and three one-dollar bills. Bill wondered if there was any symbolism to her gift, some hidden message of support, but he didn't get a chance to ask her. For the next four years, Estabrooks Masters kept in contact surreptitiously with her son. She would call from a neighbor's house in the middle of the day so Frank wouldn't find out. She sent money in letters to Bill at boarding school, but he never thanked her "for fear of my father finding out and making her already tenuous home life even more difficult."

Bill's abortive Christmas visit marked the last time he ever saw his father. Frank Masters died of his debilitating brain illness three years later, after Bill finished Lawrenceville and enrolled at Hamilton College. By then, Bill had distanced himself from his mother and younger brother, Frank—relationships that would never quite mend. Grimly, he learned to overcome the empty feeling when other boys left school and went home merrily for Christmas and other holidays. He focused on building himself into a man, on his own terms. He resolved to be his own creation, finding his own destiny.

At Hamilton College, the three-story brick home of Alpha Delta Phi, located prominently on the bucolic campus of this private liberal arts college, housed two dozen fraternity brothers dedicated to a good time, including Bill Masters. Everyone at Alpha Delta Phi knew him. He had matured into a strapping, cocksure adult, someone far different than his earlier years. "As a young man I was easily wounded socially," Bill recalled. But at Hamilton, fellow frat members were in awe of Masters and his manly approach to just about everything. He played football for Hamilton and impressed the crowds despite permanently damaging his knee. He knew how to box, enough to scare off nearly any challenger. He jousted verbally on the school's debate team and drove his own car on campus, a rarity in those days. Envious classmates spoke of a family trust fund that they figured paid for Bill's expenses. Though he originally majored in English, Bill picked medicine as a career. "He knew what he was going to do all the time, no doubt in his mind about what his future profession would be," claimed Addison Wardwell, who never ran afoul of him. "He didn't have a helluva lot of patience with those who were not well oriented to what they were going to do."

During college, Bill's most adventuresome times, however, were in a plane. He first flew during his years at Lawrenceville, taught by a family friend who operated a nearby flight training school. Bill worked odd jobs at small private airports in Trenton and near Princeton and gained his pilot's license. Flying was still new and quite dangerous in the days before World War II, and Masters got paid handsomely for his services. One businessman who traveled frequently around the country hired him to be a copilot for his multi-engine plane. For extra income, he flew as a test pilot, a risky task that added considerable value to a new plane once proven safe and reliable. He also bought and sold his own planes, always at a sizeable profit from the original price. He was enough of a daredevil to try skydiving. One Sunday afternoon, he accepted a bet among his pals to walk along the wing of his plane and jump over Lake Placid, New York, near Rainbow Lake. On the way down, however, Bill wound up on the wrong side of his parachute, falling from the sky, out of control. Frantically, he righted himself and floated safely to the ground. It was his first, and last, jump.

Fran Baker sometimes joined his friend in the sky and was convinced by him to take pilot lessons. Like Bill, Fran had enrolled in the University of Rochester's medical school after graduating from

Hamilton. Flying also played a pivotal role in Bill's relationship with Fran's sister. At Hamilton, Bill dated other young women, particularly a steady girlfriend named Elisabeth Ellis. But after idyllic summers at Rainbow Lake, he dreamed of marrying Dody Baker. Bill always seemed like another person in her presence, as if still gliding across the lake. His usual curt, no-nonsense manner melted. "Bill was able to show his caring for me," Dody later recalled. "He had a nice way of doing it with his actions—being thoughtful, kind, helpful, and being interested."

His intentions escalated when Dody became suddenly ill. Fran arranged for his sister, who still lived in Buffalo with their mother, to be hospitalized in Rochester for minor surgery. On a whim, Bill decided to greet her when she recovered with two dozen long-stemmed roses. Bill wanted Dody to marry him and "felt it was time to make his move," Fran recalled. When he couldn't find enough special roses in Rochester, Bill launched an extravagant plan to make him seem a "big shot" in Dody's eyes. He called New York City and arranged to pick up two dozen roses at a small airport near the George Washington Bridge. By the time he flew back to the hospital, visiting hours were over. A volunteer nurse assured him Dody would receive the roses and his attached love note when she awoke.

Early the next morning, Fran called Bill to say his grandmother had died in Buffalo, and he wondered whether Bill could possibly fly Dody home for the funeral. "Of course," Bill agreed, certain Dody would be delighted to see him. However, when he arrived at the hospital later that day, Dody appeared upset and still groggy from anesthesia. To Bill's surprise, she said nothing about his two dozen roses and love poem in a handwritten note. Dody didn't know about the gifts, because they never arrived. Perhaps the evening nurse forgot to deliver the roses or something else went amiss in the daily frenzy of a busy hospital. Bill assumed the worst and never inquired about the gesture. "He knew she was upset because of her grandmother's death, so he didn't press the issue," explained Fran. "She never mentioned the note [and roses] because she never received them, so he interpreted it as a rejection."

Dutifully, Bill flew Dody home to Buffalo in his two-seater plane. Not much was said above the dull hum of the engine. "I noticed that she was only answering questions, not talking freely with me, which made me feel quite anxious," Bill later recalled. When they landed in Buffalo, Dody graciously thanked Bill, displaying only simple courtesy. Fran whisked Dody away, and Bill climbed back in his plane to head back to Rochester alone, stunned that his proposal of love had failed. For a long time, he didn't hear anything more about Dody—whom he called the one true love of his youth—until one morning when he learned Dody had married someone else, another young doctor from Buffalo. "I could only wish her the very best and I did so," Bill wrote. "I hurt for a very long time."

Some friends and family would doubt Bill's sad, apocryphal account of this lost love, this summer romance gone awry. Was Dody Baker more of a dream than a reality, the kind of idealized image that men conjure up about the women they say they love, without any real understanding of the person behind this projection? How could a man so grounded in the exacting standards of science and medicine, with a seemingly unforgiving stare as he looked out upon the world, see this woman with such a gossamer haze? For years afterward, Bill Masters wondered how life might have been if he'd wed his beautiful blonde on the beach at Rainbow Lake. "I don't know if we would have had a happy marriage," he wrote in his unpublished memoir, "but I certainly would have liked to have tried."

CHAPTER FIVE

A Wonder to Behold

"Can we expect to have sound education without the inspiration of men who are seeking to know, through their own research, the universe in which mankind dwells and the nature of man's body and mind?"

—Dr. George Washington Corner

The human body was a wonder to behold in George Washington Corner's anatomy class. With mastery and precision, Corner surveyed the blood-pumping heart, the exquisite architecture of the spine, the vital functions of the liver, kidneys, intestines, and other marvels of muscle, bone, and tissue described in the *Gray's Anatomy* textbook. To his students, he could make a cadaver come alive.

At the University of Rochester, Corner was a renowned physician in his prime. "I took Anatomy in the first year, the first class I had," Fran Baker remembered of Corner. "He was quiet, but very forceful, very inspiring." Corner made an even stronger impression on Bill Masters. After dabbling with the idea of becoming an English professor, Masters left Hamilton wanting to become an everyday doctor, but Corner inspired him to become a scientist as well, forever testing the unexplored areas of medicine. On more than one occasion, Masters remembered Corner telling him, "Bill, you can't ever learn too much."

A Renaissance man, Corner could speak authoritatively about the history of anatomy as well as the craft. He panegyrized Aristotle as the father of biology and talked knowingly about dissection among the Assyrians, Hebrews, and Greeks. He particularly fascinated on the wonders of the reproductive system, the wellspring of all life. "When the mammalian ovum was first seen, in 1827, the discovery solved a great problem, but at the same time it revealed an endless series of new questions in which we are still involved," Corner later wrote in his autobiography.

Before founding the anatomy department at Rochester, Corner studied and taught at Johns Hopkins University, researching the histology and physiology of the reproductive system. With a historian's bent, he recognized how much religion, cultural traditions, and sheer ignorance had kept humans in the dark about sexual reproduction, and he was particularly appalled by medicine itself. "Gynecologists' efforts to treat the functional disorders of menstruation and sterility were mere puttering, scarcely advanced beyond the procedures of the Hippocratic era," Corner wrote in 1914. "How could we hope for anything better when we simply did not understand the human cycle?" In gauging his impact, one textbook later referred to the "Before Corner" and "After Corner" periods in the emerging field of obstetrics and gynecology. His work led to fundamental insights on contraception and the development of the birth control pill. Corner and his trusted colleague at Rochester, Willard Allen, discovered the role of progesterone, a key hormone in the menstrual cycle. Many expected them someday to win a Nobel Prize.

In the lab, Corner performed reproductive tests on monkeys and rabbits, where his students received their first look at how things worked among mammals.

"Masters, glad to have you aboard," Corner said as he entered the professor's office. "Do you know whether rabbits menstruate cyclically?"

Masters appeared clueless. "Dr. Corner, I haven't the vaguest idea," he admitted.

Although one of the most accomplished scientists in his field, Corner remained humble and soft-spoken, with the air of a cheery grandfather looking out for his charges. He decided to let Masters off easy.

"Neither have I," Corner said with amusement. "When you find out, let me know."

Initial attempts by Masters to get rabbits to menstruate didn't go very far. "I was spectacularly unsuccessful," he recalled. "They just wouldn't do it for me." But direct observation of rabbit love in the lab did yield its rewards. Masters eventually discovered that the female rabbit involuntary ovulates while being mounted by the male.

Soon Corner left Rochester for an even more prestigious position at the Carnegie Institute of Embryology in Baltimore, where he influenced many young researchers, including Alfred Kinsey of Indiana University. Corner's connections with the government-sponsored Committee for Research in Problems of Sex in the early 1940s helped Kinsey, then an entomologist specializing in gall wasps, gain key funding from the Rockefeller Foundation for his landmark surveys on human sexual behavior. He urged the committee to support Kinsey generously, even though he later described him as "the most intense person I ever knew outside of an institution for psychiatry."

About the same time, during the spring vacation of his third year at medical school in 1942, Masters received an invitation from his old teacher in Baltimore to attend meetings of leading reproductive biologists from around the country who visited Corner's lab. Without saying a word, Masters absorbed their lively discussions and plotted how he, too, might make a mark in medicine. During lunchtime chatter, Carl Hartman, a longtime Corner associate who had developed Carnegie's primate testing lab, discussed his difficulties in getting a female monkey to have sex with a male, even though she was in heat. After a time, the frustrated monkey became angry at Hartman's promptings and bit him on the thumb. Waving his wounded finger, Hartman sought some answers for his dilemma and then turned to the young medical student in the room.

"Masters, while I was talking about trying to get this female in heat to mate, you had a bemused look on your face—what were you thinking about?" Hartman demanded.

Masters possessed the spellbound look of a research scientist engrossed in an eternal question.

"I was wondering about the human female," Masters replied, "and if there could be a cyclic mating heating pattern in women that has not been identified?"

There was no laughter, no initial response at all. At the lunch table, as Masters later recalled, there was dead silence. The idea of testing a woman, exploring her physiology and sexual response, sounded like a sure ticket to professional ruin and possibly criminal arrest. No one dared go beyond the testing done on rabbits and monkeys.

For the rest of his stay in Baltimore, Masters consulted with Corner and the other experts about exactly what it would take to do a study of human female sexuality. Any professional foolhardy enough to try it, they told him, would face boundless dangers. Ever inquisitive, Masters pressed these wise men of medicine for a way they thought it might be done. Eventually they arrived at a four-point criteria: this sex researcher must be a married man, they said, and close to age forty with ample seniority. ("I've been bald since twenty-three, so that helped!" Masters later quipped.) More important, this sex scientist needed to prove himself an accomplished researcher in a related medical field and have the institutional backing of a university, preferably its medical school.

Unlike these older scientists, who had come of age saddled by the constraints of the Victorian era, Masters viewed himself as a modern doctor unafraid of such a challenging topic and what others might think. But he would follow their advice, convinced of its worthiness. "My experience at the Carnegie Institute was a major factor in my life," Masters wrote. "The criteria that the men in Baltimore had developed certainly influenced my thinking." With this long-term plan in mind, Bill returned to Rochester to finish his last year of medical school, wondering whether to seek his internship in psychiatry or in the field of obstetrics and gynecology.

Elisabeth Ellis waited patiently for the day she would marry Bill Masters. Ever since they'd danced at an Alpha Delta Phi party during his junior year at Hamilton College, she had indicated he was her special intended one. When Masters went off to medical school in Rochester, the young couple continued to date—sometimes sporadically but never with complete interruption—while she worked as a factory secretary in Utica,

New York, more than one hundred miles away. If she knew about his longing for Dody Baker, she didn't let on. Nor did she seem to wonder whether her fiancé might be marrying her on the rebound, to overcome the lonesome hurt of someone else's rejection. The smart, athletic, and hard-working Bill Masters was someone she felt she could count on, the kind of man Elisabeth Ellis had sought all her life.

Betty Ellis—known as Libby or just plain Lib, as Bill often called her—treated him more lovingly, with more genuine regard, than any woman in his life. She remained steady in temperament and resolutely true to those she loved, no matter how much they might disappoint her. Though not a natural beauty, she was a thin, pleasing young woman with luminous eyes and generous lips who wore her dark, curly hair carefully coiffed. She dressed as well as her modest finances allowed, enough to look as if she'd stepped out of an advertisement for Marshall Field's or Talbots, the women's store. As they both knew, Libby was the kind of proper young lady suitable for a doctor's wife. Addison Wardwell, Bill's fraternity mate at Hamilton, said the feelings of affection were mutual. "They had a big romance while Bill was in college," recalled Wardwell. "From what Betty said, they had been seeing quite a bit of each other during college. But Bill never talked a great deal about what he was going to do or what he was planning." Years later, Bill described the genesis of his relationship with Libby as less a romance than as two fates joined. "We began dating on an irregular basis," Bill wrote, "but the more we saw of each other, the more we felt we had an important future together."

Hamilton strictly limited fraternization with what educated gentlemen called the weaker sex. Dances at Alpha Delta Phi were held just twice a year. A cautious separation between men and women was enforced. Men on the second floor of the house surrendered their rooms for those young ladies staying overnight, supervised and guarded by a militia of chaperones. Undoubtedly, the notion of meeting a local girl like Libby behind the nature garden, perhaps kissing and necking in the moonlight amidst the flowering trees, outside the purview of a forbidding housemaster or pesky resident adviser, appealed to Bill. Wardwell remembered one instance in which Bill inadvertently challenged the social code of wholeness and purity between the sexes at Hamilton, reflected at other colleges as well before World War II. During a vacation, when most of the frat brothers were gone, Bill awakened early in the morning to tend to a science project before picking up Libby at her home nearby. When the couple stopped by Alpha Delta Phi, it was late morning. Bill decided to check on his project, which involved putting eggs in an incubator to observe the development of a chick embryo. He pulled out one of the eggs and began breaking it apart at a table. One of the crusty old professors assigned to keep an eye on the fraternity espied the young couple peering into one of the heated eggs and quickly concluded the worst. "Being a stern type, he assumed that there had been some misconduct going on," Wardwell recalled. "He had assumed that Bill and Betty had spent the night at the house and were getting up, having breakfast." The professor didn't confront Bill and Betty but later addressed the entire fraternity house, lecturing them about what Hamilton men shouldn't be doing with female guests.

Bill held his tongue during the old professor's admonishments. Life had given him a stony poker face, controlled enough not to reveal shame, embarrassment, or other emotions. When the professor left, though, Bill gave out "a happy roar," with a wide, bemused grin.

"The old boy knows all about it—he knows all the rules!" Bill said, laughing in mockery.

Long before she met Bill Masters, Elisabeth Ellis had experienced plenty of disappointment and heartbreak. Her mother died when Libby was about ten—an age old enough to miss her mother's memory, but too young to benefit from her worldly advice. Her death was a blow from which Libby and the surviving Ellis family never recovered. After her mother's passing in the 1920s, her father, Guy Ellis, disappeared. Without any warning or explanation, he just got up and left. He ditched Libby and her two sisters, Marjorie and Virginia, and their once-comfortable life in Grosse Point, Michigan, the toniest suburban lakefront enclave surrounding Detroit. Guy Ellis took off for Florida, a warm climate hospitable to a man fleeing his responsibilities. For Libby, her father became a phantom lost forever.

Libby and her sisters wound up living with the family of Uncle Steve, a very wealthy, kindly neighbor and his wife who were no relation but took pity and made room for them in their house. Before she could finish high school, the Depression brought more tragedy for Elisabeth and her new family. When the 1929 market crashed, Uncle Steve's sizeable fortune collapsed with it, sending him into a steep emotional decline that resulted in his suicide. After witnessing the shocking end of both her natural and adoptive families, Libby was ready for a man who had learned to overcome life's cruelties and thrive.

After nearly five years of waiting, Masters finally proposed to Libby. Over summer vacation before his fourth year at medical school in Rochester, he married her in a modest ceremony in Detroit, the only place she'd known as home. "He told her that he could not really get serious because he had a lot of education and work to do to establish a name," recalled her younger cousin, Townsend Foster Jr. "He really discouraged her but she hung on long enough and they got married." The newlyweds rented a small apartment within walking distance of Rochester's medical school and hospital. "Finances were tight, but we were contented and happy," Masters recalled. When graduation finally arrived, he considered where he might go for his medical internship. Despite World War II's being in full gear, Masters had received a medical release from the military. He wanted to take his hospital training in the field of obstetrics and gynecology, to understand the anatomy and physiology of the human reproductive system, though he knew it would take him only so far on his intended path. "I had no illusions that I would learn anything about sex in the ultraconservative medical specialty of Ob/Gyn," he wrote. Once again, he reached out to his old mentor, Dr. Corner, for advice. During their telephone conversation in February 1943, Masters confirmed his commitment to doing sex research.

"Well, why not go and see Willard Allen?" Corner suggested.

Masters explained that his "grades were not absolutely top flight" to be accepted into Allen's program at Washington University. At the time, Allen reigned as one of the top reproductive endocrinologists in the nation. Masters said he would love to go out to St. Louis, working in an internship with Allen, but he doubted he could overcome the competition for that position.

Allen had been Corner's first research fellow at Rochester when they studied the impact of hormones on the female reproductive system. They discovered the hormone progesterone, prevalent both in ovulation and in pregnancy, by teasing it from the corpus luteum (the bloody tissue released from ovarian follicles during the menstrual cycle) of rabbits. Proving that there was more than one sex hormone, estrogen, in the body catapulted Allen's reputation into the rarified academic air occupied by his teacher, Dr. Corner. Eventually, Allen left Rochester's faculty to become the department chairman of obstetrics and gynecology at the Washington University medical school. About a decade older than Masters, Allen was considered a brilliant and skilled surgeon with a pleasant, if somewhat bland, demeanor. He became one of the nation's youngest medical school department chairmen when he arrived in St. Louis. Though their careers took them in different directions, Allen never lost contact with his trusted and brilliant colleague, Dr. Corner.

"Bill, are you rushed for time?" Corner asked Masters over the telephone. "If you will wait for about five minutes, I will call you back."

Within minutes, Corner returned with good news. "The internship is yours," he announced, quite pleased with his behind-the-scenes handiwork.

Masters remained stunned and deeply moved that Corner might care enough, have enough faith in his ability and future, to extend such a helping hand. "I had very wet eyes for the next several days musing over my incredible good fortune and the kindness of Dr. George Corner," he remembered.

By the summer of 1943, Bill and Libby Masters moved to St. Louis, where the young couple planned a new life for themselves and to start a family. In arranging this internship, Corner gave Masters's medical career not only a boost but also a ringing endorsement to chart the unknown corridors of human sexuality. If such a wise and learned man as Corner recognized his plan's scientific worth, Masters knew he could convince the world.

CHAPTER SIX

The Fertility Expert

Motionless on an operating room table, the young woman had already lost her fetus and was dying in a pool of blood. She kept hemorrhaging from *placenta percreta*—a rare catastrophic condition in which the placenta penetrated the uterine wall, invaded other organs, and starved her baby of life-giving nutrients. Whatever rescue the three young doctors tried on the fourth floor of Maternity Hospital, nothing seemed to work. They performed a cesarean section to remove the remains of the woman's placenta. They stuffed numerous packs into her uterine cavity to stop the profuse bleeding, without success. If the doctors didn't think of something soon, they knew she would die on their watch.

"It was the worst case that I had seen," recalled Ernst R. Friedrich, a resident doctor that night. "We gave her multiple blood transfusions. There was a danger that, if the blood didn't clot anymore, she would bleed to death."

A desperate call went out to the faculty member on duty from Washington University's medical school, the prestigious teaching institution affiliated with the hospital. Although their plea came late at night around Christmas, one of the school's most skilled practitioners soon appeared, to the residents' relief. Bill Masters rushed through the door. "He took his clothing off in the hallway, put on a scrub suit that some nurses threw at him, and he went right into the operating room," Friedrich remembered. "Dr. Masters came in, saw what the problem was, and he knew what to do.

He didn't discuss it, didn't procrastinate. He did what was necessary and got us out of trouble."

After some tense moments, Masters saved the woman's life through sheer talent with a knife, his understanding of the complexities of a woman's reproductive system, and his unflinching manner that never showed doubt. Friedrich felt so relieved that he grabbed a small camera, meant to take pictures at a Christmas party, and snapped an image of the doctors involved in this miraculous recovery. "Everyone was wading through blood," he remembered. "The photos showed how bloody some of us looked." Medical reputations were made of heroics like this, a virtuoso performance by a surgeon at the top of his form, earning Masters respect from his faculty peers and gratitude from fledgling doctors in his training.

By 1950, William Masters had achieved the necessary preparation proscribed by George Corner before studying human sexuality. Appointed an assistant professor of obstetrics and gynecology at Washington University, Masters enjoyed a prodigious rise through one of the most esteemed medical schools in the Midwest. Looking older than his thirty-five years, he emerged as the department's second in command, right behind chairman Willard Allen. Masters and his wife, Libby, moved to a comfortable place in Clayton, and then a larger house in Ladue, an affluent suburb of St. Louis, in anticipation of starting their own family. He built up an enviable coterie of wealthy patients who revered him through each pregnancy, labor, and successful delivery. Among his peers, Masters developed impeccable credentials as a surgeon, a teacher, and an expert in the emerging science of fertility.

Though under six feet tall, Bill retained a broad-shouldered vigor from his college football days, running each morning before work. He wore stiff, starched shirts and always a bow tie, and carried himself like a gladiator. His walleyed gaze seemed merely a sign of his studied detachment from those around him. In class, he didn't smile easily. He would sort of smack his lips and draw them in toward his teeth, in a tight, even keel. "When you got a smile or a chuckle out of him, you felt like you were being accepted, like your father just patted you on the head and said, 'You're a good boy!'" described Dr. Mike Freiman, a medical school fellow assigned to Masters. The prep school adolescent who once seemed so unsure of himself, who refused to go home, had emerged from his self-contained cocoon. "He was an extremely proud man, and all of his clothing was custom-made," recalled Dr. Francis Riley, another fellow assigned to him in the 1950s. "That was the nature of Masters. He used to change his white coat twice a day and he used only white ballpoint pens. He never used any other color pen. He was an independent man who wasn't exactly reserved, but he didn't do a great deal of talking." Some thought Masters more than a little arrogant, though no one had the nerve to say it to his face. "Not only did he think he was better than everybody else as a doctor, but he also meant it as a person," said Dr. Eugene Renzi, another ob-gyn resident during the 1950s. "His ego was big." Renzi and Riley recalled the stylish black sports car, an MG convertible, in which Masters tooled around campus. When the rain fell, Bill kept the top down and put the car's tarp around his waist, whizzing by them, impervious to the downpour.

Late Friday afternoons, Washington University's ob-gyn faculty and residents gathered to discuss surgical techniques and case management. No nurses or medical students were allowed at these frank discussions. Masters enjoyed mixing it up, playing the devil's advocate. "He would stand up and say, 'No, I'd do it *that way*' just to provoke, to show there's not always one way to do something in medicine," said Marvin Rennard, another former resident. Masters challenged medical orthodoxy, as only a superb practitioner could do. "If there was a problem at Maternity Hospital, the guy we most wanted to see walking down the hall was Bill Masters," said former resident Robert Goell. "He had superb judgment, the bridge between the old time and the new."

One Friday, cesarean sections were vigorously debated, particularly why the rate jumped from 3 percent to 6 percent of all cases during a six-month period. Today, a cesarean procedure—removing the baby through a surgical incision to the mother's abdomen rather than risking complications if delivered vaginally—is far more common, with many hospitals having a rate of 25 percent or more. But in the early 1950s, most seasoned obstetricians relied exclusively on vaginal deliveries, no matter how long labor lingered for the suffering mother. Senior faculty trained in the 1930s—when penicillin and blood banks hadn't been developed, and when anesthesia could prove disastrous—warned their young staff not to be "knife happy" with C-sections, partly because they were unaccustomed to the procedure. During a memorable exchange, debate focused on how best to handle dystotic labors, where the agony of childbirth could last more than thirty-six hours and seem never-ending. Doctors expounded on how they could "manage" a woman enduring more than a day of labor. Someone finally asked, "Dr. Masters, what would you do?"

Masters gave a wry grin and curt reply. "I wouldn't have had this problem," he declared flatly, in a loud voice. "I would have sectioned her out *long ago*."

Though his skills were admired (he seemed nearly ambidextrous with a scalpel), Masters wasn't "one of the boys" after hours. Among the predominantly male faculty, he wasn't inclined to go out for a beer or sign up at the golf links for a Sunday-morning party of four. He seemed present at Maternity Hospital all the time, a relentless researcher and practitioner of the craft. Masters didn't suffer fools gladly, as doctors, nurses, and sometimes patients could attest. If a patient arrived more than ten minutes late for an appointment, Masters refused to see her. She would have to reschedule, and if tardy a second time, she was banned permanently. As an expert in the new field of fertility treatment, Masters insisted women bring their husbands along for treatment. "He was very rigid on this," recalled Dr. Ira Gall, who worked as a fellow under Masters in the mid-1950s.

Behind his gruff veneer, Masters could be very empathetic, especially to women vulnerable to life's indignities. As a new physician in training, Mike Freiman accompanied Masters on his rounds and entered an examination room where they did a routine gynecological checkup on an older black woman. St. Louis was still very much a segregated city in the 1950s, and Maternity Hospital had its own "Negro" floor, where women of color and their babies were treated. Freiman vividly recalled the exam's lessons. The tiny, slight woman was a widow more than eighty years old who, despite her age, retained a hint of her youth. She clutched her lace handkerchief as the doctors methodically quizzed her about her health. Near the end of her visit, Masters cleared his throat, as he often did at this point, to pose a question.

Masters began, "When was the last time you had intercourse?"

The elderly woman, who had been looking down at the floor, suddenly lifted her gaze and stared Masters right in the eye. Then she let slip a slight, almost grateful smile.

"Dr. Masters," she replied, "at my age, it's hard to find a good friend."

Freiman was struck by the poignancy of this exchange. For men in white robes dealing with the most confidential secrets of a woman's health, Masters showed it was imperative to act in a professional manner, yet to be sensitive to each patient's humanity and emotional needs. "That was very valuable to me," recalled Freiman. "What I learned from him, as he said, 'If you are proper in the way you ask a question, you can ask just about anything.' By asking, he recognized her as a sexual being and still attractive."

By the mid-1950s, Masters's constant innovations to ob-gyn surgery earned him a prominent place in the field. He became one of the first in the country to use caudal anesthesia—applying a local anesthetic to the caudal canal, located in the lowest part of the spine, to relieve the pain of childbirth. It avoided the dangers of a pregnant woman losing consciousness while going under with ether or general anesthesia, the preferred approach for complicated cases. He coauthored a 1953 scholarly article about that technique, analyzing more than five thousand deliveries over an extended time. In 1955, Masters and Willard Allen wrote in the *American Journal of Obstetrics and Gynecology* about a new operating technique to help thousands of women suffering from pelvic pain related to uterine scars, usually left over from previous pregnancies. This condition became known as the "Allen-Masters" syndrome and sometimes switched as Masters became more prominent. His mind so inventive, his hand so sure, Masters boldly championed new surgical answers for the most desperate of patients, such as creating an artificial vagina for seven women born without them. Particularly in these cases, Masters realized how much sexual function could affect a patient's mental health. Dr. Marvin Grody, a faculty staff member, recalled a patient in her late teens, given an artificial vagina by Masters when the procedure was still quite new. She expressed her profound gratitude, as if she'd been granted a new life. "The patient couldn't have children," Grody recalled, "but could at least enjoy intercourse."

Willard Allen proved the perfect patron for Masters's research into hormones, fertility, and the underlying sexual lives of patients, which the hidebound field of obstetrics and gynecology often ignored. "None of this would have happened without Willard Allen—he was the boss," explained Dr. John Barlow Martin, who also served as a fellow under Masters. "He and Bill Masters had a very close relationship and that's how Bill was able to do it." In the name of science, Allen could take a principled stand himself. At Maternity Hospital, Allen respected the wishes of any woman who, after delivery, said she wanted to be sterilized with a tubal ligation (so long as she had "enough" with five or more children, her husband agreed, and her blood count was at an acceptable level). Decades later, "tube-tying" became commonplace among women wanting to prevent pregnancy. But in 1950s St. Louis, Allen's policy directive stunned both staff and patients. "That caused a revolution here because this is a Catholic community and the university backed him," said Martin. "So Allen was accustomed to being controversial." Initially, Masters joined Allen in researching hormone replacement therapy, testing how the return of estrogen and progesterone to an aged woman's depleted system of hormones could revitalize her and avoid difficulties after menopause. In all, Masters had his name on more than forty academic articles during his first decade as a full-time Washington University faculty member. To Ira Gall, whose two children Allen delivered, it was striking that these two men, so different in personality and temperament, could be close friends united in a common goal. "Willard Allen was an easygoing guy and it took a lot to really upset him," said Gall. "Bill Masters was a very capable person and the patients who got pregnant because of [his medical attention] thought he was a saint. But when it came down to it, he was not an outgoing, jovial person."

By his tenth year at Washington University in 1953, Masters focused increasingly on fertility, helping couples to procreate. He introduced the Infertility Research Program at Maternity Hospital and set up one of the first sperm banks in the nation. Harvard, Columbia, and a handful of other teaching hospitals around the nation had similar operations, but none more advanced than at Washington University. Masters's sophisticated skills were viewed as a godsend to those desperately trying to conceive. "We have a child because of Bill Masters," said Dodie Josephine Brodhead, who along with her husband, John, became friends with Masters, mainly through his wife. "It was feast or famine in families, and it was famine in ours. We didn't have a child for eight years. And we went to Bill Masters, and thanks to his astuteness and understanding of the whole field of sterility, I became pregnant and we had a child. As a matter of fact, she was born on his birthday."

Dodie Brodhead had difficulties in conceiving, and her husband had a low sperm count, perhaps as a consequence, she theorizes, of the gravitational forces endured during his days as a Navy dive-bomber pilot. At the Infertility Service, the initial session for couples like the Brodheads began with a rudimentary lesson in sex. "It was surprising to me how little people knew about getting pregnant," recalled Freiman, then a fellow who accompanied Masters during these sessions with couples. "He helped women understand when they were most fertile and how men should behave."

In those days, fertility treatment carried a certain social stigma. "Typical male jokes were made about it," recalled Dodie Brodhead. "The joke was that everybody who came to Bill Masters to be tested, they came with a paper bag over their head." Facing long odds, most successful couples willingly shared details from their intimate lives, hoping to win in the baby sweepstakes. Masters spoke plainly but compassionately, with practical advice even after her baby girl was born at Maternity Hospital. "Now, Dodie, don't think you've found the magic number and put off having another one—try again right away," Masters reminded her, aware of secondary infertility, which can sometimes impede women after they bear their first. "When you're in the pregnant mode, it can happen again quicker, better."

Rita Levis and her investment banker husband, Ed, sought out Masters, worried she might be sterile. "I wanted to have kids—

there's no question about it," Rita Levis recalled. "When I wasn't getting pregnant, the doctor I was going to suggested [Masters] to me. Nobody ever talked about sex in those days." Masters arranged prompt appointments and very private surroundings, so Rita never saw other patients exiting. "I think he did it to protect his clients," Rita Levis said. "People just didn't want anybody to know that they were having problems." Rita became indebted to Masters. "I got pregnant—that's what I call success for a fertility man," she said. "He delivered the baby." If success didn't happen soon, couples followed a number of methods designed to improve their chances, recalled Dr. Elfred Lampe, another of Masters's junior assistants. This to-do list included instructions on how to pivot in the missionary position to increase a would-be mother's receptivity to the downward crawl of spermatozoa. Getting pregnant usually involved maneuvers and contortions "that the normal couple wouldn't even have to think about," Lampe explained, "like going through the vaginal smears to optimize the time that ovulation would occur, and the husband getting the specimen either through masturbation or collecting it in a condom." Husbands arrived with their sperm specimen in a small paper bag, as if carrying their lunch to school. As a last resort for women married to infertile men, medical students were the preferred donors at the sperm bank, where the rate of success was very high. "We told people that our sperm bank was the student body of the medical school of the University of Washington and that we would try to match hair and eye color and basic background, but we would allow the dean of the medical school to select for intelligence—a little bragging," recalled Dr. Thomas Gilpatrick, another resident who worked with Masters. "With our donor insemination, our success rate was in the 90 percent range."

As word of Masters's triumphs spread, patients looking for reproductive expertise arrived from all over the country and, in several cases, from overseas. During an appointment in the mid-1950s, Dodie Brodhead remembered waiting in the examination room until Masters finally showed up, apologetic and upset. Dodie, a social friend of Libby Masters, inquired why.

"I've had the loveliest lady here and I just had to tell her that she's sterile and will never have children," Masters confided. Nothing could be done, he explained, his voice full of frustration. He said the woman's husband would go to any lengths to have a son. Then, after a pause, he added, "It's especially sad when she's the Shah of Iran's wife and you have to have an heir."

Though it sounded fanciful, Brodhead didn't forget Masters's account. A few months later, she read in the newspapers about the sad fate of Princess Soraya Esfandiari Bakhtiari, the wife of the Shah of Iran, exactly as Masters had explained it to her. During the 1950s, Soraya was the obsession of paparazzi in Europe, a woman of legendary beauty who filled the tabloids in the same way later generations obsessed over Princess Diana of Great Britain. In 1951, she married Mohammed Reza Pahlavi, the last Shah of Iran, and joined the world of the Peacock Throne in Tehran. Implicit in this agreement was that Soraya would produce a son. From the moment the Shah met Soraya, however, the two seemed genuinely in love. The Shah's first wife was an Egyptian princess, a loveless marriage arranged by their families that produced a daughter but no male heir. Within a short time, Soraya's difficulty in becoming pregnant became clear. Politicians and religious leaders in Iran pressed the Shah for a male child capable of someday leading their nation and maintaining political stability. This urgency heightened after a failed assassination attempt against the Shah, an American-friendly monarch installed during a CIA-provoked coup d'état.

On a trip to the United States, the Shah's wife visited top fertility experts, hoping for a solution. One doctor suggested an untried, possibly life-threatening form of surgery with a long-shot chance of success, ultimately rejected as too risky. Masters didn't offer any miracle cures. When he examined the X-rays of Soraya's fallopian tubes, Masters quickly determined the hopelessness. In 1958, the Shah divorced this one true love, believing it would save the throne. Soraya, barren but not penniless, spent the rest of her days with the title of princess, a constant wanderer living in Europe's finest hotels. Years later, before the Shah was deposed by the Ayatollah Khomeini and his Islamic revolution, his doctors would come to see Masters again for further training.

Though a few friends knew of his consultation in the Shah of Iran's quest for an heir, no one was more impressed than Dodie Brodhead, who was surprised when Masters later mentioned he was changing the focus of his research. At a neighbor's crowded cocktail party, they chatted about his successful fertility clinic, the concerns of would-be parents, and the fascinating aspects of bringing a child into the world through artificial means. Then at some point, Masters confided that his intended goal, as a logical sequence, was to study sex itself.

"People are sent from all over the world to you—why are you switching into something so controversial?" asked Dodie, a bit taken aback.

"Well, almost everything that really needed to be known, or can be known, is done, and I want to make a discovery," Masters stated plainly. "I want my name in history."

Dodie stared at him in amazement.

"Wow, you *do* have an ego, Bill!" she said.

They both laughed at his audaciousness. But it was something she would always remember.

CHAPTER SEVEN

The Good Wife

"The greatest of all curses is the curse of sterility, and the severest of all condemnations should be that visited on willful sterility. The first essential in any civilization is that the man and woman shall be father and mother of healthy children, so that the race shall increase and not decrease."

—THEODORE ROOSEVELT

Marge Foster rejoiced when the Masterses moved next door. She had known Betty ever since their early days together in Michigan and they shared a bond of kinship. Marge was the sister-in-law to Betty's oldest sister, Marjorie. Their husbands were brothers, Torrey and Townsend Foster. She regarded Betty as a longtime friend and wonderful wife to Bill, a respected university physician. Betty and Bill had everything in their lives except children. The brick, two-story Dutch colonial at 34 Oakleigh Lane in Ladue, Missouri, would be an ideal place to raise a family, they all agreed.

When the Masterses first came to St. Louis, Marge helped them find an apartment near the university and Maternity Hospital. And when the house next door became available in Marge's neighborhood of Ladue—one of the most affluent and prestigious suburbs in St. Louis—she tipped off Betty and Bill, who promptly put down a deposit for its purchase. "We lived next door to the Masterses for years, so we were very close," Marge recalled. "She tried to do everything in the world to make him happy." To Torrey Foster, Marge's impressionable teenage son, not a hair, weed, or word seemed out of place at the Masters house. "Like a lot of women of her generation, I don't know that she saw her role as being anything but being the homebody that supported the family and letting Bill do his professional work," recalled Torrey, who shared his father's first name. "Being a good wife meant a lot to Betty."

The Masterses gave the impression of being to the manor born, emanating from a higher caste in the social strata. This notion was perpetuated by Betty's affluent friends from St. Peter's Episcopal Church in Ladue and by those who knew Bill as a card-carrying Republican member of the squash club, seen on certain mornings with a racket in hand. "I would describe her as a patrician woman, a good-looking individual who was not overly friendly but was proper," said Dr. Francis Riley, who had known a fair number of Brahmins from his Harvard days. "Libby was very well connected socially," insisted Dr. John Barlow Martin, who himself graduated from a private school in St. Louis. Bill's patients seemed drawn from the carriage trade—well-to-do women in St. Louis who favored the droll, bow-tied Bill as their preferred obstetrician-gynecologist. Phyllis Schlafly, the starchy archconservative, relied on his services, apparently without much satisfaction. "I don't have anything good to say about him," she recalled. Most women, though, enjoyed Bill's no-nonsense, direct manner that gave them the feeling, whether in the stirrups or chatting upright on the floor, that they'd been to the best in town. From his wife's friends and acquaintances, from the country clubs, prep schools, and word-of-mouth on the upper-class society circuit, Bill built enough of a practice that he could later delegate patients to his junior colleague, Dr. Martin. After a few months, Martin consulted Bill about one topic these patients always wanted advice about—sex.

"Bill, you've referred all these socially prominent ladies to me—and they are all unhappily married," Martin said, both frustrated and perplexed.

Masters smiled as if they were still in the classroom, as professor to student. "You simply tell her, 'I'm terribly sorry that you're unhappily married. You have three choices—you may continue as you are, get a divorce, or have an affair. Thanks for coming, just pay the girl on your way out,'" he explained.

Martin adopted this mantra as gospel from Masters, his mentor.

When they first arrived in St. Louis, Elisabeth Masters worked as a secretary for Dr. Otto Schwartz, an older physician who had been Washington University's ob-gyn department chairman before Willard Allen. Libby's job gave her some sense of her husband's life at the hospital, an inside knowledge of the influential faculty members. Within a few years, "Lib felt it was time to have a family," Bill recalled. During the holidays, Libby Masters played the charming hostess to cheery, stylish parties at their home. They invited neighbors, friends, and colleagues from the medical school, including those serving under Bill. "At that time, it looked like a lovely marriage," recalled Dr. Marvin Grody, a fellow in the Infertility Research Program. "They wanted children very much, to have two children. They were very devoted to the idea of having a family."

There was only one problem—the Masters couple couldn't get pregnant. Like most having fertility difficulties, they preferred not to talk about it, at least not to others. When Addison Wardell, their old friend from Hamilton College, visited shortly after they arrived in St. Louis, the notion of starting a family was already in the air. "They did not have any children, and Bill's mind got working to figure out why, what the problem was," recalled Wardell, who said Bill's interest in fertility stemmed in part from his concerns at home. "I kind of gathered, from what Betty said, they did consider it a problem and were trying to get around it." Wardell didn't pry enough to find out the source of their fertility problem.

Later in life, Dr. Masters never mentioned his personal history with fertility problems. Even when the topic came up and he rendered his opinions professionally, he never hinted about struggles with conception in his own marriage. To Virginia Johnson, however, Bill went further, with a version fundamentally misleading. He suggested Libby's reproductive system was at fault. Bill told Virginia that an acidic "lethal factor" inside Libby's vagina killed his sperm, and only through his scientific handiwork did the Masterses wind up with two children. A daughter named Sarah Masters, often called "Sali," was born in 1950, and a son, William Howell Masters Jr., "Howie," the following year. "They had two children—they are thirteen months apart—and it was courtesy of his infertility work," Virginia recounted. "That's probably why he went into fertility, because she couldn't get pregnant." Bill developed a "capping" technique—one of the first physicians to use such an approach. His sperm were collected in a plastic "cap," then inserted through Libby's vagina into her cervix, allowing Bill's seed to be planted safely in her fallopian tubes. "He was one of the pioneers of doing that," said Johnson of the capping technique. "It wasn't that she wasn't fertile or that his sperm wasn't perfectly active and fine. It was just the vaginal environment." This heroic version about the genesis of the two Masters children, a tale Bill confided to Virginia, dovetailed nicely with his innovative reputation as a fertility expert. Somehow Bill found success for Libby, whom he suggested couldn't bear children without the circumvention he devised.

But in truth, the fault wasn't with Libby, but with Bill himself. "Elisabeth had trouble becoming pregnant and Bill Masters was responsible for her infertility because he had oligospermia, a low sperm count," remembered Dr. Grody, who coauthored a medical study with Bill about the "cervical cap" for treatment of male infertility. Bill recognized the potential to cure his own fertility problems when he heard of an earlier study using the cervical cap and launched a follow-up experiment. Their study counted Betty and Bill among its human guinea pigs. "Bill told me that he had a low sperm count and that's why he used the cap," explained Grody, who prepared much of the detail cited in their May 1952 article published in the *Journal of the American Medical Association.* In the paper, the two pregnancies of Elisabeth Masters were cited only with the initials "E.M.," like the other successes listed in a chart with just patients' initials. The study underlined Bill's remote chances of becoming a father naturally at that time. It described a sperm count of sixty million per cubic centimeter as "the arbitrary lower limit of the normal range." Of the thirteen other husbands mentioned in the study, the average sperm count was thirty-six million/cc. But Bill Masters—the husband of "E.M."—had a sperm count of only five million/cc, the lowest in the study.

Admitting to a low sperm count may have been impossible, perhaps as some admission of male weakness, a chink in his carefully structured armor of masculinity. Men like Bill Masters, the former college football player who got up early each morning to run a few laps around Oakleigh Lane before going off to work, weren't supposed to be faulty vessels of potency. Perhaps Bill felt his own male infertility, if it were known, might affect his status at the university's infertility clinic. In the political and sexually repressive atmosphere of the 1950s, the clinic's euphemistic goal of "making babies" in a lab still involved keeping the nitty-gritty, socially forbidden details of sex wrapped in secrecy. Beyond his obligatory mention to Grody, Bill decided to either say nothing or concoct a variation of the truth. "It had nothing to do with low sperm count—quite the contrary," Virginia insisted when told of the study, citing the husband of "E.M." with the deficient sperm count. "Believe me, it was very hard not to become pregnant with him!"

Sure of his facts, Grody could only laugh years later at the different accounts left by his old friend. "That may have been what he told Virginia, but it was wrong," said Grody of the claim that Libby was the reason why it took years for the Masterses to have a child. "All I know is what Bill told me, that he used it [the cervical cap] and that he was successful." Indeed, Grody assisted in the delivery when one of the Masterses' babies was born.

Libby Masters, hopeful of becoming a mother, quietly trusted her husband's judgment. "The only thing I know truthfully is that they had a hard time getting pregnant," explained their son, Howie. Masters never discussed sex with his son, except once when Howie, near age thirty, sought his father's practical advice about a similar matter. "The only thing I remember of him talking to me about sexuality was when I was married and trying to get pregnant and having trouble," explained Howie. "He finally said, 'Jesus Christ, do A, B, C, D—and laid it all out, if you were going to have a better shot at conceiving.'" To conceive, Libby and Bill, like other couples desperate for a child, endured the petty humiliations and crude, recipe-like methods of artificial insemination as then practiced by American medicine. At the medical school's infertility program, each couple was "simply exposed to a discussion of *when, how frequently,* and *how to* have intercourse in order to have the best chance of conception," Masters recounted in his memoir with special emphasis. For example, Masters advised couples, quite counterintuitively, that they shouldn't have intercourse every fleeting moment during the female's fertile period. Instead, he suggested "a staggered coital schedule" about thirty-six hours apart—usually the twelfth night, fourteenth morning, and fifteenth night within a woman's normal twenty-eight-day menstrual cycle. "It often takes the male thirty to forty hours to return his sperm count to whatever normal levels might be," he advised. As a fertility expert, Masters counseled each woman to begin by relaxing on her back, with a pillow just so beneath her hips. During intercourse, as the male approached "the stage of ejaculatory inevitability," Masters suggested a rather abrupt and definitive finish. "He should make the deepest possible vaginal penetration, stop the actual process of coital thrusting, hold the penis in the depth of the vagina, ejaculate, and then withdraw *immediately*," Masters instructed. No dawdling here, no waiting for a magical moment. Sex in this scenario resembled the swift final incision of a swordfight, or inflating a tire with a hose, rather than any expression of tenderness. Seminal fluid should not be wasted, Masters warned. Following this confluence of two bodies, the female should bend her knees and rest them on her chest for about an hour, so no precious emissions could escape the vaginal canal. These how-to pointers could make a big difference, he suggested, helping to create the miracle of life no matter how graphic or demeaning the advice seemed to the participants.

At the infertility clinic, his little sex talk worked wonders. Merely by reciting the basics, one of every eight cases resulted in a pregnancy within three months. Masters enjoyed telling colleagues the story of a couple, both high school teachers, who thought they could become pregnant by sleeping together in the most literal sense. The husband complained about "the acrobatics associated with sex" but he and his wife dutifully followed Masters's instructions, resulting in a pregnancy by the second month of trying. "I do realize it is almost impossible to believe this story," Masters later wrote. "It certainly was for me initially, until I got to know this couple better."

Masters's case was more complicated, and more desperate, than most. A footnote in the *JAMA* article described "E.M." and her husband as "an intensively treated couple with a seven-year sterility problem with marked oligospermia who achieved conception twice by capping." Their remarkable success, however, obscured the long odds they faced. As in most sterility research, this study found chances of getting pregnant "inversely proportional" to the length of time spent waiting for it to happen. Of fourteen couples who endured more than three years of sterility, only five wound up conceiving. Before being enrolled, they endured at least one year of therapy with another physician for this problem and followed the infertility clinic's advice for six to twelve months before trying the cervical cap. Quite clinically, the paper described the bedroom obstacle course confronted by couples like the Masterses with each pregnancy attempt. For starters, rectal thermometers and vaginal pap smears checked for just the right time in Betty's monthly ovulation. In anticipation, Bill, like other males in the study, observed a "three-to five-day period of abstinence" before, as the paper described, masturbating "directly into a clean, wide-mouthed glass tube." Within twenty minutes, his semen was placed in the cap, ready for entry. Meanwhile, Betty followed the route of other women in the study by "douching with a specially prepared neutralizing solution shown to be optimally favorable for sperm survival."

With a clean rubber glove, the fleshy folds of Betty's labia were spread apart, enough for the cap filled with ejaculate to enter. Then the truly tricky part began. Still wearing the glove, the doctor—or in this case, presumably Masters—slipped two fingers up along the back wall of the vagina, balancing the open cup horizontally in its grip to keep it from spilling prematurely. When the two fingers reached the cervix, the cap was properly fitted in place. From there, the wiggly sperm raced their way toward the ripe and awaiting ovum, just as nature intended. Not all uteruses and vaginas were alike, as the study acknowledged, offering an even more elaborate Plan B if necessary. In this alternate scenario, a clean empty cap entered first, secured against the cervical opening. Then the cap was injected with semen drawn into a twenty-gauge syringe, with a curved needle to avoid puncturing the cervix. Once the cap was filled, the waiting game began. For all would-be mothers, these caps had to stay in place for a minimum of eight hours and removed usually within sixteen hours. Some couples repeated this process up to seven times before success. The majority of "Individual Failures"—as the study identified this unfortunate lot—went through this ordeal more than ten times, with one couple doing it nineteen times over two years without a pregnancy.

The Masterses were lucky, statistically speaking. They repeated the insemination procedure twice to produce their first child, and only once with their second. They were among four couples in which the husband was a physician, taught to use the cap at home rather than coming into the hospital clinic. "All four wives, no longer subjected to the procedure in the confines of a professional environment under the management of persons other than their husbands, promptly became pregnant," the study noted. Another couple, who went on vacation, also relaxed enough to become pregnant. With an eye toward the future, Masters's study suggested a link between fertility and female sexual response. Some women who faced this capping procedure over and over, usually without luck, developed vaginismus—the conditioned reflex of the pubococcygeus muscle preventing vaginal penetration, even with something as seemingly innocuous as a tampon. "Much attention has recently been focused on the psychic aspects of sterility, and certainly the unusual circumstances of insemination procedures, as compared with ordinary coitus, can initiate or intensify unusual emotional reactions which may, in turn, become manifest organically by localized muscle spasm and vascular congestion," explained Masters in the paper. One can only imagine how such a tense clinical atmosphere for a woman anxious to become pregnant, with a husband looking for results and a male doctor with a rubber glove on his hand, could hinder her receptivity.

Masters showed more compassion toward his patients than ever, understanding from experience their desperation to have a baby. He didn't offer any remedy that Bill and Libby hadn't already tried at home. The intrinsic connections between mind and body, between fertility and sexual habits, were all part of these efforts, he recognized. In another earlier 1952 paper about infertility cowritten with Grody, Masters explained how careful questioning of a couple "either too embarrassed or too inhibited to voluntary disclose" their sex habits could greatly affect the results. Particularly for the infertile couple dogged by expensive but ineffectual therapies in the past, he advised, "the initial interview should instill in the couple a feeling of enthusiasm." As a fertility doctor, Masters devised a plan to interview each couple together and also separately as individuals to maximize his understanding, a format he later refined as a sex researcher. "When you work in infertility, then you have a great deal to do with the subject of sex—we were indoctrinated into that subject with Masters," recalled Dr. Riley, another of his young physician fellows at the clinic dealing with about 100 infertility patients. "You had a considerable amount to do with the sexual behavior of these couples."

As always, Libby Masters lived up to her wifely duties, consenting to virtually any means her husband devised to become pregnant with his faulty sperm. She agreed to plastic caps, special soaking solutions, rubber gloves, and resting on her back for hours with knees in the air, so they could start a family. As a research subject, she even agreed to have her experiences and her children's birth cited by initials in his medical articles to enhance his career. However, once the two Masters children were born—the fruit of their long odyssey through the infertility desert—Libby decided she'd had enough of medicine. She left her job as a secretary to Dr. Otto Schwartz at the university. She also let Bill know she wouldn't be able to help him in his research as it moved increasingly from hormones and fertility to the largely unexplored terrain of human sexuality. "He offered that opportunity to her and she turned it down because she felt her obligation was to the home and the children," recalled Townsend Foster Jr., her nephew. Her decision reflected Libby Masters's personality as a homebody, her deepest desire to establish a settled family life after so much heartache and tumultuousness growing up. "In her heart of hearts, she wanted to be supportive in any way she could be, but she was never going to make a significant contribution to the work," explained their son, Howie. "She was interested in being a really terrific wife, supportive of a guy who was pursuing a rather precarious medical profession. And knowing full well, as they talked about it, that this whole thing could have *easily* blown up."

CHAPTER EIGHT

Academic Freedom

"It is only through truth that man can build with strength. As the University motto has it, 'Per veritatem vis.'"

—ETHAN A. H. SHEPLEY

During the McCarthy era, Ethan A. H. Shepley's defense of academic freedom never wavered. A Republican who later ran for Missouri governor, Shepley never went along with the anti-Communist jeremiads of U.S. Senator Joe McCarthy from Wisconsin, or insisted on loyalty oaths from his faculty. He loved Washington University, his alma mater, too much to do anything but encourage the best in intellectual pursuit. In 1954, Shepley took over as chancellor after he joined the school's search committee for a new leader and they eventually turned to him. Shepley was a towering figure, with broad shoulders, a square jaw, and a high, sloping forehead that hovered above his black horn-rimmed glasses like an iceberg. "One of the things that he liked about the job was that he could encourage academic freedom and research," recalled his daughter-in-law, Peggy Shepley. "So he was the perfect backdrop for Bill Masters."

Masters was nearly forty years old, a teacher at Washington University's medical school for a decade. His work on hormones and infertility proved first-rate, his surgical skills were unimpeachable, and his academic reputation in the field of obstetrics and gynecology comparable only to Willard Allen, the department chairman. With Shepley as chancellor, Masters realized the timing was right to propose an extensive study of the physiology of human sexual response. At Indiana University, Alfred Kinsey had published a book in 1948 about male behavior and a second about the human female in 1953. Masters's proposal seemed in that same vein, building on Kinsey's much-publicized research. "Without their original foot in the door, we would have never been allowed to work, there's no question about that whatsoever," Masters later said of Kinsey. "Obviously, there was a precedent set."

Unlike Kinsey, who gathered eighteen thousand personal histories from a Gallup-like questionnaire about sexual behavior and attitudes, Masters proposed to directly observe the body's functioning during sex—meticulously tracking each pulse, breath, thrust, and quiver. Studying men and women in the flesh would provide a far more definitive understanding of human sexuality than the notoriously inexact and often misleading process of an opinion survey. From his countless interviews with infertility couples, Masters knew people didn't always tell the truth about sex—far from it. Lies, half truths, delusions, wishful thinking, faulty recollections, and significant omissions were all part of patients' accounts of their sex lives. As every scientist knew, the most valuable information—the only thing that could really be trusted—was clinical observation, documented proof for each assertion. Since their early days together, Allen had known of Masters's intent to concentrate on female sexual response. Masters referred to it obliquely in hundreds of pregnancies and fertility cases, and in tiny footnotes in medical studies. As an obstetrician-gynecologist, Allen and Masters saw female sexuality as the anatomical underpinning of their specialty, a reality all practitioners had to contend with but refused to investigate. Tradition, taboo, and the penal law itself prevented such study. Allen warned him of the possible consequences.

"Since you are determined to do this type of research, I am not going to stand in your way, but I must tell you that I am deeply concerned," cautioned Allen, a kindly man not given to bluster. "Both you and I know that you may be committing professional suicide if you do this work." The medical school dean, Ed Dempsey, also expressed concerns to Masters about professional ethics and in-house politics that might cripple his efforts. But both Allen and Dempsey agreed to pass along his proposal to the next level. After listening to Masters's pitch, Chancellor Shepley agreed to take it to the trustees. "I will be back to you when I have something to say," Shepley promised.

Several months passed before Masters received an answer.

Chancellor Shepley, a smart lawyer well acquainted with the conservative mores of his native St. Louis, didn't provide many specifics to his board of trustees. He knew Masters's study of human sexuality would entail a much different approach than Kinsey's—one worthy of the intellectual freedom the medical school could provide. But this approach also carried greater risk, public scorn, and possible legal charges. Shepley told them only what was necessary and that Bill Masters deserved their backing. Washington University officials "were terrified . . . but had they known what we were going to do, they'd have been even more so," Masters recalled. "They thought it was going to be more of the same, but we weren't about to play in the Kinsey league."

On June 26, 1954, Masters received a letter from Shepley, telling him to come by at his convenience. After such a lengthy wait, he assumed the worst.

"Bill, we whipped them," Shepley announced as soon as Masters walked through the chancellor's door. "I am just delighted. I must tell you that I was a little surprised that you did get permission."

Masters felt elated. Now he would get the chance of a lifetime, to finally do something for which he had worked and prepared his entire career. His happiness, though, was short-lived. Shepley admitted the board's vote wasn't unanimous. He explained the trustees' nervousness about losing vital alumni contributions if news leaked out about Masters's sex study. Masters would have to find his own source of funding and keep the program secret. Most important, though he'd given his trustees only a general outline of Masters's intent, Shepley made Masters promise to keep him informed regularly of his future actions. "Needless to say, that was a rider that I was delighted to accept and said so," Masters later recalled. "Above all else, I wanted to use the chancellor's good offices and mature judgment whenever I had a problem."

Six weeks later, Masters reported back to the chancellor. During that period, in August 1954 Alfred Kinsey had died of a heart attack. The way seemed clear for Masters to become the new pioneer in sex research. When Masters walked into his office again, Shepley wore a bemused, friendly smile, hardly the mask of a worried bureaucrat.

"What have you got to tell me about sex?" the chancellor asked half-jokingly.

Masters remained serious. "Well, sir, I have to tell you," he began, "I am overwhelmingly aware that I don't know anything about sex. And I don't believe you do either."

Shepley roared with laughter.

The two men discussed the difficulties of conducting a medical study of human sexuality, and why it was so long overdue in America.

After gaining approval, Masters visited the medical school library, looking for any book, medical article, or dissertation he could adapt to his plan. "I realized that there was really nothing that had been written or researched that was going to be of any help in working out the physiology of human sexual response," he later observed.

At Washington University, Masters found just one title about sexual functioning to shed some light. The textbook had been written by a former University of Illinois department chairman of obstetrics and gynecology who, as Masters learned, waited until retirement to publish it. Washington University kept this book on the reserve shelf. When Masters asked to see it, the librarian refused.

"I'm sorry, Dr. Masters, I cannot do that," she told him.

Puzzled, Masters thought she had misunderstood him. "I do not want to take it out," he explained. "I just want to look at it."

The librarian wouldn't budge. The textbook contained sketches—thin line drawings—of male and female genitalia, which the library superiors worried might be pornographic. As an associate professor, Masters wasn't eligible to see it. Only full professors, heads of departments, and librarians could remove this book from the reserve shelf, he was told. He promptly marched over to Willard Allen's office and asked him to borrow the library book on his behalf. This small incident, Masters later reflected, "represented all too well medicine's fearful approach to the subject of sex."

For centuries, talk about sex had focused solely on reproduction, its only sanctioned purpose being to breed a family, tribe, or nation. Though many wondered in poems, plays, and treatises about the allure and differences between the sexes—with religions, philosophies, and political tracts defining love between a man and a woman as a cornerstone of civilized culture and often the meaning of life itself—few in medicine had studied its basic fundamentals. Dating back to the ancient-Greece days of Hippocrates, the "father of medicine," human sexuality remained perpetually misunderstood, ignored, vilified, or condemned to punishment. Yet everyone had a theory. Plato distinguished between "vulgar" lust and the noble "heavenly" form of eros as the motivating polar attractions between men and women. "The only difference between men and women is one of physical function—one begets, the other bears children," Plato said in *The Republic*. As a doctor, Hippocrates hypothesized that both men and women produced semen, emanating from the spine, with a child's sexual identity determined by which parent's seed was more dominant. Some self-emasculating Greeks tied up left or right testes, believing it would determine an infant's gender. Although egalitarian in love, Aristotle wondered about sex differences and, based on his animal studies, envisioned a process of male semen awakening the tiniest of babies already formed and dormant in the female. According to the prevailing science of his time, Aristotle advised couples, before getting together, to check the weather. "More males are born if copulation takes place when north than when south winds are blowing," he wrote. "For in the latter case the animals produce more secretion, and too much secretion is hard to concoct; hence the semen of the males is more liquid, and so is the discharge of the catamenia."

During the Renaissance, Leonardo da Vinci magnificently illustrated the anatomical changes of sex and pregnancy, with enough technical realism to be replicated in glossy medical textbooks many years afterward. Undoubtedly, to even the most chaste observer, the sensual, fleshy images found in the work of Michelangelo, Botticelli, Reuben, and other great artists of Western Europe hinted at the mix of pleasure and procreation in sexual love. But even in this lush era, medicine remained a captive of political and religious dictates, both of which kept a careful reign on sex outside the confines of marriage. After a misspent youth of fornication, described in his autobiographical *Confessions,* a repentant St. Augustine ("the bubbling impulses of puberty befogged and obscured my heart so that it could not see the difference between love's serenity and lust's darkness") influenced centuries of church teachings about sex, warning of its potential for evil even among married couples.

Invariably, sex became enwrapped in a wider debate about women in society. The Jansenist condemnations in France—with their suggestions that revolutionary politics had been fueled by unrestrained sexual urges—were echoed by the Calvinists in England and Puritans who made their way to the New World, conducting witch hunts on childless women whose infertility, they alleged, was caused by the devil. Even Martin Luther, the great Protestant reformer who denounced celibacy within the church's ranks, viewed women as inferior, passive receptacles for men's sinful cravings and their ceaseless desire for lineage. "A woman does not have complete mastery over herself," Luther summarized in a letter to three nuns in 1524. "God created her body that she should be with a man and bear and raise children."

As the industrial age dawned, migration to the city allowed more time for leisure, beyond the constant backbreaking grind of rural life. The economic drive of sex to provide a succession of farmhands faded. In urban settings, the very nature of family life changed. Women's drive for equality emerged in schools and at the ballot box, while other progressive concepts, such as a childhood free of manual labor, entered the public consciousness. Increasingly, medicine focused on the body rather than the heavenly soul. An early pioneer, John Hunter, a physician often credited with establishing modern surgery, rejected the common view that "a practice so general" as masturbation could lead to impotency. Willing to dissect corpses exhumed from graves, Hunter (a favorite client of the "body-snatchers" before such thefts were outlawed) learned about the internal organs of the reproductive system. According to biographical legend, Hunter claimed the first successful case of artificial insemination and even enlisted himself as a guinea pig in an experiment testing for syphilis and gonorrhea. It supposedly backfired when he tried inoculating his own penis with "venereal matter" from a prostitute and contracted disease. Along with legitimate doctors, numerous medical quacks offered "cures" and potions for whatever sexual inadequacy might afflict the public. Scotsman James Graham became famous for claiming to solve the Duchess of Devonshire's infertility. Her gratitude helped finance Graham's Temple of Health retreat, where Londoners could hear lecturers about potency, read selections from his book (*Lecture on Love; or Private Advice to Married Ladies and Gentlemen)* or be stimulated with mild electrical shocks. For today's equivalent of about $50,000, the Crown's wealthiest couples could spend a night of ecstasy in a vibrating "celestial bed," a contraption in which "the barren certainly must become fruitful when they are so powerfully agitated in the delights of love," as Graham guaranteed.

Early American society, spawned largely by Western European influences, embraced both a fundamentalist view of sex in public and a far more iconoclastic, utilitarian view in private. From the pulpit, Cotton Mather and others thundered with fire-and-brimstone sermons, warning of an eternity in hell for those who gave in to their basest urges. "If any person . . . falls into a scandalous iniquity," scolded Mather, the son of Harvard's president, "let the rebukes of the Society be dispensed unto him." Just in case anyone forgot these lessons, Nathaniel Hawthorne's 1850 novel, *The Scarlet Letter,* portrayed the passions, sexual repression, and Puritan condemnation symbolized by the big "A" worn by the heroine, who had committed adultery. Despite these unambiguous warnings, however, sex in the thirteen former colonies was a far more complicated matter. On southern plantations, at least one white Founding Father inflicted himself upon his Negro slaves, while in the north, Benjamin Franklin, as worldly as he was brilliant, suggested experience in bed might be more valuable than the loss of youthful beauty. "In the dark all Cats are grey, the Pleasure of corporal Enjoyment with an Old Woman is at least equal, and frequently superior, every Knack being by Practice capable of Improvement," advised Franklin.

The American penchant for mixing sex with theocratic beliefs emboldened the polygamous Mormons to seek refuge in Salt Lake City, a place where they could pine for each other and intermingle. This driving force also prompted John Humphrey Noyes to establish his "free love" Oneida colony in upstate New York during the 1840s, based on the ideas of "Christian Communism," eugenics, and sharing wives for "amative" rather than "procreative" sexual intercourse. The Victorian era of the late 1800s placed a damper on the sexual license of the western frontier, with its boom towns, brothels and gas-lit boardinghouses run by ruined southern belles. But scorn for illicit sex didn't prevent Grover Cleveland's election as U.S. president despite allegations of having fathered an illegitimate child ("Ma, Ma, where's my pa?" jeered his opponents. "Gone to the White House! Ha ha ha!"). In New York City, Anthony Comstock launched his crusade against sin and vice, determined to stamp out any sign of obscenity in the library, in the mail, or onstage. Several early feminists, notably Victoria Woodhull, championed sexual equality as much as women's suffrage. A writer and newspaper editor, Woodhull was arrested under the Comstock Act for exposing the sexual liaisons of famous preacher Henry Ward Beecher with his best friend's wife—a tawdry affair that drew the kind of lurid headlines later reserved for a sitting president and his female intern. By the turn of the twentieth century, medicine had barely adapted to the sexual lives of patients, especially women. In 1900, a physician proposed an article about the sexual response of female adults but the editor of the *Journal of the American Medical Association* magazine rejected it. In 1916, Margaret Sanger, who had worked as a nurse and midwife, railed against women's lack of power over their own reproductive lives. Sanger challenged the legal bans against contraceptives endorsed by leading church figures and physicians. "When the history of our civilization is written, it will be a biological history, and Margaret Sanger will be its heroine," predicted historian H. G. Wells, about the woman who later led Planned Parenthood.

As Bill Masters read further in the library, he realized the field of obstetrics and gynecology had a peculiar aversion to matters of sex, as if doctors preferred only the happy outcome of babies being born, rather than the more indelicate matters leading to their arrival. In Great Britain, physician Havelock Ellis prepared a lengthy history about the psychology of sex, underlining the toll that ignorance exacted from men and women. As he wrote in 1927: "The ignorance of women of all that concerns the art of love, and their total lack of preparation for the natural facts of the sexual life, would perhaps be of less evil augury for marriage if it were always compensated by the knowledge, skill, and considerateness of the husband. But that is by no means always the case." In America, Masters knew from experience that gifted doctors like George Washington Corner and Willard Allen wouldn't go near the topic of sex, even though so much of their study encircled it. Masters underlined a quote he found in the library from Dr. Robert L. Dickinson, former president of the American Gynecological Society, who wrote in *JAMA* during the mid-1920s: "In view of the pervicacious gonadal urge in human beings, it is not a little curious that science develops its sole timidity about the pivotal point of the physiology of sex. . . . Considering the incorrigible marriage habit of the race, it is not unreasonable to demand of preventive medicine a place for a little section of conjugal hygiene that might do its part to invest with dignity certain processes of love and begetting." Dickinson's circuitous language in another 1940s *JAMA* piece allowed him to advocate the hygienic qualities of newly developed tampon products. To overcome parents' moral objections about an object being inserted into their daughters' vaginas, he argued that the old pad, used as a "menstrual guard," rubbed up against the vulva too provocatively. As Dickinson wrote, the old pad-and-belt system "in addition to applying some degree of heat within a confined space, is responsible for rhythmic play of pressure against surfaces uniquely alert to erotic feeling."

As a matter of professional pride, Masters didn't want to engage in euphemisms or elliptical arguments of the past. He wanted to learn the truth about human sexual physiology, as best as medical science could portray it. When he first spoke with Chancellor Shepley, he didn't dwell on specifics about the proposed sex study. He positioned his plan as a matter of academic freedom. Now that he had Shepley's conceptual approval, however, he felt duty-bound to tell him exactly what he had in mind.

After some friendly banter during their meeting, Shepley finally asked, "What do you want to do about this business?"

Masters's first request was a sabbatical. He explained that he needed to leave the St. Louis area frequently during this time and that Willard Allen had agreed to relieve him of teaching responsibilities. Masters then revealed his plan. Over the course of the next several months, he would interview and observe prostitutes in St. Louis and elsewhere in the nation. The chancellor "turned deathly pale," as Masters later wrote, and stammered out a response.

"The prostitute population—but why?" the chancellor asked, with a trace of dread.

Masters held firm. "They are the only experts on the subject of sex that I can identify," he said. "This certainly indicates how little any of us know about the subject."

Shepley, champion of academic freedom, was in no position to argue the point.

CHAPTER NINE

Through the Peephole

As chief of police, H. Sam Priest understood how the morally righteous denizens of St. Louis felt about prostitution. He also knew how his wife felt about Bill Masters.

Prostitution had a sordid, sometimes violent history in St. Louis. In 1850, a mob became so enflamed by the painted ladies and their illicit sex that it smashed through all the city's brothels in a frenzy to enforce standards of public decency. For decades afterward, Missouri's law considered prostitution a felony. Violators in the flesh trade were sent to jail and bawdyhouses were shut down permanently. In 1955, however, Priest decided prostitutes who assisted Dr. Masters in his Washington University research study were going to get a free pass—no arrests, no police raids, not even threatening knocks at their doors. This grant of immunity was particularly odd because the wiry, hard-driving police commissioner was credited with a decrease in the city's crime rate while that of the rest of America went up. But Priest trusted their doctor.

Inside the Priest home, Bill Masters was beloved for delivering their second child. Margaret Priest admired Masters for his sure-handed skills and his down-to-earth manner, with the implicit high regard for a person who brings your baby into the world. Sam Priest, a cop's cop, shared his wife's esteem for Masters, regardless of possible rebuke for his department's lack of prostitution enforcement. "Sam felt it was important work and he just didn't allow the prostitutes to be locked up or mistreated in any way," recalled Margaret. "If he [Masters] wanted to interview them or get any information about them, as long as it didn't impinge on their rights, that was all right with my husband." Masters enlisted the police commissioner as a secret ally of his sex study, running political interference. Priest's detectives recommended prostitutes willing to be studied and kept the sordid details away from the press—all because Masters asked him so. "My husband was not a scientist or a doctor—he was a politician in St. Louis," explained Margaret, whose husband was not above seeking advice from academia to improve his department's effectiveness in the streets.

Recruiting the St. Louis police commissioner as a special adviser on a consultative board, along with several other prominent figures in the city, proved vital to Masters and his work, according to lawyers who later represented him. "Priest was supportive of his work and as a consequence, when the prostitutes were acquired, the police were told, 'Let 'em have them—you don't have to raid the [Masters lab],'" recalled Torrey Foster, the young man next door who became Masters's first attorney. To Walter Metcalfe, the lawyer who later represented Masters and his clinic, the enlistment of Priest highlighted Masters's persuasiveness. "He was extremely dedicated, had a long-term plan, and the authorities and others bought into it," said Metcalfe. "He was striking in his sincerity and his conviction. He'd say, 'This is where I'm going to be, and I have to go to these places to get there.'"

Along with the police commissioner, the advisory board included Richard Amberg, publisher of the *St. Louis Globe-Democrat* (then one of the city's two newspapers), as well as the Episcopal bishop of Missouri and the most senior rabbi in the Midwest. Washington University Chancellor Ethan Shepley agreed with Masters that such high-powered advisers would be invaluable in preventing trouble.

"Tell me, Bill, what damn fool are you going to ask to head this board?" asked Shepley.

"Sir, I thought *you* might," Masters replied.

Shepley stood motionless for a moment—perhaps contemplating how a new university chancellor could find himself in the position of overseeing a research study using prostitutes—and then started to laugh at the absurdity of it all. "If you have enough nerve to do this to me," Shepley said with a chuckle, "I have enough nerve to join you in your venture." He directed Masters to secure the cooperation of the Catholic community because of its large numbers in St. Louis. The next day, Masters called the St. Louis diocese, asking to meet with the archbishop, whose secretary responded with a flustered voice when told the subject was "sex research." Masters assumed his attempt to talk had failed, but three days later, the same secretary called back to say the archbishop would be pleased to see him.

In the Catholic Church in America, Joseph E. Ritter, a slightly built man with a gentle voice and rimless glasses, was that rarest of breeds—a liberal who had risen to the top. Upon becoming archbishop in 1946, he ordered parochial schools to integrate, while many Missouri public schools remained segregated. When opponents threatened court action, Ritter promised to excommunicate them if they challenged his decision. "The cross on the top of our schools must mean something," insisted Ritter, who eventually became a cardinal. Masters visited Ritter in the mid-1950s, when only slight rumblings existed about birth control—certainly far from the political divisiveness found in the church after its 1968 ban on contraceptives, the 1970s battle over abortion, and the more recent public outing of pedophiles in its ranks, all of which seemed to militarize the Catholic hierarchy on the subject of sex. Most parishioners kept mention of their carnal sins for the confessional. In his meeting with Masters, the archbishop welcomed serious research into marital tensions afflicting couples. "I realize all too well that the security of millions of marriages in this country and abroad is threatened by sexual problems," Ritter told him during their two-and-a-half-hour meeting. The Catholic leader said he couldn't accept an official appointment to Masters's consulting board but would assign a priest as a liaison to keep his office informed. As Masters departed, the archbishop thanked him. "I don't have to tell you that some of the research techniques you described could not be approved by the Catholic Church," he said. "But I can tell you that the Catholic Church will be very interested in your results." Ritter promised he wouldn't say anything publicly about his work without first speaking to Masters.

With the police commissioner, the archbishop, and the Washington University chancellor on board—each in his own way a believer in medicine—Masters finally felt comfortable relying on prostitutes as his experimental subjects.

As in other American cities, female prostitutes in St. Louis were portrayed as fallen women perpetuating a social evil. Their male patrons were seen as victims of feminine wiles (never their own willful actions), unwittingly infected with syphilis, tuberculosis, and other venereal ills, which they carried back home to their families. In 1895, the St. Louis health commissioner's annual report reflected the prevailing view about the prostitution trade: *"For the maiden who in a moment of passionate love renders up the jewel of her chastity, there may be some commiseration; but what excuse or palliation can be offered for the woman who abandons her body to every comer, for money? The vice is as ancient as history, and a universal and incurable evil, that must be tolerated, and should be, as far as possible, palliated."*

By the 1950s, most doctors in St. Louis still wouldn't dream of dealing with prostitutes. But the world of streetwalkers, whorehouses, and anonymous men craving sex soon became Masters's lab. During his first twenty months of research, he interviewed 118 female and 27 male prostitutes, from St. Louis and other cities. He carefully noted their encounters and their medical histories. Masters said he never paid for their cooperation, though doctors assisting him say prostitutes received compensation for their time as research subjects. From this group, he selected eight women and three men for "anatomic and physiologic study"—watching various sexual acts. Even though he was a senior faculty member at a leading medical school, Masters realized how much he didn't know about the complexities of copulation. Their streetwise frankness was far different than the stiff anxiety of his upper-middle-class patients who visited his office for a pelvic exam. These prostitutes, conscripted with the vice squad's help, knew exactly what aroused a flaccid penis and stimulated a dry vagina, and how the two might come together with maximum efficiency. "They described many methods for elevating and controlling sexual tensions and demonstrated innumerable variations in stimulative technique," Masters wrote. These "laboratory-study subjects" helped him through the trial-and-error period of his investigation, as he realized how to record the most basic anatomical aspects of sex.

In bordellos, with the police department's blessing, Masters met "three men who, to a significant degree, controlled the professional prostitution population of St. Louis." These pimps became convinced Masters wasn't part of some law-enforcement sting but rather a university professor intent on learning. Masters was struck by the honesty of prostitutes discussing customers and their own experiences. In their early or mid-teens, many "started out having sex with various partners" as "payment-in-kind for being taken to a movie or other social engagements," he observed. Because men rarely wore condoms, diaphragms were the most common form of contraception, with a surprising number of women sterilized. When interviewing male prostitutes, however, Masters often felt lied to, especially about "coital frequency and functional capacity and efficiency." Unlike their female counterparts, these men claimed a sexual prowess beyond the realm of believability. When Masters felt a male prostitute's story was "more fantasy than fact," he refused to accept him into his study. Nevertheless, these interviews provided Masters with more insider detail than he ever imagined. "I could usually determine what questions to ask by letting their questions arise from my obvious ignorance of many patterns of sexual behavior about which I had little or no knowledge," he explained.

Direct observation in the bordellos gave Masters a ringside seat into the world of paid sex, a view that no interview session could offer. Initially, the vice squad donated some pornographic "stag" films confiscated during raids, depicting sex both graphic and rather joyless. But Masters explained he needed "to observe sexual function in order to develop a significant degree of objectivity." Masters's ability to convince pimps and prostitutes to go along with such a request—and not reject him as some pervert—was testament to his evident sincerity and the clout of his powerful supporters.

From the shadows, Masters followed the mating calls of prostitutes and watched how men responded. In houses of prostitution, he peered through peepholes or two-way mirrors, which had been placed strategically and discreetly so that voyeurs might watch a couple in action, or madams and pimps could keep an eye on rowdy customers. "I was always interested in why the prostitute approached a targeted male the way she did," he explained, like an anthropologist about an unknown distant civilization. Some prostitutes showed "an attitude of overt indifference," he noticed, while other women made "an obvious effort to stimulate, encourage and please the particular partner." After a few moments alone, prostitutes invariably asked their customers, "Where are you from?" Masters learned that query was more than friendly—if the patron hailed from somewhere local, these courtesans exerted extra effort to please, increasing the chance for repeat business.

Peephole watching was a cramped, tension-filled endeavor for Bill Masters. To see adequately, he had to put his eyeball right next to the hole, sitting behind walls or in catty-corners, without much circulation to relieve the stagnant, hot air. "It was the damnedest, least sexy thing you could imagine," he would later tell curious colleagues. As he squatted in hushed silence, Masters checked the amount of time in a sexual encounter, the points of entry and departure, and even the degree of bouncing around on the bed. He envisioned how to use an electrocardiogram, respiratory monitors, and other available medical equipment to measure the bodily changes taking place. Afterward, in his car or hotel room, Masters scribbled down his observations. Between 1955 and late 1956, Masters expanded his study in such St. Louis neighborhoods as the Central West End to interviews with call girls in other American cities, such as Chicago, Minneapolis, and New Orleans. The usual arrangement called for a police moratorium on arrests the week before, the week of, and the week after Masters's visit. As part of the exchange for information, Masters always offered to conduct a physical exam of each volunteer, including cultures of her throat, vagina, cervix, and rectum.

But eventually Masters realized prostitutes weren't suitable. The sample group was too small and not representative of the average American woman. Prostitutes frequently suffered from inflammatory disease and chronic pelvic congestion, known as Taylor syndrome (named for the Columbia University medical professor who wrote in the late 1940s about patients suffering temporary build-up of blood in the pelvic area without relief). Masters felt he couldn't make any definitive statements about the sexual response of women based on this atypical sample. More troubling, if he acknowledged in an academic paper that he had relied on prostitutes, he would face "an extremely negative response from the local St. Louis community," a firestorm sure to lead to professional ruin. Nevertheless, Masters believed that so-called ladies of the night provided numerous insights and were worth every second on the learning curve. "Interrogation of the women involved was quite productive, especially for someone who was essentially uninformed about female sexuality," he later conceded. These limits as a male doctor, trying to understand the response of women, were never so apparent as when he interviewed a "most attractive" college graduate, an intelligent, inquisitive woman who majored in biology. As Masters recalled, she was "amplifying her income for an impending marriage" by dabbling in the sex trade and became a clinical volunteer in Masters's study. One day, she offered a suggestion that changed everything.

Inside an examination room at Maternity Hospital, this young woman had manipulated herself into a lather ("auto-manipulation" was Masters's clinical phrase for it) until she appeared to climax—all while being recorded and analyzed by Masters's equipment. During a follow-up interview, they discussed her curved toes and tingling sensations but also her deepest emotions during sex. His purpose was to "identify with the subjective aspects of an objective response pattern." The young woman described what orgasm felt like and said the successfulness varied depending on who and what was doing the stimulating.

"What if I fake it?" she suddenly asked.

Masters seemed completely befuddled. "I don't know what you mean," he wondered, after a lengthy pause.

"That's what I do for a living—*I fake orgasms*," she stated bluntly, as if explaining to a child there was no such thing as Santa Claus. Often her sole objective in sex, she said, was "to hurry up and get the man to come, get paid and get rid of him."

Although he was a married man with hundreds of female gynecological patients, Masters remained perplexed. The young woman's description of orgasm—and the possibility that she might fake her reaction just to get the whole thing finished—seemed beyond his comprehension. "I simply could not understand her," he recalled. "I'm not sure I ever did."

After much frustration with this otherwise brilliant doctor, who monitored her orgasm but couldn't grasp her explanation of how it felt, the young woman finally declared that she had been patient enough with him.

"You really need an interpreter if you are serious about doing this research," she lectured the doctor pointedly. "You would certainly benefit by having a female partner."

Masters listened without reply. He seemed struck by lightning, as if hit in the head by a truth so obvious that he couldn't see it until now. Yet the more he pondered her suggestion, the more it made perfect sense. If he was to understand the "psychosexual aspects of female sexuality"—the *terra nova* region of this medical investigation upon which he was willing to risk his career—then he absolutely needed a female research partner. Masters knew he couldn't ask his wife, Libby. She had quit her job at Maternity Hospital to focus on their two young children.

Instead Masters decided to seek an assistant, a complete stranger, by placing an innocuous help-wanted notice with the Washington University recruitment office. After several weeks of hit-and-miss interviewing, just before Christmas in 1956, Masters finally found the helper he was looking for.

PHASE TWO

Bill and Gini on the couch

CHAPTER TEN

The Matrix

"But the thing has to be done scientifically, or the last state of the aspirant may be worse than the first."
—GEORGE BERNARD SHAW, PREFACE TO *PYGMALION*

Most mornings in early 1957, Virginia Johnson jotted down patients' names, ages, and addresses at a bulky metal desk situated on Maternity Hospital's third floor, like a lonely island in a sea of linoleum. Mrs. Johnson appeared just another nameless secretary, hired temporarily to sort through endless paperwork. "Her job was to fill out insurance forms," recalled Dr. Mike Freiman, then a young physician. "She was the single person in the department of ob-gyn whose desk was not in an office but actually in the hallway."

Johnson wanted to better herself by getting a sociology degree. But with this job, she didn't have any more ambition than to earn some money. "The medical world just didn't appeal to me in any way, shape, or form," she explained. "I always liked the doctors I knew as a kid growing up. But it meant nothing to me."

When medical students or young resident doctors walked through the hallway, Johnson occasionally looked up to acknowledge them with a glance. She befriended nurses in their twenties or early thirties, and, for a moment, she might chat with these women about their young kids, like her own. But when the senior doctors walked by, Johnson learned to perk up with an engaging smile and greet them by name. Within a short time, she knew all the major players in Washington University's ob-gyn department—

Dr. Willard Allen, the department chair; Dr. Alfred Sherman, the specialist in gynecological oncology; and especially Dr. William Masters, who had hired her. "To me, she wasn't any different than anyone else," recalled Dr. H. Marvin Camel about the new secretary who quickly made herself known. "Bill Masters saw something in her that no one else did."

At first, Johnson paid little mind to the happenings inside the physician offices. Before she took the job, friends told her Masters was a run-of-the-mill ob-gyn, specializing in fertility and hormone-replacement cases. She had no idea this bald physician, who always wore a properly drawn bow tie and an astringent face, shuffling busily from one appointment to the next, was doing something more. No one informed her about the clandestine sex experiment by her boss, a university professor secretly prowling through whorehouses. Masters never revealed this information when Johnson was hired. Nor did he mean to tell her four months later when Johnson rose from her hallway desk and went to lunch.

For her, the hospital cafeteria meant relief from the humdrum of filling out forms and the chance to circulate among the doctors and nurses. Seated next to those in white, she could be treated as nearly an equal, as close to social parity as any secretary or "research assistant" like herself could achieve. Mingling day after day, Virginia impressed the staff favorably. She dressed quite professionally, perhaps a reach above her lot in the hospital's pecking order, with only the slightest hint of sensuality. Her shining-smooth brown hair, expressive eyes, engaging manner, and sonorous voice made her a hit among the mostly male resident doctors. In the cafeteria, Camel remembered, Virginia always seemed in the middle of conversation among doctors and nurses. Johnson was "not unusually pretty but I think she looked rather sexy—she was friendly," recalled Camel. Sandra Sherman, wife of Dr. Sherman, recalled Johnson as a dark-haired beauty reminiscent of actress Ava Gardner, with a classy presence felt throughout the room. "Just her whole demeanor—the way she would even talk, to men in particular—that's the kind of sexuality that we're talking about." In the 1950s, when most doctors' wives were at home with their families, such an attentive divorcée hobnobbing at lunch with married staff members could be perceived with peril. Secretaries were not viewed fairly for their skills or acumen but as potential husband-hunters, she said, using their wiles to upset happy homesteads. Some men formed their own impressions about Johnson, including Dr. Sherman. "I saw her day in and day out—she was a nice secretary and she was very close," he said about Johnson's early tenure, when she performed secretarial duties for him and Masters. "After once or twice, I think she tried a little bit to get me involved sexually with herself. But I think she laid off and went to Bill because he seemed to be more interested in it." Camel heard rumors "that she had relationships with other men in the department but I'm not really sure it was true."

One of her closest friendships developed with Dr. Ira Gall, a short, energetic, often brilliant young doctor whose future success seemed certain. Their daytime shifts at the hospital often matched and soon the two began commuting to and from work together. Sitting in Ira's 1948 Plymouth, Virginia shared some of her life story, confiding details about her previous marriages, her experience as a singer in George Johnson's band, and about being a single parent raising two children with the help of babysitters. This very human portrait differed from the nearly anonymous secretary who chirped "good morning" from her hallway desk. Johnson impressed Gall and he offered his insights about medicine, the inner workings of the hospital, and the ob-gyn hierarchy at Washington University. Johnson proved a quick and able student, recognizing chances to improve her situation. "She talked herself into a good job," said Gall. "The original job was secretarial and filling out insurance forms. But when they were looking for a research assistant in this project, there wasn't any question that she would get it."

Lunchtime chatter one afternoon turned to Masters's covert sex study, provoking the usual inside gags among the house staff. Johnson smiled but didn't quite follow the humor. "They were kind of joking around about it within my presence a few times," she recalled. "I didn't ask a question. I didn't plan to stay" in that job. In her mind, Masters's infertility clinic certainly brushed against the topic of sex, but only as the necessary means for creating babies. "I had heard of Masters and his work with infertility, and that's what I thought I was being hired for when I took the job," she recalled. From the beginning, Johnson compiled the personal histories of patients, just as Masters instructed, and showed a genuine affinity, a curiosity about people's lives. Intimate questions seemed consistent with what she believed to be an infertility study. Nothing caused her to think otherwise. Her conversation in the lounge that day opened her eyes.

"Why are you doing this, Virginia?" one of the young male staffers asked her.

The medical residents assumed she knew all about the carnal goings-on in the soundproof rooms with research subjects paid for their services.

Virginia's genial reply didn't reveal her ignorance. As they conversed, however, she realized the full extent of Masters's secret sex study, with enough basics bandied about in undeniable detail.

At that point, Masters, dressed in his white lab coat, wandered into the room. He quickly surmised what was being discussed. Some staffers realized they had blundered by speaking so candidly. Everyone stared at Johnson, awaiting her reaction. Her eyes and other facial features didn't reveal her thoughts.

In front of his staff, Masters felt obliged to explain that the patient histories she had assembled for the past several months were part of a study of human sexual response and that some engaged in sex for the purpose of clinical analysis. "When he first told me what he really planned to do, that infertility was not going to be the prevailing work, that it was going into sex research, the question essentially posed to me was—'Is that going to bother you?'" she remembered.

Johnson appeared nonplussed. "I can't imagine why," she answered plainly. "But why does anyone need it?"

Her reply stunned Masters. Other men in the room, all medical residents in their twenties, grinned. A few chuckled belatedly, as if slowly comprehending the punch line to a joke. Masters didn't look amused, but rather pleased at her response. "That was the endearing line—I could never understand why anybody needed to know anything [about sex]," remembered Johnson, sounding like the Missouri farm girl who had witnessed enough animal lust in the barnyard not to be surprised by humans. In her world, sex had been long separated and kept apart from love, as perhaps only a divorced woman with two small kids can understand. She didn't look upon intimacy with either ferocity or dread, or the illusion of bliss. "I took it for granted," she recalled of her uncomplicated view about sex before working with Masters. "It was important but I never categorized it that way. To me, it always was a natural requirement, *a need*. It didn't shock me."

In retrospect, Virginia's calm, agreeable reaction in 1957 was a decisive factor in the partnership that became Masters and Johnson. "That, presumably, labeled me as the perfect person because I had no problems with it," she recalled. Characteristically, Masters offered a more detached description about her selection. "The nonmarried female inevitably is a professional virgin, and I couldn't deal with someone who doesn't find sex a totally comfortable subject," he explained with more than a little condescension, as if he were Professor Henry Higgins to Virginia's Eliza Doolittle in George Bernard Shaw's play *Pygmalion*. Here was an untrained female assistant who knew next to nothing about this explosive subject, someone Masters seemingly carved out of the public's bedrock ignorance about sex, and polished and refined to his liking.

Ideally, Masters preferred a female physician as his partner, but such a candidate—far more qualified than Johnson—was too difficult to find. Presumably, Masters knew a female physician would likely demand more equanimity as a partner, more control over the research guidelines, and perhaps a more cautious attitude than the energetic but unschooled enthusiasm Johnson exhibited each day. Years later, Johnson recalled how much she'd been crafted as an ideal companion. "I'd ask, 'Why didn't you get one of the women MDs?' [and] he'd say, 'When women went to medical school at that particular time, an MD was so hard-won they would never have jeopardized it, being associated with sex research.' Which was, more or less, probably true. So he created me."

From the outset, Masters and Johnson's remarkable success sprung from their dual approach, the matrix of male and female therapists exploring the boundaries of human sexuality together. For all of his brash confidence as a gynecological surgeon, he maintained a certain humility about sex research. "At a very early age, I learned something most men never learn—that I knew nothing at all about female sexuality," he explained. Although a neophyte in medicine, Johnson soon recognized her own importance in the clinic. "The presence of the two sexes in the laboratory team makes the difference," she later said. "The volunteers feel at ease; he or she does not have suspicions about our motives. There is, if I may say so, a certain dignity in having us both present."

Whenever Masters explained himself to patients or other doctors, Johnson remained faithfully at his side. "He was smart enough to bring me aboard—a *woman* aboard—because it's what made the difference," she said. And eventually, she felt comfortable enough to quiz Masters about his reasons for choosing her. Given the study's volatility, she wondered why he didn't entrust his wife, Libby, as a female counterpart.

Masters, not warm to personal inquiries, kept his composure and authoritative tone. "Actually I did [ask her] at one point," he replied. "But she had no background and no interest whatsoever."

What Masters sought most, his wife could not give him. He convinced himself that Johnson shared his extraordinary commitment, with the same passion he brought to this pursuit. As her boss, Masters was willing to train her—teach all the intricacies of anatomy, biology, and physiology—so that she would be conversant in their field. He cajoled her to work endless hours, day after day, with no free weekends and few holidays. She gathered endless personal histories and observed copulation after copulation among strangers. And she did so unflinchingly, as if she'd found her life's vocation.

Before the end of her first year, Virginia Johnson's importance to Masters had grown rapidly enough to be invited to the doctor's house for a party. Shortly after she walked through the door, Masters introduced Virginia to Libby, who chatted amiably but briefly with her. Johnson mingled with top doctors and professors from Washington University and several well-known people in the city. She stood unobtrusively in a corner of the large living room, sipping on a drink with her date for the evening, when suddenly she detected a boisterous older woman fast approaching.

"I want to meet this paragon—*this perfect woman*—that Bill Masters has found," announced this woman, within listening distance of everybody. Johnson felt mortified. "She was practically shouting it across this fairly elegant setting," she remembered. "I just turned away from her. That was within the first few months of my starting to work with him."

To his wife and family, Masters said he was merely extending a gracious hand to this woman who seemed hardworking and sincere, if a bit down on her luck. "As a very young boy I remember her," said Howie Masters, who was no more than six or seven years old when Mrs. Johnson accepted his father's invitation for a weekend visit. "She would come over sometimes to the house on Sundays, bringing her own two kids." One Thanksgiving, Masters even invited her parents, Edna and Harry, along with Johnson and her children. The Eshelmans had moved from Springfield to be closer to their daughter, and often provided relief by watching her two children, Scott and Lisa, if a babysitter wasn't available. Although she'd been married twice, Johnson still hadn't fully escaped her mother's emotional orbit. At the dinner table, Masters turned his persuasive charm on Edna.

"You raised Virginia just the way a woman *should be* raised," he told her with doctoral certainty.

Edna had never met Masters before, but she seemed validated by his compliment, as if her daughter were still a teenager living at home. "She was so flattered—she thought *she* had been given an accolade," Johnson remembered. "And he meant that, in a way, because I *was* the most obedient human being ever created." However, contemporaries remember Johnson as enthralled by Masters and his research, as if she had found something she'd always been searching for. She didn't appear manipulated or coerced. Quite the contrary, they say, she turned into an avid student. Masters even brought her into the operating room so she could witness basic anatomy in its rawest form, and where she gained a sense of his superlative skills. "He put me into the OR in order that I would know what fallopian tubes looked like and where things were located—much to the chagrin of the chief of surgery, who would run screaming when I was over there," she recalled. "Masters was a superb surgeon. The surgical staff adored him. He really could put Humpty Dumpty back together again."

Johnson's enthusiasm became palpable to doctors, nurses, and staffers who listened to her insights at the hospital cafeteria tables. With evangelical zeal, she seemed to have read and absorbed, chapter and verse, every published work about sexuality. "We all met at lunchtime many times, and the subject of sex came up," said Dr. Sherman. "She discussed it pretty well, particularly the Kinsey Report." She convinced Sherman to let them also use his third-floor medical offices, across the hall from Masters's office, after he departed each night at six. In his desk drawer, Sherman left the key to his examination room so the two could observe people having sex as part of their research study. "I had no hesitation," recalled Sherman.

As a not-very-distant observer, Sherman marveled at Johnson's rapid transformation within her first year, from the once nonchalant secretary at a desk sorting through papers to a savvy, creative assistant who helped gain some early funding from a New York–based foundation sponsoring reproductive research. Because Masters still maintained the hospital's infertility clinic and his own ob-gyn practice, he relied increasingly upon Johnson to keep their sex study progressing. "Bill was the name at the top of the research project, but it was really Virginia doing all the work," recalled Sherman. If Masters provided the theory and the intellectual framework, Johnson provided the common sense and practical communication skills needed to succeed. If once disposable, she was now indispensable. In exploring the outer reaches of human sexuality while paying her bills at home, she unabashedly became Masters's *de facto* partner.

CHAPTER ELEVEN

The Experiment

A young woman wandered into the examination room garbed in a white terry-cloth robe and a pillowcase over her head. Two ragged holes carved into the linen allowed her to see. She wore nothing else. Casually, the mystery female walked across the bare floor. She dropped her robe and stretched herself across a padded chaise longue, tilted slightly back. In repose, she appeared only slightly anxious, as though she had done this many times before—but never with a hood on her head.

Masters and Johnson, both clad in white medical jackets, introduced the woman, without revealing her real name. The sight of this nude volunteer bewildered their guest, Paul Gebhard, the Harvard-trained director of the Kinsey Institute for Sex Research. "Maybe she wasn't counting on me being there, so they had to improvise a mask quickly," Gebhard recalled with amusement.

For a few moments, Gebhard found himself exchanging pleasantries with the naked young woman lying on the chaise longue, while Masters and Johnson fiddled with their medical devices, wires, and gauges assembled together to record her sexual response.

"I'd say she was a perfectly average female," Gebhard remembered. "She wasn't obese or skinny. She just looked like what you'd expect a graduate student or nurse to look like. She didn't have shaved pubic hair like a model might. She had normal pubic hair."

The most conspicuous object in the room was a long cylindrical plastic mechanism created by Masters and attached to a small camera. It resembled a baker's rolling pin formed of clear acrylic Plexiglas, with an optical eye made of plate glass. Without revealing the nature of his experiment, Masters enlisted the help of another professor, well versed in miniature photographic equipment. To anyone in the room, the purpose of this elaborate device was quite clear. "It was a dildo," Johnson explained. "Bill was never reluctant if he thought something would work."

No one had ever photographed the inside of a woman during coitus, documenting the female reaction to the entry and penetration of the phallus. This rather ingenious contraption allowed for cold-light illumination, enough that Masters and Johnson and their staff could observe the vaginal cavity, filming in living color without distortion. The electric equipment could be adjusted for physical variations in each woman's size, weight, and vaginal development. "It looked like a serious piece of medical equipment, and rather cleverly done too," said Gebhard, who marveled at the fastidiousness of Masters and Johnson as they checked each detail. "You had to watch the wiring or you'd electrocute somebody. It was fairly simple, with an electric motor and a handheld rheostat to control it. It had some pretty good adjustments; otherwise it might have been painful."

Moments before the young woman inserted the device into herself, Johnson went into an adjoining room. She returned with something rather thoughtful, as only a female scientist might consider under these circumstances. She "came in with a warm, moist towel and draped it over the phallus for a few minutes," Gebhard recalled. "Sort of reminded me of a hot towel in a barbershop."

Then the experiment began.

By the late 1950s, most faculty and students still harbored only a vague idea what was going on with Masters and Johnson. In hushed voices, they spoke of experiments in snide or sinister tones.

"Everybody was interested but they thought he must be crazy," remembered Dr. Robert Burstein, an obstetrician-gynecologist on the school's faculty, never taken into Masters's confidence.

One of the few outsiders granted access was Gebhard, a tough-minded scientist with a gravelly voice and Clark Gable mustache, whose professional approval Masters coveted. In 1956, Gebhard had taken over the mantle of his boss at Indiana University, Alfred

Kinsey, who had died of a heart attack two years earlier, leaving the future of sexual research in doubt. As *Time* declared with Kinsey's passing: "His staff may or may not complete the projected series that, he had hoped, would free another generation from old misunderstandings and fears about sex." Despite Kinsey's own personal peccadilloes—including exhibitionism, bisexuality, and a masochistic penchant for filming himself masturbating while tugging at a rope around his scrotum—journalists and biographers later portrayed him as a figure of immense cultural significance. In America, Kinsey became a martyr for greater understanding about human sexuality.

Privately, Masters considered Kinsey's sex studies as brave but flawed, relying on patients' recollections rather than clinical observation. Masters believed Kinsey's lack of medical research undercut his search for definitive answers. Critics pointed out that many Kinsey volunteers lived in jail or prisons, hardly the social setting for the average American. During Kinsey's lifetime, even potential allies, such as anthropologist Margaret Mead, fired potshots at him, saying his dry clinical language (using the word "outlet" for sexual activity) "confused sex with excretion." Mindful of such attacks, Masters kept an aura of secrecy around his work, aware that any news might hamper his efforts or frighten away supporters like Washington University Chancellor Ethan Shepley. "I have often wondered how Kinsey was able to tolerate the highly prejudiced critical evaluations of his work as well as he did," Masters observed. "In my opinion, he may have made a tactical error by attempting to respond, in good faith, to each and every published criticism." Masters vowed not to repeat the same mistakes.

Masters and Johnson made clear distinctions between themselves and Kinsey, with a medical approach based on facts and not fuzzy inexactitudes. In their first book nearly ten years later, they spelled out the essence of their inquiry:

> Although the Kinsey work has become a landmark of sociologic investigation, it was not designed to interpret physiologic or psychologic response to sexual stimulation. These fundamentals of human sexual behavior cannot be established until two questions

> are answered: What physical reactions develop as the human male and female respond to effective sexual stimulation? Why do men and women behave as they do when responding to effective sexual stimulation? If human sexual inadequacy ever is to be treated successfully, the medical and behavioral professions must provide answers to these basic questions.

Inside his small, wood-paneled office, Masters provided an overall vision, charting each twist and turn of the body during sexual response with the precision of a cartographer. This clinical approach fascinated Gebhard. Before Kinsey died, Gebhard had discussed with him a similar study of basic anatomical and physiological questions, but neither man was trained as a medical doctor, so they couldn't perform such firsthand research. Nor did they think the deans at Indiana University would ever consent to it. So Gebhard wondered how Masters had launched such a wildly ambitious experiment.

Seated next to Masters, Johnson listened attentively without saying a word. "Gini," as she now preferred to be called, watched him discuss some initial findings, written down in notebooks kept along a bookshelf. She nodded her head with supreme confidence, as if she could bear witness with her own eyes to his descriptions. "It was a complete revelation—nobody had done anything as intensive as this," Gebhard said. "They validated what little we had studied ourselves in terms of blood pressure, respiration, and, of course, the reaction of the organs themselves. They just educated us." In strictest confidence, Masters mentioned how they employed prostitutes and other paid volunteers to study female orgasm, perhaps their biggest mystery.

"How do you get to see the interior of the vagina and the cervix during sexual activity?" Gebhard inquired.

At that point, Masters revealed they had come up with a device to document a woman's orgasm on film. "Would you like to see it?" he pried.

Gebhard, a bit dumbfounded, nodded his head. Bill and Gini motioned for him to follow them into a green examination room nearby. In the middle of this sparse, almost empty room was the chaise longue, a baseboard riddled with electrical outlets, and another machine, best described by Gebhard as "a motor-powered, Plexiglas phallus." Masters, a proud progenitor, beamed with satisfaction as he explained its gadgetry.

"Well, do you want to see it in action?" Masters demanded.

Though the question caught him by surprise, Gebhard quickly agreed. Johnson disappeared into another room and returned several minutes later with the anonymous female graduate student wearing the pillowcase over her head.

When everyone was ready, the young woman rested on the leather-padded lounge chair, with her feet in stirrups and her body nearly flat. Her pink, bare skin was fitted with numerous dark wires connected to a bulky electroencephalograph machine, which hummed, whirled, and beeped. A tiny television screen tracked the swirling patterns of electrical impulses coming from her brain. Little sensors attached to the woman's breasts monitored each heartbeat, recorded in squiggly lines across white paper rolling out slowly from an electrocardiograph machine. These tools served as a kind of sexual polygraph, as detectors of the truth in an area so often filled with exaggeration and lies.

In the meantime, Masters grabbed a metal office chair, which he placed in front of the chaise. He instructed Gebhard to sit down if he wished to observe the inner actions of the vagina and cervix during this experiment. Gebhard found himself within two feet of the young woman's opened legs, close enough to stare through the optical lens of the long-stemmed device.

"Keep your eye some distance from the end of the phallus or you'll get poked!" Masters advised, after Johnson removed the warm towel. Masters allowed a slight grin before returning to his studied grimace.

With the machinery in place, Masters gazed around the room. He made sure the color camera was turned on and his staff was ready to register and tabulate each reaction. Once settled, the young woman was handed "Ulysses"—the nickname given to the cylindrical plastic device. Among the staff, it seemed only natural to call this one-eyed monstrosity by the same name as a recently released Kirk Douglas movie featuring a giant cyclops. Gebhard viewed the fully illuminated vaginal cavity through the cameralike lens with remarkable clarity. "It was completely transparent," he remembered.

At her own speed, the young woman in the chair rubbed Ulysses against her labia, first gently and then firmly. She massaged the moist outer lips of her vagina, enough so that the plastic device made a slight scratchy sound against her pubic hair. She followed a prepared routine, as if she had been trained to perform certain practices for the benefit of her clinical audience. Eventually, she felt a rush of blood and energy with her vulva feeling lubricated. She slipped the device inside almost effortlessly, with barely any pressure at all.

For the next few minutes, the entire room seemed caught up in a minuet of movement, syncopated to the young woman's thrusting of Ulysses into her vagina and the chronicling of each impulse it provoked. As tension rose and her climax neared, the woman's body glistened with sweat. The room's warmth, monitored carefully by Johnson, now felt even hotter. In those days, Maternity Hospital didn't have air conditioning, and climate control became a critical factor in testing the volunteers' physiologic response. The young woman threw her head back, wiggling her hips up and down, sideways and back. To reach the stated goal of orgasm, she'd been instructed beforehand on controlling the motorized device, increasing the rapidity and depth of its plunging as she desired. Rather than convulsing in ecstasy, however, she appeared relatively calm. Her simulated lovemaking appeared almost workmanlike.

Gini and Bill scribbled notes while watching the machines and the young woman's gyrations. Gebhard kept watching through the Plexiglas device with utter amazement, enough that he lost track of its thrusting motion. "She speeded it up too much, and the phallus came back and hit me in the eye," Gebhard recalled. Flustered after being struck by a mechanical dildo, Gebhard "kept my eye a little further away from the phallus so it wouldn't happen again." Despite years of study at the Kinsey Institute, Gebhard felt as if he were observing sex for the first time. As the woman neared climax, he recalled, "I got to see the cervix sort of retreat up into the recesses of the uterus and become more prominent. Eventually she did have an orgasm and that did not take too much time."

Through this looking-glass widget, Gebhard confirmed Masters's significant discovery that dispelled a longstanding—but fundamentally incorrect—medical belief about a woman's body prior to orgasm. Masters and Johnson showed that vaginal lubrication during intercourse didn't pour forth from the Bartholin's gland, located in each of the minor labia, as believed by organized medicine. Nor did it come from the cervix, as others theorized. Instead, they discovered "a transudation-like reaction" of mucous material, seeping or "sweating" through the walls of the vagina. It formed a smooth, glistening coating, like perspiration on an athlete's forehead. It left a woman sufficiently lubricated usually within less than thirty seconds of initial sexual excitement. This basic misunderstanding about a woman's sexual response existed for decades before being corrected with their direct scientific observation. As Gebhard said, "You had to have a researcher like Bill, because no other way were you going to find out."

When the young woman finished, she put her clothes back on, picked up her money, and returned to life on campus. Masters and Johnson counted her among more than a dozen women recruited in the early days of their study. Gebhard never learned her name. Her identity remained a tightly kept secret. "Bill said nothing—*he watched*," Gebhard remembered of the solemn demonstration that day. Once the experiment was completed, however, Masters beamed with inventor's pride. "Males hate this machine," he quipped, "because invariably the females speed up the machine at a rate that no male can equal!"

Gebhard couldn't resist a laugh. "I can understand that," he replied.

Years later, Masters defended the supreme practicality of this Rube Goldberg–like device. "Doctors put mirrors inside the stomach to study the stomach," he observed. "You do the same thing with the vagina and people say, 'How *dare* you do that?'"

Over time, Gebhard remembered Virginia Johnson more than the young woman with a pillowcase over her head. Initially, Gebhard thought of Johnson as only a helper, not the serious, innovative collaborator she would become. "He was a full-fledged MD with a practice in gynecology and she was simply his assistant whom he had educated," he recalled. Gebhard returned occasionally to St. Louis for meetings and training with Masters and Johnson, and they would travel to the Kinsey Institute in Indiana. Bill Masters wasn't an easy fellow to know or like. Each time they met, he acted like a stranger. "It would be funny [that] when I would meet him, we became friends, ultimately," Gebhard described. "Then, when we'd be apart for a year or so and I'd meet him again, he'd revert to his original, distant, imperious self." With each successive visit, however, Gebhard noticed Johnson's role had increased, an amazing advancement to Gebhard. While her comments once had echoed Masters's, she now began expressing her own opinions.

Although Masters and Johnson discovered all sorts of new anatomical information about sex never mentioned in textbooks, Gebhard remained most fascinated by their relationship. It seemed Bill and Gini were their own experiment into the dynamics between men and women. Gebhard wondered about the underlying tensions and attractions, the loyalties and betrayals that seemed to drive their partnership. At dinner with them during subsequent visits, Gebhard noticed how they finished each other's sentences, as if they were of one mind. They seemed inseparable even when apart. To Gebhard, what happened between them remained an enigma.

CHAPTER TWELVE

Volunteers

Gini Johnson had no peer as a recruiter of university coeds, hospital staffers, and faculty wives willing to perform prearranged sexual acts in a way that prostitutes would do only for pay. Certainly her boss posed no real competition. Before she came along, Bill Masters depended on prostitutes by offering a "get out of jail free" card—a respite from arrest arranged with St. Louis police. When Masters realized these prostitutes, with their inflamed uteruses and engorged, chronically congested pelvic areas, didn't reflect "anatomic normalcy," he feared his experiment might be doomed. For nearly a year, research languished.

After she became his assistant, Johnson threw herself headlong into recruiting well-educated females in their twenties and thirties willing to engage in a sex study in exchange for a nominal fee and the promise of anonymity. Many believed Johnson when she proclaimed, with her infectious enthusiasm, that they were breaking through a cultural barrier, bequeathing a gift of themselves to science. By discovering truths about their bodies, Johnson envisioned, they would benefit all womankind.

Gini's powers of persuasion became obvious one day to Dr. Mike Freiman, a fellow in the fertility clinic, not the sex study, when called into the examination suites used by volunteers. In those early days, Masters and Johnson relied on several women who also cooperated with their separate studies on contraception and fertility. In this particular case, Freiman said a young volunteer tested Emko foam, a vaginal contraceptive used to kill sperm, while simulating sex using the electronic vibrating device with the camera.

The internal camera recorded how the foam thoroughly covered the vaginal walls during intercourse, causing the sperm sample from a male volunteer to be chemically neutered. To prevent pregnancy, she was fitted with a plastic cervical cap. After the round of simulated sex, and after the woman washed herself of any remaining foam, Freiman heard Masters beckon him. "Dr. Masters was busy in the operating room and it was time for this young lady to leave, so they asked me if I could go in and remove the cervical cap, which I did," Freiman recalled.

Although aware of the secretive testing, Freiman had never visited this room before, certainly not while occupied. When he entered, a naked young female volunteer appeared, wearing only a mask. "The lady's body was very nicely built and looked familiar," he remembered. As Freiman moved forward to remove the cervical cap, the young woman bolted up. She acted as if he'd done something wrong, and quickly tore off her mask.

"Hi, Mike!" she yelped with the joy of recognition. Her folksy smile beamed as if she'd found some old friend at a backyard barbecue.

Freiman immediately recognized the face of this student nurse. As he remembered, "I had *dated* this young lady!"

Most memorable, though, was how Gini Johnson convinced this earnest student nurse to participate in the first place. When Freiman inquired, the young woman's reasons sounded altruistic rather than hedonistic. "She made me feel that not only was I getting paid, but helping my gender," the nurse explained about Johnson's recruitment. Freiman admired Gini's gumption as he heard similar explanations. "A lot of women from around the university were involved," he said. "Some looked upon it as a badge of courage—sort of like, 'I'm supporting something that is very worthwhile.'" During the stagnant 1950s and early 1960s, when adventurousness for women meant wearing capri pants, Johnson's call for sexual freedom as a basic right made sense. As Freiman recalled, "She made people feel they were doing God's work."

A female nurse and a male medical student were two volunteers known to Dr. Robert Goell, then a young resident at the hospital. "They used to have intercourse on a regular basis, which Gini Johnson would monitor, with heart rates and all sorts of other things," Goell said. This obstetrics nurse "was quite upfront in talking about it. She said it was very quiet and there was usually two of them having intercourse and Gini Johnson would come in and do readings [on medical equipment], being very quiet not to interrupt them." Ira Gall, another young doctor, said he knew Johnson's friend from McDonnell Douglas, an aircraft manufacturer with a St. Louis–area facility, who after hours became "an active participant" in the study. "Virginia had a good appreciation of sex," said Gall. "She had a very wide view, a worldly view, and she was very interested in it."

Gini's sincere manner made people comfortable. She possessed a remarkable talent for discussing intimate subjects they'd never dare bring up in mixed company. Her winning style emboldened many women to volunteer willfully, almost gleefully, for the explicit sexual calisthenics demanded in their research. Johnson would escort new recruits through the lab and introduce them to all the gadgets they would stick onto their most sensitive body parts and flesh. She'd acquaint them with other unknown masked partners with whom they might have intercourse, and still keep these volunteers committed as ever. "Gini Johnson was particularly effective at this phase of the work," Masters wrote. "She was able to relax many anxious, neophyte study subjects and measurably improve their confidence and comfort levels." As part of her recruiting drive, she pinned little notes on bulletin boards throughout the university, seeking those willing to "engage in overt sexual activity in a laboratory environment." As word spread throughout St. Louis, Masters recalled, they gathered "more volunteers than I could possibly handle efficiently and effectively." About two-thirds of those interviewed eventually became research subjects. Because the study's central focus was sexual response, interviewees who had never had an orgasm—or were unsure—were weeded out. "Our rule of thumb was if they're not sure about it, they probably haven't had it," Masters explained.

All volunteers were expected to become accustomed to nudity in the lab and to function sexually in front of the medical staff. Some joined to improve their sexual performance, while a number of female participants told Masters "the research program represented a way to release sexual tension." Despite psychological screening, Masters conceded that "in all probability we did work at times with an occasional voyeur or exhibitionist." Research subjects, like good little guinea pigs, were first put into an exam room by themselves, before "mounting episodes" occurred, as Masters described in his scientific jargon borrowed from rabbits. "When they first began interacting sexually, the research team was never present," he wrote. "In time, however, the sex play would lead to mounting episodes. Orgasm, if it did occur, was identified and appreciated, but not made much of. We were trying to make sure that any potential for the development of sexual performance pressures was personally neutralized before it could develop into pathological proportions." By contrast, Gini spoke candidly about sex, funny and appealingly, without ever losing her dignity and sense of honesty. Her gentle eyes and honeydew voice exuded a warm, relaxed spirit that avoided the kind of self-consciousness or professional hard sell that others might bring to such an endeavor. "She wouldn't hesitate to talk about what kind of a study should be done," explained Alfred Sherman, who shared many lunchtime conversations with her and Masters. "She wouldn't hesitate to talk about using the word, if you will please excuse—'screwing around.' She did not hesitate to bring up sex and what made women sexually attractive and what made things sexually stimulating."

Once Bill and Gini invited Dr. Sherman to observe the after-hours testing going on in his daytime offices. Through a one-way mirror installed in the soundproof examination rooms, they watched female volunteers engage in masturbatory techniques designed to calibrate their sexual reactions. Johnson did most of the coaching, always listening for Masters's direction in the wings. "The patient was put into the stirrup, and a speculum was put into the vagina," recalled Sherman. "Early in the study, they were just doing a massage of the clitoris, massaging the vulva, going up toward the cervix to see if the woman got excited or even had an orgasm. She [Gini] would have the patients stimulate their vaginas, pretending that it was a penis, or using an instrument that was like a penis."

As the testing moved on to actual sexual intercourse, the circle widened to include secretaries for other professors and wives of doctors as active participants, Sherman said, along with medical students and resident doctors looking to pick up a few dollars in research fees. Whatever their motivations, nearly all volunteers seemed drawn to Johnson's unflagging interest. Years later, she portrayed these volunteers in the same idealistic, almost heroic tones she undoubtedly had used to convince them. "In the laboratory, we worked with ordinary people—or perhaps we should call them extraordinary—because they cared enough to contribute time to the effort to replace myths with facts," Johnson recalled. "We could perceive so clearly the desperate need for the information we were accumulating, and we were so confident we were right, that we were doing 'A Good Thing.' We lived in a bubble of conviction that isolated us from all doubts."

Under the glare of lights and scientific scrutiny, some seemingly healthy and virile male volunteers suffered impotency, premature ejaculation, or what the two researchers politely called "fears of performance." Four of every five "failures" in the program—those incapable of successful sexual performance—were male volunteers, records showed. "In my wisdom, I had decided that the female would be much more difficult to work with," Masters later explained. "How wrong we were! The male is infinitely more difficult to work with in the laboratory than the female." Masters's clinical attention to performance and results could turn a relaxed Saturday-night endeavor into Monday morning at work. "All of the assigned couples were very direct and goal oriented," with little or no foreplay during the experiments, and "moved right to the genitals," Masters recalled. By comparison, their no-frills approach led to "twice the failure rate of committed couples when it came to intercourse." As a scientist, Masters seemed to prefer sex as a humdrum, loveless matter in which "intercourse was just a mutual masturbation exercise for the assigned couples." Eighty percent relied on the missionary position, with no variation. Among the men, Johnson demonstrated as much patience as she did with female participants. She allowed anxious volunteers to visit the clinic offices, just to read, talk, and shoot the breeze inside until they felt comfortable. Some stopped by three or four times, with no demands placed on them. With a hearty laugh, she brought a sense of humor to the proceedings, reassuring young men uncertain of themselves that everything would be all right.

One morning, a volunteer who was a Washington University medical school student rushed through their door in a dither.

"Is Dr. Masters here?" he asked urgently. "I want to see Dr. Masters!"

Only Johnson was in the office. "Geez, I think he's in the OR at this point," she replied, aware of Masters's surgical schedule. "Can I help you with anything?"

The male medical student shook his head and quickly left. An hour or so later, he returned with the same pressing concern.

"I don't know when he'll be back," she explained. "Can I help?"

The young man stared for a moment, not sure he could trust her. Then he blurted out, "I think I've lost it."

"You've lost *what*?" Gini replied in puzzlement.

He returned her question with a look of obvious frustration.

"I think . . . I can't perform anymore."

Johnson recognized this polite, charming volunteer, who acted more like a country boy than a city sophisticate. She had compiled his personal history as part of the routine background questioning before he entered their program. He hailed from her hometown, she recalled, and was "raised by a very conservative family, as an only child" with a limited social life. "Until he got to the second year of medical school, he had hardly dated," she said. Once he discovered sex, though, this volunteer, like other young males his age, became prolific in his desire for more, like a once-thirsty man who suddenly wanted to swallow the ocean.

On the morning he showed up looking so desperate, the medical student had engaged in thirty-six hours of sexual encounters with two separate women and rendered himself completely exhausted. His physical unresponsiveness left him mystified and very alarmed. As an emergency intervention, he sought Masters's help.

After listening patiently, Gini determined this young man "had just gone through a marathon," she said, and then endured "the refractory period," a condition unique to men that involves, as Masters and Johnson later described, a temporary "psychophysiologic resistance" to more sex immediately following orgasm. For some men, no matter how many female overtures, their penises remain on hold for about an hour. Some actually hurt if they try again too soon. Their tests showed women didn't endure such a "refractory" problem. Johnson showed a bit more sympathy for this young man's condition. "I just reassured him that he had overshot his quota," she explained, as if a firing-range instructor. "He was really deeply, deeply upset. He just hadn't encountered the inability to function under any circumstance."

In this respect, the young man from Golden City wasn't alone. Many volunteers offering their bodies "really hadn't had a vast experience or a vast range of anything," Johnson said. "Having sex at the clinic seemed a way of answering questions about themselves, alleviating apprehensions about the opposite sex, or overcoming their own shyness or curiosity." Certainly that would be the case with volunteer Thomas Gilpatrick.

A married, Harvard-educated, thirty-two-year-old resident physician, Thomas Gilpatrick worked in the infertility clinic overseen by Dr. Masters. Although his tall physique suggested some familiarity with athletics, Gilpatrick wore dark, horn-rimmed glasses to help his weak brown eyes. He kept his wavy, dark hair tightly combed in an orderly but unimaginative way. Gilpatrick seemed next in line for a gray flannel suit in this nondescript era burdened by Cold War fears, McCarthy witch hunts, and old, drab Dwight Eisenhower in the White House. Beginning in 1955, Gilpatrick assisted infertile couples who paid a then-sizable yearly fee of $250 for Masters's expertise. Repeatedly he listened to his mentor's introductory speech to childless couples, in which Masters promised results either though a successful pregnancy or through his direct connections with adoption agencies and other physicians. "We can't guarantee you'll become pregnant, but we can guarantee you'll have a baby," Masters said many times.

Being at the cutting edge of medicine appealed to Gilpatrick, who admired Masters's superlative abilities and confident style. Growing up in Washington state, Gilpatrick applied to Harvard and was accepted for the class of 1946. After his freshman year, Gilpatrick served in the Army's Signal Corps during World War II before returning to Harvard, where he graduated in 1948. That spring, Gilpatrick married "my first real love," Audrey, whom he met during his Army service. During the next several years,

Gilpatrick went to medical school at Washington University, interned at an Army hospital, and eventually landed a residency in obstetrics and gynecology back at Washington University. By the time he began his fellowship with Masters in 1955, Tom and Audrey were the proud parents of a girl and a boy. When Gilpatrick arrived, Masters was still conducting his preliminary sex research with prostitutes and discussed some findings with his young assistant. With Gini Johnson's hiring, the research gained momentum and expanded rapidly. In getting things done, Johnson had a way of ingratiating herself to medical students, residents, and doctors—nearly all of whom were men—and bending them to her wishes. "Virginia was quite attractive, not knockdown gorgeous but she exuded a certain sexuality about her," Gilpatrick recalled. "She didn't flirt exactly but, yeah, she did. This was kind of her nature. There are women for whom this is just the way they are."

One afternoon at the infertility clinic, Johnson assisted Gilpatrick as he placed a speculum into a patient's vagina. The shiny metal, funnel-shaped instrument had a tiny little bulb attached to it, almost like a Christmas light, but it wouldn't flash on. Gini stepped forward, brushing slightly against him, and grabbed the unconnected electrical cord.

"Oh, doctor, I need to plug you in," she murmured, grinning both innocently and somewhat lasciviously, as she inserted the prong into an outlet.

Gilpatrick never forgot her wisecrack. "It was obviously a little double entendre, either accidentally or intended," he said. "And we laughed about it afterwards." Perhaps she sensed his interest, but Johnson always remained professional at work, understanding where the subtle social lines were drawn. "She was confident in her sexuality and so it showed, that it was part of life," he recalled. "Gini was, in a sense, ahead of her time."

In her recruiting efforts, Johnson learned of Gilpatrick's extramarital affairs during the night shift at the hospital, while his wife stayed home with their two small children. Once she knew of Gilpatrick's willingness to engage in sex outside of marriage, Johnson approached her colleague with an offer to become a volunteer. She suggested that their inquiry into sexual response among strangers was a natural, logical follow-up to his fertility research.

Gilpatrick didn't need much convincing.

On his first occasion, the naked female volunteer rested next to Gilpatrick on the twin bed, stretching her legs across the tautly made sheets of mint-green linen. The woman's supple breasts, her smooth light skin with a few goose pimples, her hands that began to caress his body were all a mystery to him.

"Get me ready," she asked of him.

Before entering the exam room, Gilpatrick had removed his street clothes. As he passed through the door, his last remaining stitch of clothing, a thin, breezy hospital robe, was left behind.

"We got undressed separately," recalled Gilpatrick. "Gini introduced us by first names." After the introduction, Johnson left the room and presumably went behind the one-way mirror.

As was the custom, the nude woman who greeted him wore nothing except a paper bag over her head, just as he did. Promptly they agreed those should come off, too. "We started to use them but we both said it was silly," Gilpatrick recalled. A covering over your face made it too taxing to pant and breathe, he said. Besides, they had never seen each other before, and they weren't likely to do so again.

Unlike other volunteers, Gilpatrick didn't need warm-up sessions to alleviate his nervousness. Plenty of times before, he had been in this examination room, tending to female patients as a resident physician. He knew just where the electrocardiogram machine could be found, the wires with the electrodes, and the placement of the one-way mirror where everything could be seen by Dr. Masters and Gini Johnson. "I knew we were being observed, but I can't say that there was anxiety," Gilpatrick remembered. "This was for science." He believed enough in Masters to overcome doubts about his own appearance in the buff. He realized the project could easily wreck his budding medical career if rumors of his participation ever leaked. But he figured many great scientific achievements had involved some degree of calculated risks, even if this one involved a kind of voyeurism. "I don't think Bill was getting his jollies out of this," Gilpatrick reflected. "I think he purely felt that this was an area of unknown physiology and the eventual recognition of this would win a Nobel or some similarly scientific [award]."

Getting erect in the lab posed no trouble for Gilpatrick, who considered himself a healthy, red-blooded American male. However, his naked partner's initial request for help in "getting ready"—some reasonable effort at foreplay—went beyond his limited expertise in bed. "I learned later, though I was married, that I was relatively inexperienced," he said. His female partners, during separate but repeated half-hour sessions, did little to steer him in the right direction. These women may have been equally as raw and relatively inexperienced. "I don't recall any [conversation] other than comments about the weather," he said. "Not anything like 'that feels good' or 'do more of that.'"

In the wings, Gini Johnson could be heard giving directions, as she watched Gilpatrick pump furiously atop his partner. Her instructions focused on ensuring the electrodes didn't fall off, that other recording instruments picking up bodily responses did not become disengaged as they bounced and wiggled on the mattress. And after viewing a rather rushed engagement between Gilpatrick and one of his female partners, Johnson coached him gingerly. "She said afterwards, the next day, that 'couldn't I go longer?' or words to that effect," Gilpatrick remembered. "Maybe I wasn't the stud that they were really looking for."

The faces, bodies, voices, and sweet smells of volunteers who copulated with Gilpatrick, anonymous women in their late twenties or early thirties, faded into distant memory decades later. The only one he recalled vividly was the pregnant, presumably unwed woman from Oklahoma who journeyed to St. Louis to give up her baby for adoption. In the process, Bill and Gini converted this expectant mother into a sex-study volunteer, taking recordings of the electrical activity of her uterus during orgasm and later comparing it to childbirth. "She was probably twenty or twenty-one, probably a college student," Gilpatrick recalled. "Her physician in Oklahoma had been a friend of Bill's and had suggested that she might be a candidate." Gilpatrick didn't mind having sex with a pregnant woman. Out of deference to her protruding belly, he combined "a little three-quarter" approach with his usual missionary position. "She was not big enough to be uncomfortable—four or five months [pregnant], I'd guess," he recalled. "I don't think we would have done it at seven or eight months, risking prematurity." Masters and Johnson's inquiry into sex response among pregnant women "had been going on for a little while when Gini asked me."

Why did this Oklahoma woman agree to become a sex volunteer with Masters and Johnson? Did her pregnancy and personal finances make her more susceptible to agreeing to such activity? And how did the screening process of Masters and Johnson—which they assured skeptics was deliberate and weeded out potentially unsuitable candidates—give ample consideration to the possible psychological impact of sex with strangers for this young woman? Gilpatrick, however, a man of medicine, asked few questions. His physical urge to have sex with the pretty, pregnant woman with enlarged breasts didn't allow for such ponderous concerns. "I'm sure Bill and Gini made her feel that she was contributing to scientific knowledge," he explained. "There was a suggestion of 'Don't try and figure out who someone is.' There was that admonition from Gini, probably not Bill, that this was to be anonymous."

A few months later, in early 1958, Gilpatrick assisted as a resident physician when the young Oklahoma woman gave birth in the hospital's maternity ward. Mother and child turned out fine, he recalled, but the blessed event allowed Masters an opportunity for a scientific follow-up, comparing electrocardiogram tests during birth with those of her having sex. "Our tracings from her labor contractions—the electrical activity—were very similar to that during orgasm," Gilpatrick recalled. Over the next several years, Masters and Johnson interviewed 111 women about their sexual responses during pregnancy, and they would arrive at numerous insightful, groundbreaking conclusions, including assurances that sex among couples during pregnancy posed no real hazard to the fetus—dispelling a longtime myth. Their study documented the increase in sexual interest among women during the first two trimesters of their pregnancies. And with the help of real-life examples, they detailed noticeable changes with a woman's breasts, external genitalia, and internal organs during pregnancy. However, only six pregnant women were used in their study for the "anatomic and physiologic evaluation of sexual response during pregnancy and the postpartum period." All were married, they reported. Of these six women, four had been volunteers prior to becoming pregnant, allowing for a comparison of their uterine contraction patterns in both conditions. For whatever reasons, Masters and Johnson decided not to include the pregnant Oklahoma woman in their final results.

As he had hoped, Gilpatrick's fellowship with Masters set him on the right course professionally. When Gilpatrick's successful tenure in St. Louis ended, he moved with his wife and children back to Spokane, Washington, where he began a practice in general obstetrics and gynecology, including infertility, endocrinology, and pelvic cancers. By the mid-1960s, he had helped start a Planned Parenthood chapter in Spokane and carried on a rewarding medical career.

In his private life, however, his time as a volunteer for Masters and Johnson proved a mixed blessing. "I had that stupid, egotistical feeling that if the wife didn't know, it didn't matter—and that, eventually, was the problem between us," Gilpatrick reflected. His freelancing in the lab eroded the trust between his wife and himself. "I had many affairs in Spokane and learned a lot that I didn't know with different teachers—I was seduced very easily," he said. On weekends at the shore during the 1960s and 1970s, he cruised along in a hydroplane, a powerful motorboat that soared across the water, and picked up women at various outdoor events. His time as a sex volunteer and a weekend libertine carried consequences he never anticipated. "I think that affected me in a way, and damaged and ended my first marriage," he reflected. "You get to thinking nobody knew." But he found nearly everyone in his life became aware of his sexual infidelity, including his children.

Before he left St. Louis, Gilpatrick had hoped to get involved with a particular woman but never did—Gini Johnson. He thought of her fondly for years but never had the nerve to seek her company outside the hospital. A few years after he left St. Louis, however, Gilpatrick traveled back to Washington University for a gala dinner honoring Dr. Willard Allen, the chairman of the department who had played such an important role in Masters's career. Many doctors, residents, and nurses who served under Dr. Allen, a giant in the field of obstetrics and gynecology, promised to be there. On that particular night, though, Bill couldn't attend. Gilpatrick called Gini and asked if she would like him to accompany her to the dinner. She agreed.

At the end of the night, after the dinner celebration concluded, Gilpatrick drove his old associate home and walked her to the door. "I took Gini back to her apartment and kissed her goodnight and hugged her," he recalled decades later. "I said something to the effect, 'We should have gotten together before.' And she said that she realized that I was sexually active and that certainly now was not a time to go back to that." He didn't press her for any further explanation before bidding her farewell. Johnson remembered Gilpatrick more as a friend and young assistant who worked with Masters than as a volunteer in their study. "He was very close to us," she said. "I liked him too, but I wasn't that nice to him, in a way, because I was always so involved."

Johnson avoided getting too close to those who volunteered for sex in their lab, mindful of Freud's admonitions against "transference"—the psychological projection of love and strong emotions by a patient onto a therapist. Amid all the nude men and women she encountered in the clinic, amid the observation of coitus and acts of self-gratification, despite her knowledge of their most intimate secrets, Gini always kept her professional distance. "I was curious, I was not appalled by anything," she explained. "My job was to reassure and explain and have no personal interest of our own."

As he left Gini Johnson's place that night, rebuffed for more than a kiss, Gilpatrick sensed there might be another reason. Although Bill and Gini always acted very dispassionately in public, with never a hint of anything more between them, that night Gilpatrick felt Masters's looming presence. As he recalled, "I was aware that if they were not together, they were probably going to be."

CHAPTER THIRTEEN

Noah

On an impromptu blind date, Gini Johnson met Judge Noah Weinstein, a man nearly twenty years her senior, about the same time she gained employment at Washington University Medical School as Dr. William Masters's assistant. She found time to see Noah during weekends, or after hours when she got home from the clinic. Their improbable relationship soon escalated and became serious. "He was an older man but a wonderful sexual partner—very innovative and fun," she recalled.

Unlike earlier men in her life, Noah wasn't diffident, the wishy-washy sort inclined to be pushed around by others, including Gini herself. As a young man, Noah had graduated from Harvard University and its law school, practicing as an attorney for twenty years until Missouri's governor appointed him to the bench. As a respected judge on the St. Louis County Circuit, he became known as the "cannonball of the courthouse"—reforming the city's juvenile justice system, demanding public defenders for those accused unable to afford a lawyer, and pioneering marriage counseling for those seeking a divorce.

Noah was raised as a Jew in small towns in Kansas and western Missouri, a place not far from Golden City, where his religion drew the ire of bigoted Christians wanting to beat him up in the name of Christ. Weinstein came of age with the Ku Klux Klan resurgent in America, and he didn't shy away from those who confronted his Orthodox Jewish background. But he was freethinking enough to eat bacon, a violation of traditional rules, as a breakfast-time declaration of his own independence. "There were not many

Jews where he grew up," recalled Weinstein's youngest daughter, Joan Froede. "It was very common among Jews to fight ferociously for your religion and then not observe it at all."

Noah impressed Gini, with the kind of gravitas she wanted after two failed marriages and with two young kids at home. Certainly Noah approached his career more seriously than had George Johnson. When it came to men, Gini didn't follow a single, standard type. "Different things for different men," Gini later explained about what she found appealing. "Accomplished men have always attracted me, but they weren't all certainly in the same way." Based on their recent pasts, Gini and Noah both felt a sense of vulnerability. Their first date took place only a few months after her divorce. A slightly longer amount of time had transpired since Noah and his two teenage daughters had grieved over the loss of his wife, Lena, who had died a year earlier. "She was the first serious person that he dated, certainly the first person I met," said Joan, whose father introduced her to Gini upon arriving home from college that year. After so much sorrow in their house, Noah's daughters noticed that his mood—capable of being sullen and down-spirited—seemed happy again. "I think it was love," recalled Joan.

The tangible differences between Gini and Noah were stark. He was a bull of a man, not very tall but stocky enough to project an imposing figure. In his mid-fifties, he had thin hair that became whiter and more sparse by the day. His double chins and jowls were, at times, covered by a goatee. Noah's deep, widely set eyes looked tired, his skin gnarly and aged. Between his thick, fleshy lips hung a pipe with a perpetual plume of smoke. He seemed an odd choice for a woman in her mid-thirties whose intelligence and vivaciousness other, much younger men found alluring. Yet Noah seemed enchanted by his new companion, who possessed a womanly style that his teenage daughter immediately noted. "He felt she was extremely attractive," said Joan. "I remember her having brownish hair, often pulled back. She was probably the kind of woman who wished she'd lose five or ten pounds, but in those days, she was just right. She had great warmth to her."

One evening at a restaurant, Gini took Joan into confidence inside the ladies' room. That night, Gini wore a casual black summer dress, with a halter top that pushed up her breasts and plunged just enough to show some cleavage. "My dress is too tight," she moaned once the bathroom door closed.

Joan helped Gini out of the formfitting garment and then, with a bit of adjustment, to climb back into it. "It was one of those dresses that are a little tight but you hold your breath and zip it up and half an hour later you're really sorry," the adult Joan described. Nonetheless, she felt pleased to be entrusted with at least one secret by her father's new girlfriend.

Around Noah's daughters, Gini kept an amiable but respectful distance. She never talked about her job or what tasks she performed with Bill Masters. Inside the Weinsteins' suburban home, she maintained an air of impeccable propriety, despite the subtle undercurrents of something more. "In my presence, she was reserved," Joan recalled of her father's courtship with Gini. "People were not very public with their affection in those days. I wanted him to get married. I don't think people should be alone. I didn't care because I was pretty much out of the house."

One Sunday morning, when young Joan was away at college, her sister, Lois, showed up unexpectedly at their father's house. Lois, who had married that year and lived nearby, found a surprise in her old bed. "She found Virginia asleep in a separate bedroom from my father—which is just amazing that they'd done that," said Joan, who vividly recalled the account of Lois, who died twelve years later of breast cancer. "My sister—who was much more aware of the world than I—was appalled." Maybe the sleeping arrangements that night were all very innocent and Gini acceded to Noah's plea not to drive home late at night and instead stay in his daughter's empty room. Or perhaps Gini had heard Lois at the doorstep, dashed into another room, and pretended to be in slumber, after having spent most of the night in Noah's bed nearby. Whatever the case, the sight of a woman with nearly all her clothes off inside her bed startled Noah's oldest daughter, who fought back a tearful outburst and left without stirring her father's houseguest.

Gini's interest in Noah faced obstacles more difficult than a bedroom farce. Because of his age, Noah remained reluctant about entering parenthood again, becoming a stepfather to Gini's son and daughter. "He didn't want children and I didn't address any of the issues," she recalled. Still, Noah tried his best to endear himself to her kids. One time he treated them to a local carnival and accompanied them on the rides—all as an expression of his affection for their mother. Religion also proved troublesome. In St. Louis, Noah's Judaism remained a factor in a reelection bid for the judgeship he'd held for eight years and coveted his whole life. It was a strange paradox for a man who didn't consider himself a practicing Jew. No matter how much he cared for Gini, he feared how marrying a twice-divorced Gentile almost half his age might play with the electorate. "It was a political thing; he actually mentioned it to me," recalled Joan. " If he married a non-Jew, he could in those days lose all of his Jewish supporters, or so he felt. They would think it was horrible for him to marry a divorced woman outside his faith."

The most insurmountable schism between the couple, however, was not about children or beliefs, but another man. His name was Bill Masters. As Gini's research work became more encompassing—as her hours grew longer and her devotion to the sex clinic's aims became more intense—Noah undoubtedly felt Bill's dominance in her life. Noah didn't show any overt jealousy or dissuade her from pursuing her professional goals. Nor did he condemn or pass judgment on her work as unladylike or too risky, even though the judge knew it involved such potential illegalities as retaining a prostitute or observing people having sex. "He was very open and nothing shocked him," explained Joan, who once visited Gini at the clinic with her father. "He was worldly and open-minded."

During one get-together at the Weinstein house, located off Warson Road near Gini's home, the judge chatted amiably with Bill and Gini, discussing various titles for a book to be compiled someday from their research. Both Bill's and Gini's suggestions were dull titles derived from medical or technical terms.

"Why don't you just call it—*Sex*?" Noah asked, tongue-in-cheek.

They all laughed heartily in response, realizing the impossibility in those times of such a title.

Like competing attorneys who momentarily share a light moment in a courtroom, Noah remained wary of Bill Masters as an adversary. "My gut reaction is that he didn't like Bill," said Joan. "It might have been a man-to-man thing, where he saw him as a threat."

Gini's relationship with Bill didn't seem to go any further than the hospital, nothing more than a paycheck to finance her college degree. An "all work and no play" physician, Bill seemed married more to his job than to his wife and children out in the suburbs. He seemed someone who could spend the whole day with Gini Johnson and never break into a smile. In this respect, Noah represented everything Bill was not. "I didn't get any sense of warmth from Bill Masters," Joan remembered. "I did get a sense of warmth from my father towards Virginia, the kind which said a lot. He was a pretty tense person, but he was less tense than normal with her. She had a real comforting effect on him."

Noah Weinstein seemed the right man for Virginia.

CHAPTER FOURTEEN

Masks

After her husband's death, Estabrooks Masters changed noticeably in her eldest son's view. Bill's mother no longer shunned social activities, as she once did for fear of enraging her domineering husband, Frank. This small but energetic woman attended the symphony, played a smart game of bridge, and gathered an engaging group of friends. She embraced them with newfound enthusiasm, as someone whose burdens had lifted. "She obviously thoroughly enjoyed her freedom from domestic slavery," Bill later wrote in his unpublished memoir, resentful that any man could hold such power over a woman, especially his mother. By the time Estabrooks moved to an apartment in St. Louis—to be closer to Bill, Libby, and the kids—she had become "an entirely different person than the one I knew as a youngster," he wrote. "In truth, I had two different mothers."

Around Maternity Hospital, Estabrooks became a familiar sight to Bill's staff, far more than his wife. His mother lived close enough that her son and his research team sometimes stopped by for a late-night home-cooked meal. Cramer Lewis—the medical school's illustrator who filmed sexual encounters at the clinic—frequently accompanied Bill and Gini for a bite to eat. "If we got through the research at, say, ten o'clock, we would go over to her house and she would have a meal prepared for the three of us," said Lewis. One night, as Bill and his colleagues talked obliquely about their work at the hospital, Estabrooks realized what they were doing. Instead of getting upset, Bill's mother offered, in her extremely practical fashion, to help in the best way she knew how.

"Oh, those poor women!" she said, imagining the volunteers in the buff, without a stitch of privacy. "They need something to cover up their faces!"

Within a few days, she designed and created silk masks for the volunteers to wear for their couplings. Men and women given these masks, made of the same Eastern silk as Bill's bow ties, graciously accepted her handiwork to replace the paper bags and pillowcases with carved-out holes.

Keenly aware of appearances, Bill maintained a careful aura of dignity about his work. Even on the hottest, humidity-soaked summer day in St. Louis, he never loosened his tie or took off his starched white lab coat. His reputation for excellence, his own exacting demeanor, and the probity of his close-knit staff provided a protective shield. At home, Bill reigned as the all-knowing father, leading a life of four-square 1950s American domesticity in which Libby served as queen, housemaid, and adoring spouse. To visitors at their Dutch colonial home in Ladue, Libby appeared as comfortable in her role as Bill did in his. "Libby was a Junior League lady, very much the correct kind of person," recalled Sandra Sherman, the wife of Dr. Alfred Sherman, Bill's colleague in the ob-gyn department. Her lasting impression of the Masters marriage emerged the night the Shermans were invited to their house for a small dinner party. Bill greeted them near the door, while other guests were taking off their furs and topcoats.

"Come in, put the coats on the bed," Bill said, as friendly as all get-out. He motioned to the master bedroom as he continued shaking hands with the latest arrivals.

Sandra and Alfie followed Bill's instructions. In the bedroom, Sandra spotted something odd. "They had twin beds that were separated and I thought, 'Good grief! And *he's* going to talk about sex?'" As Sandra recalled, the thought of separate beds in the Masters household seemed incongruous.

Bill's friend Mike Freiman remembered a gathering when the guests included Dr. John Rock, the Harvard physician and fertility expert famous for developing the birth control pill. (Rock later served on a Vatican commission favoring the pill's use for Catholics, a suggestion rejected by Pope Paul VI in his 1968 encyclical *Humanae Vitae*.) For Freiman and others at Washington University, being in Dr. Masters's inner circle meant getting to meet Rock and other renowned medical practitioners. Everyone began with cocktails at Gini's place and then moved over to Bill and Libby's house for dinner. "They acted very cordial, very proper, very Presbyterian," Freiman recalled of the Masterses. "He was a proper gentleman who had a proper marriage, had proper children who went to the proper school—and Mrs. Johnson was the work associate."

Within a few years, Gini had learned the medical world's jargon and carried herself in the lab like a full-fledged professional. Her importance could not be overstated in their project, in which 55 percent of all volunteers were female (not including the prostitutes). As Masters later wrote, she "provided the coaching necessary" for female patients to gain "a sense of confidence in themselves as sexually responsive individuals" so they could "verbalize freely and comfortably, about what had been, up to this point in their lives, a private experience." Bill relied on Gini's insights with increasing frequency and appreciated her suggestions. The intensity of their debates was memorable. "One time they came across to my office from their sex research," recalled Freiman. "They were exhausted and they were having a discussion about what an orgasm is all about." Bill seemed to be lecturing, drawing upon his clinical knowledge of female sexual response. As Freiman recalled, Gini sat impatiently, rolling her eyes in disagreement, until she couldn't stand it anymore.

"Well, I ought to know," Gini exclaimed. "*I* am a woman and *you* are not!"

Bill admitted to a certain tone-deafness with the sounds of love. "In my opinion, Gini's most important contribution," he later said, "was her patient orientation of yours truly to multiple aspects of the female psychosexual personality. Hers was not an easy task, for I had developed a significant degree of cerebral tension in relation to this subject." In his obstipated medicalese, Bill acknowledged needing Gini as a translator. She proved a godsend, a woman who rightfully had earned a spot by his side. "Gini worked very hard to absorb as much material as she could as fast as she could," he later wrote.

Gini's role as Bill's assistant expanded to the social realm. She accompanied Dr. and Mrs. Masters to hospital fund-raisers and holiday events sponsored by the medical school. "They would come through the door as a trio," recalled Sandra Sherman. "I felt there was something more to it than that. Some men need harems." As they chatted at the table, Sandra gained a sense of both women. She enjoyed Gini as a lively conversationalist and a good listener. Gini's dress and demeanor stayed well within the narrow confines of social acceptability among the doctors and their wives, but she knew how to present herself as someone special. "She was dressed in good taste but always a little more colorful than Libby," explained Sandra.

Friends wondered what Libby Masters might be thinking. How could she not be puzzled by her husband's decision to escort another woman along with her to such special events? No matter how many assurances by Bill, no matter how cordial and nonthreatening Gini may have acted toward her, how could Libby not suspect her husband's relationship with his female associate was more than just professional? "She was very bright," Sandra recalled of Libby. "She *must* have been aware."

While late-night dinners with Estabrooks Masters provided some collegiality for her son's research team, there were evenings when only Bill and Gini slipped away for a meal. In these uncharted waters of sexual research, there seemed a constant need for dialogue and evaluation. After their regular daytime shifts at the hospital, the two researchers shared dinner until volunteers arrived for the evening appointments devoted to sexual activity. Bill preached endlessly about the dangers of their work, avoiding the deep emotional currents just below the surface. Patients must be protected from any invasion of privacy, he insisted, and their tiny staff must not allow themselves any prurient thoughts during their sessions. Nothing less than professionalism beyond reproach would do.

The constant observation of sex in a lab, though, electrified Bill and Gini themselves. Despite their austere, white-robed demeanor with the volunteers, the intensity of the evening carried over into their discussions afterward about what they had witnessed. The sight of men and women twisting and thrusting, sucking and kissing, fondling and copulating; the warm, musky scents emanating from the exam room with the aroma of perfumes and cologne; the spectacle of intertwined flesh and passionate embraces in front of their eyes as they stood behind a one-way mirror, eventually breached the walls Masters had constructed for his experiment. After everyone had gone home, the theoretical talk between Bill and Gini about sexual techniques and their research subjects soon turned to what they could learn among themselves. In less than a year, Bill initiated a major change in their working relationship. Sex for Virginia Johnson would become part of her job.

Wary this kinetic attraction in the lab might result in some improper "transference" with patients, Bill suggested their pent-up, revved hormones be aimed at each other. He made it sound like a release valve on a runaway locomotive, a way of diverting a major explosion down the track. Better to get it out of their systems discreetly and with no detection, he argued, than to run the risk of entanglement or obsession with some patient. Perhaps Gini's awareness of Freud's theories about transference seemed a convenient excuse for Bill's suggestion. Or perhaps the indecorous interest in Gini shown by some male patients and doctors set off Bill's internal alarms. True to his nature, Bill cast his proposal in his stern professorial voice, as a perfectly reasonable, detached, and perfunctory way of advancing their scientific understanding. "He made a case that made sense," she recalled years later. "Anything that Masters and I did together was usually couched in professional attitudes. When he introduced intimacy he said, 'We must never, *ever* identify with our research subjects' and that the focus would be on one another. He posed that as the reason for being close. Living in an intensely sexual environment, where that was the focus of the interest and the activities, you must not develop any attachment or relationship with your patient or research subjects. And we never did. A lot of doctors, of course, were having and continued to develop relationships with patients and it's lethal. Shame on the doctor that does it."

By engaging in sex themselves, Bill said they could test out the most effective methods of reaching orgasm or forestalling ejaculation. Rather than just relying on photographic documentation, they could see for themselves what the "superficial vasocongestive skin response to increasing sexual tensions"—which they coined as a "sex flush"—really felt like, so they could more accurately explain it in writing. Masters pitched his idea purely in the name of medicine, part of a long history of practitioners practicing on themselves.

One night, after the last research subjects departed, Dr. Masters and his female associate disrobed and, atop the single bed with green hospital sheets, acted out the physiology responses they were seeking to comprehend. Not yet thirty-five, Virginia Johnson could not have been more appealing to her boss—a sensuous woman full of verve and emancipation, yet attentive to every detail and eager to please at the office. With his little bow tie unraveled and his starched white shirt undone, Bill possessed the stout body of a former athlete who had kept himself in shape over the years. In this moment, he knew exactly what he wanted to do and did it with authority. With their clothes off, he instructed Gini to remain as professional as possible. These encounters should not venture beyond the scope of their scientific inquiry, not into the messy realms of emotion. By cooperating as his assistant, by having sex with him for purely clinical reasons, Gini once again confirmed her commitment to their approach. Or so Bill contended. "We weren't emotionally tied at all," she recalled. "He was building me into this 'team' person, into this research person. That's essentially what he presented."

At Maternity Hospital, colleagues suspected Masters might be having an affair with his aide, just as other doctors did with their nurses, but no one uttered such provocations within earshot. Some assumed Gini to be the instigator, as a divorced woman scheming to lasso a hotshot doctor. Others who knew them well said the nature of their work—observing hundreds of sexual intercourses in the lab—overwhelmed them and any pretense of objectivity. Dr. Roger Crenshaw, a psychiatrist who later teamed with his therapist wife at the clinic, heard what happened from his private conversations with Bill. "As a therapist, the only time I saw a patient nude was during the physical examination, but the circumstances that surrounded Bill and Virginia's beginning relationship involved fairly explicit sex, and I can see where a lot of libidinal energy may have gotten released," he explained. Mike Freiman, as friendly with Gini as he was with Bill, said the sexual energy from their experiments drove them together. "It was like watching a stallion and a mare—it gets everybody excited," he stated. "They were dealing with very exciting things. There was no question that they were emotionally and sexually involved early on." If Freiman needed any confirmation, he discovered it on his own wedding day in early 1961. After the ceremony, Mike and his bride stayed at a motel near the hospital before they left for their honeymoon. The Freimans went to dinner in an upstairs restaurant and after a couple of drinks made their way to their room on the first floor. As he fiddled with his key, Mike heard a noise nearby—and Bill and Gini suddenly emerged from the room next door.

But these assumptions and sightings didn't explain the half of it. In the beginning, there wasn't mutual consent between them, and certainly not the provocateur role to Gini's involvement that some male colleagues presumed. Instead there was a forced agreement that both were reluctant to admit. Their closest aide, Dr. Robert C. Kolodny, who worked for two decades with them and coauthored several books and medical articles, considered writing a biography of them and asked extensively about the origins of their partnership. Only after hours of conversation with Bill, whom he considered his mentor and friend—and after comparing it to Gini's version—did Kolodny gain an understanding of what transpired. "Bill made it plain to her, fairly soon after she took the job, that being sexual partners was a requirement," Kolodny said. "Bill saw it as a consensual involvement. He indicated that he had been the instigator and Gini agreed with that. But Gini perceived it, as she put it, as a matter-of-fact, expected part of the job. And my suspicion is that had she not gone along with this, she might not have been employed too much later. I bet she knew that and sensed that." Bill envisioned a "blueprint," as Kolodny called it, in which his female associate would engage in sex with him, as a way of further comprehending all that they were learning through observation. He exacted this demand early in their working relationship, when Gini was still essentially a nondescript figure hired off the street. For all of her insights, she was still no more than a friendly paper-pusher with some typing skills, with whom he treaded lightly until he was sure she would go along with his plans. If Gini "opted out of that," Kolodny realized she "would have been replaced." In the late 1950s, "that early in their work together, she had made no significant contributions," Kolodny explained. The sense of Gini's invaluableness to their work arrived only after this private pact was reached. Bill believed, naively and erroneously, that his concupiscence could be contained to the lab. Despite their working dinners, Bill offered no pretense at romance. He seemed oblivious to his own wedding vows with Libby, and to Gini's courtship with Judge Noah Weinstein. No one would ever find out, he urged, if they kept this secret between themselves. "I don't think either one of them felt it was a romance," Kolodny said of their beginning. "It was pretty pure sex."

Decades later, Gini paused for a moment when told of Kolodny's recollection, as if she'd heard an unpleasant truth. Because this version varied so much from the official version Masters and Johnson portrayed to the world, because it revealed so much more than she'd ever said before to friendly questioners, or to the version she had told her children and her parents, or tried to convince herself, Gini seemed taken aback. Kolodny was Bill's friend, someone with whom she didn't always agree and often argued. The emotion in her voice revealed a longtime hurt. "Bill did it all—I didn't want him," she insisted about his subtle depredation, her normally modulated voice tinged with anger about the origins of their sexual relations. "I had a job and I wanted it."

To Virginia Johnson, the rewards for her outward enthusiasm and private acquiescence would be quite impressive—a research appointment in the city's most prestigious university, an exciting and intellectually rigorous job far beyond her credentials, and enough money to raise her children without ever having to rely on anyone else. By 1960, Gini shared a coveted byline with Bill in a medical study titled "The Human Female: Anatomy of Sexual Response," published by a journal run by the Minnesota State Medical Association. It was a remarkable coup for someone with Gini's modest background, placing her on the same platform as Marvin Grody, Willard Allen, and other Washington University doctors who had shared a byline credit with Dr. Masters. A succession followed of further medical publications with a joint byline, generous raises, and important duties for Gini. Her prominence in their work—the seeming transparency of giving her boldly stated credit—belied rumors suggesting her contributions might be more than just empirical observation in the lab. What other doctor would be so magnanimous, so progressive, so *enlightened*, as others would later say, to share his well-earned spotlight with a woman? But these perks and plums came at a cost she never dared mention. "He was elevating me and I was always being rewarded," Gini explained. "I wasn't qualified at all."

Particularly for a generation of women younger than Gini, such a proposition might be considered not only improper but illegal sexual harassment, the impetus for a career-ending lawsuit. "It might have been [sexual harassment], but I really hadn't thought of it that way back then," she conceded. "He was a senior medical person." In the late 1950s, newly hired secretaries didn't accuse the hospital's top-ranking physicians of sexual indiscretions. Many didn't say no to whispers over dinner. And if these women didn't agree to stir it up after highballs, their day jobs often abruptly ended, either by quitting or getting a pink slip at week's end. Gini had enrolled at Washington University to build up her life after two wrecked marriages and with two kids in tow. She wanted and needed to find a new life for herself through education. She said she couldn't afford to throw it away. Forced into compliance by personal circumstances and the tenor of her times, Gini didn't act offended or recalcitrant in having sex with Bill. She accepted his overtures without complaint, part of a rationalization to herself. "No—I was not comfortable with it, particularly," she insisted. "I didn't want him at all, and had no interest in him. I don't know how to explain it." By then, Gini had enough experience in life to know that sex for women came in many different forms and arrangements. The facade of utter professionalism was just another mask she embraced quite willingly, by all appearances. She knew her dilemma couldn't be shared with anyone. "I was in an emergency situation and the perks kept coming along," she recalled. "People would ask why he hired me, and he said, 'Because she knew where babies came from.'"

The artifice surrounding their sexual affair presented numerous awkward moments, particularly for Gini and the other woman in Bill's life—his wife, Libby. Increasingly, their private lives became more intertwined. Rather than an occasional guest for dinner, Gini Johnson became a familiar fixture around the Masters house. Libby sometimes acted as the caregiver for both sets of children when Bill and Gini went out of town to a medical conference. "My children would stay with Lib when we started traveling," Gini recalled. "That was 'Aunt Lib' to [them]. She was wonderful to my kids."

In a vague parallel to Gini, Libby also found herself placed in an unfair predicament by Bill, boxed in by happenstance with few options. As a forty-five-year-old mother of two, Libby was older than Gini, with less independence and little experience outside the home. The Masterses' suburban life in Ladue, with the country clubs and leafy backyards for the kids, seemed so serene that she didn't want to disturb it. There was no sense upsetting her hard-won family life if she could say to herself that she had no proof of her husband's infidelity. She liked Gini Johnson and had tried to befriend her husband's associate from the very start. Showered by so many kindnesses, Gini couldn't help but be fond of Libby. At times, when the two women were alone, Libby reached out to her as a friend, woman to woman. She figured Gini had seen her husband's coldness, his gruff demeanor, and probably knew a lot more about his activities at the hospital than she did.

After one holiday dinner around 1960, the two women stepped away from the table, beyond Bill and his mother, Estabrooks, and the noise of the kids. In the stillness of the kitchen, Libby confided in her.

"I made the right choice, didn't I?" Libby asked. After fifteen years together, had she made a mistake in marrying Bill Masters? Her naked inquiry almost required its own silk mask. Gini fidgeted and shrugged.

"Geez, Lib, how can I answer that?" she exclaimed.

Libby immediately backed off her question and returned to her chores for the evening. Gini didn't get the sense Libby was trying to coax some admission from her about an illicit relationship with Bill. Rather, the directness in Libby's eyes, the sincerity in her vulnerable voice, seemed touching, as if she really did consider Gini her good and trusted friend.

"He broke all the rules—he was not a loyal husband at all," recalled Gini, who would claim she had little to do with it. "I was always close to Lib. She always tolerated me, because he wouldn't tolerate anyone's objection to me in any way. I was 'Aunt Gini' to his kids."

This duplicity didn't square with Noah Weinstein, however. He dated Gini quite seriously in 1959, attending parties with her where the Masterses were also invited, and they wound up chatting together. Gradually the judge sensed something amiss. His political friends, concerned about his future on the bench, also expressed worries about his courtship with Gini. So they did a little sleuthing of their own. "One of his associates called me and wanted to know what I knew about Virginia Johnson because of her relationship with Judge Weinstein," recalled Dr. H. Marvin Camel, Bill's ob-gyn colleague at Washington University who could vouch only for the professionalism of Gini's work and knew nothing of her private life. "They were concerned because of her damning his reputation, I guess. It was a friend of the judge's and they got my name from someone. At the time, there was some serious talk about them [Gini and Noah] getting married. And that was what the problem was."

But a wedding between Gini and the judge never materialized. Instead, in 1960 Noah met and married a widow named Sylvia Lefkowitz, who had none of Gini's complications, including a different religion. "She was a very vivacious woman and she was the perfect wife to the judge because she knew how to entertain," explained Harry Froede, Noah's son-in-law. Sylvia was financially independent enough that she didn't need to work, certainly not the long hours demanded of Gini. She was the kind of accommodating wife who would make Noah his favorite peanut butter–and-jelly sandwiches for lunch and be sure to trim off the bread crust, just the way he liked it. When asked years later about Virginia Johnson, Sylvia demonstrated the discretion some jurists prize in a spouse. "Yes, I knew that she was part of his [social] group, but I never asked questions," she said. "It was none of my business."

After the judge married, Gini remained in the picture, though never with Sylvia's participation or consent. "Bill and I used to invite them out to dinner but she wouldn't come because she knew what my role had been in his life and she didn't want the competition, or the presumed competition," recalled Gini. "If we showed up at the same dinner party together, she wouldn't even speak to me. He would join me for dinner himself because he said Sylvia just wouldn't come. So we stayed in touch. We just stayed good friends."

A few years later, when Noah's daughter Joan married Harry Froede, Gini invited the newlyweds over for dinner at her house for old times' sake. Joan knew Gini was still not married and said the judge's relationship with Sylvia was "bumpy" at the time. It was just the three of them—the judge was away on business and Gini's two children were absent. Joan was so pleased to see her father's old friend that she didn't grasp the dinner's subtext or how much Gini might be curious about the state of Noah's marriage. "I'm sure she wanted to know about my father," Joan recalled. "I was just too naive to realize it at the time."

But the increasing role of Bill Masters in Gini's life prevented Noah from ever really having a chance. Noah was smart enough to sense the pull that Bill possessed over her, and proud enough to cover his hurt with a joke or by acting as if he didn't care. One night the judge invited Joan and Harry over to his house and the conversation soon turned to the new book Gini had published with Bill, based on their sex research. In his living room, with Sylvia by his side, Noah was asked if he'd seen the book.

"Yeah, I got an autographed copy from her," he replied dryly, referring to Gini.

What did she say? Harry and Joan wondered aloud.

Noah smirked and blurted out: "To the man who taught me everything—Virginia."

Everyone laughed uneasily.

In fact, Gini's inscription on Noah's book, which Joan obtained years later with his passing, underlined how much the judge meant to her. "To Noah, who from the beginning was there when it mattered," Gini signed.

Her regrets about Noah lingered for years, as the one that got away, the man she should have wed. At the time, however, Gini believed too much in Bill's vision and was too caught up in their exciting, pioneering work together. "In retrospect, it would have been a nicer life, a more enjoyable life if I had married that judge," she reflected years later. Or perhaps she was just fooling herself—maybe she really did, as others suspected, want Bill Masters for herself.

CHAPTER FIFTEEN

Leaving School

"I must confess no object ever disgusted me so much as the sight of her monstrous breast."
—JONATHAN SWIFT, *GULLIVER'S TRAVELS*

Enlarged across a movie screen, the giant flickering image of a naked woman's torso, quivering in living color, galvanized all in the darkened hospital conference room. Nearly twenty male doctors, many with a martini glass in hand, stared like curious Lilliputians at the massive pimpled areola, the engorged pink nipples hardening, and huge fleshy orbs pumped with blood, indicating this celluloid woman's breasts were aroused. At these late Friday-afternoon seminars, featured speakers often discussed their anatomical research in frank detail before Washington University's faculty of obstetrics and gynecology. To illustrate, some relied on slides or scribbled on the blackboard with chalk. But no one had ever seen anything quite like this. "It was a film that showed the erection of a nipple during orgasm and they were showing the blood vessels in the neck and on the chest filling up, and why these areas look red during sexual excitement," recalled Dr. Ernst R. Friedrich, who like the other young residents just sat there dumbfounded. "You couldn't see her face on the film. It was from her neck to her thighs."

As the host for this presentation, Dr. William Masters stood proudly at the podium, while Virginia Johnson fluttered around the room, ushering late arrivals to their seats. Rather than offering the usual can of beer for these Friday sessions, Masters upgraded the refreshments to his favorite dry vermouth and other mixed drinks. In front of an audience of his peers, he performed at his surefire best. “He was good as a showman,” said Mike Freiman, another doctor in the audience that afternoon. “He was trying to introduce his sex research. He showed a movie about a woman whose motions indicated that she had her finger in her crotch and was rubbing it. The focus was on the breast, which was showing nipple erection. Then he pointed out that little infant males have erections. He was making the point that it was a common factor in human physiology that things become erect, whether it be an infant boy or an adult woman who is sexually aroused.”

What might seem commonplace to Masters, after five years of observing human sexual physiology in all its splendor, was still quite jarring to his fellow faculty. After the close-up of jiggling breasts with electrodes attached, the film segued to increasingly intimate shots of female genitalia, with the eye of the camera revealing the cavernous interior walls of the vagina. The narrow-framed lens focused on a headless female torso, then moved on to another. Although Masters narrated soberly throughout this gynecological journey, with its first-rate cinematography steady and clear, it possessed an unsavory quality, suggestive of a grainy stag film at a frat house. “I was shocked initially,” said Dr. H. Marvin Camel. “He presented it in a very matter-of-fact way, like any other scientific presentation most people would give. It wasn’t how he presented it. It was the *content* that shocked some people.”

Masters assumed his peers would be impressed by his scientific discoveries, the kind of groundbreaking research bound to be of interest to any ob-gyn physician. Just as he had with Paul Gebhard from the Kinsey Institute, Masters outlined how the different physiological aspects of orgasm might be understood far more accurately. He also disproved several long-held beliefs about female physiology. Masters hoped for the support of his colleagues and certainly didn’t expect any criticism. He should have known better. “Why did I choose to present material in Ob/Gyn circles first?” Masters later wrote. “In retrospect, it was certainly a judgmental error that I did not realize at the time.”

Prior to this presentation, the leading journal in their field, *Obstetrics and Gynecology*, had rejected an article containing his sexual research. His work on estrogen and endocrine therapies had appeared in this same publication—commonly called the "Green Journal," published by the American College of Obstetricians and Gynecologists—but this new research was considered too risqué, too threatening. Masters felt the nation's ob-gyn doctors would welcome clear-cut medical information that had taken him years to compile. Instead, Masters realized his brethren "have always accepted the fact that conception and delivery of children are natural functions, but have been extremely reluctant to consider the means of conception as a natural function as well." Americans were ready for a Dr. Spock to tell them how to raise their children, but didn't want to hear how they got there in the first place.

When the lights went up in the conference room, the unsettled buzz began. The harsh condemnations of Masters's movie soon reached Willard Allen's office. "What the film did was alert the rest of the department," recalled Dr. Alfred Sherman. "That's when he [Masters] started getting into trouble." Allen, the department's chairman, had been an ally of Masters's research, allowing him great academic freedom with virtually no oversight. But the stark reality illuminated on the movie screen startled even Allen. "There were rumors that Willard Allen was quite shocked," remembered Dr. Theodore Merrims, another colleague. For critics who had heard rumors but weren't certain of the facts, Masters's presentation, with all of its explicit detail, handed them a sword. "While it brought great notoriety, it wasn't the kind of academic pursuits that certainly the anatomy professors and the biochemistry professors particularly cared for," said Dr. Robert Goell, another contemporary, about the medical school's reaction. "We were suspecting that strange things were going on in his sexual research down there—that he was actually studying people while fornicating, taking their blood pressures and all sorts of other things, but we were never privy to it. Bill just went ahead and did it and no one stopped him."

Irritated and defensive, the faculty also felt Masters had exposed a gaping hole in their medical training. It revealed how unprepared physicians really were in answering fundamental physiological questions, how little so-called women's doctors really knew about women. Some preferred to keep the hallowed ground between doctor and patient unchallenged. "I was relatively sheltered when I heard this stuff—we were kind of confused about what it meant," recalled Dr. Robert Burstein, then a junior faculty member who considered Masters reckless. Like that of the older teachers, Burstein's lack of aptitude about his patients' everyday sexuality was underlined by this study. "I did not do much sexuality work," he explained. "If I did anything, it was when a young woman, who was pregnant or close to, had some kind of troubles. You'd sit and let her verbalize. You listen and you nod, and give her some instructions and a mild sedative. And in the old days, you gave her a hug and said, 'You'll be all right.' You'd be surprised what you could do with a hug." The old-fashioned country doctor approach, while personable and comfortable for male doctors, would no longer be adequate, as the Masters and Johnson study suggested. Doctors could no longer hide their ignorance behind a veneer of affability. In their fury, a sizable portion of medical students—about 20 percent to 25 percent by Masters's later estimates—raised an objection to the study's propriety, as did three members of the senior faculty.

When Masters finally discussed the reaction with Allen, his old friend told him not to worry. "Bill, they're just *complaining*—they didn't put it in writing," assured Allen, who depended on Chancellor Ethan Shepley to back him up. He referred Masters to the university's guidelines. "Down here in the small print," Allen explained, "it says I don't have to bring it up with executive faculty unless I have it in *writing*." Masters admired the "deansmanship" exhibited by his old ally in defusing this dustup. But while Allen took no immediate, direct action, the med school opposition was only beginning for Masters and Johnson. If Masters believed a candid presentation would squelch "unsubstantiated rumors" about their research, that plan backfired, only creating more rumors—including the persistent gossip that one of the naked, headless women in the movie was Gini Johnson.

"We recognized her fingernails in the film," said Friedrich, recalling how colleagues felt sure they had identified Johnson from her manicure. "The makeup color, the nail color that she used, and the shape of her fingers. We saw her fingers often enough that we knew them. So we said, 'Oh, that's Gini up there. Gini Johnson!' We residents all agreed it was her." Even friends like Mike Freiman believed her to be the mystery woman. After the film faded to black, Freiman walked over to Gini, turning his head to whisper. "I said to her, 'Gini, that looks just like you,'" Freiman recalled, "and she smiled, as if I was saying something that would make her happy."

Several people familiar with the film's production, including its photographer, Cramer Lewis, and Johnson herself, deny she ever appeared as an anonymous model. "They were all volunteers (seen in the film)," Johnson insisted. "Good Lord, I was the one who wired people up for sound. I was just a functioning research assistant. No way in the world was I ever involved in any demonstration, nor did I practice anything." But the laughter and conversation concerning her possible involvement reflected the intensifying opposition among the medical staff to Masters's pet project. Inside the clinic, secrecy increased. Lewis, a technician from the medical school's Department of Illustration, and physiology professor William Slater, who checked patients' breathing and other vital signs, sat discreetly behind movable screens, monitoring their equipment rather than the faces of those before them. Slater, a dour sort with bushy eyebrows, appeared none too comfortable in his job, perhaps because, as Lewis allowed, "some of these people may well have been prostitutes." Nevertheless, both Lewis and Slater were talented professionals who heeded Masters's warning never to discuss their work. They admired Masters as a doctor and friend, and for bringing them along on this late-night adventure at the hospital, which earned them a few extra bucks. Lewis made repeated efforts to improve the technical quality of his intravaginal photography until its fuzzy images became crystal clear. He made sure Eastman Kodak processed his films under the strictest confidentiality, as if they were replicating the Manhattan Project in their lab. Masters's detractors in the department knew Lewis could be a potential source of incriminating detail if he turned informer, ratting out his colleagues. "Some of the other doctors would come to me and tell me to tell them what I had observed—and I refused to do this," Lewis said. "I considered it a privacy thing and I was just involved in doing my job." Masters and Johnson stumbled across a number of humorous yet unnerving attempts to find out more about their activities. One night, when Gini returned from the hospital cafeteria with a snack and some beverages, she took the elevator back up to their clinic. When the doors opened, she spotted another doctor—a vociferous critic of their work—standing with his stethoscope against the wall of their medical suite, trying to hear anything inside.

"Why *hello*, doctor!" Gini boomed, her mellifluous voice squeezing out every piece of irony. The doctor, alone in the darkened hallway, seemed to shrivel in the glow of her big, amused smile. Doctors from other parts of the hospital wandered by inexplicably, making it their business, perhaps on a voyeuristic impulse, to see what might be happening. In a more ominous encroachment, Masters and Johnson received in the mail several large photographs of their shaded clinic windows, taken surreptitiously across the street from the old Maternity Hospital. As Masters later observed, "It was amazing to what lengths people would go to, trying to find out what was going on."

At Washington University, Masters convinced the medical school to require a course on human sexuality for all students, one of the first institutions in the nation to do so. But not everyone appreciated the importance of learning about sex to help patients plagued with problems. Despite Willard Allen's assurances, antipathy toward their study escalated over the next several months—not only on propriety and medical reputation, but ultimately on the question of money and the advancement of Gini Johnson.

From the outset, the university provided no direct financing for the late-night research sessions, the slight compensation for volunteers, and the wages for Slater, Lewis, and especially Johnson. By special arrangement with Allen, Masters diverted his fees for ob-gyn services, especially the fertility treatment in the early days, and used this money to subsidize his study. Generally, any income generated by full-time faculty for their medical services was considered property of the medical school, and not to be pocketed by individual doctors for their own projects. As the faculty resentment grew about Masters's venture, the university decided to end this special financial arrangement, presumably with Allen's consent. Although Masters gained some grant money for his physiology studies, he realized the clinic's future income would depend on fees from therapeutic sessions with patients facing sexual difficulties. The department also didn't want Masters devoting all his time to the sex clinic at the expense of his other duties as a teacher and a surgeon. His enormous devotion to work still wouldn't cover this gap. Another reason involved Johnson's place by his side. Before publishing their long-term research project on human sexual physiology, Bill felt they needed some kind of academic credential for Gini, to recognize her pivotal role. Every time she tried to kick-start her academic career by signing up for courses to gain her undergraduate degree, she said, Masters demanded more of her time, already in short supply as a single parent with two growing children. But the school didn't budge, despite Masters's entreatments. It wouldn't hear of any appointment for Johnson to its medical school faculty, no matter how honorific. The very suggestion caused some to mock and jeer them, reprising the unfounded rumors that her naked torso had been up there on the movie screen. Soon, Masters's old champions made way for younger men who didn't look kindly toward his work. "The powers that be at the hospital wanted to get rid of Masters because he had very explicit photographs and that got the hospital administration very distressed," remembered Marvin Grody, his former resident and co-author.

After twenty years at Washington University, Masters concluded he could no longer stay. Reluctantly, he gave up his tenured professorship and high-ranking status in the department, maintaining only a nominal affiliation. He ended his surgical practice at the hospital and eventually referred all of his ob-gyn patients to a friendly colleague, John Barlow Martin. There would be no capitulation, no turning back. Although George Washington Corner once had advised him that a university setting for such daring research was essential, he'd once again learned a hard lesson—the truth about sex is often unpalatable to many, including those in academia and the healing arts. From now on, Masters resolved that he and Johnson would face a skeptical world alone.

CHAPTER SIXTEEN

A Matter of Trust

Moving out of the old Maternity Hospital, Masters and Johnson and their tiny staff relocated across the street to a white-pillared building at 4910 Forest Park Boulevard. They gave a euphemistic name to their sex clinic (Reproductive Biology Research Foundation), as discreet as the small sign outside its door. Masters made sure his new nonprofit foundation included trustees with a personal loyalty to him and gratitude for his services as a physician. Following his bittersweet departure from Washington University, filled with rumors and recriminations, Masters wanted only those he could trust.

Typical of this admiring coterie, Torrey Foster became the foundation's new lawyer, despite a lack of experience. He had known the Masterses since he was a young boy living next door in Ladue. Before their own children came along, Torrey's wife depended on Masters as her first gynecologist. Given their long history together, Masters never doubted Foster's allegiance or his ability to keep things confidential. Foster's first assignment took him to Washington, D.C., for a meeting with the Internal Revenue Service, to see if the new foundation's inquiry into sex might hinder its bid for tax-exempt status. The clinic's cash flow from voluntary contributions and outside grants would be vital, especially without the university providing a hospital suite and other indirect support. "We were as candid as we could be about the nature of the subject matter," Foster said of the IRS meeting, "but we did not get into a lot of detail about how it was being done—and they didn't ask either."

On the board, Foster joined another steadfast friend of Masters's—Ethan A. H. Shepley Jr., the son of the former Washington University chancellor. Young Ethan became chairman of the foundation. Like his father, he believed strongly in the importance of Masters and Johnson's research, and in providing a protective environment free of any intellectual intimidation. "There were board members who were brought in because it was such a sticky wicket in St. Louis," recalled Peggy Shepley, his widow. "People were embarrassed to say that they had been to Masters and Johnson. So in this way, it became dignified because Ethan's family had a very good reputation, not only in the academic community, but in the St. Louis community." Other early trustees brought their own intellectual heft and academic proficiency to the foundation, such as Dr. Ray Waggoner, a University of Michigan psychiatrist who later headed the American Psychiatric Association, and Emily Mudd, the well-known family therapist who founded the Marriage Council in Philadelphia. But most trustees, like police commissioner H. Sam Priest or insurance executive John Brodhead, signed on mostly as a favor to Masters and because their wives had been his patients. "I was really a friend of his wife, Betty," explained John Brodhead, who had known her for years, ever since their families vacationed together in upper Michigan. "Bill felt that he needed some establishment figures to take what could be offensive sexuality out of it." Before he joined the board, John's wife, Dodie Brodhead, said they discussed the ramifications. "It was a controversial board to be on, and my husband did it out of kindness," she said, grateful for becoming pregnant with the help of Masters's fertility treatment. "He felt that Bill Masters was a brilliant man and maybe was getting into a field that was not going to be quite acceptable at that point in time, in the society that we lived. He wanted to make sure that we waved the flag of friendship." At board meetings, the foundation's trustees remained remarkably quiet, deferring to Masters's judgment on day-to-day matters. If Johnson chimed in, she did so only to elucidate his points or to remind him of one he may have forgotten to mention. Trustees "knew what he was interested in and what he was going to write about," recalled John Brodhead, "but I was not privy to any more details than I had to be."

Aside from stealth and daring, a progressive aura surrounded the foundation, as if embarking on a mission as noble as America's mid-1960s space program, cloaked in promises of better living through science. But Masters kept many secrets from them, including previous use of prostitutes in the research—a fact that Foster as attorney didn't learn until years later. "Bill wasn't as upfront with his board as he could have been," Foster said. "I don't think he wanted for us to get challenged in any way about whether we knew these things. He just did it." Foster's youthful, unsophisticated endorsement of family friend Bill Masters obscured more subtle undercurrents. He didn't sense the complexity of Bill's relationship with Gini and instead depicted their collaboration only in heroic terms. "I took it on faith when I got involved that she was coming over in a professional way and I didn't realize they had that close an intimacy," Foster said. At family gatherings, Libby Masters privately confided concerns about her husband. Foster's own mother, Marge, also shared her friend's qualms. Torrey discounted these fears by defending Bill's honor and integrity.

At one event, Libby, her face drawn and anxious, quizzed Torrey Foster repeatedly about her husband's activities.

"Do you think these late nights at the clinic are really necessary?" she asked, as Foster recalled it. Libby could barely bring herself to mention Gini Johnson's name. She worried why her husband had left the university's medical school under a cloud and phased out his lucrative practice. "I'm uncomfortable with this whole business of sex," Libby told him.

As they conversed, Libby wondered whether Bill was risking both his medical career and implicitly, without daring to say so, their marriage.

In all earnestness, Torrey assured Libby her fears were unfounded. Emphatically, he said Bill could be trusted.

"Everything that they're doing is on the up-and-up," Foster explained. "What Bill is doing is legitimate and very important. I have every confidence that you don't have anything to worry about." Libby appeared satisfied with Torrey's answer. Or perhaps she knew better and just decided to drop her inquest of their former next-door neighbor, who clearly admired Bill professionally and couldn't view him without blinders. In time, Torrey and Bill's other trusting board members proved far more clueless about the personal inner workings of the clinic than Libby. "I was a bit naive, frankly, about what was going on," Foster admitted decades later. "She had concerns about Bill's work and the direction it was taking him personally, particularly with Gini. And she turned out to have had the right instincts."

Around dawn each morning, Bill Masters could be seen jogging past the dew-drenched lawns and empty streets of Ladue, before he showered and spent a full day at work. His steel-blue eyes and his overall stern demeanor projected the kind of self-discipline he'd prized ever since his days on the Hamilton College gridiron. "The Masters look is hard, penetrating, an X-ray look that discourages frivolity and commands immediate candor," the *Atlantic* later observed. In the wake of his unofficial ouster from the medical school, Masters redoubled his efforts at the clinic, seemingly driven to prove he would not be a loser with the biggest gamble of his life. "He would do whatever it took to achieve what he wanted to achieve—it didn't matter what it was," Johnson explained. "He had to win."

When the most prestigious journals in his field refused to publish his sex research, Masters kept pushing for acceptance. He pitched his articles to editors until he found a small medical periodical—the *Western Journal of Surgery, Obstetrics and Gynecology*—willing to include him in its pages. The snub by his most esteemed peers made him furious. Masters cursed their myopic denial, their curt dismissal of his scientific discoveries, which he felt could very well win the Nobel Prize in medicine. "This was indeed a severe blow," he wrote years later, still stinging. "This rejection of research material was not only an act of censorship but consisted of a deliberate attack on my personal integrity." The *Western Journal* was neither peer reviewed nor well read beyond its Portland, Oregon, headquarters, but its editor, Dr. Robert Rutherford, was a hero in Masters's eye for "his kind offer" to publish their research. Similarly, Masters refused to take no for an answer at the annual get-together of American obstetricians and gynecologists. At a Chicago convention in the early 1960s, Masters was told he couldn't impart their findings to the society's elders. In a harsh rebuke, he recalled, "it was requested that I not discuss the contents [of their sex research] during the society's regular meeting hours." So Masters rented a small suite at the convention's hotel to make an impromptu presentation when the formal program wasn't in session. "Masters was treated miserably by his own discipline, even though they had published many of his groundbreaking works in both obstetrics and in surgery," Johnson recalled. "No one wanted to be associated with sex." Sandra Sherman, who attended the same convention with her husband, came away appalled by the profession's reaction. "They were shunned as though they had some terrible disease," she recalled. "And I thought, 'Good grief, what's the matter with these people?' This is a very important part of living and how wonderful that they [Masters and Johnson] could talk about it and help."

With a vengeance, Masters wanted to prove his detractors wrong about Virginia Johnson. After the medical school rejected his request for a faculty appointment for her, questioning her credentials and ability to get involved in such sensitive research, Masters insisted on demonstrating that Johnson was more than capable. He would show the world that she belonged at the table of his peers. At their newly formed foundation, free of the university's meddling, he upped her title from assistant to research associate and continually improved her salary. Some doctors at Washington University wondered why Masters, usually so exacting, had permitted such unwarranted advancement for his former secretary. "It was very unusual because she was being called Dr. Johnson and she really didn't have any kind of degree at all," said Dr. H. Marvin Camel. "I don't think it was innocent because she allowed it to go on, without setting the record straight. If people called her this, she never told them otherwise." Years later, Gini denied ever calling herself Dr. Johnson, an easy mistake for laypeople when addressing therapists dressed in white lab coats.

Like a proud impresario, Masters gave Virginia Johnson equal billing in their scientific productions. He let doubters know that she had provided many original insights, not only about female sexual response, but also therapeutic solutions for various problems with intimacy. Few at first believed him. Only a handful of friends understood the dynamic between the two researchers, how one's ideas were shaped and augmented by the other. "She was young and green," recalled Peggy Shepley, Ethan's wife. "It had to be great for each of them to learn from one another. He gave her all kinds of credit." Yet even at professional conclaves, Johnson felt inferior, as if one sharp question might puncture her smooth deportment and expose her as a fraud. When she wasn't asserting herself, she told Masters that she felt in over her head, that she just didn't have the needed background for these sensitive cases. Masters wouldn't have it. He bolstered her confidence by providing private tutorials that prepped her about human anatomy, physiology, and medical terminology. By 1965, they routinely rehearsed prior to any professional appearances, going over lines and phrases that she could add to supplement his comments during their dual presentation together. After nearly eight years together, Johnson had picked up enough medical knowledge and lingo to expound beautifully before onlookers. "Since she had a very good command of the language, she gave a very good impression," said Dr. Ira Gall, a close friend.

In turn, Johnson pushed Masters to achieve their ambitious research program—with hundreds of volunteers and thousands of recorded sexual encounters—which they might never finish without her constant prodding. "She was the catalyst," explained Gall. "Because of her, the experiments that proceeded I don't think would have occurred without her. She was the encouragement to Bill Masters." There was something about the two of them together that seemed more potent than either could have been alone. Even Masters's family understood her singular importance to his accomplishments. "She was someone who had a tremendous drive and real brainpower," described his son, Howie. "If she hadn't been as smart as she was, and as driven as she was, it would never have turned into what it was." The improbable Pygmalion-like rise from a lowly secretary to medical research partner—though made possible by Masters—was primarily motivated by Johnson herself, as a strong woman determined to push their project to success. "She also came with edges; it's not like she was a perfectly refined Eliza Doolittle," Howie said of his father's bond with Johnson. "There was something that made it work—and it worked powerfully for a time—and there was something in there as well that made it die."

Virginia Johnson's search for equality in her professional life with Masters mirrored the transformations in their personal relationship. No one knew how sex with him had been imposed upon her as part of the job, because Johnson gave no hint of unhappiness, if indeed any existed. Over time, their intermittent encounters developed into a steady stream of intercourse. Still, these sexual exchanges were far more of a workplace compromise than a romance, a creation of the heart. Somehow she had managed to take his improper sexual dominion over her and turn it to her advantage. Old friends noted subtle changes in Johnson—in her physical assertiveness and self-possession with Masters, who no longer acted as a solitary professor and deferred to her more often. Some assumed they were having an affair and that these changes emanated from the bedroom, with Johnson as the initiator. "Gini had a very commanding presence," explained Mike Freiman, always impressed by her willpower. "She was sort of muscular and stood in a way that made you feel she was tough. She sort of leaned forward toward you. She wasn't laid back, wasn't quiet. Her wishes had to be known."

As the personal and professional intertwined, family gatherings between the Masterses and the Johnsons became increasingly complex. Libby's kindly offer to care for Gini's kids while the two researchers were away on business took on a more ominous tone when Libby called her husband's hotel room late one evening and Johnson answered. Friends and neighbors, confronted with the unspoken reality of Bill and Gini's affair, strained to avoid the subject, especially in Libby's company.

Next door, Torrey Foster's mother was appalled by Bill's behavior toward his wife, whom she still called Betty. When school ended, Bill encouraged Betty and the kids to go away on vacation while he stayed home, Marge Foster recalled. Masters seemed indifferent to the predicament he placed on not only his wife but also his neighbors. "We were friends with both of them—until he began making Betty go up to Michigan for the summer with the children and then Virginia Johnson would move out to the house," Marge said. "I became rather disgusted with him, I guess." One summer morning, she spotted Bill and Gini, both in terry-cloth robes, relaxing on the backyard furniture. "They used to carry out the breakfast tray and eat outdoors," Marge said. "From my kitchen window, I could see them. She stayed there all summer while Betty was away. Lived in the house!"

Dodie Brodhead and her husband, John, who was still a trustee on Masters's foundation, sometimes vacationed with Betty and the kids in upper Michigan. When both families returned home and school started in the fall, Dodie and Betty shared a car pool, driving their children to class. "You'd have a few minutes to chat, and Betty was a great chatterer," Dodie recalled of her friend. "I genuinely loved her and felt sorry for her."

During one conversation, Betty confided that her husband wasn't home alone while they were vacationing on Michigan's Upper Peninsula. "She told me with naiveté, 'Wasn't it nice that when I was in Michigan, that Gini was taking care of the house?'" Dodie recalled, still incredulous at her friend's statement. "Was it a cover-up, who knows? She was like so many lovely, old-fashioned ladies who kept their heads high and looked the other way. That has been done a lot, in a number of generations." Dodie brought home this disquieting news to John, who had joined Masters's board out of personal loyalty to Libby, and now debated whether he should stay.

Increasingly, Libby Masters was confronted and embarrassed by evidence of her husband's infidelity. At the Country Day School, the prestigious private school attended by young Howie Masters and Johnson's son, Scott, along with generations of future governors, senators, and corporate titans, Johnson showed up for a parents' meeting wearing a vicuña coat, a smooth, luxurious wrapping of very expensive wool.

"Oh, that's a beautiful coat!" admired one parent.

"Yes, Bill Masters gave me this," Johnson replied regally.

Standing in the same circle of parents, Libby looked mortified, hearing about her husband's gift to another woman. Gini didn't seem to give her a second thought.

If Libby felt lonely in her suburban house because of her husband's long hours, that feeling of estrangement became worse with the gnawing sense her husband was cheating, caught up in an intricate relationship with Johnson that couldn't be easily ended.

For the first time in her life, Johnson earned enough money to provide a comfortable lifestyle for herself and her children. She gained credit for the groundbreaking research that Masters willingly put her name on. And the once unwanted advances slowly became the mainstay of a physical relationship that she learned to enjoy. "We were really sexual athletes," she later told friends. To his male colleagues, Masters seemed the beneficiary of that old medical tradition of keeping a wife at home and a girlfriend on the side, usually an attentive nurse or nubile aide. Not only did they have sex at Johnson's house but also the foundation rented a small apartment for guests where, unbeknownst to the trustees, they would stay the night when the bed was empty.

His arrangement with Johnson carried far more weight than a run-of-the-mill affair, however. Gambling that his sex research would lead to fame, Masters invested all of his professional capital into the Reproductive Biology Research Foundation, and she proved a vital, irreplaceable component in its success. At this critical stage of their work, Masters could no longer think of replacing her as he became increasingly dependent. In many respects, she was leading the way, fashioning a more thorough, integrated approach to dealing with human sexuality than he ever envisioned.

Faced with this reality, Libby Masters turned her gaze elsewhere. Good wives, she believed, ignored their husbands' ugly betrayals and focused their attention on their children's lives. They poured their unappreciated energies into the intricacies of homework, the bustle of after-school car rides, and the companionship of mah-jongg or bridge with female friends. Faithful to her marriage, Libby hoped her heartache would fade away someday. "I think she was too understanding and too forgiving—too good for him," said Marge, who shared many conversations with her about Masters. "I think he actually was the love of her life."

CHAPTER SEVENTEEN

Revealing Secrets

"If I am asked how we should account for the unusual prosperity and growing strength of this nation, I would reply that they must be attributed to the superiority of their women."

—ALEXIS DE TOCQUEVILLE, *DEMOCRACY IN AMERICA*

For nearly a decade, their secret remained safe. Rumors of a lab study devoted to sex, operating in the heart of St. Louis, never appeared on television or radio or in print. As a personal favor to Masters, *St. Louis Globe-Democrat* publisher Richard Amberg vowed his daily newspaper wouldn't breathe a word to its readers. The city's other competing paper, owned by Pulitzer, stayed mum. Reporters for the Associated Press and United Press International, the two wire services beaming scoops across the world, also knew of this sensational human experiment but refused to say anything to the American public.

St. Louis's media agreed to a blackout until the highly controversial research could be completed. In many ways, this self-censorship was an easy decision. Sex was still the private domain of the marital bed, with strong religious and political retribution for those who strayed. Daily newspapers, general interest magazines, and television stations regulated by the government wouldn't dare venture into the raw clinical descriptions of Masters and Johnson's work. The word "pregnant" could be bleeped from any television show. Sex education was kept out of the classroom. America frowned on mothers who worked, banished homosexuals to the closet, outlawed contraception for unmarried adults, and made abortion a crime in all fifty states. During these baby-boom years, Americans steadfastly believed virginal Doris Day and Rock Hudson were the ideal Hollywood couple.

Despite highly technical articles by Masters and Johnson in arcane medical journals, and an unheralded appearance before a New York science academy, no one breached this publicity blackout. Masters and Johnson's ensemble of sexual performers proceeded unmolested by press notoriety or official condemnation. Few noticed when the pair signed a deal in September 1964 for a book summarizing their physiological and anatomical findings. With the sparest of illustrations, this textbook-like compendium, called *Human Sexual Response,* published by the medical book department of the distinguished Boston publisher Little, Brown and Co., was designed primarily for doctors and residents in need of basic training. Contractually, Johnson shared in a third of whatever royalties came their way, with an equal measure to Masters, and another third given to their nonprofit foundation. Their publication schedule provided plenty of time to finish their research without a rush. No sooner had the ink dried, however, than their undercover status was blown wide open. "I knew we were playing with dynamite," Masters later explained. "We wanted to be able to do our work and collect a body of data before the roof fell in. We're surprised it wasn't sooner."

In November 1964, *Commentary* magazine, a journal of politics and culture, featured Freudian-trained psychiatrist Leslie H. Farber's exposé on the dirtiest little secret in St. Louis. He wrapped his bombshell in a literate, sometimes humorous discourse about the separation of eros from true love in modern American life. "My conviction is that over the last fifty years sex has for the most part lost its viability as a human experience," Farber concluded sadly. Putting sex under the scientific microscope was "removing it from all the traditional disciplines, such as religion, philosophy, literature, which had always concerned themselves with sex as human experience." As Exhibit A in his indictment, Farber described the carnal calisthenics in Masters's lab and the "colored motion-picture photography . . . used to record in absolute detail all phases of the human sexual response cycle." Farber depicted naked, faceless female volunteers who clearly preferred "automanipulative technics" to reach climax on their own, rather than the traditional missionary methods of yore. The mysterious power of the female orgasm revealed in the film both fascinated and horrified poor Farber. His essay—a far cry from *Commentary*'s usual anti-Communism screeds and the latest crisis in the Gaza Strip—provided enough details to prompt another magazine writer to call it "a juicy item of highbrow pornography." With feigned outrage, Farber expounded on the ills of American sex. He mourned the death of centuries-old romanticism that "willfully insisted on soft lights, Brahms, incense and poetical talk." Instead of a "Queen of Courtly Love," he wrote, each maiden in the St. Louis experiment became a "Lady of the Laboratory" who could turn her sexual ardor on and off like a faucet. "I should make clear that Dr. Masters' project itself interests me far more than his exact findings," Farber confessed. "This project strikes me as one of those occasional yet remarkable enterprises that, despite its creator's intentions, quite transcends its original and modest scientific boundaries, so that it becomes a vivid allegory of our present dilemma, containing its own image of man—at the same time it charts a New Jerusalem for our future. Such an enterprise, when constitutive, is apt to be more relevant and revealing than deliberate art."

For all his fussing, Farber correctly sensed a cultural watershed afoot. By the mid-1960s, a genuine American revolution was being fueled by the newfound freedoms and expectations aroused by the newly developed birth control pill, available to American girls at the same drugstores where boys had bought their condoms for years. Orgasms now seemed a battle cry of individual freedom, a birthright for all. "Of all the discoveries sexology has made, the female orgasm remains the most imposing in its consequences," Farber wrote in the least ironic and most understated line of his critique. Indeed, without Farber's admitting it, his article seemed to recognize the clinical evidence being assembled by Masters and Johnson would shatter the pseudoscience of Freudian theory. Those who plodded through Masters and Johnson's vast docket about human sexuality would soon realize the folly and latent misogyny of the old Viennese master, with his conjecture that assumed men's sexuality superior to women's.

For nearly sixty years, a mountain of psychoanalytic books and articles in America had repeated Sigmund Freud's doctrine about a distinct difference between clitoral and vaginal orgasms. During sexual development, as a young girl's emotional attachment shifted from mother to father, Freud said, her sexual feeling focused on the clitoris as the "true substitute for the penis." During these immature days, he wrote in 1910, the girl's nascent sexuality seemed a "wholly masculine character" in which "she obtains pleasure from her clitoris as a boy with the penis." Freudian psychoanalysts built a whole schema, a psychosexual house of cards, around these unverifiable claims. Women who preferred clitoral orgasm were seen as butch, neurotic, "frigid," or some combo plate of tossed emotions, while women who engaged in vaginal orgasms were feminine, mature, and normal. Reflective of how Freudian psychoanalysis grew into a secular religion during mid-twentieth-century America, this contention became a largely uncontested matter of faith among many psychoanalysts, causing untold emotional pain for their female patients.

Whatever Freud's analytical merits on the couch, Masters and Johnson decided he was wrong on medical facts in the bedroom. The incontrovertible, see-it-for-yourself evidence of the pair's color movies disproved Freud's views, which delineated between supposedly more satisfying vaginal intercourse and a less fulfilling, "immature" orgasm based on clitoral stimulation. When so many imbibed Freudian psychology from the schools, media, and popular culture, however, such a challenge was no small feat. A later study by two Chicago academics of a dozen 1960s-era medical textbooks found that two-thirds "continued to state, contrary to Masters and Johnson's findings, that the male sex drive was stronger." Half of textbooks by gynecologists and other doctors serving women cited "procreation" as the main purpose of sex for most females. Two texts said most women were "frigid" and another two repeated Freud's view that vaginal orgasm was the only "mature" sexual response. Masters and Johnson said previous studies of sexuality were unfortunately "the result of individual introspection, expressed personal opinion, or of limited clinical observation"—a barb clearly aimed at Freud and his acolytes. Their proof in the lab seemed undeniable. As the electrodes and other devices showed, the multi-orgasmic potential of the American female far outpaced that of the male, who faded, at least temporarily, after only one shot of glory. Based on medical fact, Masters and Johnson's exhaustive research offered to free Americans from cultural superstitions and the Freudian imprisonment of female sexuality. No wonder their apparatus with its optical eye looked like such a monster to Farber.

Armed with empowering information and an array of new contraceptive methods, young American women dramatically changed their sexual attitudes. Farber's fellow Freudian, University of California–Los Angeles psychiatrist Ralph R. Greenson, tried to alert a 1966 American Medical Association convention of the impending tsunami. "It is my definite impression that women are becoming sexually more assertive and demanding, and men are more indifferent and lethargic," he warned. "Apparently, as they have gained greater freedom, they feel entitled to equal sexual satisfaction along with their other equal rights." At its most popular point, Freudian psychoanalysis was being disclaimed by clinical medicine, as much as observations through a telescope once threatened church orthodoxies about the heavens. "Masters and Johnson treated sexual problems more swiftly and effectively than anyone in psychiatry recognized," declared Dr. Fritz Redlich, a psychiatry professor at Yale University School of Medicine. "They have turned the tables on Freud and exposed the weak underbelly of his theories about sex." No matter how much Farber tried to update Freud's views for an American clientele or ridicule Masters and Johnson with an amusing article that sought to tantalize and diminish, there was no way around this empirical repudiation.

In the American media, Farber's commentary stirred curiosity about the little-known male-female team of Masters and Johnson, the two unmarried researchers who had convinced hundreds to drop their pants in the pursuit of human knowledge. "What of those self-effacing scientists behind the camera who conceived and guided this research?" Farber wondered. "Do they too reflect who we are and who we would become? We know as little about this research team as we know about the volunteers." Into the maw, other inquisitive reporters ventured. They knocked on the door of Masters and Johnson, who remained determined not to repeat

Alfred Kinsey's mistake of constant rebuttal and public debate. "I plan not to defend myself against attack nor to comment on them except to continue publishing data," Masters replied, seemingly unprovoked. But in fact, the Farber essay was a proverbial shot across the bow, energizing them to revamp their schedule, expedite their research, and aim for a new publication date of April 15, 1966.

Their secret lives in St. Louis would never be the same. The anonymous efforts of so many volunteers would soon be immortalized in print, mapped on charts, and reduced to case histories named "Subject A," "Subject B," and so on. After twelve years of effort and a lifetime of preparation, Bill Masters's dream of becoming famous for a medical breakthrough—made possible only with Gini Johnson—had finally arrived.

CHAPTER EIGHTEEN

The Human Response

In their landmark book *Human Sexual Response,* Masters and Johnson began with a primer on the sorry state of knowledge concerning human sexuality and what little society had done to remedy it.

"How can biologists, behaviorists, theologians, and educators insist in good conscience upon the continued existence of a massive state of ignorance of human response, to the detriment of the well-being of millions of individuals?" they implored. "There is no man or woman who does not face in his or her lifetime the concerns of sexual tensions. Can that one facet of our lives, affecting more people in more ways than any other physiologic response other than those necessary for our very existence, be allowed to continue without benefit of objective, scientific analysis?"

These idealistic strains echoed a young Bill Masters, appalled at America's ignorance about sex and resolving to do something about it. But the book soon sounded like a seasoned medical explorer planting a flag on *terra nova*, rightfully claiming credit for new insights. Their thanks to Alfred Kinsey, dead a dozen years by then, was kept in respectful but comparative terms. While Kinsey and his team "published a monumental compilation of statistics reflecting patterns of sexual behavior," Masters and Johnson made sure the reader understood Kinsey's effort was mere sociology and not medicine. Indeed, they suggested "future evaluation" by historians might conclude Kinsey's biggest contribution was as a precursor to their own work, "opening the previously closed doors of our culture to definitive investigation of human sexual response."

Masters and Johnson even managed to dig up a quote from Freud that sounded like a clarion call for their work: "*Biology is truly a land of unlimited possibilities. We may expect it to give us the most surprising information and we cannot guess what answers it will return in a few dozen years to the questions we have put to it. They may be a kind which will blow away the whole of our artificial structure of hypothesis.*"

By implication, Masters and Johnson's book of biological discoveries was just the incendiary device that Freud foretold. Rather than theories or supposition, they would provide plenty of facts in *Human Sexual Response* to back up their claims. Its first section stressed a commonality between men and women during sex, with its increased blood flow and muscle tension. Despite the obvious anatomical differences, they said, "again and again attention will be drawn to direct parallels in human sexual response that exist to a degree never previously appreciated." Along the way, like birdwatchers from a distance, they noted changing hues and shapes among the plumage, such as the "plateau-phase color changes of the minor labia in the female and the coronal engorgement of the penis in the male." Although Johnson described case histories near its end, the heart of this 315-page text dealing with the physiology and anatomy of sex was Masters's, relying on language as "noninflammatory" as possible, particularly in describing carnal acts.

Most significant, Masters and Johnson outlined a general framework about sex, with four separate stages of human response. When stimulated sexually, both men and women pass through an excitement phase, a plateau phase, an orgasmic phase, and a resolution or refractory phase. These four phases could vary widely in duration and intensity between individuals. But as a way of corralling the unruliness of sex, this generalized "human sexual response cycle" served as well as could be expected. The ambitiousness of their approach rivaled Freud's grand theories, yet its elemental reduction into four steps seemed familiar enough to even the most uninitiated lover. In men, excitement announced itself quickly, they affirmed. Young males could expand from a flaccid state to a full erection within three to five seconds of their libidos being kindled. While older men waited two or three times as long to become ready, and their firmness might waver a bit, the most obvious embodiment of excitement in males never changed. Evidence among young women emerged first with nipple erection, fuller breasts, and the vaginal lubrication within ten to thirty seconds of being aroused, with a lengthening of the vaginal barrel in anticipation of more to follow. Although excitement was a bit slower for older women, the researchers found that with the right stimulation, "these reactions may continue into the 80-year age group"—undoubtedly a surprise to the geriatric set.

On this highway to ecstasy, aspirants soon found themselves in the plateau phase, a temporary condition best described as a way station for the main event. Among women, the vagina moistened further as the "sex tension color change" turned the minor labia and surrounding tissue bright red to burgundy. Most significant, the clitoris, regulating sexual response in the female, tightened up considerably from its normal state, with the glans and shaft retracting behind a protective hooded foreskin. In this plateau phase, the male remained erect, with his testes enlarged and somewhat elevated, releasing a few drops of mucous-like fluid. Both genders usually experienced a "sex flush" during this plateau, reflecting "increasing sexual tension" with a temporary measles-like skin rash across the torso. Replete with medical terms, enough to require a glossary for the lay reader, one writer called their book "an almost impenetrable thicket of Latinate medicalese"—pointing to such lines as "This maculopapular type of erythematous rash first appears over the epigastrium," which a popularist might have described as the sex flush across the belly.

With orgasm, both sexes were in bloom, the rhythms of life in full gallop. In the male, heart and breathing rates jumped considerably from normal, with a "sensation of ejaculatory inevitability" in the prostatic urethra, just prior to the propulsion of seminal fluid through the penis. In women, orgasm took somewhat longer to express. However, once her crescendo arrived, the wavelike contractions in her uterus and the outer third of her vagina repeated themselves four to eight times in intervals of 0.8 second—about the same time as the "expulsive contractions" of male ejaculation in orgasm—before the quivering diminished. Masters and Johnson discovered among aroused women that the anterior vaginal wall moved backward and upward, creating a "tenting" effect, along with a near doubling of the uterus, to accommodate the penis. In both sexes, contractions of the pelvic tissue were followed by the rectal sphincter moving in harmony.

After this pinnacle, a release of muscle tension and the easing of blood flow from the engorged sex organs marked the fourth phase, resolution. This finale was most noticeable in the male, as the hardened penis quickly lost steam. The amethystine male organ remained somewhat inflated for a brief period, until it shrank completely to an unaroused natural state. For females, while some blood flow and skin discoloration soon faded, a refractory period was barely perceptible and "extended over many minutes," they reported.

Masters and Johnson orchestrated these four phases like Vivaldi concertos, even though their claim of a comparable sexual response between men and women seemed a bit strained. "The parallels in reaction to effective sexual stimulation emphasize the physiologic similarities in male and female responses rather than the differences," they contended. Rather than portraying the sexes as polar opposites, as different as Adam and Eve, Masters and Johnson found that each adult having sex was "homogeneous in their physiologic responses," regardless of their own individual likes or dislikes. They based their reasoning on similar "vasocongestion"—blood rushing through the veins to the sex organs—as well as observable secondary traits like heavy breathing and muscle contractions. Skeptics doubted their four-stage construct and wondered whether parallels between men and women were forced and categorized a bit too neatly. For instance, the similar 0.8-second contractions among men and women, as if tested by stopwatch, was a "finding [that] is not practical but symbolic," historian Paul Robinson noted. "It suggests that at the supreme sexual moment men and women are in perfect harmony. They march to the same drummer." The book contained a pleasingly egalitarian tone, without directly confronting the medical profession's mistaken view about male dominance in sex.

Nevertheless, the book's most important, exhaustively detailed finding, derived from watching 382 female and 312 male volunteers over nearly a decade, couldn't be denied—in the rigors of sex, women were superior to men. The book's very structure underlined this point with 141 pages devoted to female sexual response, triple the amount spent describing the male. Its clinical descriptions and illustrations provided a road map through the wonderland of a woman's body, detailing new insights into the unexplained physical mysteries of lovemaking. Their landmark findings about female sexual response would prove the most lasting aspect of their clinical work, carrying profound consequences that helped to define and inspire America's sexual revolution over the next two decades. Fascinated by the multiorgasmic capability of women, Masters knew this evidence would shake the totems of a male-dominated American culture, obsessed with what he called its "phallic fallacies" and fantasies. After their first climax, men waited up to an hour or more, enduring a temporary impotence during the politely named resolution period, before they could resume. But most orgasmic women were ready for more immediately, again and again if the mood fit and opportunity existed. "The female has no such refractory period," they wrote, comparing responses between the sexes. "She usually is capable of return to repeated orgasmic experience without postorgasmic loss of sexual tension." Further descriptions of multiple orgasms among women were mentioned throughout *Human Sexual Response* and their earlier clinical writings. "As contrasted with the male's usual inability to have more than one orgasm in a short period, many females, especially when clitorially stimulated, can regularly have five or six full orgasms in a matter of minutes," they reported. In this scenario, women's potential fireworks display in bed far exceeded the single little firecracker of the men beside them.

Before Masters and Johnson, medical literature portrayed the so-called weaker sex as "frigid" or frail, as if women were incapable of keeping up with men. Although one of every six female interviewees mentioned multiple orgasms to Kinsey, as well as a comparable number in a separate study of married couples by Stanford University psychologist Lewis M. Terman, this phenomena was still dismissed by most critics as a minor sideshow, as an anatomical oddity, or, most amusingly by male critics, as not a true orgasm. Masters and Johnson proved the biological reality was quite the other way around. Among multiorgasmic women, they discovered, each climax didn't differ physiologically from the another. If anything, their orgasms became better as they went along. "When female study subjects were interrogated in the laboratory after multiorgasmic experiences, the second or the third orgasmic episode usually was identified subjectively as more satisfying to more sensually pleasurable than the first orgasmic episode," they wrote. Some women enjoyed orgasms in succession without a break, while others slipped into another phase, like excitement or plateau, before revving up for another orgasm. "One of the important things we established—to our own satisfaction, at least—is that the female is naturally multiorgasmic," Masters later said. "This had not been emphasized before."

In divining the mysteries of female orgasm, Masters and Johnson delved into the intricacies of the clitoris, that little stout bundle of fibrous love, and how it reacts in heat. Unlike previous male doctors—including the author of the venerable *Gray's Anatomy* textbook, who described the clitoris as a "homologue of the male penis"—Masters and Johnson underlined its singular, unmatched qualities. "The clitoris is a unique organ in the total of human anatomy," they wrote. "No such organ exists within the anatomic structure of the human male." A clitoris wasn't some little brother or female phallus, as errant anatomists declared. Nor was it, as the Freudians theorized, the "immature" love object of masturbatory girls before they married and engaged in the preferable bliss of vaginal orgasm. Instead Masters and Johnson said these so-called expert writings about the clitoris amounted to "a potpourri of behavioral concept unsupported by biologic fact" and that "decades of 'phallic fantasies' have done more to deter than to stimulate research." The two researchers probed the interconnections between the clitoris and vagina during sexual response and found no difference in orgasmic response. "Are clitoral and vaginal orgasms truly separate anatomic entities?" they asked. "From a biologic point of view, the answer to this question is an unequivocal No." Nor was there any sense in comparing the clitoris during sex to a man's penis, they added. While vaginal lubrication might occur close to the time of a man's arousal, Masters and Johnson insisted "the widespread belief that the clitoris responds to sexual stimulation with a rapidity equal to that of penile erection is fallacious."

Their evidence was hard to refute. Spread out over several pages, rudimentary pencil drawings of engorging breasts and female genitalia—including the retracting clitoral hood, glans, and shaft prior to orgasm—provided a guide for the untrained. One reprint of an electrocardiogram traced a racing heartbeat during orgasm, sometimes soaring to as much as 180 beats per minute. Women were observed having sex in the supine, superior, and knee-to-chest positions. They were manipulated manually by themselves or by a spouse, or when mechanically aroused with the clinic's optical device. The artificial penis worked just fine when women received it flat on their back, but it became "technically impossible" if they tried the superior pose. So female volunteers who preferred to be on top had to rely on orgasm the natural way—with a real, live partner. Whether up, down, or sideways, the results all stressed the magnitude of female sexual response.

Orgasm for women was a bodywide sensation—with an "intense clitoral-pelvic awareness" and "often a feeling of receptive opening"—than for men with their narrow, centralized focus on erection and ejaculation. Contrary to old wives' tales or the prejudices of male doctors, women in all stages of life could enjoy intimacy. Pregnant women could have sex without fear of hurting the fetus, their study showed, and in some cases increase the potential orgasm, especially during the second trimester. Older women didn't have to end their love lives either. Among sixty-one active female participants over the age of forty-one, including three between seventy-one and eighty, the results suggested aging might slow, but never extinguish, the intensity of passion. "There is no reason why the milestone of menopause should be expected to blunt the human female's sexual capacity, performance, or drive," they stated. Masters and Johnson also tested the outer limits of female sexual response. In a wounding arrow to male pride, the researchers found the most intense orgasms for females were not with their guys but when they masturbated alone. Along with the possibility of multiple but separate orgasms, some women were capable, in rare circumstances, of "status orgasmus"—an extended peak of orgasm lasting from twenty to more than sixty seconds without returning to a plateau. (On an accompanying page, an electrocardiogram of one such episode appeared, presumably to quell any accusation of exaggerating.) The book didn't cite women who could fantasize to orgasm without being touched, but they later found and tested three such women after it appeared on shelves.

Most volunteers in Masters and Johnson's study were no strangers to sex or their physical feelings, a factor that undoubtedly influenced the results despite the researchers' insistence on a wide sampling. "The women's personalities varied from the very shy through the agreeably independent" and their previous sexual encounters ranged from "single to many," the book reported. But the unblinking physiological data underlined the possibility of orgasm for every American wife living in a "marital unit." Women considered "frigid"—an imprecise, pejorative term that Masters and Johnson didn't like—were quite capable of orgasm during sex. If anything, they were likely to be victims of religious or cultural inhibitions rather than some anatomic flaw or personal incapacity. With enough information and encouragement, free of society's condemnations, they too could be led into the land of sexual fulfillment. It was a message most women had never heard before. "Neither totem, taboo, nor religious assignment seems to account completely for the force with which female orgasmic experience often is negated as a naturally occurring psychophysiologic response," the authors assured their audience, more in the tradition of American self-help manuals than a medical textbook. "With orgasmic physiology established, the human female now has an undeniable opportunity to develop realistically her own sexual response levels."

Sexual fulfillment, they emphasized, was all in her own hands.

By comparison, the male sexual response portrayed by Masters and Johnson could seem inferior and in constant need of reassurance. "The 'fear of performance' developing from cultural demand for partner satisfaction has been in the past uniquely the burden of the responding male," they wrote, as if imagining Hercules carrying the world on his back.

Erection could be an uncertain adventure, no sure bet especially for the aging male, their testing showed. Ejaculation proved limited and fleeting. Some men could not control its premature release, leading to their partners' frustration. On the way to orgasm, women could exhibit a multifaceted control, able to stop and go seemingly at will, while men often rushed ahead like a runaway train. "In contrast to the fact that orgasmic experience of the human female can be interrupted by extraneous psychosensory stimuli, the male orgasmic experience, once initiated by contractions of the assessory organs of reproduction, cannot be constrained or delayed until the seminal-fluid emission has been completed," they observed.

Masters and Johnson also dispelled other dark "phallic fallacies" with the light of their scientific findings. To men who fondled themselves in private, they assured such "automanipulation" would not drive them crazy. Uncircumcised men did not show any greater ejaculatory control or less impotency than those who were circumcised. To the delight of locker rooms everywhere, they shot down the "wide-spread concept that ejaculation, whether accomplished through masturbation or coition, is detrimental to the physical condition of men in athletic training programs." And for men worried about their potency as they grew older, the maxim of "use or lose it" seemed to apply. "The most important factor in the maintenance of effective sexuality for the aging male is consistency of active sexual expression," they counseled. One section titled "The Penis"—like other genitalia afforded their own subchapters in the book—tackled the widespread factual ignorance surrounding its mythic importance in a male-dominated American culture. "The penis constantly has been viewed but rarely seen. The organ has been venerated, reviled, and misrepresented with intent in art, literature, and legend through the centuries," they observed. "Our culture has been influenced by and has contributed manifold misconceptions of the functional role of the penis. These 'phallic fallacies' have colored our arts and, possibly of even more import to our culture, influenced our behavioral and biologic sciences."

The overall portrait they painted was of a rather moody sex organ. During the excitement phase, they reported, penile erections could be lost easily due to "a sudden loud noise, vocalization on an extraneous subject, or an obvious change in lighting, temperature or attendant personnel." Given these conditions, any wife might wonder how a married man with bills to pay, kids in the house, and a TV on in the bedroom could ever get excited. Unlike the hardy, endlessly responsive female in bed, excitement for the male could be maintained for "extended periods" only by "carefully controlling variation and intensity of stimulative techniques"—in short, by not getting too excited too quickly. To satisfy a woman, a man's control of the ejaculatory impulse was often essential, their investigation found. After the seminal release, some semblance of an erection could be maintained if the man stayed for a time in his partner's vagina rather than quickly bidding adieu. But a rapid departure—or any activity in which this easily distracted, refractory fellow "walks about, talks on any extraneous subject, or is otherwise diverted in an asexual manner"—meant a certain return to flaccidness.

Aware of the defensiveness of men, Masters and Johnson refuted one more common fallacy—that those with bigger penises were more effective lovers. The lore and laughter surrounding tales of men with huge or tiny penises were the stuff of comedy roasts, urinal walls, and worrisome trips to the psychoanalyst. "The delusion that penile size is related to sexual adequacy has been founded in turn upon yet another phallic misconception," Masters and Johnson declared. Yet for reasons of their own, they deliberately avoided a clear answer to the most frequently posed question about male anatomy—the average size of a penis. To be sure, such prognostication was precarious for two researchers already employing a mechanical dildo as part of their studies. Historically, medicine avoided this topic as if it were radioactive. Masters and Johnson cited the late Dr. Robert Latou Dickinson (Masters had studied his anatomical book years earlier), who concurred with the 1899 measurements taken by a German physician named Loeb. In comparing height, penis length, and foot size, Loeb had reported a flaccid penis ranged from 8.5 to 10.5 centimeters, with the average length translated to 3.7 inches. Masters and Johnson did their own homework with willing volunteers but didn't share all the results. Routinely an investigator, armed with a tape measure, was assigned to check the top surface of what amounted to eighty different penises, gauging them in length from base to tip, both erect and at rest. In this tally, forty flaccid penises in the smaller category ranged from 7.5 to 9 centimeters, while the larger flaccid group extended to 10 to 11.5 centimeters. When erect, however, the smaller men nearly all doubled in size, while the larger men did not inflate proportionally, gaining about a 75 percent increase, according to their results. The biggest winner in this derby was from the smaller group—a volunteer with a penis less than 3 inches long. He experienced a 120 percent growth, and repeated this measure all three times he was checked.

Despite their efforts at quality control, Masters and Johnson conceded the nature of such testing was rushed, "crudely clinical at best," and bordered on unreliable. One third of the penile measurements were taken during "automanipulation," with presumably enough room for accuracy. But the rest were taken when men were near ejaculation. They pulled out during "active coition," to be measured fully engorged, in theory if not practice. "While the information returned obviously is not definitive, there certainly is no statistical support for the 'phallic fallacy' that the larger penis increases in size with full erection to a significantly greater degree than does the smaller penis," they concluded. But that limited disclosure about penile length was as far as the researchers would allow. They evaded any gold standard for the typical American male standing naked in the mirror, wondering whether his member might be deemed big, small, or just right. "When we published *Human Sexual Response,* we purposefully did not include information about the average size of the penis," Masters explained more than a decade later. "To some degree, we hoped that by not doing so, we would neutralize the concept that penis size is crucial to sexual response." Of course, Masters and Johnson had figured a median size for the average American, but they refused to say. "We won't ever tell," Masters joked, quite seriously. "It's our contribution to the security of mankind! No matter what we said, every man would reach for a tape measure."

Instead, Masters and Johnson aimed for a more expansive lesson, for men and women alike. In sexual intercourse, no matter what size a penis may be, the vagina seemed to know what to do. "Full accommodation usually is accomplished within the first few thrusts of the penis, regardless of the penis size," they wrote. For anxious men, the bottom line was that size really didn't matter and, in a breathtakingly counterintuitive notion, perhaps was even a detriment! Men with a smaller penis could enter the vagina easier and earlier in the excitement phase, they suggested, acting as a "dilating agent" for their spouse. Meanwhile, considerate men with a larger penis would have to wait and delay their entry until their wife became ready, somewhere further along the human response cycle. With sufficient care and stimulation, the vagina could accommodate a visitor of virtually any size. This proof was displayed by female volunteers who used the "artificial coition" device, as the color photography showed convincingly. The wondrous powers of the female anatomy seemed a marvel of self-actualization, a phrase coined by psychologist Abraham Maslow, whose work on self-esteem and female sexuality was cited in their book. "It helps to realize that the vagina is a potential, rather than an actual space, in its unstimulated state," Johnson later explained, almost existentially. "Actually the vagina is virtually an infinitely expandable organ. After all, it goes from a collapsed state to a size large enough to accommodate a baby's head."

For all their claims of a four-phase framework steeped in equality, the hard evidence in Masters and Johnson's book suggested a female's sexual prowess, in nearly all forms and at any age, outdistanced that of her male counterpart. Their view of human sexuality was simply revolutionary; it turned the existing order on its head. Their account, offered jointly by a man and woman, reflected both perspectives as never before. While they muted their explosive findings in obtuse medical phrases, while they deferred to the vanities and wary fortress of the male ego, while they stepped lively around the minefields of psychoanalysis and never confronted old man Freud by name, while they paid homage to Kinsey and cited 329 other references, and while their arguments were shaped in the conventions of organized medicine and their morally conservative times, their proof was stark, frank, and incontrovertible.

After ten long years, Masters and Johnson succeeded as none of their contemporaries ever achieved or dared to try. They escaped the firings, arrest, and professional revilement their detractors had predicted. Their book offered a new way for men and women to look at themselves and communicate with each other. It was a remarkable achievement unlike anything medical science had ever seen in this realm, or was likely to repeat in the future. Now, after toiling in near anonymity and secret confinement, they could only hope that America noticed.

PHASE THREE

Masters and Johnson with their book *Human Sexual Response*

CHAPTER NINETEEN

The Excitement of Release

The old Ritz-Carlton Hotel exuded a certain Brahmin charm in Boston, beholden to starchy traditions reaching back to British colonial rule. High tea was sipped late in the afternoon, while swells crowded in the restaurant's dining room, wrapped in furs, diamonds, and pearls. Upstairs, a fireplace warmed the majestic suites, as butlers tended to the blaze and turned down the plush linens just before bedtime. For out-of-town medical experts, these amenities were part of the mystique of staying at the Ritz while doing business at nearby Harvard, MIT, or the *New England Journal of Medicine*.

During a visit to see their Boston-based publisher, Masters and Johnson enjoyed this grand hotel and were delighted when it became their book's launching pad with the press. In facing skeptics before, they'd tried a similar swank approach without much luck. They had chartered a spacious hotel suite to present their findings in Chicago when banned from a national obstetricians and gynecologists convention there. They also served libations for the "Wash U" medical faculty when showing their filmed lab results. Both proved disasters. Still, these past experiences prepared them well for the challenge they were about to endure. They didn't want to be panned in Boston.

In April 1966, Masters and Johnson presided over an almost quaint series of press conferences at the Ritz that seemed more like informal seminars than a ritualized media grilling in front of a microphone. Sitting in comfortable chairs beside a long, draped window, they discussed their findings during two-hour sessions, which turned out both lively and convincing. They deliberately reserved two separate bedrooms for themselves at the hotel to avoid gossip.

During these sessions, skeptics were impressed with Masters's crisp authority and technical virtuosity. Johnson, with her trained vocals, further elucidated in plain English. Their publisher invited several influential journalists, including John Corry of the *New York Times,* Albert Rosenfeld of *Life* magazine, Arthur Snider of the respected *Chicago Daily News,* and Earl Ubell of the *New York Herald Tribune*—a core group that would influence the rest of the media coverage. While some findings had been leaked already, these lengthy, relaxed discussions at the Ritz became Masters and Johnson's first formal encounter with the press. The outcome couldn't have been better. "Dr. Masters' and Mrs. Johnson's face-to-face confrontation with the nation's science writers yielded an extraordinarily favorable reaction to their book," concluded *Harper's* magazine in its own laudatory profile, "The Sex Crusaders from Missouri." These once-obscure researchers were now described in Nietzschean superhero terms, as "endowed with exceptional sensibility, nerve and persistence" in educating a nation. Reflecting his paper's unexcitable manner, Corry's dispatch in the *Times* stressed numbers that were almost unimaginable. During the eleven-year study, Corry noted, some ten thousand orgasms were tracked through "direct observation" of hundreds of men and women "engaged in coitus and masturbation." In mentioning the uncounted prostitutes from Masters's preliminary research before Johnson arrived on the scene, Corry advised readers that "a more accurate and conservative estimate" might be between twelve thousand and fifteen thousand orgasms, figures that boggled the mind. Corry, like the other science writers, underlined that Masters and Johnson were the purest of white-coated scientists, a sober-minded, male-female team that had "taken pains to purge the book of anything that might be considered salacious." But not everyone agreed. Critic Albert Goldman, like Farber and others, pointed obsessively to the "plastic dildo" and the study's coldhearted description of human intimacy. In his review of their book, Goldman complained it should have been called "Sexual Body Mechanics," as even the elderly seemed hypersexed. "One wishes that we could return to the wisdom of an earlier time that accepted physical decline and sought compensation in pursuits that transcend the physical," Goldman lamented. "Perhaps a genuinely prophetic imagination is declaring itself in the book's most indelible image, that of a woman mating with herself by means of a machine."

Of the seven hundred reviews and notices about *Human Sexual Response*, the biggest stamp of approval came from the *Journal of the American Medical Association,* the kind of professional publication that once shunned their work. "Why was this study so long in coming?" asked the *JAMA* editorial. "It is no more reasonable to teach students the anatomy of the reproductive organs and ignore the way these organs function during their ordered activities than it would be to study the anatomy of the stomach but disdain any knowledge of [how it works.]" In the whiz-bang scientific era of the 1960s, admirers such as psychiatrist George Krupp suggested Masters and Johnson's findings illuminated the world of sex that seemed, in retrospect, like the dark side of the moon before NASA documented its deep curves and crevices. "If we are inclined to regard sexual union as something so sacrosanct that it should not be open to investigation, we should remember that a similar view was taken regarding the stars in Galileo's day," insisted another reviewer. Although Alfred Kinsey had provided the broad outlines of American sexual practices and others, such as Dr. Mary Calderone, had pushed for sex education in the classroom, Masters and Johnson produced hard-science answers for specific questions that went unasked by millions. As sociologist John Gagnon observed, "Everybody seems to be in favor of sex education, but they're against doing the research that would give us the knowledge to educate people *with*."

In interviews, Masters downplayed the pall of constant scrutiny and secrecy they'd had to bear for so many years. Although this success was a personal affirmation, the kind of achievement he had long sought, his public persona remained calm, grounded, and humble. He could take fierce pride in their findings, but he didn't seem hungry for the limelight. "The most important thing is that the work was done," he said simply. He told the press that hate mail amounted only to about 10 percent of all letters they received. Most letters arrived from people desperate for advice about personal problems, he said. But decades later, Masters conceded the "drop dead" mail that arrived after the publication of *Human Sexual Response* ran at about 75 percent, something closer to the truth. "The mail was horrendous," recalled Mary Erickson, who joined their staff four years after the book's release. "A lot of it was nasty and awful."

Uncontested was the textbook's commercial success, which publisher Little, Brown originally shipped to doctors in a plain brown paper wrapper. It soared onto best-seller lists, with 300,000 copies sold within a few months. "We feel for the first time that we are working with the support of public opinion, not against it," Johnson told *Newsweek,* which later called their effort "the most daring and explicit experiments ever conducted in the scientific studies of sex." *Human Sexual Response* transformed the public discourse about sex in America, opening a new era of candidness never seen before in the media. Although ridiculed for their turgid prose, Masters and Johnson relied on medical terms and clinical descriptions that didn't offend readers. They stayed away from vulgar phrases that would have invited censorship. Wary of being too provocative, in their book they mentioned fellatio only once and avoided anal sex entirely. And the media could repeat their language without appearing lascivious themselves. "You must remember that in publishing this book we were concerned primarily with acceptance—that is the reason that it wasn't in English to start with," Bill joked.

Masters and Johnson's mechanical approach, rooted in the American reverence for science, made their book palatable to a tongue-tied nation. Specific sexual information suddenly became part of the standard fare for newspapers, magazines, and television talk shows, which recognized the audience appeal for this sex talk involving Masters and Johnson. "When receptivity to sex-related material started increasing, people weren't as threatened by it," Johnson later noted. "They began to listen, instead of reacting emotionally. This evolution was paralleled by the media's awakening to the idea that this was a very saleable product." Some women's magazines remained wary of the topic in the mid-1960s, so they profiled Masters and Johnson themselves, until the sexual revolution gained greater public consent. "Then the floodgates opened,"

Johnson recalled. "All of a sudden the whole magazine—every single magazine—was being sold on the basis of sex. A little food, a little fashion, a little parenting, and all the rest is sex, so the media actually created the concept of a revolution."

In the 1960s, America would convulse with the assassinations of the Kennedy brothers and Martin Luther King Jr., massive civil rights demonstrations, and bloody race riots in the streets. The conflict in Vietnam brought about widespread draft resistance, the repudiation of one president (Lyndon Johnson), and the election of another (Richard Nixon) who eventually would resign in disgrace. In this swirl of political and social drama, the traditional definitions of sex, love, family, and commitment seemed an open question too. The media chronicled a whole new world of hippie love beads, antiwar love-ins, free-love utopian communes, unclothed flower children at Woodstock, revealing miniskirts, thigh-hugging go-go boots, midriff-baring bellbottom pants, skin painted in psychedelic Day-Glo colors, explicit movies such as *I Am Curious Yellow* and Broadway shows with nudity, such as *Hair,* which screamed of sexual freedom not seen before. "The Sixties will be called the decade of orgasmic preoccupation," declared Masters, with only a little irony. Even pent-up suburban wives such as Mrs. Robinson in *The Graduate* seemed emboldened by the book. "Masters and Johnson's view of women as sexual athletes capable of multiple orgasms suddenly harmonized with the spirit of sexual freedom or, more accurately, sexual experimentation, sweeping the country," observed author Jane Gerhard about the era.

Soon after the book's publication, Masters and Johnson embarked on an extensive tour at several medical schools and colleges, usually before standing-room-only audiences. Bill didn't kid himself about the prurient interest driving sales of *Human Sexual Response.* As he often quipped, "This is the most purchased, least read book in history." Masters insisted they soon get back to work at the Reproductive Biology Research Foundation clinic. Now that they had mapped the basic physiology of human sexuality, there was so much more to do.

CHAPTER TWENTY

Focusing Feelings

"Man survives earthquakes, epidemics, the horrors of disease, and all the agonies of the soul, but for all time his most tormenting tragedy has been, is, and will be—the tragedy of the bedroom."

—LEO TOLSTOY

"Have you ever been orgasmic? Under what circumstances? Tell me, what were your feelings during that experience?"

On the first day of therapy, Virginia Johnson sat opposite an unhappy wife and started asking about her sexual difficulties. Across a wooden table, she opened a manila file and stationery pad. She jotted down a running stream of notes. A microphone placed between them captured every question and answer. It was connected to a large tape-recording machine located elsewhere in the building, where reams of tapes from all sessions were stored for further review and analysis.

For the next two hours, Mrs. Johnson, dressed in a white lab coat with her dark auburn hair pulled back in a bun, stared sympathetically at this troubled woman, posing a litany of inquiries designed to reveal the hidden story of her marriage.

"How has this sexual problem affected your partner? When do you recall this first happened? How have you handled this problem?"

"Have you ever noticed your husband having problems getting an erection or ejaculating?"

"How has your husband attempted to pleasure you sexually? What were the results?"

"What is your idea of the appropriate female role in the marital bed? In other aspects of your daily married life?"

"How do you think your husband would answer these questions?"

In a nearby suite, Dr. William Masters performed the same task with the woman's husband. He explored the husband's feelings about experiences with dating, marriage, divorce, and child-rearing; his religious affiliations; and the couple's educational and social backgrounds. He then posed even more sensitive questions about possible sexual encounters before marriage, whether he masturbated, or whether he summoned up specific images and fantasies during intercourse with his spouse. Masters asked whether the husband, in the past, had witnessed his parents having sex, either by accident or on purpose. Had he played "doctor" as a "sex game" with other kids, or woken up with nocturnal emissions in his shorts? Did he ever have a homosexual experience? Masters asked him to describe what initially attracted him to his spouse, what their honeymoon was like, how often intercourse occurred, and what sights, touches, sounds, and smells he associated with lovemaking.

On the second day, Masters and Johnson switched partners. She talked with the husband, while he chatted with the wife—repeating the same format of questions, which they called "history-taking." Learning about the needs, wants, and desires of each couple was an important first step in the Masters and Johnson "dual therapy" program. By gaining a view from both sides, the overall portrait of a couple's sexual history emerged much faster. Masters and Johnson could begin to mend the couple's relationship, filling in the vast differences between partners. By the third day of their two-week therapy program, they would compare and contrast replies to their most revealing questions:

"What do you want from this therapy program for your husband or wife?"

"How interested is your spouse in the sexual part of your marriage?"

"What does your husband (or wife) want most from you?"

The answers provided clues to the puzzle, glimpses into the heart of a marriage, which they believed a single therapist, usually male, could not divine. While some interviewing techniques mirrored Alfred Kinsey and others suggested Sigmund Freud, the dual-therapy approach devised by Masters and Johnson was remarkably unique. To many, they offered practical insights for healing marriages, the power to change lives far beyond the capabilities of the average therapist or religious counselor. By the mid-1960s, with their physiological testing nearly completed, the most intimate moments at the Masters and Johnson clinic happened with clothing on, rather than off.

"Their work was totally innovative—the 'dual therapy' model was terrific," said Dr. Alexander N. Levay, a clinical professor of psychiatry at Columbia University's medical school, who was first a patient with his wife and then later a trainee of the program. Levay first heard Masters and Johnson speak in New York soon after the publication of their groundbreaking book. As a newly minted man of medicine, he wasn't sure what to make of their presentation. Levay had finished medical school and entered his third year of training in internal medicine, a specialty that prides itself on knowing all functions of the human body. Yet organized medicine seemed ill-prepared on sexual matters, certainly compared to the effectiveness of Masters and Johnson's breakthroughs. "It was obvious that these people were either crooks or they were onto something really new," he recalled. Levay and his wife, Matilde, journeyed out to St. Louis, seeking their own miracle, as if venturing to Lourdes. "Matilde had never had an orgasm, it was as simple as that," said Levay, who also couldn't overcome his own sexual hang-ups. Originally from Hungary, Levay was educated as a teenager at a Benedictine abbey, where he lived until he graduated at age nineteen. "They said, 'Give the first kiss to the mother of your children,'" he recalled of the cleric teachers' limited wisdom about conjugal love. "Matilde had the same background, because she came from French nuns in Peru. So this [therapy program] was a big eye-opener for us." To Levay, the revolutionary idea of a male-female therapy team guiding a married couple made all the sense in the world.

From the very beginning, the purpose of understanding the science of sex was to help people overcome their difficulties in lovemaking—what Masters and Johnson called "sexual dysfunction." In allowing their initial studies, Washington University agreed with Masters's premise that "the greatest handicap to successful treatment of sexual inadequacy was a lack of reliable physiological information in the area of human sexual response." A simple logic guided their strategy—before they could fix things sexually, they had to know how it worked. In January 1959, after years of studying how the human body responded anatomically and physiologically during sex, Masters and Johnson launched a therapeutic experiment to improve the faulty love lives of American couples. Their methods were so uncertain that they didn't charge any fees. While the first study of human sexual response played to Masters's strengths as a researcher, this second study underlined his weaknesses. Neither he nor Johnson had any prior psychotherapy training (even though *Time* magazine identified Johnson as a "psychologist"). Masters's closest formal education involved a three-month Department of Psychiatry course on interviewing techniques. Johnson had even less experience—an assortment of undergraduate classes that touched on matters of the heart and mind. Yet curiously, their lack of training—especially when medical school–trained psychiatrists were inculcated in Freudian theory—allowed wide latitude to experiment, to be free of orthodoxies. "We didn't know what couldn't be done, and that was a tremendous advantage," said Masters.

Virginia Johnson's instinctive understanding of human behavior far exceeded Masters's grasp and proved invaluable in this unexplored land of sex therapy. As the smiling, friendly hostess of their clinic, she had witnessed the deepest cravings, longings, and fears of people having sex, and absorbed the lessons of how to counsel, comfort, and educate them on a daily basis. She had a certain practical credibility that leveled the playing field between them, giving Johnson the chance to exert herself more as Masters's equal rather than as an "associate" or other replaceable accessory. She suggested several effective methods that seemed to him like brilliant eureka moments. Instead of sifting through the childhood roots of an adult's neurosis, she observed sex through their one-way mirror and came up with applied solutions, like some anatomical plumber repairing the pipes. "At least 70 percent of the therapy was her idea," Masters later said. Johnson incorporated the theories of others, notably psychologist Albert Ellis, who pioneered counseling with couples in the 1950s, and Temple University's Joseph Wolpe, whose behaviorist theories reflected the views of B. F. Skinner, John Watson, and Ivan Pavlov. Masters's colleagues scoffed at his claim that their revolutionary therapy model derived mainly from Johnson's imagination. Masters realized they were forging a new path—what others would call cognitive behavioral therapy—to gain improvements within a short, defined time span. They didn't experiment with dogs or lab rats, or zap patients with electric currents. To change bad habits, they adapted such ideas as Wolpe's "systematic desensitization"—slowly learning to relax and overcome fears and anxieties—with their own regimen. Masters never shied away from supporting Johnson or tried to claim her ideas as his own. He increasingly listened to her therapeutic ideas and intuitive hunches, which proved their worth.

Johnson championed this dual-therapy approach, particularly its stress on involving both marital partners from the outset. In the past, therapy had focused only on the spouse with a "dysfunction," such as a male's impotence or a female's inability to reach orgasm. The other spouse remained in the dark about the treatment and usually avoided any responsibility for the problem. A wife with an impotent husband didn't know when, or if, she should wait for a sexual advance or take the initiative. Similarly, a husband with a nonorgasmic wife might wait endlessly for a clue, worried that he might be accused of being too demanding or having lost all interest. But Masters and Johnson knew better: "There is no such thing as an uninvolved partner in any marriage in which there is some form of sexual inadequacy," they concluded.

Over time, Johnson convinced Masters that many men just didn't understand the underlying dynamics of female sexuality. This became glaringly apparent in roundtable discussions when everyone compared notes. Johnson believed their dual-therapy approach could balance the inequity between sexes. In a world so tilted in the male direction, this was not an easy task.

"We're producing men who know damn well they don't understand women . . . ," Masters once explained to a reporter.

" . . . and are willing to accept a woman's interpretation of *herself* as a woman," Johnson added, finishing the equation. "The fact that more than 95 percent of all the interpretations and definitions of female sexuality and responsivity have been produced by men is something that I personally reject because the content is often inaccurate."

Gini's insights sprang from her history-taking with patients, the endless hours spent asking about personal background, their likes and dislikes, attempting to detect a pattern in their behavior. Whereas Bill could be very businesslike in his rudimentary questioning, Gini enjoyed the give-and-take, mining different layers of a patient's life. The difference in styles could be dramatic. "He was very brief and very brusque—forty-five minutes was a history to him," she remembered. "The first one I took, I was up to the third hour when he called through." During each session, a telephone was available in the room so a therapist could be contacted. Picking up the receiver, Gini heard Bill's voice. "He said, 'I think you're going to put yourself and this person to sleep.'"

Gini couldn't dim her own natural curiosity, the wonderment about people she had developed as a young girl in Golden City. For a couple having trouble with sex, each story provided clues toward an answer. In essence, the therapists were holding up a mirror at the couple so they could see themselves honestly. While listening intently, she realized there was "lots of pain in these interviews and hundreds of things that needed to be addressed."

After the initial sessions, Masters and Johnson unveiled their most powerful tool on the third day of therapy. They called it "sensate focus"—a series of touching exercises conducted outside the clinic, usually in the couple's home or a hotel room, aimed at restoring intimacy between them. Particularly for women, the sensate focus exercises—with no immediate demands of intercourse—allowed many to reacquaint themselves with their natural sensuousness. So many patients had been taught that sex was wrong that it rendered them unable to make love in a mature or even adequate way. "What is totally foreign to effective sexual development, in spite of centuries of practice, is the notion that sex is dirty, supplemented by various controls exercised through fear, rejection, ignorance and misconception," Johnson later said. Indeed, the inspiration for sensate focus came from her own high-strung childhood, when her mother calmed her down after a long, stressful day. "When she would want me to go to sleep or anything, she would do things like tracing my face or my hands, or drawing and writing words on my hands—little things like that, nonsensical nothings, but they were all sensual and they always ironed me out, calmed me down," explained Johnson. "That was kind of the origin of it [sensate therapy]. I'm not talking about anything sexual. I'm just talking about hands-on, the way animals comfort their babies, nothing more or less."

In the confines of a bedroom, alone together, the couple followed the sensate instructions, given as "homework" by Masters and Johnson. They remained unclothed throughout these sessions. One spouse was designated as the "giving" partner, with the job of tracing, massaging, or fondling whatever body part was requested by the "getting" partner—except for the genital areas or the wife's breasts. As the process was repeated, switching the giver and the getter roles, the couple stayed away from any specific "sexual stimulation" in favor of a gentle trial-and-error meant to be simply pleasurable, free of stress and anxiety. Particularly for women, these full-body exercises allowed them to think and feel sensuously, without the pressure to "make something happen."

On the fourth day, the couple discussed with therapists what had happened the night before. The loosely structured therapy was deliberately designed to give a couple creative freedom to explore their own bodies. While most women were accustomed to their husband's genitalia, many men were mystified by their wife's "external pelvic anatomy" and were invited to examine her, without shame or guilt. Respecting religious and moral values remained paramount for therapists, though they found that cultural constrictions by married couples were a constant obstacle. "The feeling that sensate pleasure at best represents indolence and at worst, sin, still permeates society sufficiently to influence the affectional, sexual patterns of many marital relationships," Masters and Johnson found. Gini and Bill also relied on olfaction—the sense of smell—to facilitate a couple's touching and feeling experience. Husband and wife received moisturizing lotions—

unscented or perfumed—to spread along the skin, both to smooth any dry, rough hands to the touch and to ease the way toward sexual union.

This breezy "game" of sensate focus, as Masters and Johnson described it, allowed couples to express themselves, perhaps as they had never done before. Although no concrete goals were set, no performance standards to measure, by the fourth day therapists gently pursued inquiries that suggested the direction of where all of this manual manipulation was headed. Each couple was asked questions such as: *"What, if any, degree of erection (husband) or lubrication (wife) did you notice while you were pleasuring one another yesterday?"* Over the remaining two weeks, sensate focus treatment served as a therapeutic sounding board to address premature ejaculation, vaginismus, primary and secondary impotence, orgasmic dysfunction, dyspareunia (painful intercourse), and sexual inadequacy in aging men and women. It opened up their feelings toward each other, if indeed a troubled marriage could be saved.

For Alex Levay and his wife, their stay in St. Louis transformed their marriage and became a turning point in his career, incorporating their methods into his own New York practice. As he learned, Masters and Johnson "had tons and tons of people who had never had an orgasm" and were helped with their innovations. One method for women with vaginismus—an involuntary tightening of the vaginal muscles preventing intercourse—relied on slowly inserting a tiny plastic penis into the vagina. Causes of vaginismus could range from physical discomfort from endometriosis or laceration of the broad ligaments, to psychological trauma from rape or incest. During treatment for this problem at the clinic, a female partner was asked to move into a gynecological examining position, and the condition was reviewed with her husband present. When they returned to the bedroom, the couple used a series of Hegar dilators—essentially black, heavy plastic dildos available in various sizes numbered one through five. At the wife's instruction, the husband cautiously inserted the dilators, which increased over the next few days to a man-sized replica. Some women kept the larger dilators inside themselves for several hours each night. Within a month or so, this practice led to success. "It was a way of increasing their sexual intimacy and sexual comfort with each other,"

Levay said. "The husband and wives were always partners in the treatment."

This success offered more hope than ever imagined. Outsiders like Levay, who learned of the researchers' still-unpublished discoveries, were thrilled. For a second astonishing triumph was emerging from the Masters and Johnson clinic—a new psychosexual treatment to rival Freud, with far better results.

CHAPTER TWENTY-ONE

Sexual Healing

For Robert Kolodny, one fascinating lecture changed his whole life. Before a group of Washington University medical school students in 1967, Dr. William Masters explained how patients every day pose questions about human sexuality and why they must be ready with answers. "Bill was surely one of the most electrifying speakers I have ever heard," recalled Kolodny, then a medical student from New York sitting in the crowd. "He spoke with immense presence, with clarity, and a logical flow to his presentations. He used no notes whatsoever."

Until that moment, Kolodny had planned to become a dermatologist. He wanted a comfortable nine-to-five medical practice, prescribing pills to pimply skinned adolescents and old people with rashes. He didn't want the exhaustive hours of his father, Dr. Maxwell Howard Kolodny, a respected internist at Mount Sinai Hospital in Manhattan, whom he admired but rarely saw at home. "When I wanted to spend time with my dad, I either went on house calls with him or made hospital rounds with him," he recalled. The community's respect and adulation for his father—the oldest son of Jewish Russian immigrants—impressed young Kolodny enough to follow in his path. "I made up my mind by age five that I was going to be a doctor."

Masters and Johnson seemed a revelation to Kolodny, a bright, well-read young man already conversant with Sigmund Freud's theories concerning sex. Within a short time, he landed a position as the first medical student to study at the clinic. "I was absolutely astonished by the success rates they were having, which ran totally counter to everything in every psychiatric manual at that time," he recalled. "That's what prompted me to change my career plans completely." Like many familiar with psychoanalysis, Kolodny believed "sexual dysfunctions were only surface manifestations of deeply-rooted, unresolved psychological issues and that there was no way possible to treat them in the short term, that it would take years and years of psychoanalysis to address the underlying issue."

With almost religious certainty, the America-based disciples of Freud said the Oedipal complex, penis envy, castration anxiety, and a stubborn chain of neuroses must be overcome before any bedroom healing could be achieved. Masters and Johnson proved otherwise. Kolodny, like others who joined the staff during these early days, was enthralled with the new therapy's grand potential. At the clinic with tape recorders rolling, Kolodny sat next to Masters as they listened to another staff therapist interview a patient. Masters provided his own running commentary, critiquing each move. He explained why the therapist asked such a question, pursuing one inquiry over another. He also pointed out errors, if the therapist missed a chance to further clarify or illuminate a patient's problems. At times, Kolodny felt like a young analysand in Vienna during Freud's era, starting at the ground floor with something truly momentous. As much as he admired Masters, Kolodny realized Johnson's innate intelligence was often the treatment's guiding hand, even with no more medical knowledge than perhaps a first-year nursing student. In those days, their remarkable success with patients seemed almost unbelievable. "If you go back to the 1950s and early 1960s, the sexual therapy of choice was five to ten years of psychoanalysis—and the outcomes of that were abysmally poor," he said. "Here was Bill and Gini, who had worked out a modality for seeing people with longstanding chronic problems—fifteen or twenty years of problems—and treated them over a two-week period and getting 80 percent of them better."

Johnson became Kolodny's first partner in sex therapy. After six weeks, the young recruit was called into Masters's office. As was typical, Masters got right to the point.

"You and Gini are doing a case tomorrow," he declared. "Are you ready?"

Kolodny, with a sense of propriety that kept his youthful ambition in check, initially resisted this opportunity.

"Wait, Bill," Kolodny told him. "I'm no more ready to do this than I would be to do a hysterectomy tomorrow because I've watched six hysterectomies done."

Masters wouldn't have it. "No, you're underrating yourself," he said, his reedy voice becoming insistent. "And don't forget, Gini invented this field. She's going to be there in the room anytime you're not sure what to do."

The next day, Kolodny donned one of the white robes worn by the clinic's small band of therapists and joined Johnson in overseeing the care of a married couple with profound sexual problems. Kolodny, conscientious almost to the point of priggishness, tried to conceal his uneasiness. To his great surprise, the couple never seemed disappointed. "I was astounded!" he recalled.

After earning his medical degree from Washington University in 1969, Kolodny moved to Harvard for his internship and residency, intending to return to St. Louis for a permanent position with Masters and Johnson. In confidence, Masters suggested that Kolodny might take over for him someday, while others tried to steer the young doctor away. "A mentor of mine in medical school told me, 'You're throwing your medical career away,'" he recalled. "In 1969, it [sex therapy] was regarded as some frivolous, almost voyeuristic area that no serious person would ever engage in." Colleagues conjured up fantasies about the sex clinic, only to be disappointed by the humdrum reality. "Sex therapy was not watching people getting undressed and having sex together," he explained. "I was taking care of people with sexual illnesses, consulting with people."

Along with his idealism about the Masters and Johnson mission, Kolodny, an endocrinologist in his mid-twenties, possessed a personal intelligence and dedication that seemed to ensure a bright future for the clinic. "Dr. Kolodny was basically the heir apparent," said Della Fitz-Gerald, who later trained there with her husband. "He was helping Masters and Johnson expand their efforts. He really is quite a walking encyclopedia regarding all aspects of human sexuality." Among the small full-time staff, Kolodny was exceptional because he had also received a medical degree and training from a top school. "The people who came there for any length of time—social workers, nurses—some of them were physicians, but most of them were non-degreed people," said Rose Boyarsky, a clinical psychologist with a PhD from Duke, who worked at the clinic for four years in the early 1970s. "Bill certainly liked Bob very much and took him into his confidence a lot." Masters's rhetoric about a multidisciplinary staff conveniently veiled a harsh reality—their still-unpublished sex therapy wasn't lucrative or prestigious enough for most physicians. Many considered "sexology" a potential disaster. Eventually, Masters and Johnson held seminars to review their work, inviting several top psychiatrists and psychotherapists from around the nation. But in the early days of the therapy, only optimistic young doctors like Kolodny or somewhat flawed practitioners, like Dr. Richard Spitz, joined them on a regular basis. In the case of Dick Spitz—a pediatrician and ordained minister—his judgment was apparently eroded by alcoholism.

Spitz was a tall, handsome fellow with impressive therapeutic skills. But Johnson took a dim view about any staffer who drank, and Masters wasn't pleased with Spitz for violating another unwritten rule. During his tenure, Spitz romanced Mae Biggs, a pretty, blond nurse with a sociology degree, who might have been the clinic's most talented female therapist next to Johnson. Despite his own relationship with Johnson, Masters wouldn't tolerate interstaff dating. By the late 1960s, Masters had heard plenty of gossip about Alfred Kinsey's old staff, including rumors of wife-swapping and bisexual encounters, and felt any such behavior at their clinic would lead to ruin. Their dual-therapy approach, with male and female staffers together, relied on professional cooperation. "He had a serious, almost intimidating cautionary talk with about-to-be new hires, basically saying, 'I don't care what you do in your personal life, but what you do here in the office *is my business* and I will not allow anybody to besmirch our reputation,'" recalled Kolodny, who, like everyone else, became keenly aware of the double standard. The office's somber administrator, Wanda Bowen, enforced the no-fraternizing rules in the staff assignments. "They alternated—there were no pairs," said Bowen. "Even VEJ [Johnson] and Doctor [Masters] were paired off with other people." Though Spitz and Biggs had worked together as a team, their relationship soon deteriorated as Spitz's health worsened.

For perhaps too long, Masters disregarded Spitz's alcoholism. "He stayed much longer than he should have," said Bowen about Spitz. "He did drink a lot but then when he became ill . . . he died a terrible death, lingering with cancer. . . . Doctor [Masters] kept him on until he said 'that's all I can do.'" Spitz died in the early 1970s, soon after Kolodny returned from his Harvard residency and the line of succession at the clinic became clearer.

Despite their weaknesses, Masters and Johnson, as a team, were more than the sum of their parts. Their potent personalities—the very notion of a man and woman together, jointly and equally, helping couples sort through their most intimate problems—became the clinic's center of gravity, the astonishing force that kept everything in place. After five years of not charging for their untested therapy, they became confident in its results and started collecting increasingly steep fees. Still, Masters made sure couples in need could be treated. Based on their income, about 25 percent of couples were given adjusted rates and another 25 percent were not charged at all. After screening each patient, Masters and Johnson supervised the staff's assignments, ensuring that newly arrived therapists, such as Roger Crenshaw, didn't feel overwhelmed. Masters cautioned therapists to keep their moral judgments and personal feelings at bay while discussing each patient's problems. Increasingly, they received cases of greater complexity, from sexual failures to fetishes. Crenshaw worried he might be ill-equipped to deal with a patient's sexual dilemma. Like a stern father, Masters set him straight.

"You know," Masters replied drolly, "if someone says they like to have sex with a seal, I want you to ask them—'Is it on the north side or the south side of the island?'"

Crenshaw laughed heartily at Masters's humor, part of his tough-guy charm and wit that many staffers found endearing. Soon, Crenshaw found himself confronted with just such a circumstance. "It wasn't much more than a week later when a guy comes in and says, 'I'd rather have sex with my dog than with my wife—and that's my problem.' And I said, 'German shepherd or collie?' So learning to be nonjudgmental was probably the first big hurdle."

At their working luncheons, the staff sometimes shared lighthearted moments in between the tales of human woe. "I remember one couple that I treated in therapy—sweet, sweet people—but they kept referring to their genitals as 'Gentiles,'" recalled Kolodny with a chuckle. "Little things like that happened all the time. But because of the subject matter, you couldn't wait until you got into private to burst out laughing."

Premature ejaculation was widespread in the fast-paced world of postwar America, a condition the bedeviled Romans once called *ejaculatio praecox*. Though definitions varied, premature ejaculation usually meant losing control shortly before or soon after entering the vagina. Men often had hurried sexual experiences with girlfriends "in the back seat of cars, lovers'-lane parking spots, drive-in movies or brief visits to the by-the-hour motels," Masters and Johnson noticed, hastened by the fear of getting caught or discovered. With their clothes on, couples would "pantomime intercourse" until the friction caused the excited male to ejaculate in his pants. Other times, their sex play might involve *coitus interruptus,* with "a few frantic pelvic thrusts" from the penis into the vagina, quickly "withdrawn as a means of contraception."

In a 1956 medical journal, Dr. James H. Semans of Duke University described his "stop-start" method for treating the overexcited male, which Masters and Johnson soon melded into their own therapy. At Duke, Semans was known as a skilled urologist married to Mary Duke Biddle Trent Semans, the socially prominent granddaughter of the university's cofounder, tobacco magnate Benjamin N. Duke. Few talked about Semans's innovative technique, even though premature ejaculation afflicted at least one-third of all young men engaged in sexual relations. "You had to cloak your wording very carefully, even in a hospital, to get your point across," recalled Mary Semans about her husband's efforts. His lesson came right out of behaviorism's school for wayward reflexes. As a matter of bedroom conditioning, men were instructed to have their erect penises stimulated manually by their partner, up to the point of near ejaculation, and then cease all activity until that sensation of inevitability subsided. The starting and stopping were repeated until a sense of control over the ejaculatory reflex was developed during arousal. Eventually, the couple performed this "stop-start" method during vaginal penetration, sort of a coital hokey-pokey, until ejaculation could be prolonged enough for a wife's sexual satisfaction.

Masters earlier had discovered a variation of this start-stop approach while in the whorehouses of St. Louis and elsewhere. He learned many men were introduced to sex by prostitutes, who urged their clients to complete their business promptly so they could service their next customer. After just two or three visits, he observed, an "inexperienced male became conditioned to this pattern of sexual functioning, a life-time of rapid ejaculatory response might be established." Some men couldn't be touched on the genitals "without ejaculating in a matter of seconds," while others burst at the sight of a nude woman in person or in a magazine centerfold. By watching through peepholes and two-way mirrors, Masters later wrote, "I was able to identify a technique that, with minor alterations, proved to be of extreme importance in helping men contending with premature ejaculation obtain voluntary control of their ejaculatory process." In their own writings, Masters and Johnson called it the "squeeze method"—a detailed way for married couples to solve this frustrating problem together. "We weren't even the originators of it," recalled Johnson, who added the technique to their repertoire of "sensate focus" exercises in the bedroom. "Prostitutes knew how to do it." Female partners were crucial for men in overcoming this predicament. In fact, men were warned the "squeeze method" wouldn't work if they tried it alone.

Masters and Johnson presented "PE" in epidemic-like terms with tragic consequences because of its impact on married life. "Probably hundreds of thousands of men never gain sufficient ejaculatory control to satisfy their wives sexually, regardless of the duration of their marriage or the frequency of mutual sexual exposure," they estimated. While some medical experts defined "premature" as any ejaculation during the first minute of vaginal penetration, Masters and Johnson refrained from "stopwatch" measurements. Instead, they defined the condition as any man who couldn't contain himself long enough to satisfy his partner in "at least 50 percent of their coital connections." Unlike that of other experts, Masters and Johnson's advice about this male dysfunction reflected a woman's perspective as well. While some wives, particularly those from poor backgrounds with little education, were afraid to complain about their domineering husband's haste, many did show their sexual frustration. "She verbalizes her distress by accusing her husband of just using her as an object for sexual release; in short, of being selfish, irresponsible, or simply of having no interest in or feeling for her as an individual," they observed.

Sensitivity to a woman's view was one of Johnson's many triumphs in developing a new sex therapy with Masters. Many wives followed an unwritten "don't touch" policy concerning their husband's genitals. Sensate focus exercises were designed to overcome their shyness and cultural conditioning about such intimacy. With the "squeeze" method, a wife began by sitting up in bed, with her back against the headboard cushioned by a pillow or two, with her legs spread open and relaxed. Meanwhile, her husband rested on his back, with his head situated near the foot of the bed. He then placed his pelvis in front of her, his legs over hers, giving her "free access to his genital organs," as the therapy team prescribed. For a time, the wife fondled his penis and scrotum, enough to arouse her husband. When full erection was reached, the wife held the penile shaft, placed her thumb just below the coronal ridge, with her index and forefingers against the other side of the shaft. Like a good sport, she held his penis like a curveball or a Havana cigar. Then slowly, for maybe three or four seconds, she squeezed—not painfully but strong enough to lose his urge to release. With a short rest of up to thirty seconds, the same method resumed. Once again, a wife enlivened her husband's penis and then held the shaft firmly until all signs of quick ejaculation had subsided. After twenty minutes—repeating the same techniques up to five times in the first session—couples usually discovered premature ejaculation wasn't as inevitable as before.

After two or three days of practice, the squeeze method usually provided the kind of control men needed to move to the next important step—pleasing their wives, or what Masters and Johnson called "nondemanding intromission." In this scenario, once an erection was achieved and the squeeze employed twice or three times, a woman mounted her husband, almost like a wrestler pinning an opponent to the floor, with her knees adjacent to his chest. Then leaning toward him at a 45-degree angle, the woman slid the penis inside herself, without directly sitting on the engorged shaft. Once it was inserted, she concentrated on staying motionless, without any thrusts. This union was the most critical time—allowing the man to remain in her vagina without the immediate feeling of certain ejaculation. If he sensed an imminent expulsion, the husband was instructed by the therapists to tell his wife immediately. From this "female-superior" coital position, she could elevate herself enough to release his penis and to reapply the squeeze method.

It was a remarkable *pas de deux* in bed. For most traditional American couples, who thought men naturally assumed the dominant missionary position during sex, the arrangements were stunningly reversed. The woman on top acted as both the coach and quarterback. Instead of being the aggressors, men essentially didn't move, except to maintain an erection. In fact, to avoid a reoccurrence, men were told "the male-superior position, which places the greatest strain on ejaculatory control, should be avoided when possible." Over the next few days, a couple continued this treatment until they grew more confident in their success, eventually capable of up to twenty minutes of uninterrupted intercourse. For many longtime marriages, such a mutually pleasurable experience was unprecedented in their collective memory. "There is physical closeness and holding, development or redevelopment of communication, and markedly increased warmth of understanding between husband and wife," the researchers observed. Their words likely understated the magnitude of this shared achievement.

Some men could achieve erections, but they could not reach orgasm. For these males unable to ejaculate during sexual intercourse, Masters and Johnson offered a similar solution. Though relatively rare, "ejaculatory incompetence" usually emerged during the first sexual encounter in marriage and lingered for years. Again, many sufferers confessed deep-seated guilt, stemming from "rigidly orthodox religious backgrounds" where open sexuality was condemned. One thirty-three-year-old man from a fundamentalist Protestant background told of being whipped as a boy for nocturnal emissions and started his honeymoon by being unable to ejaculate during sex with his wife. A Catholic man, with two sisters who were nuns, was punished for masturbating as a teenager and told it was a disgusting sin. He found himself unable to ejaculate for the first eleven years of his marriage. Another man from an orthodox Jewish marriage, still unconsummated after eight years, found himself incapable of ejaculating with his wife because of his concept of the vagina as "an unclean area." Some considered sex an unpleasant duty; their physical problems intertwined with the psychological. In these cases, the therapeutic instructions didn't involve any "squeezes." Instead women were directed to "manipulate the penis demandingly," following the cues of the man lying on his back to "force ejaculation manually." Once achieved, the couple proceeded in their next encounter to sexual intercourse, with the woman in the female-superior position. "A demanding style of female pelvic thrusting against the captive penis should be instituted immediately," Masters and Johnson instructed. If the man didn't ejaculate soon, the female partner stopped her thrusting, removed his penis and began immediately rubbing it again until her husband reached "ejaculatory inevitability"—the point of no return. Unlike the premature ejaculators or those beset by impotency, these men rarely had their erections falter or wilt. With sexual intercourse lasting thirty to sixty minutes with a husband who could "maintain an erection indefinitely during coital sex play," several women became multi-orgasmic, the therapists found.

Sexual healing by Masters and Johnson and their dedicated staff brought about many remarkable improvements. Over eleven years, they treated 186 men for premature ejaculation, with a failure rate of only 2.2 percent, they reported. All of the twenty-nine women referred for vaginismus recovered sexual function, with sixteen women experiencing orgasm for the first time in their lives during the two-week therapy. If fear, worry, and shame caused sexual dysfunction, then they worked tirelessly, and inventively, to provide a remedy. Together, Masters and Johnson had charted the physical universe of human sexuality, detailing each nuance of male and female anatomy and response. Now they had discovered a therapy to help couples express themselves intimately to their own satisfaction—just as Masters had once promised in seeking Chancellor Ethan Shepley's permission for their studies.

CHAPTER TWENTY-TWO

Surrogates

"The man who has no wife is no cuckold."
—Geoffrey Chaucer, *The Canterbury Tales*

Barbara Calvert exuded sex appeal. With her enchanting English accent and good looks, Calvert turned the heads of several men at Washington University as one of the medical school's most attractive secretaries. Her husband, George, worked elsewhere in the school, in the Department of Illustration, though it wasn't certain how much he knew about his wife's activities. Most mornings, she could be found at her desk, typing up papers or arranging appointments for Dr. Willard Allen, the chairman of obstetrics and gynecology. While Allen's main secretary—a dour older woman named Mildred—had no use for Dr. Bill Masters's clinical investigation into sex, Calvert, just like her boss, agreed with the study's value. An effervescent woman, she befriended Masters and Johnson before they moved from the university to a clinic across the street.

Some afternoons, Barbara Calvert slipped away and wouldn't return to her desk for more than an hour or two. Dr. Ernst Friedrich remembered noticing her absence. "When you went in, close to lunch hour, someone else would say, 'Yeah, she's out to lunch,'" recalled Friedrich. "When you came back, after a little while, they'd say, 'She's still out to lunch' and that person would roll their eyes. In other words, you knew she had some extracurricular activity during her lunch hour. It was more or less an open secret. But I don't know if her husband knew in the beginning."

In Masters and Johnson's crusade to alleviate sexual dysfunction, Calvert stepped forward as a front-line soldier. She agreed to become a sexual surrogate partner, assigned to help men suffering from impotency, premature ejaculation, or other sexual problems.

"In present-day terms, you might call her 'the Viagra girl,'" explained Dr. Michael Freiman, who considered both Calverts as friends. "I remember seeing her come back to work like she'd just taken a shower—the way that people look in the morning, fresh and clean."

And Barbara continued to volunteer, one case after another, until her husband found out.

Female surrogate sex partners, though relatively rare in Masters and Johnson's therapy, became one of the program's most controversial but highly effective assets. In the first eleven years, they made surrogates available to forty-one unmarried men who felt sexually inadequate and could not turn to a former spouse or friend for help. To these patients, women like Barbara Calvert, earnest and anonymous, were "someone to hold on to, talk to, work with, learn from, be a part of, and above all else, *give to* and *get from* during the sexually dysfunctional male's two weeks in the acute phase of therapy," they emphasized. Thirteen female surrogates were accepted from among thirty-one volunteers screened for the assignment. Thrill-seekers or other psychologically suspect candidates were weeded out. Johnson counseled the selected women and ensured they were reimbursed sufficiently. Yet for all of her therapeutic innovations, this secret system of providing sex surrogates wasn't her idea. "It was remarkably successful but I thought it was asking for trouble," Johnson recalled.

Bill Masters displayed empathy for the fragile male psyche and those unable to perform adequately. "It was appalling to Bill that any man we could help would go untreated," recalled Johnson. Masters's affinity may have stemmed from his own travails with infertility or, more likely, from empathy for his most desperate patients. Once they agreed to accept unmarried clients, Masters argued for surrogates to achieve an acceptable success rate. Medical literature pegged their chances of overcoming sexual dysfunction at less than 25 percent. Under this new treatment, thirty-two of the forty-one men with surrogate partners—nearly 80 percent—had their symptoms reversed, a remarkable success given their chronic severity. As it had for decades, Missouri law still prohibited a man and woman not married from having sexual intercourse. But Masters didn't care much about the legal and ethical dilemma posed by surrogates, as long as their contributions led to a happy outcome for his patients. Though Johnson helped arrange the matching, the money exchanged between patients and their surrogate was kept secret. They always faced the risk some prosecutor or medical authority would liken it to a prostitution scheme. The national notoriety and financial success of their *Human Sexual Response* book only heightened the risk of what they had to lose professionally. As Bill and Gini agreed, the less said about the surrogates the better.

In the late 1960s, Robert Kolodny learned of this secrecy when he accompanied Masters to a medical ethics seminar on campus. Masters was scheduled to speak about their still-unpublished therapy, as he often did in promoting sex education among physicians. During a walk to the classroom, Kolodny suggested Masters might mention ethical concerns in using female surrogates.

Masters stopped him in his tracks. "I'm not going to go there," he replied. "It's not something I want to talk about. Don't ask about it."

Kolodny, who had been working for only a few months with Masters and Johnson at the time, didn't realize the sensitivity of his request. Nor did the trustees of the Reproductive Biology Research Foundation know much about the surrogates. Torrey Foster, the board's attorney at the time, said neither he nor any other trustees were ever told of the practice during the entire eleven years of the initial study. "He [Masters] impressed upon us the secrecy by which he conducted some of this, and that it was all very legitimate, but we never got into any details," Foster explained. "I was never brought into the legalities of the research he was doing. I never felt that Bill was totally open with us at board meetings. We were a 'rubber stamp' board, no doubt about it. We didn't challenge a lot of what Bill did. We were a board that did everything he wanted."

Masters and Johnson extolled their sex surrogates as Florence Nightingales of the night, with their own altruistic sense of calling. They were mostly local white women, from varied economic and educational backgrounds, whose ages ranged from twenty-four to forty-three. "The one common denominator that they all have, as women, is great value and great pleasure in their sexual identity," explained Johnson at the time. Half the surrogates had performed previously in the human sexual response study; the other half volunteered specifically for this task. All but two of the thirteen surrogates had been married at some point, and three-quarters were mothers of at least one child. While some had graduated from high school or formal secretarial training, more than half were college graduates or had a postgraduate degree. One of Masters's favorite surrogates was a female physician "frankly quite curious" about the role, he recalled. She volunteered several times over a three-year period, evaluating the program "for herself *and* for us." Johnson fondly described another surrogate—a nurse she called "Mary"—who had been a volunteer in the earlier study. As the victim of sexual abuse, Mary remained grateful to Masters for a minor gynecological repair that had restored her injured tissue. "She would have done anything for us—for him," recalled Johnson. Mary wasn't alone in her troubled background. Several surrogates had a "history of sexually oriented trauma in the immediate family." Three surrogates themselves had been married to sexually dysfunctional men, including one husband who had committed suicide and another who had become an alcoholic.

The surrogates worked as part of the therapy team, prepped about all aspects of male sexual response, including psychological concerns. Fears about performance, "spectatoring" during sex with emotional detachment, and the devastating impact of sexual dysfunction were all discussed in advance, along with techniques that put "an anxious, tension-filled man at ease socially as well as physically." Each surrogate learned basic information about her client's history and sexual problems, but not his name or any other identifiers. They met for the first time at a restaurant, intended to help each become more comfortable in the other's company. At the table, patients discovered what the surrogate looked like, her tastes in clothes and manners, and how she communicated. More than two-thirds of male patients suffered from impotency or other psychosexual malady that had caused the ruin of their previous relationships. However, the success rate among surrogates, because of their superior skills at aiding recovery, turned out far better than originally anticipated.

Despite talk of equality among the sexes, Masters and Johnson didn't offer surrogate partners to women. American society wasn't ready, they contended, nor were women themselves. In eleven years, only three unmarried women sought treatment at the clinic. All three arrived with "replacement partners," men with whom they had a relationship lasting at least six months. "Refusing to make a male partner surrogate available to a sexually inadequate woman, yet providing a female partner surrogate for a dysfunctional man, seems to imply application of a double standard for clinical treatment; such is not the case," Masters and Johnson insisted. They struggled to explain away the obvious dichotomy. A male patient regarded the surrogate's services "as he would a prescription for other physical incapacities," they contended, like some bottled elixir at the neighborhood drugstore. But for women, such simple utilitarianism wasn't acceptable. Growing up in American society, a distressed female would first need "a relatively meaningful relationship which can provide her with 'permission' to value her own sexual function," they wrote. The "extreme difficulty" of creating a "meaningful relationship" in the allotted two-week period was ostensibly the reason why the clinic forbade male surrogates. It was one risk, one battle that Bill Masters wasn't ready to take on for the moment.

Despite Johnson's ambivalence about surrogacy, she accepted the inherent contradictions in their treatment. "As far as we have been able to discern by patient interrogation, it does not fit in with the value systems of most women," she explained to reporters about using male surrogates. "We wish the male's sexual attitudes were shared by all females. It is not. Even with the freedom of communication, even with the far less rigid attitudes existing today, even with the real determination by many women to adopt comparably unfettered attitudes, female sexual responsivity is still a product of the residuals of older value systems." More than one claim by Masters and Johnson about surrogates was misleading, however.

"None of the volunteers were married when living their role as a partner surrogate," they asserted—yet Barbara Calvert and some other surrogates were married during their tenure. More significant, they said "no attempt ever was made to persuade any woman to serve as a partner surrogate." Yet among nurses in the hospital's delivery room, candy-striped student nurses, female research volunteers, and even some wives of other faculty members, Masters often encouraged their enrollment as surrogates. "He didn't set out to ask somebody to be a surrogate knowing who their husband was, but he did know these women were married because they all wore wedding bands," recalled Kolodny.

Masters and Johnson were forced to reevaluate surrogacy when Barbara Calvert's husband hired an attorney. In a $2.5 million federal lawsuit, George E. Calvert, then a former Washington University employee living in New Hampshire, said that he and his wife had been fertility patients of Masters's but that Masters and Johnson had "breached the doctor-patient relationship in procuring the said Barbara Calvert to engage in sexual intercourse" with two male patients. Court papers said she had been paid $500 for sex in July 1967 as a surrogate with a patient referred to as "John Doe I" from New York, and another $250 from "John Doe II" of Virginia for her services in January 1968. A later court filing upped the accused number to seven men. Calvert claimed the researchers knew Barbara was married and convinced her to keep her illegal surrogate activities from her husband.

To their old friends in St. Louis, George Calvert's shocked reaction seemed far-fetched. Most assumed he knew about Barbara's midday romps, just like others did around the medical school and hospital. Dr. Mike Freiman and his wife attended several parties and shared dinners with the Calverts, and he certainly got wind of her enlistment in the clinic's activities. Freiman said Barbara volunteered as a way of making a few extra dollars. "I think they [the Calverts] were under financial pressure," he recalled. " I don't think she did it because she was convinced of the philosophy or the sexuality was important. She just simply did it as a way of making money." By the time the lawsuit appeared, Masters and Johnson were famous for their best-selling sex advice, collecting princely sums in royalty checks and therapy fees. As a way of dipping into that cash, George Calvert's lawsuit claimed Masters and Johnson had benefited monetarily from the information they gained as a result of Barbara's employment.

A few newspaper stories appeared about the lawsuit, but the clinic's new lawyer, Walter Metcalfe Jr., advised Bill and Gini to stay quiet. "Our reaction is that any such charge is ridiculous," they said in their only formal statement. "We can prove it." Metcalfe convinced a judge to seal the record in the case and deftly pressed for an out-of-court settlement, sealing all lips from speaking to the press. The Calvert lawsuit threatened to expose the clinic's myriad secrets—the sex between unmarried couples, the money funneled between patients and surrogates, and the questionable actions of America's two reigning experts on sex. If this information became public, state medical authorities might have taken away Masters's medical license, or he might have been forced to resign from academic or professional affiliations. The clinic's board of trustees learned of the practice years after it began. " I think he finally admitted using surrogates and said maybe it wasn't a good idea," lawyer Torrey Foster recalled.

For all of Bill Masters's good intentions, for all of his confidence in the new therapy to overcome sexual dysfunction, his method of relying on surrogates nearly sunk them in a legal morass and public relations nightmare. "It placed the entire program in such jeopardy," Johnson admitted two years later. "It's so sad because they're the ones who need the most help."

Chastened but unbowed, Masters and Johnson promised publicly never to rely on surrogates again.

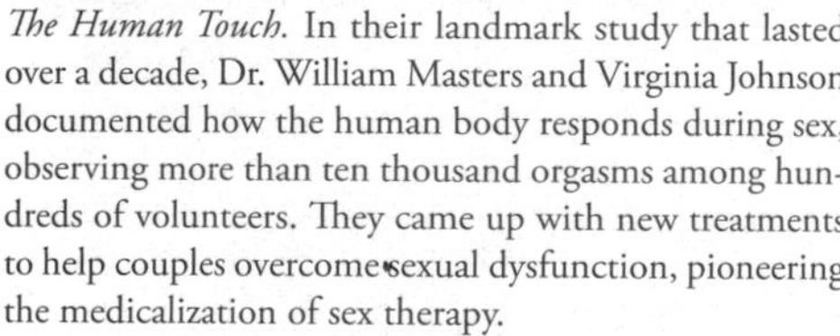

The Human Touch. In their landmark study that lasted over a decade, Dr. William Masters and Virginia Johnson documented how the human body responds during sex, observing more than ten thousand orgasms among hundreds of volunteers. They came up with new treatments to help couples overcome sexual dysfunction, pioneering the medicalization of sex therapy.

Self-Made Boy. Having been abused by his father, young Bill Masters left his Midwest home at a young age to attend school in the East, determined to make something of himself.

Golden City High. As a farm girl in Missouri, the young Mary Virginia lost her virginity to Gordon Garrett, her high school sweetheart. Despite predictions in their yearbook, they never married. Fifty years later, Virginia would search for the whereabouts of her lost love.

Bill and Libby. Bill Masters's marriage to Elisabeth Ellis lasted more than two decades and produced two children, thanks to his fertility lab techniques. Libby considered Masters the love of her life but was wary of Virginia Johnson's influence on him.

Bride and Groom. George Johnson, Gini's second husband, was a local bandleader and the father of her two children.

Limelight. As the singer in a band, Mary Virginia Eshelman professionally renamed herself "Virginia Gibson," after the Gibson coffee company that sponsored her radio program. "I literally didn't go out with anyone, to any degree, that I didn't have a sexual relationship with," she later recalled.

Seeking a Degree. Gini Johnson, a twice-divorced working mother at age thirty-two, came to Washington University in St. Louis, seeking a college degree she would never earn. Instead, she became the trusted female assistant to Dr. William Masters, the school's top ob-gyn surgeon and fertility expert.

Volunteers. Gini convinced dozens of nurses, students, doctors, and faculty wives to volunteer in research on human sexual intimacy. The Masters and Johnson ten-year study revolutionized medicine's understanding of sex and underlined the power of female sexuality.

Family Man. Bill Masters showed great empathy toward marriages troubled by sexual problems, but his own union was plagued by adultery, indifference, and his workaholic tendencies.

Unmarried Researchers. Masters and Johnson were often portrayed by America's media as two unmarried researchers objectively studying sex in a lab. Their secretive affair continued for years, until Gini's interest in another man prompted Bill to leave his wife and family.

A Sex Therapy Better Than Freud. After studying the physical aspects of human intimacy, Masters and Johnson developed a two-week treatment program that claimed an 80 percent success rate, far better than traditional psychoanalysis.

Feminist. Gini Johnson proved a pioneer in improving women's understanding of their own sexuality and debunking old myths—a crucial part of the 1970s feminist movement. Like some modern Pygmalion tale, Johnson's mercurial rise impressed those who previously knew her as a secretary. Her creative insights were key to the successful sex studies that earned worldwide acclaim.

Couple of the Year. Time magazine celebrated Masters and Johnson with their 1970 best-seller, *Human Sexual Inadequacy,* which brought fame, wealth, and celebrity clients to America's leading experts on sex and love. The two married in 1971.

Master Doctor. Bill Masters became legendary at Washington University in St. Louis. He championed a greater understanding and acceptance of human sexuality, pushing for training in med schools, and paving the way for Viagra and other medical-based treatments for sexual dysfunction. But his research techniques were often as radical as they were effective—from observing volunteers copulating and using vaginal cameras to document orgasm, to relying secretly on sex surrogates after disavowing their use as unethical.

Bill and Gini. Among staffers, Masters and Johnson were an enigma—charming and inspiring one minute, cold and hypocritical the next. But together they earned the heartfelt gratitude of those who benefited from their advice and treatment. Some patients even sent photographs of themselves in flagrante, demonstrating their success. "We tell them that we are willing to take their word for it," Masters once quipped.

Lost Loves. On Christmas Eve 1992, William Masters, age seventy-six, told Virginia Johnson he wanted a divorce after more than twenty years of marriage. He then wed his beloved Dody, the girl he had adored during summers at Rainbow Lake a half century earlier. Though Masters and Johnson said they were content with their separation, their famed partnership as sex experts soon fell apart.

Remembrances. After Bill's death in 2001 from Parkinson's disease, friends held a memorial for him at Washington University, but Gini found it too painful to attend. In a lengthy obituary, the *New York Times* declared that Masters "revolutionized the way sex is studied, taught and enjoyed in America." Now living under the name Mary Masters, Virginia Johnson remains both grateful and resentful for the ways Bill Masters changed her life.

CHAPTER TWENTY-THREE

Playboys and Patrons

The Playboy Mansion in Chicago resounded as home to the most provocative imaginings of American sexuality in the late 1960s. Its owner, Hugh Hefner, emboldened a more open, commercialized approach to sex, beginning with the first edition of his hugely successful magazine, with a reclining, nude Marilyn Monroe on its cover. At the mansion, the late-night bacchanals, the in-house pool with a sliding pole from the floor above, and the constant catering to every corporeal appetite were all part of its lore. This seventy-room redbrick townhouse, dating back to the Victorian era, was America's pleasure dome, ground zero for the explosive sexual revolution being heralded in its pages. At age forty, Hefner had a brash yet sophisticated persona—often seen puffing a pipe and wearing a tux on his television show *Playboy After Dark,* a far cry from the stuffy, professorial style of Bill Masters and his partner, Virginia Johnson.

In early 1968, the mansion's atmosphere provided a bit of a shock to the two researchers from St. Louis. Upstairs, several young Playboy bunnies, stuffed into tight-fitting costumes with a little cotton tail, stayed as guests for weeks on end. In the downstairs living room, a constant flow of celebrities from Hollywood and the sports world attended endless parties, getting a glimpse of whether the libertine fantasies surrounding Hef's "*Playboy* Philosophy" were really true. On the front door, a brass plate warned in Latin, *si non oscillas, noli tintinnare* ("If you don't swing, don't ring"). Masters and Johnson arrived in the Windy City for none of that. Their stark, scientific focus on sex was never glamorized or viewed through a gauzy lens. The women they'd seen naked often had cellulite along their hips and sagging breasts. The men worried about flaccid penises and unmanageable expulsions. As a team of male and female researchers unmarried to each other, Masters and Johnson agreed to stay at the mansion strictly as a matter of business, not pleasure.

"For propriety's sake, they always took adjoining bedrooms, rather than sharing a single bedroom," recalled Hefner. "That was a source of some amusement for us."

The unlikely alliance between these midwestern researchers and America's media satyr revolved around a shared admiration and support. During their visit, Hef stayed up for hours chatting with Masters and Johnson, and they discovered a mutual indebtedness to Alfred Kinsey. Before he founded *Playboy* in 1953, Hefner studied at Northwestern University, where he wrote a sociology paper comparing Kinsey statistics on male sexuality to the law in America's then forty-eight states. "I made the case, statute by statute, that if the laws were effectively enforced most of us would be serving time in prison," Hefner said with a chuckle. "My own prejudices on this subject came early."

As a loose scholar of human sexuality, Hefner recognized the landmark importance of their scientific work. "Prior to Masters and Johnson, there really were no significant studies related to the physiology of sex—one of the most important parts of our lives, and something we knew almost nothing about—because studying it was taboo," Hefner recalled decades later. The plain-spoken advice for couples unable to show affection rang true with Hefner's personal experience. "I was raised in a very typical midwestern Methodist home—with a lot of repression and very little hugging and kissing—and very early on I saw the hurtful side of all of that," he explained. "That's why it became a cause celebre for me."

During the 1960s, *Playboy* expanded beyond glossy nude pictorials to discuss the pill, women's rights, abortion, and other cultural controversies. Yet, Hefner realized that *Playboy,* for all its purported knowledge and worldliness, had never mentioned the term "clitoris" in its pages until Masters and Johnson agreed to be interviewed. "I mean, the very nature of orgasm, climaxes, the fact that women had orgasms—what is more fully understood now—that information really didn't exist before Masters and Johnson," Hefner recalled.

In the May 1968 *Playboy* interview, conducted by senior editor Nat Lehrman, Masters and Johnson provided unprecedented answers from their untraditional study of age-old questions:

> PLAYBOY: Traditionalists also complain that investigations such as yours destroy the mystery of sex. Do you think that's true?
> JOHNSON: We happen to think that the realistic, honest aspects of sexuality are a lot more exciting than the so-called mystery. The mystery to which the traditionalists usually refer has to do with superstition and myth. A knowledge of sex doesn't impair, but *enhances* it.

In Hefner's mind, what took them beyond Kinsey was the very presence of Virginia Johnson as an equal partner. Unlike the tanned, nubile blondes on display *au naturel* elsewhere in the magazine, here was a remarkably well-informed forty-three-year-old woman with her dark hair clipped tightly off her face, wearing little makeup and dressed in the same clinical white jacket as she had appeared in *Life, Time,* and *Newsweek* magazines. She argued passionately for the sexual equality of women, not as objectified Barbie-like dolls but as loving, active participants in the bedroom. "All the names on the Kinsey book were male, but the fact that Masters and Johnson—the male and the female—were involved in the studies and the research, the results turned into more than just a male's point of view," Hefner realized. Johnson's willingness to sign on with Masters as *Playboy* consultants provided a degree of journalistic ballast that pleased Hefner, which he happily rewarded. "In 1965, I founded the Playboy Foundation and, because the magazine and the company was doing very well in the 1960s, we started funding all sort of things, including Masters and Johnson," he explained. "They became good friends."

Despite her practiced calm and sophisticated manner, Gini could barely contain her amazement inside the Playboy Mansion. "There was a blue and a red room—all the rooms were different colors," she remembered. "Hef was terribly bright and accomplished. I liked staying at the mansion. What I loved about it was that the chefs were on duty twenty-four hours a day. At three o'clock you could count on wonderful new cookies being baked because Hef stayed up almost all night and slept into the day. He was wonderful to us." Even though she and Masters would regularly sleep together on out-of-town trips, Johnson specifically asked for two adjoining rooms. "I was always very concerned about my public image and my family," she recalled. "I just didn't want to be known in that way." During their stay, Lehrman was impressed with how enthusiastically Hefner lavished attention on them. "There was a joke about him being up for five days and then, when he went to sleep, he'd say 'Don't wake me unless it's a call from Frank Sinatra or Lyndon Johnson!'" Lehrman recalled. "He was very difficult in those days, very difficult to reach. He rarely saw people, but he was there for them and very proud that they considered him a peer."

Masters and Johnson realized the magazine's cultural impact in the 1960s, particularly with millions of young male readers. "*Playboy* is probably the single most important source of sex information in America today," Masters proclaimed. "We're glad to help them make it accurate information." Along with popularizing their own advice, Masters and Johnson's chronically underfinanced research clinic received a big boost from their *Playboy* alliance. During the next decade, the Playboy Foundation contributed a total of $300,000 to the Reproductive Biology Research Foundation "to develop a comprehensive training program for health care professionals in the treatment of sexual dysfunction." As the intermediary who had first met Masters and Johnson at a medical convention, Lehrman flew to St. Louis to iron out the arrangement. He also wrote a paperback called *Masters and Johnson Explained,* published by *Playboy.* "Our relationship was *quid pro quo,*" explained Lehrman, who often called St. Louis seeking technical advice for the "*Playboy* Advisor" column. "When he [Masters] needed money, he came to me and I usually got it for him. When they needed information for any part of *Playboy,* I would go to him. It was a fantastic thing for *Playboy* and I'm sure Hefner was very impressed."

America's endless skirmishes about sex prevented government subsidies from reaching Masters and Johnson's program. Unlike most university-based medical clinics, especially those favorably reviewed by the press and professional peers alike, "it soon became evident that the chances of getting federal grants to support sex research were little or nonexistent," Masters recalled in his unpublished memoir. "Ours was the type of research that we would have to support individually in some manner." From 1959 until 1970, Masters used nearly half of his physician's income to support their clinical research. "We need between $250,000 to $500,00 a year to do the job we want to do," Masters said at the time. "We've never had nearly that much." Successful therapy patients showed gratitude in various ways, but rarely with notable donations, even those with considerable wealth. "People who were patients were never anxious to become public, so, for the most part, they didn't make contributions to the institute," recalled former staffer J. Robert Meyners. "It had a very hard time raising money, except for the fact that it charged a lot for two weeks of treatment. Each of us who were therapists only saw two or three patients at a time, so you don't build up a lot of money that way. It was never a money-raising operation."

While politicians in America prevented tax dollars from going to sex research, Masters himself didn't help matters. His scrupulous pride in their work and his unwillingness to flatter bureaucrats killed off potential funding. After he applied for a grant from the National Institute of Mental Health (NIMH), for example, the agency dispatched a young, somewhat officious psychologist to review the clinic. As recalled by former staffer Dr. Thomas Lowry, this meeting with Masters proved brief.

"As a condition of having this grant, of course, you'll have to turn all your records over to us," explained the civil servant.

Masters froze on the spot.

"Well, thank you very much but I think our discussion is over," declared Masters, with the chilliest finality.

For reasons of patient confidentiality as well as staff training, most physical records of their therapy were on reels of recording tape, and not extensive paper files. Masters wasn't going to allow a bureaucrat to go through those tapes and run the risk of exposing their patients' identities. "They didn't turn their records over to anybody," said Lowry.

In the early 1960s, Paul Gebhard of the Kinsey Institute helped Masters, still full time at Washington University, to apply for a federal grant. But the frankness of their physiology and anatomy studies seemed unacceptable to those holding the government's purse strings on research. "He [Masters] said he needed [federal grants] for research purposes, that he couldn't just depend on the university subsidizing his work forever," Gebhard recalled. "We had been successful in getting NIMH money, so I encouraged him to go ahead and apply." Masters sent "the most detailed application, even down to money to be spent on how many ashtrays, etc.," he said. Gebhard felt sure Masters's application would be approved. "The people in Washington were, of course, impressed by this but they also were worried about the repercussions." The feds sent out a review committee for a site visit, to examine Masters and Johnson's facility and determine its suitability for the American people's money. On the way back, the white-haired physicians on this review committee stopped by the Kinsey Institute in Indiana and talked with Gebhard. Just before they left, one of the senior physicians drew him aside.

"By the way, Dr. Gebhard, have you heard of a Dr. William Masters?" asked this physician in an ominous tone.

Gebhard paused and gave a minimal reply.

"Why, yes—yes, I've heard of him," he said hesitantly, as if he'd read Masters's name in some medical journal, rather than actually being a longtime friend who had helped him prepare his bid.

The senior examiner frowned and issued a grim warning. As Gebhard recalled, "This man said, 'Don't have anything to do with him! There's something twisted there!' And he walked off. Needless to say, his grant application was denied."

Gebhard suspects the feds got a peek at the artificial coition device. "He [Masters] probably showed them his machine and that probably just freaked them out," Gebhard said with a laugh. "Can you see a bunch of old Boston Brahmin physicians who'd never seen anything sexual in their lives confronted with this machine? Sex research has always been difficult to fund and easily subject to criticism."

To raise money beyond Hefner's largesse, Masters gathered limited grants from pharmaceutical companies interested in contraception and fertility research. During the 1970s, they conducted a study for Encare Oval, testing a spermicide on sixteen female volunteers, ranging in age from eighteen to forty-five, who were injected with semen from male donors and given a rubber dildo to simulate "coital activity" in determining its effectiveness.

Over time, however, Masters recognized the importance of currying favor with the few wealthy benefactors willing to have their names listed publicly. Their biggest supporters were Lou Morton Ellis and her husband, Van C. Ellis, of Dallas, who were sex therapy patients in 1970 and later returned for "refresher" therapy at their own request. Lou, an heiress to a potato chip fortune, donated to numerous philanthropic and religious causes, including her local Park Cities Baptist Church. At one time, Van was president of the family's snack firm, Morton Foods, which became a subsidiary of General Mills, owner of such familiar household brands as Wheaties cereal and Betty Crocker baking goods. "It makes us both sad and angry that there are couples who wait until it is too late to seek help because they either are too proud to admit their need, or who are unaware that sex-related problems generally can be resolved by competent therapists," said Lou, a self-described "traditional" mother of four whose photo resembled Betty Crocker herself. Their participation as Masters and Johnson's board members undoubtedly raised some eyebrows in Dallas, where their church was one of the largest in the Bible Belt. Undeterred, the Ellises tried to weave religion and strong family values into the discussion of sex. They provided money for a pilot program at the Masters and Johnson clinic related to the clergy and sex counseling, as a prelude to promising a five-year, $1 million grant. One awkward proviso, however, included their request to hire Herbert Howard as a member of their staff. "Van and Lou Ellis were friends and they knew him as a minister," Johnson recalled. The staff wasn't pleased with the addition of someone they considered unqualified. "I was very unhappy about the prospect of this guy joining the staff, even though the wealthy people wound up paying his entire salary and benefits package," said Dr. Robert Kolodny. Shortly after he arrived, Howard mumbled an obscure phrase to Masters and Kolodny that included a racial slur. "I got so upset I got up and left the room," said Kolodny. Masters saw the obvious disgust on his young assistant's face and chased after him.

"This is a guy from down South and we're not going to let him do that if he's here," Masters assured him. "But it's very important that you come back in here because we're talking about $100,000 a year for the next two years in support of our work. And we can't afford to offend these people."

By that time, after so many rejections for government grants and other prestigious funding sources, Masters couldn't turn down the support of a potato chip heiress and the relatively small request for her local pastor. He'd already learned to live with some compromises as part of his larger goals, even if it meant spending a night or two in the Playboy Mansion.

"I've listened to you on so many things," he said to Kolodny, with a calming voice. "But this time, I'm asking you to trust me."

CHAPTER TWENTY-FOUR

Repairing the Conjugal Bed

"Physiology should not be confused with psychology."
—SIGMUND FREUD

On the cover of *Time* magazine, Masters and Johnson's worldwide fame reached its height. A full-color portrait of Bill and Gini, their close-up faces luminous and triumphant, was emblazoned across the May 25, 1970, edition. Masters wore his trademark bow tie and Johnson, seated slightly in front of him, smiled demurely. Next to them, an abstract wooden sculpture of two lovers appeared in an embrace. Against a dramatic black backdrop, white lettering boldly identified them as "Researchers Masters and Johnson," with a yellow banner proclaiming "Sex Education for Adults." Four years earlier, *Human Sexual Response*, their pioneering guide to physiology and anatomy among the sexes, had become a runaway best-seller, in more than a dozen languages around the globe. It had transformed itself from a mere textbook into a cultural touchstone, catching the American zeitgeist just as the sexual revolution began in full swing. The bestowing of *Time's* cover—linked to the release of their second book, *Human Sexual Inadequacy,* and its remarkable new sex therapy—affirmed their cultural significance.

"They are the most important explorers since Alfred Kinsey into the most mysterious, misunderstood and rewarding of human functions," declared *Time's* story, titled "Repairing the Conjugal Bed." In a nation with skyrocketing divorce rates, the Masters and Johnson treatment promised a much-needed medical antidote for unhappiness in the bedroom. "The great cause of divorce in this country is sexual inadequacy," Masters said. "I would estimate that 75% of this problem is treated by the psychologist, the social worker, the minister and the lawyer. Medicine has really not met its responsibility." The team's "educated guess" was that "perhaps half of the 45 million married couples in the U.S. are sexually incompatible to some degree," *Time* reported. The article underlined the clinic's overall success rate of 80 percent, with many still reporting satisfaction five years later. Given their claims of success, *Time* placed Masters and Johnson into a gallery of other sexual pioneers, including Sigmund Freud, Alfred Kinsey, and Havelock Ellis.

During press interviews, Bill and Gini were in top form. Despite the clinic's ambitious goals, they convinced *Time* that "Masters and Johnson take a modest view of their work." The magazine described Johnson's growing up in Missouri "within the rigid sexual taboos of the back country" only to become a visionary proponent of women's sexual equality. And it portrayed Masters as a plainspoken physician, similar to the genial Robert Young character on television's *Marcus Welby, MD.* Sex in marriage was the needed balm to save the country from its troubles. "The greatest form of sex education," Masters said, "is Pop walking past Mom in the kitchen and patting her on the fanny, and Mom obviously liking it. The kids take a look at this action and think, 'Boy, that's for me.'"

By 1970, Masters and Johnson weren't alone in the field of sexual research. Advice for all interests and tastes spread like marmalade on the American palate. Best-sellers included Dr. David Reubens's popular manual *Everything You Always Wanted to Know About Sex* (*But Were Afraid to Ask),* which inspired a Woody Allen movie, Kate Millett's feminist polemic *Sexual Politics,* and *The Sensuous Woman,* a how-to book written by "J," an anonymous author. Masters and Johnson's work became a source of imitation and constant comparison. Two pulp novels called *The Experiment* and *Venus Examined* exploited their image with titillating, anonymous accounts from the clinic, as if smuggled out of a gulag. A supposedly nonfiction book, *The Couple: A Sexual Profile by Mr. and Mrs. K,* claimed to be the real-life experience of a couple who'd spent two weeks at the St. Louis clinic during 1970. In this testimonial to conjugal redemption, a man named Harold ("I'd reached a point where normal sex, with a person that mattered to me, meant frustration every single time") and his wife, Joan, thanked them for saving their marriage. Joan, portrayed as an American Everywoman, described how the sensate focus therapy led her to orgasm. "I never had true sex and true love together before," gushed Joan in her account, written by two male ghostwriters. "Take it from me, it's fantastic."

Unlike with their first book, Masters and Johnson now enjoyed tremendously favorable acceptance from the press. Seasoned reporters heralded *Human Sexual Inadequacy* as groundbreaking and portrayed them as near geniuses. The *New York Times* review, written by physician Alan Guttmacher, called it "extraordinary" and "phenomenal," and *Newsweek* praised their new therapy as revolutionary. Some women's magazines, which once had complained about the appropriateness of their studies, now jumped on the Masters and Johnson bandwagon. "Their success rate in alleviating the problems brought to them by sexually troubled couples is an astonishing 80 percent," the *Ladies' Home Journal* told its millions of female readers, suddenly willing to read about vaginismus and unconsummated marriages along with the recipes for oatmeal cookies and homemade soup.

Much of the 467-page book described different forms of impotency and sexual dysfunctions, and the specific therapies derived to treat each problem. Many marveled at the book's insistence that sex could carry on into the olden years. While a male over fifty years old might wait minutes rather than seconds for an erection, he might become a better lover because of greater ejaculatory control. And while research showed a woman might experience less elasticity in her vagina, briefer orgasms, and a shrinking of the clitoris, she too could carry on with her partner well into her eighties. Using Masters and Johnson's sensory methods, they could enjoy intimacy so long as they were reasonably healthy and had "an interested and interesting partner." Near the book's end, Masters and Johnson charted all of the program's statistics, delineating various forms of cases and their outcome. Another chapter marked "Treatment Failures" gave a clear idea of the complex psychosexual problems of some patients and the depth of their misery. "For 7 years before her marriage at the age of 23, Mrs. B. had been living in an incestuous relationship with her father, presumably appeasing his sexual demands to prevent similar abuse of a younger sister," described this section, written mostly by Johnson. "It is expected that she might find her husband's sexual approaches frightening, unstimulating, or even revolting after eight years of marriage."

Throughout this second book, far more so than the first, Johnson's voice could be heard—confident, encouraging, and quite reflective of women's experiences with sex. While she adopted Masters's anatomic language, she also provided her own vision of the metaphysical union that a loving couple might enjoy. Not content to repeat the "1-2-3 kick!" sexual instructions of marriage manuals written by men, as she described it, Johnson placed sex in the broader context of a mature, ongoing relationship. In a chapter titled "Treatment of Orgasmic Dysfunction," which hardly sounded romantic, she spoke directly to the married woman uncertain of herself. "Frequently, it is of help to assure the wife that once the marital unit is sexually joined, the penis belongs to her just as the vagina belongs to her husband," she explained. "When vaginal penetration occurs, both partners have literally given of themselves as physical beings in order to derive pleasure, each from the other."

What Bill and Gini accomplished in a dozen years—with no support from government and little from academia, and under near total secrecy—was unprecedented in the annals of medicine. They now offered a therapeutic regimen to cure chronic sexual dysfunction and distressed marriages. In their world, couples were called "marital units" and "coital opportunity" became another name for love. "The naked facts of sex are clothed in the dry, objective vestments of the scientist," *Newsweek* noted. Yet, as *Time* magazine later observed, a decade after their second book appeared, Masters and Johnson had illuminated an area of medicine kept in the dark for so long, creating a whole new field that offered hope and solutions to millions. In the still shadowy landscape of American sexuality, the publication of *Human Sexual Inadequacy* proved "one of those events that transform the clinical landscape," the magazine said. "Afterward, sex therapy seemed a brave new world and Masters and Johnson were its gurus."

On their book tour, Masters and Johnson again appeared at Boston's Ritz-Carlton for a three-day press seminar. At age fifty-four, Masters said he hoped to work for another ten years, to finish a long-term study of homosexuality, and to develop a top-flight training program for preventing sexual dysfunction. "I think I've been very fortunate over the years to be successful in something that I thoroughly enjoy—particularly in some areas in which we've made incredible contributions," he said in a rare moment of public reflection. "But the greatest thing that ever happened to me was coming up with a fish in my mouth such as Gini Johnson."

Johnson, always aware of their image as two unmarried researchers, feigned surprise at being called a fish.

"That's the first time that I've ever thought of myself in that category," she replied wryly. "Thank you."

During the book tour, Johnson revealed more of herself, more about her own independent views. Sometimes she simply brought a feminine perspective to something Masters explained. Other times she offered her own interpretation about what their new techniques meant for patients, and her own contempt for Freudian psychoanalysis. "Many psychotherapists treat inadequacy on the basis of superstition, fallacy and just good guesswork," she told *Newsweek,* an all-out frontal assault on the talking cure. While some blanched at the $2,500 base price for two weeks at their treatment program, she suggested it "may cost considerably less than years of psychoanalysis." She also said the model of two therapists, male and female, was far more effective than a single analyst. "I'm so anti-Freudian," she later admitted. "It [Freudian psychoanalysis] was a perfectly ridiculous bunch of stuff. Utterly idiotic, ridiculous stuff."

The idea of being attacked by a woman without a degree, constantly and incredulously identified as a "psychologist" lacking the usual doctorate in psychology, was appalling to some critics. "From beginning to end, the book is one vast oversimplification," complained Denver psychiatrist Warren J. Gadpaille. "The naïve acceptance of such naïve concepts would set back the understanding of human behavior and disorder by 50 years." It was bad enough Masters and Johnson's first book undermined Freud's theories about female sexuality by proving them wrong physically. Now this second book threatened to topple the entire house of Freud, the years of pondering on a couch, by offering a quick modality for sex-related problems. "Persistently negating and slurring the value of one-to-one psychiatric psychotherapy and other forms of counseling for sexual disorders is beneath the dignity of the authors," reacted Leonard Gallant, a psychiatry professor at Johns Hopkins University. Gallant was particularly distressed by their policy of encouraging husband and wife to tell each other about past sexual experiences. "Sometimes revelation will help," said Gallant, "sometimes it is tantamount to emotional rape." Critics also questioned Masters and Johnson's competency to evaluate subconscious psychosexual problems, complained that such cures as the "squeeze" method were derived from prostitutes, and rightly said the therapy results weren't scientifically valid until they could be replicated by other scientific researchers. Still, the anecdotal evidence and the reams of testimonials from satisfied couples underscored the new therapy's effectiveness. As Jane E. Brody later observed in the *New York Times:* "To those who had spent years in psychotherapy without success, such a rapid and seemingly permanent cure sounded magical."

Now with great fame in America, Bill remained grateful to Gini Johnson for finding the practical answers to questions he had raised long ago in the lab, and for achieving the acclaim he so coveted. Undoubtedly he could have found another woman to pose as his assistant, to smile knowingly, and to pretend to be an equal partner. But with the publication of *Human Sexual Inadequacy,* Gini achieved a well-deserved parity that couldn't be denied. While Bill had the vision to identify many individual components of human sexuality, she helped put together the whole puzzle. By far, the most substantial sign of Gini's ascendancy—this equanimity of power in their partnership—was also the most subtle. On the first book's cover, Bill identified himself as "William H. Masters, M.D.," but with this second work, his designation as a physician was left off. The slight change in co-bylines reflected the changing nature of their relationship. "By his dropping his MD, they were on an equal footing," explained their friend, Dr. Mike Freiman. "They did it to make the work more believable. He lowered his standards to elevate hers. It was a condition of them continuing to go forward."

For whatever reason, by the time of this new book's publication, Virginia Johnson was ready for many changes—in both their personal and professional lives together. A hint of her restlessness could be found in the *Time* cover story. It noted the seven-day workweeks, including two night sessions, leaving little or no personal time for the two researchers. "His whole life is here at the lab," she told the magazine. And as she slowly realized, so was hers.

CHAPTER TWENTY-FIVE

The Scent of Love

"Why certain bright colours should excite pleasure cannot, I presume, be explained, any more than why certain flavours and scents are agreeable; but habit has something to do with the result, for that which is at first unpleasant to our senses, ultimately becomes pleasant, and habits are inherited."

—CHARLES DARWIN, *The Descent of Man and Selection in Relation to Sex*

If birds and bees do it, then surely, Bill Masters and Gini Johnson believed, human beings rely on a sense of smell in sexual selection. Olfaction must play a hidden role in the allure between men and women, the sweet and musky odors that excite the senses and signal the inevitability of love.

Human Sexual Inadequacy underlined the "tremendous undeveloped potential" of smell in affecting human sexual behavior. Sex pheromones—scents that somehow sparked a natural behavioral response—remained uncharted territory in science. Yet food and fragrance companies, looking for possible methods to make money from this untapped chemistry of desire, turned to the Reproductive Biology Research Foundation. In a way that government refused to do, these private firms provided grant money to explore this missing link of sexual attraction. At the clinic, endocrinologist Joan Bauman investigated female scents under funding from the Monell Chemical Senses Center, a Philadelphia-based nonprofit financed by the food, beverage, fragrance, and pharmaceutical industries. "They were interested in developing perfumes that would be pheromonal—in other words, they would stimulate sexual feelings," she remembered.

In this search, the biggest supporter of Bill and Gini's work was International Flavors & Fragrances Inc. (IFF) and its charismatic chairman, Henry G. Walter Jr., better known as Hank. His multimillion-dollar global conglomerate provided smells and tastes for a wide variety of products, from lemon-scented furniture polish to chocolate flavor in Cocoa Puffs, the breakfast cereal. Most profitably, IFF provided scents for perfume makers like Revlon and Estée Lauder. By extracting the pheromones from gypsy moths, it synthesized a sex attractant used by Jovan in perfumes for women and colognes for men. Hank searched the world for a new taste or aroma to adapt to the marketplace. "In China they have floral preparations that make people go to sleep," he once observed. "Fragrances operate on the same part of the brain as opiates. Maybe we can develop odor equivalents to Valium without the side-effects." He called his business "the sex and hunger industry."

At age fifty-seven, Hank Walter exuded health and vitality, capable of riding a bicycle across Manhattan to his office with the speed and dexterity of a messenger boy. With a nest of neatly coiffed hair and tight, tanned skin, he looked out at the world through thick glasses and with a cocksure smile. A *Fortune* magazine writer later described him as "one of the most distinctive chief executives I've ever met—an earthy, saucy kind of guy. . . . His language is earthy, rich in sexual allusion." In the office, he avoided the usual gray flannel of corporate chieftains and wore unconventional red suspenders, decorated sometimes by skunks or shamrocks. During a tedious meeting with security analysts at a posh club in London, Hank stripped off his shirt and rubbed himself with IFF-scented lotion. "I think I woke them up," he later said with a gleam in his eye. Helping to create the Monell Center in 1968, Hank theorized that women emitted pheromones that weren't easily detected by the human nose. He wanted to develop fragrances that would "amplify the odor signal" or "sharpen the odor receptors." Without much difficulty, he enlisted Bill Masters to capitalize on the scents of love. They exchanged several letters over the years on this topic, with an occasional check enclosed for the clinic. Hank suggested several ideas to be pursued. "If you think the whole idea is crazy, please say so, or if you think some other variation of it is desirable, also please say so," he told Bill in foisting his grand plan.

By far, their biggest success with Hank involved IFF-scented lotions used in sex therapy. Before entering the bedroom, couples received lotions with commercial fragrances, labeled by IFF as masculine or feminine. Four bouquet scents—floral; a mossy green; a floral/woody blend; and "oriental"—were feminine. Aromas on the menu marked as masculine included lavender bouquet; modern ambery; sweet bouquet; citrus bouquet; fresh citrus plus woody, floral bouquet; and a sharp fragrance with balsamic notes. If couples found one smell objectionable, they switched to another lotion, unscented if they preferred. Of one hundred couples studied, many enjoyed the sensual experience of massaging the glistening cream along their naked skin, helping them overcome their own hang-ups about seminal fluid or vaginal lubrication. Without any clear-cut conclusions, Bill and Gini found that lotion rubbing could be an accurate barometer of difficulty ahead in the therapy. Of the eighteen couples who rejected the lotions as "juvenile, undignified, unmeaningful, or that they got nothing from the lotion," more than three-quarters failed to reverse their overall sexual problems during the two-week treatment. In *Human Sexual Inadequacy*, the two researchers called for more comprehensive olfactory research, convinced they were on to something.

While Hank applauded his company's contributions in treating sexual dysfunction, he pushed for commercial products for the general public. Imagine, he wrote to Bill, if the study of pheromones in human females could result in a "pleasurable fragrance" sprayed on millions? Were they on the verge of finding an aphrodisiac for the weary, a fountain of youth for the old and shriveled, an over-the-counter rival to the pill's effectiveness in detecting ovulation in a way that not even the Vatican could object? If they could identify the pheromone that "marks the actual date of ovulation in each cycle," women could use it as a natural early-warning system "able to avoid contraception by avoiding intercourse during the relatively short fertile ovulatory period," Hank theorized. Undoubtedly, the possible bonanza from such a natural-based enticement was well worth an occasional $5,000 or $10,000 tax-deductible check from IFF and its affiliates. As a savvy patron, Hank appealed to Bill's scientific curiosity, with the smell of money clearly in mind. "How can we best push forward this whole field of investigation?" he urged Bill. "The goals are high and the methodology does not risk interference with bodily function a la the pill or conflict with religious teachings. The end product should be very cheap."

While Bill valued this monetary contribution to the clinic, Gini steadily grew interested in Hank Walter himself. After the publication of *Human Sexual Response* in 1966, Hank's staff contacted Bill and Gini "as an exploratory thing, knowing who we were, by publicity," she recalled. "They wanted to know if there was any interrelatedness between the kind of developmental work that they did and what we did." With Hank's help, Gini developed the idea of rubbing lotion across the skin as a "medium of exchange" between lovers during sensate therapy sessions. At times, she sounded like an Avon lady, talking so effusively about Hank's specially designed product. "Gini was doing the smell research with the sensate [therapy] and at times it was as if she had trouble staying focused on the therapy," said Dr. Marshall Shearer, one of the staffers in the early 1970s. "She would spend fifteen minutes talking about these scents, and another fifteen minutes interviewing them about which they liked better."

Like Noah Weinstein, Hank was an older, yet virile man of considerable accomplishment who showered Gini with attention and delighted in her presence. More handsome than Noah and loaded with money, Hank promised to go anywhere in the world as long as she followed. But Hank was also married. For a time, his marital status may have made it easier for her to consider just a fling. Eventually, though, Hank came along on Gini's family vacations, such as a trip to a dude ranch, where their romance intensified and they conversed about being together permanently. "Wherever I traveled, he would always join me, and that developed it," Gini said. "He said, 'It's going to cost me several million to really divest myself of this marriage I am in, but I will do it because I want you with me all the time.'"

Despite her fame and increasing fortune after *Human Sexual Inadequacy* appeared, Gini had never felt so vulnerable, so open to such a tempting offer. With Hank's sophisticated charm, his affection and sexual magnetism, he offered her both love and escape. After twelve exhausting years, she longed to leave her partnership with Bill, to give up the ceaseless scientific expedition. She knew full well that Bill had given her so much, the satisfaction of seeing her own theories translated and amazingly accepted by organized medicine. Yet her personal relationship with him, for all of its physical and professional intimacy, never had the tenderness of real love. She had learned to have sex with Bill—at first as part of the implicit job description, but eventually as a way to satisfy her own desires as an unmarried forty-year-old woman with children. She'd learned to become watchful of his moods, anticipate and tend to nearly all of his needs. But now that they had achieved their goals—appearing on television, newspapers, and the cover of *Time* magazine—she wanted to let go, be free of Bill Masters. "I probably never had loved him," Gini reflected years later. "We had in common a real devotion to a sexual relationship and that was probably the strongest common denominator that we had."

Regardless of the complexities of their lives, getting married to Hank might be just the answer her family needed. Deep down, Gini felt remorse about the time she had spent away from her children while they were growing up. "The amount of time she spent in research laboratory was unbelievable," Bill later wrote. "She was either actively working or on call seven days and three nights a week. In addition, she had two small children at home for whom she was responsible. To this day, I don't know how she managed." She went through a series of housekeepers and babysitters who stayed with Scott and Lisa. Now that her kids were teenagers, she hoped to make up for lost time. In this new life with Hank, she could change her name once more, so no one would bother her or her family.

Over time, however, their secret affair only became more tangled. During a business trip to New York, Hank invited Bill and Gini to his spacious Manhattan apartment where he lived with his wife, Rosalind. During World War II, Rosalind worked as a riveter building fighter planes on Long Island and supposedly inspired the song "Rosie the Riveter."

"Roz was a dear lady and Bill and I were good friends with Hank," Gini recalled. "We were in their home quite a lot." Neither

Bill nor Roz seemed to sense a romance brewing between Gini and Hank. "She didn't guess because she used to confide in me a lot," said Gini, who felt a tinge of discomfort listening to Hank's wife talk of their marriage, just as Libby talked about Bill. "It was a weird position to be in. He was charmed by her and she was a lovely, charming woman—I liked her very much. But they were just so out of tune with one another. There was nothing I could tell her. I couldn't fix it. I couldn't make her into what he wanted, or vice versa." Years later, when asked about Gini's claims that she'd considered marrying Hank, Rosalind Walter gave a blunt reply. "It makes sense," Rosalind said. "She could join the group—a lot of ladies admired my husband." Upon reflection, Rosalind expressed dismay about such claims, suggesting it was no one's business, but acknowledged she was none the wiser at the time. "My husband was an extraordinarily intelligent and interesting person," she said. "He was interested in the work that they did because of his business with IFF. He did pursue it and write about it and read everything they wrote and visited them. Other than that, I know nothing."

Back in St. Louis, most staffers had no idea of Gini's affair with one of their wealthiest patrons. In a clinic filled with secrets, this was the least known. Gini assumed Dr. Robert Kolodny might figure out what was going on because he dealt regularly with Hank on the clinic's studies, yet she didn't actually confide in him until years later. "Gini at an earlier time told me that she seduced him," Bob Kolodny recalled. "I think she sort of hinted around at that. I find it very hard to believe [though] that he would have divorced his wife." While very different in style, Kolodny liked Hank Walter, who spoke with the confidence of a self-made man and fancied himself a bit of a Casanova. "He talked with me rather boastfully over a few dinners and a bottle of wine about his sexual escapades around the world," said Kolodny. "He certainly painted very clearly that he felt he could seduce just about any woman around. And he recognized part of that was the allure of his wealth."

Bill remained clueless until Hank took one of his visits to the St. Louis clinic. Usually on these occasions, Masters and sometimes Kolodny would join Gini in taking their New York patron out to a local restaurant. On this particular night, though, Gini left her kids with the housekeeper so she could entertain Hank alone. That night, she had a marvelous time with him, laughing and conversing about their dreams of seeing the world together. Nights like these reminded her of how much she enjoyed being with him. When she finally arrived home, Gini discovered that Bill had telephoned her all night, to no avail. "I got home and my housekeeper had a whole series of notes of the time of that evening that he called—all these messages from my housekeeper, with the times 11:30, 12:45, 1:50—the number of times that Bill had called," recalled Gini. "That night, I wasn't home and he knew that this man was in town, so he [Bill] put two and two together. He was not a stupid man. So he read the handwriting on the wall there, and that's when he got into gear."

The next day at the clinic, Bill confronted her about Hank. She had never seen her partner so upset with her. His face wasn't angry as much as worried; his whole demeanor appeared thrown for a loss. "Bill was really afraid that I would marry him," she said. "He was startled."

She made no attempt at hiding the truth of her relationship with this other man. Whatever doubts she harbored about marrying Hank, she didn't show them. At this point, Bill didn't deserve any more information than she was willing to reveal. She didn't want to be manipulated or talked out of doing the right thing for herself and her children. For years, he'd known of her intent to marry again. Bill's own actions seemed to assume she would never act upon her personal wishes as long as their work remained compelling, as long as their duplicitous affair remained satisfying and concealed, as long as Libby stayed home with the kids, and as long as the income and renown continued from their Masters and Johnson name.

"If you leave, the work will be destroyed!" insisted Bill. He looked like a man who was about to lose everything.

For the first time in his life, Bill wasn't sure what Gini might do. He knew Hank was a formidable contender, a man quite capable of providing anything she wanted or needed. Perhaps Bill felt jealous, suddenly realizing that the "perfect woman" he had trained and elevated was about to leave him. He didn't plan to stand around and watch their partnership fall apart. Convinced this threat was real, Bill resolved to do something about it.

CHAPTER TWENTY-SIX

Betrayals

Coming home one day from school, sixteen-year-old Howie Masters found his mother in inconsolable tears. He'd never seen her like this before. He pleaded with her to let him know what could be so wrong.

Libby Masters, her eyes reddened, gazed sadly upon her son.

"We're getting divorced," she cried. "Your father has moved out."

Howie looked around and noticed a disturbance in the serene, orderly atmosphere of their house. All of his father's belongings were missing. "He was gone, had moved his stuff out," Howie recalled.

Until this day, the life of young William Howell Masters III had seemed ideal. Not far from their large suburban home, Howie attended the prestigious Country Day School in St. Louis, where his friends included Gini's son, Scott. He chose to attend Hamilton College, his father's alma mater, but didn't harbor the pent-up anger that had driven his dad at the same age. He was thoughtful, soft-spoken, and considerate, more like Libby Masters in temperament. Yet Howie became enraged to see his mother so upset, to have their otherwise happy life turned upside down. He demanded that his mother tell him where his father could be found. She eventually mentioned the address of a small apartment.

"I remember jumping into a car and driving downtown and finding him in whatever place he was, and storming in and sitting him down, sitting right in front of him, and giving him a real earful," recalled Howie.

For quite a while, Bill Masters listened to his son's irate words. He paid polite attention to Howie's rant until enough time had passed, allowing him a chance to respond. Bill maintained an even keel and spoke dispassionately, as if he were conducting a psychotherapy session with some adolescent stranger rather than his own son. Bill began by stating the hard, irreconcilable truth. As Howie recalled, his father "communicated to me that the relationship was over with my mother. Regardless of whether he had fallen out of love or into some new love, whatever the reasons, it was over—and it was something that wasn't going to be salvaged."

Bill never mentioned Gini Johnson's name. Instead, he carefully explained to his teenage son how two adult people can slowly drift apart in a marriage. He spoke calmly and considerately. "What he told me was honest and completely made sense," remembered Howie. "He didn't pull the punch. He wasn't somebody who was going to lie to me or tell something that wasn't true, or tell me what he thought I needed to hear to make it easier." Bill informed his son he had been considering this move for years. He didn't attack Libby or blame her. He treated Howie like a young man, worthy of his respect, without adult condescension. Yet persuasively, perhaps even manipulatively, he made his son realize that the quietude in their house had been partly the missing bond of communication between a husband and wife.

Because of his demanding career, Bill wasn't home very much. His absence made his presence and words even more valued by his son. Howie very much wanted to believe his father, particularly at this awful moment, the fracturing of their family life. Years later, Howie could talk in hindsight about how his father calmly handled this confrontation. "It was something I appreciated, actually, because he could defuse a young kid who was confused and angry and left with a teary mother who was sort of a basket case," Howie remembered. "I had to go home now and pick up those pieces. My life had changed and my role had changed. What would any kid feel when you come home and life as you've known it has exploded? That doesn't sit too well. I felt it warranted an explanation—and I got it."

Elisabeth Masters knew deep in her bones about Bill's infidelities. For years, Bill's audaciousness with his sex research, his drive to become recognized in his field, and particularly the absent nights and personal indignities of his intimacy with Virginia Johnson were painfully apparent to Libby. She recognized enough telltale signs, so she didn't want to know anything more, as if to keep her old image of Bill intact. "She just loved him very much and she had nothing but respect for him," recalls her friend Dodie Brodhead, whose husband, John, served as a foundation board member. Perhaps Libby hoped her husband's recklessness would all go away. Perhaps the sex studies would cease, his need for Gini's assistance would dissipate, and his everyday life as an ob-gyn doctor based at the university would return. "She acted like this was a stage he was going through and it would pass," explained Judith Seifer, a therapist friend who later helped Bill prepare his unpublished memoir. "And so, if you pretend like it's not there, it will all go away." Bill's nonstop work schedule undermined their marriage, never allowing for much of a home life with Libby. "From January 1954, when I started the clinic to December 1971, I never missed a day of work, seven days a week," he said. In asking for a divorce after twenty-nine years of marriage, Bill could be clinical in his postmortem: "Ultimately, my wife and I had to face the fact that our relationship was essentially nonexistent."

Libby's life, however, was devoted to her children and her community of friends and neighbors. "She was fiercely devoted to us always, but certainly after [the divorce]," said Howie. "She lived for us." To not disturb this universe, she sacrificed and worked hard to keep her family intact. She tended to Bill's mother, Estabrooks Masters, until she passed away in the 1960s. She encouraged Bill to remain in touch with his younger brother, Frank, a plastic surgeon who lived in Kansas City. At age fifty-four, Libby remained thin and active, though her hair had turned gray and her appearance increasingly more reserved. She was true to her Episcopal faith, enough to make sure their children were confirmed, even though her husband didn't encourage church attendance. "My father preferred—in the best years of our little insular family's lives—that on Sundays, we'd go bowling," said Howie, who tagged along with his sister. "We thought it was a riot that—out there in the suburbs of St. Louis—people went to church on Sundays and we'd go bowling instead." As attentive as she could be to her husband's needs, Libby perhaps felt no match for Gini Johnson, a younger woman, more vibrant and more crucial to Bill's ambitions.

Yet Libby couldn't bring herself to dislike Gini, no matter how uneasy she might feel in her presence. "Gini and Betty were friends," recalled Peggy Shepley, the second wife of Ethan Shepley Jr., then the foundation's chairman. "That's the damnedest thing of all time. I can't imagine being friends with the first wife. Normally there isn't any love lost between the first and second wife. But Gini and Betty became friends." Intuitively, Elisabeth Masters seemed to understand she and Gini shared Bill, that he had defined both their lives, and they would always be under his sway. "I knew her well and we liked one another in a way," Gini said of Libby years later. "I think we would have been pleased to conspire against him, but she didn't quite have the sophistication to do that."

Those who knew of the long-running personal affair between Bill and Gini wondered about Libby's reaction at home. "I never quite understood why Bill left Libby," admitted Bob Kolodny. "It didn't make sense to me. Was something missing from their marriage? Was Bill put upon in some way? I never heard Bill say something critical of her." At work, Kolodny sensed that Gini envied the stable, upper-class lifestyle the Masters family enjoyed in the suburbs. "She undoubtedly was somewhat jealous of someone who was securely married, lived in a nice house, and everything seemed to be hunky-dory," he said. "Gini lived in a different world than Libby." In an emotional match with Gini, some believed Libby never stood a chance of retaining Bill's fidelity, no matter how long they had been married. "I'm not so sure that Betty Masters and Bill had that sexual intimacy that he needed, that he may have found with Gini," said Torrey Foster, who always distrusted Gini while he served on the foundation board. "Maybe it was one of the ways that drew him towards her, as opposed to staying with Betty. There was a very bright sexual attractiveness to Gini, and Betty Masters was a very plain Jane. . . ."

After Bill moved out of their English Tudor house in Ladue, several months elapsed before the divorce became final in December 1970. In the meantime, friends of Betty Masters rallied to her side. They expressed outrage at Bill's actions and voiced their previously whispered contempt for Gini. By then, many had heard of Gini's summer stays at the Masters house, while Betty was away in Michigan with the kids. "He just brought Virginia into the house, just blatantly was there with her—I think that's a pretty ruthless thing to do!" said Dodie Brodhead. "Betty was a lovely person who never understood something could happen, because she loved Bill and assumed he loved her that much. But Virginia was the other woman—*cherchez la femme*—who wormed her way in and Betty was out, which devastated her. And it was very hard on the children too."

Dodie's husband also felt his friendship had been abused. At considerable risk as a local businessman, John Brodhead agreed to join Bill's sexual research foundation as an original board trustee, mostly as a favor to Betty. John had known Betty as a teenager, when their families vacationed in Michigan, when she was "a marvelous girl, very gregarious, energetic type." He admired how Betty had overcome the adversity of her mother's death and her father's abandonment, and had grown into "a remarkably well-balanced and resilient person." Although grateful to Bill for their successful fertility treatments, the Brodheads were offended by his callousness toward Betty, prompting them to choose sides. After six years as a trustee, John resigned from the Reproductive Biology Research Foundation. Nearly everyone knew why, but no one on the board asked his reasons for leaving. "I got off the board when Bill and Betty split," he said. "It was pretty hard to be neutral. If there had been any discussion of who was right and who was wrong, we decided it was Betty."

The Masters family, and their seemingly serene life in Ladue, were never the same again. At the time her parents split, Sali Masters, a year older than her brother, Howie, attended boarding school. She had been sent away for school because her parents decided the nasty phone calls and snide remarks from the community about what transpired at her father's clinic were too much for a young girl's ears. "Our children were socially ostracized," Bill later recalled. Too often, he said, Sali heard other parents tell her friends, "I don't want you hanging around with that Masters girl—her father's a sex maniac!" Years later, Sali declined to talk about her experiences but Howie remembered her situation well. "Sent away, my father would always say, because he wasn't sure what would happen with his work, that she could ultimately as a young girl be put into too many difficult circumstances if she was around home, so it was safer to have her at boarding school," he said. Sali came home to find that her father would never return. Bill compounded the hurt with coy, deceptive comments about his reasons for leaving. At least once, he denied Gini's involvement in the breakup. "After my divorce, you won't see us running off to Mexico or anything like that," he told *The Atlantic* magazine, the same month his divorce decree was finalized by a judge. "But I may take it upon myself to chase as many women, eighteen years and older, as a slightly fat, bald, fifty-four-year-old can catch."

Libby adopted her own defensive posture. She never accused Gini of wrecking her marriage. "If she did expect that Gini was, say, an 'interloper,' she never said it. If she was jealous, she held it pretty close," recalled Howie. "She would have stuck it out longer with my father if he hadn't walked. She was a loyal sort, one of her great strengths and one of her great faults."

During Howie's last year at the Country Day School, the Masters house in suburban Ladue was even quieter. Libby tried to carry on, but the central focus of their family life had been shattered. Not wanting to lose contact altogether, Howie traveled occasionally into the city to see his father. They talked at length but never discussed Virginia Johnson or whatever Bill had in mind for his own future. "I'd go down and have dinners with him, wherever his new digs were, his new apartment, and scold him or talk to him about whatever was going on," Howie said. "Pretty soon after that [divorce], I was gone. I went away to college and started my professional career. But it didn't have anything to do with St. Louis."

CHAPTER TWENTY-SEVEN

The Marriage Compact

On a visit to the Kinsey Institute, Bill Masters strolled around the Indiana University campus with his old friend Paul Gebhard, chatting about work and their personal lives. A decade had passed since their introduction in the mid-1950s, and Gebhard felt free enough to pose a delicate question that he wondered privately.

Did Bill's wife know the extent of his relationship with Gini? he asked.

Bill barely broke stride.

"My wife?" he replied confidently. "It's quite nice about this relationship, that she's so *understanding*."

Gebhard, who had seen private extramarital affairs upset Alfred Kinsey's staff, laughed reflexively. "Well, that's great, Bill," he declared in his husky voice. "You're a fortunate man!"

For several years before his divorce, Bill had been, in effect, balancing two lives: at home with Libby and the kids, and with Gini at work and after-hours. Many of Bill's assumptions had proved wrong. "At one point he was happy that his wife was accepting his relationship with Gini, but that turned out to be erroneous," Gebhard recalled.

Bill carried on his pretense with Libby by inviting Gini everywhere in public, playing the part of a benevolent employer rather than a secret philanderer. "Part of it may have been a very clever strategy on Bill's part—that if he had kept Gini totally hidden outside of the hospital, his wife may have become suspicious that something was going on," explained Bob Kolodny. "I suspect Bill was enough of a pragmatist that he would have seen that as the smart thing to do." Before events precipitated a divorce, Bill seemed quite comfortable with his double life and double standards. Even after becoming famous, he appeared in no hurry to upset this balancing act between the two women. "We all knew what was going on," recalled Dr. Alfred Sherman. "There was a time—before Bill divorced his wife and married Virginia—that Bill had already strayed a great deal from that. He was virtually living with her."

In Ladue, Gini resided with her two children a little more than a mile from the Masterses. Gini's home was big and private enough, with its own swimming pool outside and a circular, wrought-iron stairway inside, that they would entertain visiting celebrities. Late some nights, Bill wound up staying in the downstairs room, while Gini's children, Scott and Lisa, barely in their teens, slept upstairs, near their mother's bedroom. "Gradually, Bill wasn't just an occasional sleep-over guest in that downstairs room," said Kolodny, who eventually bought the Salem Estates house from Gini. "Within not too long, he moved in with her." Once, while Bill and Gini were away on a lecture tour, Bob and his wife, Nancy, offered to stay overnight and babysit at Gini's house. A bit naively, the young Kolodny couple discovered to their surprise Bill's belongings throughout the house. "Bill's still married and here his clothes are in the one closet in the master bedroom, and his shaving cream and stuff are here in the bathroom," Bob recalled. "It was very clear that they were living together in the late 1960s."

Bill's duplicity wasn't seriously challenged until Hank Walter arrived on the scene. The possibility of Gini marrying this international businessman, willing to snatch her away from their familiar, provincial world in St. Louis, goaded Bill into action. He showed more apprehension about the future of their world-famous partnership than personal jealousy. He never displayed the desperate kind of emotion of a lover threatened by a rival. Passion seemed amiss, devoid of any intensity, even at this crucial point in their relationship. But he would do whatever was demanded not to lose her, even destroy his own family. "He knew that I was going to marry someone else eventually and that's when he took great measures to insinuate himself into my life even more," Gini said. "He refused to lose me. And I didn't realize how manipulative and clever he was about it all."

Certainly not everyone believes Gini's account. "That's a lovely story that would make her look like a lily-white bird, wouldn't it?" chided Dodie Brodhead, who offered her own version. "She came to St. Louis without a husband and was looking around hard and wanted something more than she had and she worked to get it." Gini's detractors in the refined upper classes of Ladue suggested she sought out marriage to Bill as a means of bettering her precarious economic position as a divorced mother of two. "I think she always wanted to be married to Bill," concluded the foundation's original lawyer, Torrey Foster. "I was always a little naive about their relationship at first. But it was apparent she was after him." Even some friendly with Gini believed she pushed for Bill's divorce. "I think it was a condition of them continuing their work, and he saw that if he didn't divorce Libby, his work would be over," said Mike Freiman, who marveled at Libby's response. "When it came to divorce, she [Libby] did not try to make it difficult for him or try and take him financially. She respected Bill's need to marry this woman."

Undoubtedly, Gini exerted considerable influence over Bill, even when she felt abused by his demands, the long hours, and the lack of a social life beyond the clinic. Those who disliked her felt she was given far more than she ever deserved and that she enticed Bill to obtain each promotion, each opportunity. Such comments always presumed Gini in an inferior role to Dr. Masters, as the upstart secretary or the rapacious divorcée. After two best-sellers, however, Gini could afford financially to leave, to be more present in the lives of her teenage kids, to settle down with a man who said he loved her. If truly committed, she could again transform herself, to change her name and occupation once more.

After *Human Sexual Inadequacy* was published, Hank Walter pressed Gini for an answer. So did Bill Masters, who, soon after leaving Libby and moving into his own spartan bachelor's apartment, made it clear he wanted to marry again. If Hank proposed based on love, Bill's offer seemed constructed on business commitments, maintaining their enterprise in a lucrative embrace. Ultimately, Gini's decision had little to do, she claims, with her own personal desires. Instinctively, she knew Bill wanted to win this little competition, to prevail over his wealthy patron. Like their books together, he never mentioned the word "love."

"I could have cared less about staying in the work," Gini admitted. "The man I was going to marry was exceedingly wealthy, but he wanted me to do for him exactly what I did for Masters—which was to travel with him everywhere, all the time." Despite Hank's tempting invitation, Gini was tired of time spent in hotels away from home, and the sense that parental control over her teenage children had slipped away. "I finally told this man that I couldn't marry him, bemoaning the fact that Masters was insisting that we marry," she recalled. "He knew why I didn't marry him, and Masters never did." Bill never inquired again about Hank. He didn't want an explanation, only the assurance their partnership was safe and intact.

Though Bill's two children endured some maliciousness, Scott and Lisa Johnson remained particularly vulnerable to what the neighbors whispered about their mother. Gini's celebrity provided plenty of fodder. In the *Ladies' Home Journal,* Gini referred to her daughter in making a larger point about sex education. As the magazine's millions of readers learned, "Mrs. Johnson, the mother of a teenage daughter, wants to reassure mothers and fathers that by not applying repressive sexual fears, they do not necessarily encourage their 12-year-old daughter to cohabit casually with assorted strangers." In Ladue, these lessons weren't appreciated. "People seemed to censure their work and them personally and because of the double standard, Gini with no credentials was looked upon askance," explained June Dobbs Butts, a former clinic staffer in whom Gini confided. "Whereas with Bill, he had been well-liked when he ran the ob-gyn clinic—something of a society doctor married to a well-known socialite—and because he had that halo around him, he didn't take too much of a negative view. But with Gini, her two children suffered a lot of social ostracism." Another friend, Peggy Shepley, agreed Gini's kids "lived under that cloud and it had to be rough. They [Gini's kids] took the brunt of it. They were mad at her for even doing it [the sexual research] and she needed the money."

Bill's argument that her departure would destroy their work had its intended effect, particularly when couched in financial terms. Their second book's success brought a new wave of public endorsements, surplus book royalties, big-name speaking fees, and the creation of a whole new field of lucrative sex therapy, based on the sensate techniques Gini had developed. She rightfully felt the pride of authorship with the second book, far more so than with the first. And the money they now earned was enough to turn anyone's head, even a proud woman who had always prized her freedom. Married to a wealthy husband like Hank Walter, Gini would still be dependent on a man. Here was something she had earned, rightfully and without compromise. With a third book still years away, Bill supported virtually anything Gini wanted, so long as their joint venture lasted. "I never wanted to be with him, but when you're making $200,000 or more a year, you don't walk," she contended, as if a victim of her own success. "I was making that *myself;* it wasn't being *given* to me."

To Gini, marriage to Bill also offered legitimacy. "I thought I could redeem who I was in terms of the community," she acknowledged. "There was always the social rejection of being who we were. I thought if I married, that would probably erase some of that. That was the only sound reason that I remember having for going ahead with it, that it would redeem the children in their social life." Perhaps Bill could help her gain control of her family life during her children's tumultuous adolescent years. By becoming the new "Mrs. Masters," she would give her children a strong male influence in their lives, apart from the ethereal presence of bandleader George Johnson, her ex-husband who slipped into their lives occasionally. By walking down the aisle with Bill Masters, perhaps she could end the speculation when she entered an auditorium with him. "Because we had become so notorious at that point, in the interests of my children, I thought maybe that would put all the gossip to rest," she explained. "I knew that I didn't want to be married to him. We lived a life that was so packed, so full, and I was trying so hard to be a close mother to these children. I had long ago given up making a choice for myself, for anything."

On January 7, 1971, Bill and Gini married in a brief ceremony at a friend's home in Fayetteville, Arkansas. For years, Masters and Johnson's views about human intimacy had been proclaimed on the front pages and television screens of America. The wedding of these two famous researchers was bound to attract headlines. In its planning, though, Gini didn't want this personal moment exploited. "I don't want to be married on the front page," she insisted. "I'm sick of it." Bill readily agreed. He reminded her of a gynecologist friend who happened to be a Universalist minister in Fayetteville. After a few phone calls, they decided to drive 350 miles south to Arkansas to secure a marriage license from the local courthouse. Gini stayed in the car as Bill went into the court clerk's office with the necessary paperwork. Inside, a San Francisco newspaper reporter spotted Masters, an easily recognizable figure from all his media exposure. The reporter checked the marriage license and called his newsroom with a surprising tip. Soon after, Gini recalled, "We got married on the front page of that San Francisco paper!"

America's media treated their nuptials as a happy ending to the much-publicized Masters and Johnson saga. Although some scribes noted the ceremony marked Bill's second marriage and the third wedding band for Gini, the overall message portrayed to the public was of love triumphant. Bill, and especially Gini, played along with their designated roles. "When I was without him, I was restless—I knew what it took to make me whole," Gini gushed to *The Washington Post,* a newspaper not easily snookered. "My only regret is we didn't find each other sooner."

Back in St. Louis, their marriage didn't surprise many, though close friends dismissed easy explanations. The typecasting of Gini as a homewrecker didn't quite ring true, nor did that of Bill as a doctor in midlife crisis bedazzled by her charms. A more complicated truth lay beneath their union. By the time they married, even sharp critics of Gini, such as Torrey Foster, didn't sense any passion between the two. "I think it was a marriage of business," said Foster, no longer the clinic's attorney but still on the foundation's board. "I don't think they really had a close, intimate husband-wife relationship. It was more contractual."

At the clinic, Gini had achieved equality on paper, but marriage to Bill left no doubt of her permanent standing. Where once she'd said little at board meetings or echoed Bill's comments with the staff, Gini now expressed herself freely as codirector. "I think she felt she had more clout, that she could be a little more verbal and do more things," recalled Lynn Strenkofsky, a staffer who helped make arrangements with therapy patients. Sally Bartok, who worked as a therapist with Bill and other male sex counselors, said Gini offered advice as a divorced mother like herself. "I remember her saying, 'Until the ring is on your finger, you don't really have it,'" said Bartok, now known by her own married name, Sally Taylor. "My sense is that when they married, it put her in a more secure mind-frame than she may have been in before. I don't know how much love there was, or whether it was just a comfortable working relationship. They would be the last people in the world who would allow a hint of anything like that to escape."

For a time, their partnership nearly fell apart, but Bill eventually got what he wanted. His real home, the Reproductive Biology Research Foundation, would stay in place. "I know why I married Masters—to preserve the identity and so forth of *Masters and Johnson,"* Gini later claimed. Not even their occasional sexual encounters provided a reason. "It would have not been enough to marry him," she replied, when asked about the sex between them. Whatever intensity once shared between them now seemed dormant. Soon after their wedding, Bill told a reporter about the simple pleasures of hugging in bed after a long day. As Gini declared: "The concept of sexuality as a question of only the penis in the vagina is so absolutely Victorian—it's sick."

In the name of helping American marriage, Bill Masters had shattered his own. He left Libby, his wife of twenty-nine years, alone in their old house in Ladue, just as their older children moved away. Bill rarely showed any remorse, as though his scientific mission justified his actions. "Bill was a pragmatist," said Bob Kolodny. "He was not a pie-in-the-sky dreamer, and certainly not a romantic. I would be virtually certain that he didn't fall in love with Gini. The concept of love in Bill's personal life was maybe something he felt for his kids, but it wasn't a large part of his essence at all." To those who inquired, Bill liked projecting a crusty image, as he straightened his bow tie and spoke about himself in terse, unsparing descriptions. He admitted he "wasn't a very good father," and not much of a husband either. Gini's eagerness to fit into the local social world was disdained by Bill, who preferred staying late at work or sitting home on weekends in front of the television by himself. Old friends from Ladue and the country club dropped him from their invitation lists because of what had happened with Libby. "I'm sort of a bastard," he confessed. "I'm no good with people. Never have been and never will be. By choice and design, I'm not a people person. I don't have many friends. I don't have the type of personality that attracts people." Gini could only agree. "Bill tolerates people," she explained, "and nothing more."

For Bill, the marriage compact with Gini was as much a set of compromises as it was for her. Years later, former colleague Judy Seifer wondered why the two researchers ever married in the first place. She never forgot Bill's coldhearted words.

"When you got married, when did you know it wouldn't work?" Judy asked.

"When I walked down the aisle," he stated bluntly.

"Then why did you do it?" she continued.

"I didn't know what else to do," Bill said. "And it was convenient."

The world had turned to Masters and Johnson to explain the mysteries of sex and to communicate better in the language of love. But when asked what true love meant, Bill Masters admitted he hadn't a clue.

"My dear girl, I haven't the vaguest idea," he said to an inquiring female reporter who posed the eternal question. "I don't know what love is. Do you?"

PHASE FOUR

Masters and Johnson featured
on *Meet the Press*

CHAPTER TWENTY-EIGHT

Feminist Movement

"In the years between the 'emancipation' of women won by the feminists and the sexual counterrevolution of the feminine mystique, American women enjoyed a decade-by-decade increase in sexual orgasm. And the women who enjoyed this the most fully were, above all, the women who were educated for active participation in the world outside the home."

—BETTY FRIEDAN, *THE FEMININE MYSTIQUE*

At the surprise engagement party for Doris McKee, friends and colleagues stood in hushed silence, waiting for the guest of honor to arrive. On this balmy October day, nearly every woman employed at the Masters and Johnson clinic gathered to honor McKee, a friendly, conscientious secretary who kept the tape recordings of each session the team conducted. Rose Boyarsky, a new therapist, hosted the poolside party at her house near Washington University and invited all of the clinic's female staff, including their boss, Virginia Johnson.

With the sexual revolution in full swing by the 1970s, female staffers at the Masters and Johnson clinic were in the front lines of the burgeoning women's liberation movement. Feminists embraced their transformative findings, proclaiming women were every bit as sexual as any man and entitled to the same freedoms and equality in a male-dominated culture. Television, newspapers, and magazines covering these sweeping social changes credited Masters and Johnson for bringing the sexual revolution to suburban malls and the everyday lives of Americans.

As Doris walked into the backyard with her new fiancé, everyone clapped and toasted. Howard, her future husband, remembered the jovial atmosphere, with provocative jokes that resembled a bachelor party, especially one particular artifact. "At the buffet table, there was a lovely bouquet of flowers," Howard recalled, "and in the center of it was the plastic penis that had been attached to the camera when the foundation was doing the survey of female orgasm!"

The totem-like quality of the mechanical dildo wasn't lost on anyone familiar with Masters and Johnson's research. The "artificial coital equipment," as the researchers called it, was one of the most startling aspects of the team's sex study. While conservatives expressed horror that such a contrivance would be used to define and defile human intimacy, leading feminists suggested something even more frightening—the irrelevancy of men in sexual satisfaction. These implications extended beyond what Masters and Johnson intended in their two books. "Masters and Johnson crafted an account of female sexuality that inadvertently threw into question the pervasive understanding of heterosexuality as innate and fully satisfied through intercourse with a penis," observed cultural historian Jane Gerhard in 2000. "They, like the Freudians before them, had 'discovered' a female sexuality that existed independently from intercourse with men." To many feminists, the mechanical device—with its electrical horsepower undiminished by a refractory period—symbolized the supremacy of women during sex compared to men. Scientific findings about the clitoris—debunking Freudian myth about a "mature" vaginal orgasm from intercourse with a man, rather than the multiple, masturbatory delights alone with a vibrator—didn't require males. "The human female frequently is not content with one orgasmic experience," Masters and Johnson determined in *Human Sexual Response*.

Feminists were particularly pleased Masters and Johnson's anatomical findings exposed the shortcomings of Freud's dictums. "We had to admit that Freud and the Bible were wrong, which is no small thing," Gloria Steinem quipped years later. In fact, the new bible of American feminism—*Ms.* magazine, co-edited by Steinem—had an office sign that read: *It's 10 o'clock at night—do you know where your clitoris is?* Masters and Johnson's phrases soon found their way into the political and social rhetoric of feminism. Anne Koedt's influential 1968 treatise, "The Myth of the Vaginal Orgasm," lauded Masters and Johnson for effectively redefining the meaning of women's sexuality in contemporary society. "The recognition of clitoral orgasm as fact would threaten the heterosexual *institution*," Koedt declared. "For it would indicate that sexual pleasure was obtainable from either men *or* women, thus making heterosexuality not an absolute, but an option. It would thus open up the whole question of *human* sexual relationships beyond the confines of the present male-female role system." Searching for new sexual paradigms and social orders, feminist writings—by Germaine Greer, Kate Millett, Ti-Grace Atkinson, and Rita Mae Brown, among others—echoed Masters and Johnson's discoveries. The clitoris, they argued, was the only organ in either gender designed essentially for pleasure. The proven female capacity for multiple orgasms, suggested psychiatrist Mary Jane Sherfey, should bring about a rethinking of the cultural boundaries set by men. Lions of heterosexuality roared their displeasure. In 1971's *The Prisoner of Sex,* Norman Mailer fumed over "woman's ubiquitous plentitude of orgasms with that plastic prick, that laboratory dildoe [*sic*], that vibrator!" At the same time, some feminists suggested Masters and Johnson didn't go far enough in pushing boundaries. As Greer complained, "There is no reason why we should believe that what American middle-class women taped to electrodes could do is all that could have been done."

In the late twentieth century, the women's liberation movement transformed American society profoundly, second only to the 1960s civil rights reforms. Polemics like Friedan's *The Feminine Mystique* voiced an outrage about women's lives cooped up in suburban domesticity. Organizations such as the National Organization for Women (NOW) pressed their demands into action. Equal job pay, tougher rules on sexual discrimination and harassment, greater access to higher education and climbing the corporate ladder—even the failed attempt to pass a federal Equal Rights Amendment—were all part of their social agenda. The birth control pill redefined the love lives of baby boomers who could enjoy sex virtually free of pregnancy concerns. Marriage was no longer a prerequisite. Science and sex became an inseparable pair. To the

American public, Masters and Johnson were impartial, fact-based arbiters in the perennial exchange between the sexes. From their lab, they inspired women to rethink their relationships. "Masters and Johnson have received most of the credit for the new understanding of female sexuality but they were, in a way, only providing a scientific rationale for a new social reality that women were creating for themselves," observed Barbara Ehrenreich, Elizabeth Hess, and Gloria Jacobs a decade later. Nevertheless, in assessing feminism's major influences, they said the 1966 publication of *Human Sexual Response* "was to become one of its major ideological manifestos. The women's liberation movement and mass spread of feminist consciousness were still two or three years ahead, but the designation of a sexual 'revolution' implied a change that went beyond manners and mores to fundamental relationship of power."

Masters and Johnson's books empowered women with a realistic wisdom derived from medically informed choices. If Freud, Kinsey, and Ellis presented human sexuality from a predominantly male point of view, Masters and Johnson were "the most consistent feminist thinkers" of all top sex researchers, concluded Stanford cultural historian Paul Robinson in the mid-1970s. As a middle-aged couple writing in the Midwest, Masters and Johnson represented "explicit feminism" in their rhetoric, if not their personal lives, with an "egalitarian sexual ideal" reflected in their therapeutic approach, he observed.

The feminist endorsement of Masters and Johnson surprised many, none more so than Masters himself. Despite the recent complications of his personal life, he still thought of himself as a straight arrow, not one to advocate libertine excesses. His textbooks, written primarily for medical professionals, focused on married couples mired in ignorance and dysfunction. In the national debate over abortion—even after the Supreme Court's landmark 1973 decision in *Roe v. Wade*—he remained deliberately agnostic, careful not to become embroiled. Pregnant women in need of abortions found help with Johnson, who referred them to doctors willing to perform the procedure. Masters still looked at women in a most traditional way. He expected females to defer to him, just as his mother and his wife, Libby, had most of his life. Johnson's inventive, farsighted contributions happened only within the parameters Masters allowed. In launching their sex study, he certainly didn't seek out a female partner who would espouse the kind of maverick thinking of a feminist fresh from Barnard or Berkeley. "There's no question I was a male chauvinist," Masters later admitted. The doctorly tone of their books—sanctioning women to exert their true sexual identities and not the mandate of repressive parental or religious authorities—was borne of the human tragedies from his patients' lives. What Masters heard often left him appalled, a reaction that Johnson helped him put into words. Whether or not he accepted the label, his search for medical answers had turned him into a feminist.

The widespread public reaction to their books also turned Virginia Johnson into a celebrity, a media darling. She signed a lucrative deal to become a columnist for *Redbook,* and to *Playboy*'s predominantly male readers, she exhorted the power of female sexual responsiveness: "There can be back-of-the-neck orgasms, bottom-of-the-foot orgasms and palm-of-the-hand orgasms." Increasingly, she stayed home to concentrate on her writing assignments, reducing her caseload at the clinic. Her expanding income provided an extravagant lifestyle she'd never known. She moved out of her Salem Estates Drive house and into a larger home with Masters on South Warson Road in Ladue. By virtue of her position as Masters's equal partner, Johnson was hailed as an ideal American woman, an articulate and convincing spokeswoman for the new sexual freedom. As Barbara Ehrenreich and cowriters noted, Johnson "was in her own way a feminist," though her books with Masters had become feminist classics "mainly by chance." They opened a Pandora's box of possibilities for a society ready to hear their message. "Here was a body of objective, and by most standards, respectably scientific findings on which to rest the case for a radically new, feminist interpretation of sexuality," Ehrenreich said.

To their surprise, when feminists asked Johnson to appear at rallies or benefits to promote women's issues, she steadfastly refused. By the late 1970s and early 1980s, the extreme wings of feminism had moved into the vaguely anti-male rhetoric of Catharine A. MacKinnon, who condemned pornography and its violent nature, and Andrea Dworkin, who likened heterosexual intercourse to rape. None of this mattered much to Johnson, however. She never entertained the idea of holding a protest sign or standing next to Gloria Steinem at a political rally. "I would never march with the ladies," recalled Johnson. She even declined an invitation to appear with First Lady Betty Ford in support of the Equal Rights Amendment. Since her days in Golden City, Johnson had never petitioned for what she wanted out of life, yet always found ways to get it. She came from an earlier generation of women who were completely on their own in finding a job, in convincing someone to watch the kids when they were out of the house. Though she was the driving force behind the feminist sensibilities in their work, Johnson didn't like to be labeled. Women needed to step up, be in charge of their destiny, she now preached. They were responsible for their own lives, both inside and outside the bedroom. "If a woman doesn't have an orgasm," she insisted, "it's her own damn fault!"

The rise of Virginia E. Johnson as an internationally recognized expert on human sexuality in the 1970s seemed astounding to those who remembered her as an office secretary. She became codirector of their world-famous clinic—renamed the Masters and Johnson Institute—fashioning a therapeutic modality that offered hope for thousands, if not millions of patients. Male therapists who worked as her partner in therapy sessions marveled at her ability. "She had the advantage of being the boss there," recalled psychiatrist Dr. Thomas P. Lowry, whose wife also worked on staff. "I was very much in awe of her." Young therapist Sally Bartok admired Johnson authoritative demeanor and emulated her conservative style of dress in the office. "Back in those days, women were still wearing a lot of dresses, but she wore slacks, like sort of a Katharine Hepburn look. . . . I thought she was the most remarkable and amazing woman. She probably knew more about the physiology of sex than any woman in the United States at that time. But she wasn't into 'warm and fuzzy.' She always maintained that air of professionalism."

Bill Masters deferred increasingly to Johnson as therapy became the heart of the clinic's activities, paying for much of its annual budget. As a medical researcher interested in "hard science" all his life, Masters never intended to become a full-time therapist. In a sense, he had backed himself into this corner. He failed repeatedly to secure enough government and private financing to continue his anatomic and physiological studies into human sexuality, at least in the way he intended. A decade earlier, his departure from the medical school—where once he had been the highest-ranking figure in the Department of Obstetrics and Gynecology behind his friend Willard Allen—closed off any possibility of now capitalizing on his fame. He had given away his ob-gyn practice and was no longer a top-flight surgeon. He continued reviewing data from their sex studies of homosexual patients, promising to publish a third major book, but another big publishing check still seemed years away.

Now sixty years old, Masters showed up daily at the clinic, not as the hard-driving force of yesteryear but as a less intimidating, almost avuncular figure. His colleagues valued his steadiness, certainly compared to Johnson's vague responses or unpredictable moods. "He was very supportive of his staff," remembered Rose Boyarsky. "And if you made an error, or you had a question, he would take all the time that was necessary to clarify." Around this time, Bill decided to change something about himself that many patients found off-putting. He went to a surgeon to correct his walleyed condition, the strange distant stare resulting from his childhood bout with septicemia. For the first time in his adult life after surgery, Masters could look another person straight in the eye and smile directly at the camera, not in silhouette. There was a more subtle change to him at the clinic. He took a backseat to Gini, as if part of their marriage agreement. Johnson's views became more ascendant. "In the later years, Bill didn't have the interest that she had," recalled their attorney, Walter Metcalfe. "I don't think it was necessarily a power struggle. It was kind of 'I've done my part at my direction, now it's your turn' type of thing, whether consciously or unconsciously."

However, the increasing demands on Johnson's time—talking with reporters, setting up appearances, writing at home, along with her determination to be more present in the lives of her teenage children—caused her to disappear from the clinic for days. Her schedule changed constantly. At staff luncheons to discuss patient cases, she was noticeably absent. It made her sudden appearances all the more startling to the staff. "She was definitely the power behind the throne," explained therapist Max Fitz-Gerald. "It was obvious that a lot of decisions were being made by her, deferred to her, even though we didn't see a heck of a lot of her. She was very much the power broker."

Inside the clinic, the most divided opinion about Virginia Johnson came from female colleagues. While younger staffers like Bartok admired her as a role model, staffers closest to Johnson acknowledged an ambivalent feeling—"probably a love-hate with VEJ," as office manager Wanda Bowen described it. "Publicly, people would say she was the warmer and the friendlier, particularly when they gave their lectures together," remembered Mary Erickson, a full-time therapist who, with her husband, socialized with Bill and Gini. "She comes across as more bubbly and he can be seen as pretty cold. But when you get to know them, it's very different. I always felt closer to him than I did with her."

More seasoned female staffers, particularly those with graduate school diplomas, perceived Johnson as aloof and defensive. "I always got the feeling that she was not comfortable with me because I had a degree that she didn't have," said Peggy Shearer, a well-regarded therapist with her own medical degree. Others thought Gini seemed lonely in her new marriage and wanted to become friends but didn't know how. "I was uncomfortable with her because she didn't seem sincere," recalled Dagmar O'Connor, a New York therapist who trained at the institute for two months. O'Connor preferred the company of Masters to Johnson. "She was in so much of a Pygmalion [situation] that she completely lost herself," said O'Connor, invoking the allusion often ascribed to Johnson's rise without credentials. During O'Connor's stay in St. Louis, Johnson invited her to go shopping at a local mall, where she launched into a rapid-fire soliloquy about anything that popped into her head. What seemed like a very friendly gesture by Johnson—escaping from the clinic's claustrophobic atmosphere—revealed more than O'Connor had expected. Johnson began by talking about how she relaxed at home by cleaning her closets. Then she wandered into a discussion about sex after experiencing a hysterectomy. "They always say it's the same . . . but it isn't," she bemoaned, as if imparting some personal truth about herself, a pearl of wisdom for this younger woman. O'Connor didn't appreciate these chummy asides. Soon she asked to train with another female therapist because she wasn't learning anything from Johnson. "I wasn't really interested in her orgasms or her early childhood experiences," explained O'Connor.

When America's feminist movement came into full bloom, changing the role of many women in the workplace, female staffers at Masters and Johnson felt they were still being treated with secondary status. After a long private conversation, these women decided to appeal to Virginia Johnson. But with Johnson often at home in suburban Ladue, staffers needed an emissary to relay their concerns. Rose Boyarsky was chosen. "No one else wanted to go out and talk to her," she recalled. Perhaps they felt Boyarsky—who was closer in age to Johnson and whose husband also was a doctor—seemed most sympathetic and least likely to be dismissed.

On a hot summer day, Johnson invited Boyarsky to her house to chat in her backyard. At the door, she greeted Rose graciously and invited her to join in a swim. Johnson seemed grateful to share a leisurely time with a familiar face, away from whatever matters were on her mind at home. Boyarsky remained focused solely on the problem of inequity for women at the clinic. "It was just the two of us," Boyarsky said. "I was trying to make the case that it would be nice if she could be more supportive of the women in the clinic." Boyarsky explained how other female colleagues felt dominated by the male therapists and that this sentiment could impede their patients' progress. After all, the Masters and Johnson sex therapy had been built upon shared communication between the sexes, with each partner treated equally by the other. "It was a very subtle kind of thing—it had to do with being heard," Boyarsky explained. "We were hoping that Gini would sort of stand up. There were four women and Gini, and there were four men and Masters, of course. We all worked together. And it was a rather futile attempt on my part." Marshall Shearer, who worked often as a therapist with Johnson, suggested Boyarsky was misguided, at least tactically. "If there was inequality there, they should have had enough sense not to go to Gini," he said. "I don't think Gini was going to confront Bill over an issue like that." Shearer said Boyarsky and other female colleagues would have been more effective to invite Masters to discuss the matter, for he always decided how much opportunity Johnson or any other female might receive at the clinic.

In retrospect, Boyarsky says their short-lived feminist movement was handled poorly. "[Gini] wasn't the least bit sympathetic to the women there. I don't know why. I always thought I did a lousy job of talking to her about this." Their poolside conversation also carried repercussions for Boyarsky's career. Afterward at another staff meeting, Boyarsky and Johnson exchanged angry words over Boyarsky's attempt to research the role of mental depression in sexual dysfunction. When she mentioned her ideas, Johnson immediately objected.

"That's *my* job to do the research, not *yours*," she admonished. Boyarsky attempted to defend herself, to no avail. They never discussed whether Boyarsky could arrange the needed financing, or how her proposal might fit into the overall research agenda of the institute. All of this detail seemed beside the point. Most important, Boyarsky had offended Johnson. And sitting nearby at the table, Bill Masters, who had always been so helpful to Boyarsky when she needed help, said nothing.

"I was surprised at the time, but I should have seen it coming," said Boyarsky, who soon left the clinic. "I could see how she might feel threatened. Because I had a degree and she didn't. Because I was trained, and she wasn't. I can't really tell you why she would feel threatened. I didn't stay around long enough to find out."

A similar confrontation happened with Thea Lowry, who gained a job as an interviewer for Masters and Johnson when her husband, Thomas Lowry, joined as a therapist. One day she fell into a terrible scrap with Gini. "They had a screaming match," recalled Thomas Lowry, formerly the director of a small psychiatric hospital in Las Vegas, who was heartsick about this quarrel. Until that moment in 1973, he'd enjoyed his tenure at the Masters and Johnson Institute.

After his wife's quarrel with Gini, Lowry scurried to find out exactly what had been said between the two. "Masters and Johnson tape recorded everything and I got to listen to part of the conversation between them," he recalled. "Thea said, 'What's the matter, you seem touchy about my challenging your authority?' And Gini screamed, 'What do you mean challenging my authority?' and so forth. A day or so later, I asked the office manager, Wanda, if I could listen to that tape again. And she said, 'That tape does not exist.'" Soon Thomas Lowry's yearlong training ended. He wasn't asked to join the staff permanently as he'd hoped. Lowry felt sure his wife's argument with Johnson was at least partly to blame. "Unfortunately, Thea tended to be someone who was outspoken when she didn't need to be—I think she really rubbed Gini the wrong way," recounted Lowry, who soon afterward divorced his wife. Thomas and Thea Lowry had learned the preeminent lesson at the Masters and Johnson clinic. "Gini was always the queen bee," said Thomas. "You got along just fine if you listened reverently and didn't cross her, for only one person can be boss there."

CHAPTER TWENTY-NINE

The Business of Sex

What Masters and Johnson once gave away for free, they now charged top dollar. For a total cost of $3,000, roughly one-third the average U.S. household income in 1972, couples flocked to their clinic. They endured up to six months on a waiting list with as many as four hundred names. In America, the business of "sexology"—Masters's preferred name for their emerging field—was suddenly booming. Given the ballyhooed recoveries in people's dysfunctional sex lives, it seemed worth every cent. Affluent clients stayed at the Chase Park Plaza, the city's most luxurious hotel, where they performed their "homework" assigned at the clinic, a short walking distance away. Some couples, grateful for their rejuvenation, returned with Polaroid photographs of themselves *in flagrante*, demonstrating their success. "We tell them that we are willing to take their word for it," Masters quipped.

In the early 1970s, Masters and Johnson's staff was the only one in America providing the intricate therapies that sprang out of Gini's head like Medusa, changing the way medicine thought about sexuality. "She had a different point of view than a physician would have," recalled Sallie Schumacher, one of their female therapists. "There were so many concepts that she made, especially in terms of supporting women's thinking—that sex is something that you share, not something that you do to each other." Bill and Gini struggled to keep pace with their traffic. Each male-female therapy team could handle only so many cases. Despite the flexible nature of its therapeutic approach, the Masters and Johnson method of running a sex clinic left little room for financial growth.

"It was kind of a mom-and-pop operation, which is a surprise to practically everybody given the impact that they had," remembered Rhea Dornbush, a staffer in the mid-1970s.

Masters and Johnson also felt a strong commitment to teach their methods, especially to academics and professionals with medical degrees or doctorates in psychology. "They didn't necessarily look at their work as the end of things, but more as the beginning," explained Schumacher. With demand far exceeding what Masters and Johnson's small staff could provide, many therapists quickly copied their success. At Cornell Medical School in Manhattan, psychiatrist Dr. Helen Singer Kaplan offered her own blend of Freud with Masters and Johnson's methods. In her 1974 book, *The New Sex Therapy,* Kaplan paid tribute to the pair from St. Louis by ranking their contributions above Alfred Kinsey's. "Perhaps the greatest contribution to the long overdue termination of the 'dark ages' of human sexuality came from the pioneering studies of Masters and Johnson," Kaplan declared. "Their monumental efforts have finally made basic data on the long neglected physiology of the human sexual response available to the clinician . . . opening up the possibility of the development of the rational and effective treatment of sexual disorders."

Not every Masters and Johnson follower was as diligent or distinguished. Some therapists claimed to be trained after attending a workshop of only a few days. (Masters and Johnson's decision to call it a "fellows" program hastened this confusion.) Others simply read their textbooks and called themselves sex therapists. "In 1970, Bill and Gini were in a very elite vanguard—there might have been only two or three people regarded professionally in the field," said Dr. Robert Kolodny. "By the mid-1970s, there were sex therapy programs in virtually every major city across the country." As many as five thousand therapy programs nationally offered variations of Masters and Johnson's therapy, but fewer than fifty therapists were actually trained in St. Louis. "On the whole, much of what is claimed to be sex therapy is probably useless and potentially harmful to the individual," Masters charged.

Rapidly, their conscientious medical approach deteriorated into a largely unregulated sex therapy industry. As a counter to this alarming trend, Kolodny proposed franchising authorized Masters and Johnson clinics around the country. If they could expand into a national program, he argued, they could set the standards for this new field, and they could finance the kind of continued biological research Masters wanted to do. The revenues would be far more than they ever dreamed. "I saw that not only was there a big opportunity, but that if they didn't do it, that other people who were opening sex therapy clinics around the country were going to jump on this and take the market," he explained. But Masters wouldn't hear of it. "We're a research outfit, not a production line," he insisted. Johnson's view about franchising her brainchild was even more prosaic. Pleased by the amount of money already coming in, she realized neither of them was particularly adept at business. She agreed with her husband that they should stick to their own clinic and not try to run others. "No matter how much you train, people are always going to do what they want to do as therapists, and it's just not worth it," she explained. Even those sympathetic to Kolodny's ambitious plan knew it didn't fit Bill and Gini's lifestyle together, or their sense of mission. "The idea of franchising would never have worked," observed Rose Boyarsky. "What they did was educate enough people, who then went out and did their own thing. By the time that Bob Kolodny wanted to franchise it, it was too late."

The treatment of wealthy New York real estate developer Arthur Levien and his wife was assigned to cotherapists Sallie Schumacher and Dr. Richard Spitz. Ordinarily, Bill and Gini would have handled the Levien case, particularly given their status as benefactors. But by the early 1970s, Masters and Johnson were celebrities ("at least as unshakably fixed in people's minds as Procter & Gamble or Benson & Hedges," observed science writer Albert Rosenfeld), and their backlogged schedule and constant crush of patients prompted them to assign the Leviens to their trusted lieutenants. They didn't know, however, that both Schumacher and Spitz had plans of leaving. Privately, Spitz approached other colleagues about bolting and setting up shop on their own. "Dick had tried to recruit Mae [Biggs, another female therapist] and myself to leave and start our own clinic down the street, which was such a misreading of where my loyalties were," Kolodny recalled. Schumacher, a better therapist than Spitz, planned to depart soon, though she wasn't sure when.

Schumacher, a married mother of five children, lived in the St. Louis suburbs with her husband, Al Schumacher, a teacher at a nearby Lutheran school. "They [Masters and Johnson] were interested in the fact that I was married and had children," she recalled. "They liked to have people who had families and were settled." She had earned an undergraduate degree from a Nebraska teachers' college, but in her late thirties, she decided to go back to school, seeking a PhD in psychology at Washington University. She learned of the clinic's work during a lecture by Masters and joined them in the mid-1960s. Like other staffers, she never received any formal sex education. As a sign of their loyalty, Masters and Johnson thanked Schumacher by name in both major books—the only staffer to earn that distinction.

Arthur Levien aspired to the finest, as only a man can when he builds a dull and bulky edifice on Manhattan's Fifth Avenue and calls it Olympic Tower. In the early 1970s, his real estate firm joined with Greek tycoon Aristotle Onassis (then married to President John F. Kennedy's widow, Jacqueline) to erect a fifty-two-story behemoth dwarfing the gothic spires of its neighbor, St. Patrick's Cathedral. Levien's fortune, principally derived from building shopping centers, allowed him to contribute $100,000 to Masters and Johnson's clinic. "Grateful patients were a very good source of money," explained Torrey Foster, the clinic's first attorney, remembering how Masters cultivated patrons to keep their finances afloat. But in the Levien couple's case, Bill and Gini's unavailability left a feeling of being taken for granted. "They were really upset that they were not assigned to Masters and Johnson," recalled Shirley Zussman, a therapist who later worked with Schumacher. "They were this wealthy, successful couple who were used to 'the best.' They didn't know that Sallie was probably the best, or at least as very wonderful as Masters and Johnson." To their surprise, the Leviens found Schumacher exceptionally effective, prompting Arthur Levien to take one step further. He contacted Long Island Jewish Medical Center and offered an even larger donation—$1 million—for a new sex therapy center near his home. Schumacher became its new director. "I was looking for job offers—and I took the best one that came along," she explained. "Very few people knew anything about this [sex therapy]. It was an exciting area and people wanted to start clinics."

When Masters and Johnson found out, however, they were furious and implied something unethical had taken place. "She was not exactly a loyal soul," Johnson fumed later. There were no angry confrontations, though Masters and Johnson refused to acknowledge her departure. Taken by surprise, the couple seemed oblivious to their contradictory response. After all, they had publicly committed to training others, so why couldn't colleagues spread the news about their therapy? Undoubtedly, her resignation was compounded by the loss of Arthur Levien's largesse. Schumacher insists she never did anything improper to gain Levien's backing. "I guess they weren't too happy to see someone go on their own, but they never stated that directly," she said. No reason for her departure was given to the staff.

The insular atmosphere surrounding the Masters and Johnson clinic—where rooms contained open microphones attached to tape recorders and patient privacy and secrecy were placed at a premium—became even more intense. Famous or affluent clients were no longer referred to anyone except Bill and Gini. Therapists who wanted to conduct any outside business first had to get their permission. Indeed, when June Dobbs Butts, the only African-American therapist on staff, tried to write an article for *Ebony* magazine, she encountered numerous roadblocks. "[The writing fee] was $1,000, and I said, 'Will I have to turn that money over?' And they said, 'Let us get back to you on that,'" Butts recalled. "They took it as seriously as the million from Sallie Schumacher."

Masters and Johnson's vision to teach the world about their methods now seemed undermined by staffers who abandoned them and by strangers who shamelessly exploited their techniques solely for profit. Even con artists and hacks, with their flawed offerings, referred to Masters and Johnson as their touchstone. "The amount of garbage in this field and the number of people without credibility!" Johnson decried to the press. "There aren't a dozen people in this field who know what they are talking about." It wasn't supposed to turn out this way. The collective genius of Masters and Johnson had called for sex therapy clinics run by well-trained physicians, nurses, and therapists at hospitals and universities. "There are different roads to the mountaintop, but most start from the base camp established by Masters and Johnson who, in these telescoped times, have already become to sex therapy what Freud is to psychotherapy," *Science* magazine proclaimed. But if Bill and Gini had hoped for a faithful band of disciples, that clearly wasn't going to happen. "We have almost no followers," Masters admitted in 1975. "We're still entirely alone."

In addition, most of their imitators had no medical training. California marriage counselor William Hartman and his associate, Marilyn Fithian, bolstered Masters and Johnson's methods with their own, like showing films of couples having sex, going through hypnosis, and performing "sexological" exams. To break down "negative" cultural taboos among clients, as Masters and Johnson did with their "sensate approach," Ted McIvenna, a clergyman and self-proclaimed sexologist with the National Sex Forum in San Francisco, began by showing films on bestiality, masturbation, and sadism on one day, and movies about "good and normal sexual expression" on the next. More questionable practices were examined in a 1972 New York state hearing, with evidence of phony diplomas, outrageous fees, and sexual abuse. This mishmash of unqualified experts included criminals and the mentally ill. They mixed their so-called sex therapy with ingredients like Gestalt, bioenergetics, psychodrama, and various forms of feminism, family counseling, and religion. Some self-licensed therapists simply made up their credentials or offered no published evidence that their methods would work. The worst cases bordered on rape. "We have found what appears to be a shockingly widespread pattern of 'sex therapy' wherein male therapists encourage female clients to engage in sexual activities with them, under the guise that this is necessary for the client's well-being," charged Stephen Mindel, then a New York assistant attorney general.

However, in the changing moral climate of the mid-1970s, when once-prohibited practices were now tolerated, not everyone condemned sexual contact between therapists and patients. The

American Psychiatric Association issued a stern rebuke, but most sex therapists didn't belong to this medically trained group. Among psychologists, standards seemed more vague. At its 1975 convention, the American Psychological Association declined to put a ban on therapist-patient sexual contact into its professional code of ethics. *Reader's Digest* magazine warned "a promising new field of medical research is being overrun by hordes of charlatans" and cited numerous aberrations around the nation. "The shocking fact is that anybody can hang out a shingle in any state and call himself (or herself) a sex therapist," the magazine determined. "Not one state sets minimum standards of education or experience or issues a code of ethics for them to follow."

These phony sex clinic scandals pained Bill Masters. For years at Washington University, he had warned that not enough sex training was being done among doctors and other qualified medical colleagues. His books with Johnson identified widespread sexual maladies, but few in medicine were prepared to deal with this glaring need among patients. The flood of fakes and frauds entering this new "sexology" field—largely attributed to Masters and Johnson—left him deeply upset. "The main stimulant to sexual quackery seems to be money," Masters chided in 1974. "The current field of sexual therapy is dominated by an astounding assortment of incompetents, cultists, mystics, well-meaning dabblers and outright charlatans." Before the American Psychiatric Association, Masters warned that sexually troubled patients were particularly vulnerable to being manipulated. He called for statutory rape charges against therapists who engaged in sexual relations with any patient who "isn't able to give objective permission" under the circumstances. "If more people were willing to press this charge, there would be less of a problem," Masters insisted.

Disappointed with the tepid reaction of other professional groups, Masters decided their foundation should "take the first toddling step" toward defining an ethical framework for sex therapy and research. During a January 1976 conference in St. Louis, thirty-two experts, including both critics and such longtime friends as Dr. Paul Gebhard of the Kinsey Institute, discussed qualifications for sex therapists, including stricter licensing, as well as discipline for those engaging in sex with patients. Doctors and psychiatrists joined experts in other fields, but despite their hope for consensus, not everyone agreed on ethical standards. Most frowned on the use of sexual surrogates, which Masters assured everyone their clinic had discontinued after twelve years because too many women "lost sight of their surrogate roles and assumed a pseudotherapist role."

His call for greater scrutiny and professional standards within sex therapy gradually took root. More medical schools incorporated training into their studies, and existing groups, such as the American Association of Sexuality Educators, Counselors and Therapists, expanded their focus from sex education in the schools to the need for clinical care among adult Americans. More significant, one of the field's new professional organizations—the Society for Sex Therapy and Research—was born the same year as Masters and Johnson's ethics conference. The group's first president, Dr. Don Sloan, had trained at Masters and Johnson's clinic, as had its president elected the following year—Sallie Schumacher. In 1985, the organization's first lifetime achievement award would be bestowed to Masters and Johnson, the creators of modern sex therapy. From then on, the society's annual award would be named in their honor, recognizing how millions around the world had been helped by their landmark work.

CHAPTER THIRTY

The Pleasure Bond

"When a subject is highly controversial—and any question about sex is that—one cannot hope to tell the truth. One can only show how one came to hold whatever opinion one does hold."

—VIRGINIA WOOLF, *A ROOM OF ONE'S OWN*

On the road, Masters and Johnson performed like two old vaudevillians, each anticipating the other's moves. "We developed what I used to call our song-and-dance act," Gini remembered, as if she'd finally found her stage. During the 1970s, they became a big-name attraction, touring several weeks a year around the country. They spoke at academic forums, medical seminars, nursing conventions, psychology symposiums, and universities willing to pay their hefty fees. They filled auditoriums at Tufts, Notre Dame, and the cavernous field house at Syracuse where basketball games were played, lecturing to undergraduates eager to listen. Although billed as the duo who'd inspired America's "sexual revolution," Masters and Johnson now offered themselves as something more—a happily married couple, the personification of sex and love. They appeared so harmonious, so blissfully wedded, that an audience could learn just by watching them respond to each other.

Indeed, after one lecture, an onlooker came up to Johnson and admitted that she hadn't listened to the substance of their talk because the give-and-take between the couple was so interesting.

"What are your signals?" the stranger asked Johnson. "I'm trying to see how you signal one another."

Gini laughed, "You're seeing absolute spontaneity!"

Masters and Johnson's image as an ideal married couple became essential to their enterprise. In public, their seamless exchanges veiled their often tumultuous relationship in private. They wouldn't have it any other way. They were now advice-givers more than lab scientists. After a decade of dispensing much-needed medical information, fueling society's sexual liberty, they sensed America longed for an emotional commitment that went beyond mere physical urges. Somehow their efforts to rid Americans of crippling sexual ignorance became linked with a popular culture awash in pornographic films, such as *Deep Throat,* celebrated sex dens, such as Plato's Retreat in Manhattan, and soft-core cable television glimmering nightly throughout the heartland. They now spoke of the warm and comforting interplay between sex and love in ways they'd once avoided with clinical precision. "Gone were the white coats, the carefully neutral faces," *Newsweek*'s Shana Alexander observed in 1975. "In their place sat a happily married middle-aged couple, just plain Bill and Gini, the Ma and Pa Kettle of sex therapists."

For years, they deliberately avoided the word "love," usually at Masters's insistence. "It means many different things to different people," he declared. If an emotion could not be defined and empirically observed, he didn't seem interested. "Western civilization has made it difficult for people to accept sexuality, so the terminology has come down to 'make love,'" he observed. "But sex can also be an act of hate, comfort, joy or sorrow." When psychologist Rollo May complained that their first two books obsessed on mechanics rather than emotions, Masters retorted, "Dr. May has the corner on the love market and we couldn't presume to know anything about it." But other critics hammered away on this point. Conservative writer Midge Decter called them "busy sexual engineers." Psychiatrist Natalie Shainess labeled Masters and Johnson as a "priest and priestess" who stripped "the sex act from the moods, feelings and emotions of desire and love," contributing to "the wave of pornographic literature and films."

While Masters dismissed it out of hand, this critique bothered Johnson. In therapy sessions, her advice often tried to place sex in the context of human loving. She simply didn't view sex with the same detachment as did Masters. Though she had echoed his opinions when their books first came out, she gradually had a change of heart, increasingly expressed in the *Redbook* columns she wrote in their name and in her press interviews. "I hope the whole mechanical myth will go down the drain—I'm tired of it," she said. In 1975, the combination of love and sex came together when their book publisher produced *The Pleasure Bond,* a nontechnical popularization of their advice, with the subtitle "A New Look at Sexuality and Commitment." Their *Redbook* editor, Robert J. Levin, pulled everything together, highlighting a wide range of opinions on premarital sex, extramarital affairs, divorce, child-rearing, women's liberation, and such media-hyped phenomena as suburban "swinger" couples who casually traded partners at "key parties." Masters tried to maintain his scientific objectivity, while being dragged reluctantly into sociological debate. "I'm going to dodge it—for very good reasons," he told one swinging couple who wanted to know whether their actions were normal. "We have an absolute philosophy; we must be nonjudgmental. And unless we know, or we are reasonably sure of an answer, we don't give one." Ever the medical investigator, Masters preferred to share his direct observation, such as noticing that in the first hour of sleep after intercourse, postorgasmic women tended to move closer to their male partners in bed, while men didn't move at all. But most of this book stressed fidelity, emotional attachment, loyalty, and marital commitment as key to mutual sexual pleasure. Its message was far different from self-absorbed books like Alex Comfort's *The Joy of Sex* and other how-to-manuals of the 1970s—an era writer Tom Wolfe dubbed the Me Decade. Among the happiest couples, they found, "it seems a matter of elementary logic: love leads to sex, which leads to greater love, which in turns leads to better sex—and so it goes." Free of charts, electrode graphs, and anatomical line drawings of couples in the nude, this was Virginia Johnson's book far more so than Masters's. It addressed matters of the heart as much as any organ. "We deliberately tried to keep anything warm or humanistic out of the medical textbooks," she explained, as if correcting some deficiency. "When something's wrong, couples don't want to know the heart rate."

With the freewheeling sexual revolution, they now applied the brakes ever so lightly. In one chapter titled "What Sexual Fidelity Means in a Marriage," they praised religious leaders for throwing off the old shackles of moral dogma condemning human sexuality outright. In only a decade, the birth control pill and other medical advances had allowed women far greater ability to control their own bodies, redefining the laws and social codes that once ruled their sexual lives. Yet Masters and Johnson cautioned this new freedom could go too far, creating an ethical ambiguity that discouraged faithful commitment. *The Pleasure Bond*—initially titled *Mirror of Sex*—asked readers to look at themselves, reflecting a nation still in the throes of great social change. "In the nine years since we wrote our first book, the pendulum has swung a long way," Masters observed, "and now we happen to think that it is swinging back a little." For the first time on the road as a married couple, they repeated their comforting prescription for love and sex at each auditorium, newspaper interview, and television appearance. While some criticized their wooden writing style and penchant for platitudes, the *New York Times* lauded their new book as "a clarion of sanity in a sexual revolution that has left many of us homeless, starving for something emotionally nourishing to augment our diet of more and more joyful sex and living hand to mouth on the fringes of our imagination." Mentioning "embarrassing words like commitment and love," the *Times* concluded, seemed almost as "intrepid and newfangled" as their earlier books detailing sexual function.

To America, Masters and Johnson appeared to share a lesson from their own life together. Their serene tone and upbeat message gave the impression of a couple who had found ecstasy in marriage, intent on teaching by example.

Bill and Gini could relax with the Shepleys. Nights out together were one of the few occasions when being famous didn't seem to matter. Often, they came over to Peggy and Ethan Shepley's place in Kingsbury, not far from Washington University, or the Shepleys would visit the Masterses in their house on Warson Road in Ladue. "At our house, they were frequent guests," Peggy Shepley recalled. "We made it possible for them to have an evening without other people, with a couple they liked. And we did that a lot."

Peggy Shepley first observed them as a couple on a loveseat in their living room, shortly before they married. Both seemed eager to gain the approval of Ethan, the chairman of their foundation, whose opinion they valued and trusted. Yet they acted awkward, as Bill sat stiffly next to Gini. "Sort of snuggled next to one another, not intimate but kind of cuddled together," Peggy described. "Bill Masters was not a romantic man. I didn't see that side of him. A clinician, that's what I saw."

Gini Johnson, for all of her considerable charms, seemed lonely, someone in search of a real friend. The odd combination of celebrity and secrecy surrounding the clinic made any social interaction difficult, always a bit suspect. "She was very guarded and she had to be," explained Peggy. "She didn't know who wanted to find stuff out." Although men considered Gini still captivating in her mid-forties, women continued to deem her threatening. In St. Louis's clubby social circles, wives overheard gossip about Bill's divorce, or perhaps knew Libby Masters herself, and they determined in advance not to encourage Gini's friendship. Johnson was one of the best-known figures in St. Louis, yet she wasn't like most women. Few of her post–World War II generation had worked their entire adult lives, and certainly no one had dealt so publicly with the volatile matter of sex.

The extraordinary acclaim she received for her work with Masters made her feel like a star, yet with a persistent feeling of unworthiness. After nearly two decades, Johnson had yet to accomplish what she originally had set out to do at Washington University—get a degree. "When I was applauded and asked for my autograph all through the years in this [sex therapy] field, I used to be faintly embarrassed," she admitted. For years, she talked of seeking a doctorate, and spoke with Emily Mudd, one of their strongest supporters, who had started her family counseling service in Philadelphia in the mid-1930s without an academic degree. Mudd, who eventually earned her own doctorate from the University of Pennsylvania, offered to help Johnson get a doctorate there, based in part on the professional work she'd done already. But Masters quickly nixed the idea. She mentioned a return to school so regularly that colleagues questioned her commitment. Others detected a sense of inferiority behind her polished public veneer, recognizing the constraints her husband placed on her. "Gini was keenly disturbed that she didn't have any degree—it was a sore spot," recalled June Dobbs Butts. "Bill had a lot of chauvinistic qualities. I think if he had helped Gini go back to school, he would have been helping her much more, because that was what really made her feel lacking."

Despite his publicized concerns about proper credentials among sex therapists, Masters dismissed those who pointed out his partner's missing degree, and instead pointed to her achievements. "The disciplinary background for this work really doesn't matter very much," he insisted. "There's no discipline that I can say is uniquely vital to the program." Even those who were dubious at first, like Dr. Paul Gebhard of the Kinsey Institute, credited her with forming the very successful Masters and Johnson therapeutic approach. At one summer seminar, Gebhard watched Masters give his standard talk about the physiology of sex. Masters then left the room when Johnson's turn arrived to speak about the sex therapy carrying their name. "Some of her presentations fit right in with the cultural climate at that time, and she was quite popular," recalled Gebhard, who was surprised at Masters's reaction, which wasn't overtly hostile but certainly not supportive. "Bill wasn't going to join with the audience and try to think of how many different names there were for the penis. He wasn't condemning it but he was not going to partake in it because he wasn't thinking of it as science."

Eventually, Gebhard asked Masters why he didn't stay for his wife's half of their joint presentation.

"That's not my cup of tea—that's Gini's business, not mine," Masters told him. "I'm a research scientist, interested in physical behavior. Sexual attitude readjustment doesn't interest me."

As their marriage progressed, Gini resented Bill even more for not recognizing how much a diploma would mean to her. Masters stated his objections paternally, couching his words in careful tones so as not to provoke a fight. He promised anything she liked—redo their house, move to another, give her a bigger clinic office than his—so long as everything remained the same. "I think he played me like a musical instrument," she remembered. The call in Masters and Johnson's writings for more emotional commitment in relationships—the sense that sex might not be enough without true love—undoubtedly carried her imprint. Journalists who inquired about their marriage found it curious that neither one could remember a time they wanted to marry each other.

Bill's inability to socialize and relax—to escape from the constant demands of their careers—became more egregious to Gini after they married. Though she seemed distressed with their lack of friends, he remained perfectly content. In St. Louis, Ethan Shepley felt honored to be Bill's designated "best friend," though the two men didn't have much in common beyond the foundation, recalled Peggy Shepley. "I think there was a reason why they were always researching. I think *that* was their comfort, not their own personal relationships."

At home, Masters and Johnson's married life seemed a study in contrasts. If she found enjoyment from music and the fine arts, he preferred watching professional football on television. Prominently on their wall, a large canvas in abstract colors depicted the violence of the game, with players in helmets hitting each other. "You could almost hear the bones cracking," recalled June Dobbs Butts, who stayed as a guest at their home when she first joined the staff. "I said, 'Oh my God, I don't think that painter likes football!" Masters smiled, proudly and defiantly. "That's my favorite painting!" he replied.

Football, with all its primal moves, appealed to Bill's manly instincts. Watching Sunday afternoon games, or the network broadcasts on Monday night, were one of the few truly pleasurable pastimes in his life. "He would make a little joke that when they had some time for a love session that he would have on the football game and Gini would tune out," recalled Butts. His gridiron devotion fueled his interest in the Wilkinsons, one of the few couples in St. Louis with whom Masters and Johnson socialized. For years, Bud Wilkinson was the lionized Hall of Fame coach for the University of Oklahoma football team. A handsome, curly-haired former star quarterback himself, Wilkinson joined ABC television in 1965 as a college game of the week commentator. In 1978, he returned triumphantly to the coaching ranks to lead the St. Louis Cardinals, Masters's favorite hometown pro football team. Wilkinson had divorced his first wife of thirty-seven years, Mary, in 1975 and remarried shortly afterward. Before Wilkinson moved to St. Louis with his second wife, Donna, they received a call from the

Masterses, prompted by a mutual contact. "That began a long period of friendship where we had dinner together," recalled Donna Wilkinson. "Bill would come over and watch football games with Bud. It was marvelous to have those guys as friends, that you felt very comfortable with and could rely on for both discretion and genuine support." And like other social acquaintances, Bill and Gini eventually signed up Donna Wilkinson to their foundation's board of directors. Although she knew little about medicine or psychological therapy, Donna readily agreed. The Wilkinsons settled permanently in St. Louis, though Bud's coaching job with the Cardinals didn't last long. After less than two seasons, with a combined record of 9 wins and 20 losses, the team unceremoniously fired Wilkinson. Despite this public humiliation, Gini stayed friendly with Donna and remained pleased to socialize together with their husbands. At Christmastime gatherings, Gini would get up and perform, as if at the local Army base during World War II. "We would have holiday singing parties and I would always have them because Gini had such a darn good voice," explained Donna. "My husband loved to sing, so it was great fun." Both Wilkinsons enjoyed her company but were more ambivalent about Masters. "Gini was very warm, very outgoing and very welcoming, while Bill was far more reserved," Donna recalled. "He was not one to engage in just idle conversation." At get-togethers, Masters wanted only to converse about football, and pestered Coach Wilkinson endlessly about the next game and the last. "Bud just found him tedious, honestly," Donna admitted. "He [Bill] felt he could coach himself." One time, while Donna chatted on the telephone with Gini, Bill suddenly picked up the receiver and started asking for her husband. It was clear he wanted to talk football. Overhearing his wife's comments, Bud Wilkinson's face filled with dread. He began waving off any attempts to discuss the gridiron with Bill Masters.

"Please, please," the Hall of Famer whispered to his wife. "Just say I'm not home."

Masters kept two Doberman pinschers at the house in Ladue, powerful animals he showered with affection. In fact, in his unpublished autobiography, he managed to spend more time describing his relationship with the Dobermans than either one of his wives or two children. While Bill and Gini were away one evening, her teenage daughter, Lisa, was watching television on the floor with a new boyfriend when one of the dogs attacked. "One of the Dobermans ripped her boyfriend's face open—absolutely shredded him," recalled Dr. Robert Kolodny, who lived nearby and quickly ran over to help. "I had to call the plastic surgeon and handle it on an emergency basis. It was a pretty scary situation. [Afterward] Bill was very indignant about the whole thing."

Family matters now played even less of a factor in Masters's life. For a summer or two, his daughter, Sali, worked in his ob-gyn office, helping to shuffle papers, but after college, she moved on with her life. After graduating from Hamilton College, Masters's son, Howie, stayed on the East Coast, where he maintained a relationship with his father over the telephone. At his age, however, Masters seemed increasingly ill-equipped for any life outside the lab. "He didn't go to parties, and he wasn't social," Howie recalled. "He had no other life at all. He didn't have it in his children and he didn't have it in friends." On Howie's occasional trips home to see his mother, Libby, he might stop by to see his father on Warson Road. He noticed the small changes in his father's appearance—Johnson's attempts to update his wardrobe to reflect the 1970s' more informal styles. Efforts to smooth over the rough edges of his personality seemed far less effective. "I think she tried," explained Howie. "I would see Dad dressed in ways that I'd never seen him dressed before. Gini wanted to be social. She'd drag him out but he didn't want to do it. I'm sure it lit Gini's fuse. She had a tough row to hoe if she thought she was going to change him. Obviously she didn't. But I don't blame her for trying." If Gini married Bill in hopes that he, as a stepfather, would help raise and guide her two children, she soon realized her mistake. "I don't think either of them cared very much for my father," observed Howie. "Believe me, my father wouldn't insinuate himself into that role because it wasn't a role that he relished. I can't imagine it really being a happy house. I just can't. Thank God, my sister and myself were older enough so that we could be on our own. It wasn't our lives to live."

By the late 1970s, the everyday communication between a husband and wife—the emotional connection Masters and Johnson said was so important to a "pleasure bond" in marriage—was mostly absent from their own life together. The secret between them—that they didn't love one another—now became evident to coworkers and social acquaintances who witnessed this paradox but didn't understand the underlying reasons. True happiness seemed to exist only when they appeared on stage, when they finished each other's sentences and spoke in comforting words to a crowd. "When I think of them, I think of the pressure," explained Peggy Shepley. "I don't think of them together. I think of the forces that were shaping them. I think of Gini being the mother who wouldn't be a mother, the wife who wasn't a wife. And Bill was a father and a husband, but not really. I think they were so public, I can't think of them as intimate."

CHAPTER THIRTY-ONE

Guide to the Stars

Most Americans recognized Barbara Eden as the bubbly, buxom, blond star of *I Dream of Jeannie.* In this 1960s television comedy, she played a genie who emerged after centuries from her bottle and replied, "Yes, Master," whenever the NASA astronaut played by Larry Hagman beckoned. The nation loved her and the show became a surprise hit.

When Eden's producers tried to expose her belly button with a slight glimpse above her harem pants, angry NBC television censors issued a "no navel" edict. America wasn't ready for such a shocking display, they judged, causing a publicity uproar. In the past, TV comedies about married life, such as *I Love Lucy,* were forbidden from using the word "pregnant." Only recently *Bewitched* had showed a shared marital bed instead of the standard singles of Rob and Laura Petrie on another sitcom, *The Dick Van Dyke Show.* A former beauty queen and cheerleader, Eden made the most of this notoriety. Asked about the "belly button" scandal, she teased, "I don't think the network even knows I have one!"

Sex appeal played a big part in Eden's Hollywood career. Her wholesome, all-American looks landed her guest spots on numerous Bob Hope television specials. Costarring in the 1961 sci-fi flick *Voyage to the Bottom of the Sea,* Eden portrayed a curvaceous secretary and worked with her husband, Michael Ansara, a brooding actor she met on a date arranged by a Twentieth Century Fox publicity agent. Ansara's television credits included playing a Klingon warrior who menaced William Shatner's Captain Kirk character on television's original *Star Trek* series. As a guest on his wife's TV show, Ansara played the Blue Djinn, a powerful genie with a deep, bellowing voice, responsible for putting Jeannie in a bottle when she refused him.

By the early 1970s, *I Dream of Jeannie* had been canceled on television and Eden turned to performing on stage. With Ansara, she arrived in St. Louis to star in a play called *The Unsinkable Molly Brown.* Each night, the marquee at the city's Municipal Opera headlined her appearance. By day, however, Eden and her husband arrived without fanfare at the Masters and Johnson sex therapy clinic. "Life was a bit of a roller coaster for her at that point," recalled Johnson, without elaborating. "They came for something that was not working for them. But it wasn't any inadequacy on any of their parts."

Gini loved hobnobbing with entertainers, politicians, and well-known businessmen who passed through their door. Though famous, the Ansaras were like any other emotionally vulnerable couple seeking help with their lovemaking. Gini particularly liked Eden and enjoyed her performance in the musical comedy, a fictionalized account of a girl from a small Missouri town who married rich and survived the *Titanic* disaster. At the clinic, Gini chatted with Eden about her own music experience—singing at Fort Leonard Wood and with her former husband's jazz combo. She usually ended that wistful memory by wondering what would have happened if she'd followed her heart's desire as an opera singer. Eden listened graciously and flattered her with deference. "She used to say, 'I won't sing for you because you're a much better singer,'" Johnson recounted. "It wasn't true. I hadn't sung in years. But she was a very humble person." By the time they arrived in St. Louis, the marriage of this Hollywood couple had lasted more than a decade and produced a son, Matthew, born in 1965. Eden very much wanted to repair their troubled relationship, but Johnson didn't sense the same reaction with her spouse. Two years after finishing the Masters and Johnson treatment, Eden divorced Ansara and started dating a Chicago newspaper executive whom she also married and divorced. Her third marriage in 1991 seemed the charm.

As sex therapists to the stars, Masters and Johnson provided extra measures to protect the celebrities who sought them out. Johnson masked their identities with phony names or disguises, or arranged special times when she and Masters could see them. In her own way, Gini felt like a celebrity herself. She knew only too well the corrosive intrusion of nosy reporters, some retained by tabloids paying for tips on the sex lives of the rich and famous. Occasionally, their staff spotted photographers sitting across the street with a telephoto lens, waiting for a celebrity couple to emerge. Some tabloids made up false stories. "Poor [Arnold] Schwarzenegger and Maria [Shriver] were accused on the front page of the *Globe* or something of coming to Masters and Johnson and they never did at all," Johnson recalled. "We learned early on that you don't protest anything because it just gives it more life."

Protecting privacy and avoiding detection became a central concern at the Masters and Johnson Institute. Staffers were warned not to let any outsiders know what they witnessed. "When we joined, we signed all sorts of [confidentiality] papers saying we'd never tell any secrets," recalled therapist Thomas P. Lowry. Gini made sure patients entered, moved around, and left their offices without encountering other patients. "They had separate waiting rooms for everyone," recalled staffer Sally Bartok. "They went to great lengths so that people's paths didn't cross." With CIA-like subterfuge, they sometimes encouraged patients to be misleading about their visit. From the very beginning, Dr. Robert Kolodny said, "a lot of people used a fertility cover story for going to see Bill and Gini, and even used 'fertility problem' as a euphemism." Far away from Hollywood and the media capital of New York, the city of St. Louis provided its own shield from prying eyes. "They had a kind of built-in security—an invisibility, certainly from my father's perspective," recalled Howie Masters. "Dad often laughed about it. He said, "God, I couldn't have picked a better place if I wanted to do something quietly!'" Yet inside the clinic, Masters didn't always follow his own instructions. Sometimes he discussed his cases with other therapists, some of whom were there just temporarily. Dr. Marshall Shearer heard about Barbara Eden's marriage only because Bill brought it up. Masters indicated that some famous patients never entered the clinic because he and Johnson treated them at their house.

Eventually, their Ladue home became a source of mystery. Some celebrities came for social visits, such as musician Mitch Miller, who was a modest financial contributor to the clinic, or media types, such as columnist Ann Landers, wanting insights into the world of sex. Gini was the keeper of the gate in Ladue, a preserve for their most secretive cases. "Occasionally, we would have very famous people come for therapy and they became friends," she explained. "Politically famous and a few of them were entertainers of great note. To put them into any of the hotels would have attracted so much attention." With her inquisitive nature, Johnson loved to talk with these celebrities about their careers, each leaving their own distinct memory. Through the office grapevine, staffers might hear of someone famous staying at the Ladue house but usually never learned their identities. "They rarely talked about it," explained therapist Mary Erickson. "In fact, we often didn't know—which was fine—because then I didn't have to keep secrets." Doris McKee, who monitored sessions at the clinic, learned of famous clients but said the rules were different for these cases. At Ladue, no routine tape recordings or permanent notes were kept in the files, for fear that they might be stolen and sold to a tabloid. Records were kept in a safe in their Ladue house, where the couple installed a burglar alarm system along with their two Doberman pinschers standing guard.

The Ladue house on South Warson Road was more contemporary than most, sheltered by tasteful plantings that shielded activity from the street. Upon entering, guests walked into a vestibule and could follow one of two ramps—to a spacious dining room and kitchen on one side, and to several bedrooms on the other, including the master suite with two king-sized beds placed together. In the back of the house were a large terrace, a kidney-shaped inground pool, and a stable with enough surrounding acreage for Johnson's daughter, Lisa, to ride her horse. When Cindy Todorovich later bought the South Warson house, she found a secret panel with a peephole. "I'm not saying there was anything kinky going on, but maybe it had something to do with their research," she recalled. Years later, Johnson laughed at how rumors about her house could spread so. Secrecy was necessary to protect their clients, she said, particularly those with the most to lose publicly. Keeping matters private with a particular U.S. senator from New York and his beautiful younger wife, however, would prove quite difficult.

In a lounge chair beside the pool, Jacob K. Javits relaxed in the comfort and security of Masters and Johnson's backyard. At age seventy-three, Javits, a short, bald fireplug of a man talked to Dr. Robert Kolodny about all the people he knew, all the things he'd seen. "Jack was very open with me," Kolodny remembered. He perched himself next to Javits and Masters with a sense of awe. The young therapist immediately recognized Javits as the senior U.S. senator from New York, one of the most influential men in Congress. Like Masters and Johnson, Javits once landed on the cover of *Time,* touted in the 1960s as possibly the first Jewish president of the United States. "There is no office now closed to a Jew, including the presidency," Javits noted, predicting that a member of his religion would be included on a national ticket within a decade. "It would be nice to be the fellow that it happened to."

Born to immigrant parents on the Lower East Side of Manhattan, Javits embodied the American dream—a dynamo of hard work and determination propelling himself through night classes at Columbia University, a New York University law degree, and a rise to the rank of U.S. Army lieutenant colonel during World War II. Upon returning, he was elected as a liberal Republican to the U.S. House of Representatives in a traditionally Democratic district, and later handily beat Franklin D. Roosevelt Jr. for state attorney general. He then won election to the U.S. Senate, eventually becoming the ranking Republican on the Senate Foreign Relations Committee. As a liberal Republican himself, Bill Masters shared much the same worldview as Senator Javits. They enjoyed each other's company, as much as a doctor can with a patient. "He was one of the loveliest men I've ever known," Johnson recalled. "If he hadn't been Jewish, he would have been president. I would be happy to be a Republican if they had Jack Javits in the White House."

At poolside that afternoon, the usually diplomatic Javits regaled them with randy tales from the nation's capital. He assumed nothing said in private would be repeated. A Washington sex scandal had engulfed Representative Wilbur Mills of Arkansas, then a powerful tax legislator and an unsuccessful candidate for the 1972 Democratic presidential nomination. In 1974, Mills was caught drunk with an Argentinean stripper known professionally as Fanne Foxe, who tried to escape the cops by jumping into the nearby

Tidal Basin. What once might have been swept under the rug now became tabloid fodder, forcing Mills to step down as House Ways and Means Committee chairman. Though obsessed with new sexual freedoms and women's rights, America also maintained a considerable puritanical streak, frowning on licentiousness. Sex became a weapon in America's political wars, never more so than in the years ahead, as others who aspired to the White House would learn. But on this summer afternoon, Javits, from the old school himself, repeated what he knew as a seasoned raconteur. "Jack told me that if a Congressman was walking through an office and he saw a secretary he liked, he would send an aide to go get his car," explained Kolodny. "There would be a ten-or fifteen-minute ride through the park for [oral sex], if he couldn't squeeze into his schedule bringing her back to the office or his apartment. Clearly he was telling me this to explain how Washington worked." Kolodny, a rather reserved doctor by nature, was amazed by what he heard. As the old senator described it, Congressmen were "very good at being faithful to their wives when their wives were in residence in Washington. But fidelity was a moving target." During this visit, Kolodny never met Marion Javits, the senator's wife, but learned that the Javits couple had been in counseling with Masters and Johnson for several years. "It was clear that Jack was coming back for some refresher talk," he recalled. "Marion really had her own life, which was a large part of their problem."

A vivacious woman twenty years younger than her husband, Marion Javits married in 1947 and soon had three children. Unlike the dutiful stereotypical politician's wife of her generation, Marion insisted on forging her own path. She dabbled in painting, ballet, flying, and even acting (with a bit part in the 1960 movie *Who Was That Lady?* starring Dean Martin, Tony Curtis, and Janet Leigh). When her husband went to Congress, Marion stayed in Manhattan, dismissing Washington as a "company town" too dull for her tastes. Jack came home weekends. "My husband is a giant and it's hard to live behind a shadow," she later explained. Her twice-a-week column in the *New York Post* allowed her access to all the parties and excitement of Manhattan. "I suppose I really keep searching for something that will give me complete satisfaction," she explained. Although she and the senator attended

Truman Capote's famous 1966 "Black and White Ball" together as a couple, Marion Javits became known as a celebrated fixture traveling alone on New York's social circuit. Using a popular phrase of the 1970s, she indicated to intimates that she had an "open marriage." Senator Javits defended his wife's choices, even when she was sharply criticized in 1976 for becoming a registered foreign agent with Iran. "In our respective professional activity, my wife and I lead independent lives," he said.

At Studio 54, the epicenter of New York's 1970s nightlife, Marion's party companions included Capote, Andy Warhol, and Mick Jagger, but she took a particular interest in television personality Geraldo Rivera. In his indiscreet but aptly titled 1991 memoir, *Exposing Myself,* Rivera described his long-running affair with the senator's wife. When they first met at a 1972 party, Rivera claimed, Marion quickly seduced him. Though nearly twenty years younger, Rivera recounted the "tremendous sexual pull" between himself and the forty-eight-year-old wife of the senator, with her "dark hair, bright eyes, and full lips of a gypsy." He soon learned that "the senator and Marian [*sic*] had an understanding that predated my arrival," wrote Rivera. "She had had other admirers, which was fine as long as there were no scenes and no scandals." At one dinner party inside Marion's duplex, Rivera said they slipped away for sex inside a locked, mirrored bathroom, leaving behind the guests, including Secretary of State Henry Kissinger and his Secret Service detail. "It was one of the most thrilling sexual experiences I've ever had, made magical by Marian [*sic*], of course, and by the sheer illicitness of the moment," recalled Rivera. Like some prime-time Casanova, Rivera managed an occasional rendezvous with Marion between the six and eleven o'clock news. During a party held at her husband's Watergate apartment in Washington, D.C., Marion played hostess for such A-list luminaries as Frank Sinatra but managed to slip away with Rivera "like two teenagers" while the party carried on, he reported. As Rivera boasted, "Sure, I was married, but so was she. To a Senator. If she didn't care what the others at the party thought, then why should I?" Rivera insisted he was "in love with her, without question" until their relationship ended in 1985.

In St. Louis, the Javitses tried for years to salvage the physical intimacy in their marriage. They first visited Masters and Johnson in the late 1960s and stayed in contact for the better part of the next decade, often by phone. One night in their living room, Bill and Gini were entertaining their foundation's board chairman, Ethan Shepley and his wife, Peggy, when a call came in. Gini jumped up, and Peggy could hear her muffled voice in the next room as she answered and then walked back quickly into the room.

"It's for you, Bill," she announced. "It's *the senator*."

That night, Peggy heard the Javits name discussed for the first time, but not the last. "There were so many calls from the senator and his wife, who were having problems," Shepley recalled about other nights at the Ladue house. "They [Jacob and Marion] used to come to town whenever Gini and Bill were in, and then they'd leave, and they had to be available for these conversations."

Masters and the senator talked often, while Johnson listened compassionately to Marion and established a form of friendship. They discussed the underlying reasons for an open marriage and her sexual needs. Despite their difficulties, Gini knew the senator adored his wife, and Marion viewed her husband as a great man—even if they didn't live together. Some at the clinic speculated that impotency or some other physiological afflictions might be the problem, particularly given the nature of the Javitses's marriage. "I don't know that the age difference was such a remarkable aspect of their relationship," Johnson recalled. "She was wonderful to him. She could make things happen if her heart was in it. But by the same token, her personal lifestyle was a little risqué, to say the least." During a 1975 trip with the senator's wife to Mexico City for the United Nations–sponsored International Women's Year conclave, Gini witnessed the senator's wife in action. Marion Javits joined several spouses of foreign leaders at this summit, including Jehan Sadat of Egypt, Nusrat Bhutto of Pakistan, Leah Rabin of Israel, and Imelda Marcos of the Philippines. "I loved being with Marion," Johnson recalled. "She was fun. Needless to say, I understood her well." During the Mexico trip, Johnson's interview with a local reporter was interrupted when Marion managed to make her presence known. "Somebody was interviewing me—a young man in Mexico City—and she seduced him right in front of me!" she remembered. "I said, 'Oh God, Marion, why don't you just give the interview yourself!' She'd move in on anyone she wanted. I can name the number of journalists that she took to bed along with Geraldo!"

The last time Johnson saw the two Javitses together was at a luncheon honoring the sister of Fiat magnate Gianni Agnelli. By then, the once-commanding Jacob Javits had melted into a wheelchair, suffering the effects of amyotrophic lateral sclerosis (also known as Lou Gehrig's Disease), which ravaged his body and dogged his failed 1980 reelection to his beloved Senate. Seated at a banquet table, Johnson was struck by the tenderness Marion showed her disabled husband. That afternoon, the weakened former senator offered an eloquent toast to the Agnellis. When Johnson gushed over Gianni Agnelli—calling him one of the most handsome men she'd ever seen—Marion pointed out Agnelli's wife sitting nearby, just in case Gini had any designs of her own. "I went into gales of laughter because I had been around her when she was seducing every young man who was loose and available," Johnson recalled. "It was one of the funniest experiences of my life."

Johnson enjoyed hearing tales of New York's jet-setters, Washington gossip, and the well-known politicians in the Javits orbit. The senator and his wife "became very good friends and we were with them a lot, just as friends, not as professionals," Johnson explained. Those close to Gini, like the Shepleys or Bob Kolodny, were amused by how much she seemed enthralled by the clinic's secret world of celebrity therapy. To Virginia Johnson, associating with the famous was "terribly important because she was a small-town girl—born on a farm in Missouri—and so that was a big deal," said Peggy Shepley. With celebrity clients, Masters and Johnson may have vicariously enjoyed knowing them, but their problems often were among the most desperate.

Governor George C. Wallace wanted the White House in the worst way. In 1963, Wallace became the face of the Old South when he attempted to prevent desegregation at the University of Alabama. "I say segregation now, segregation tomorrow, segregation forever," Wallace promised in his inaugural, after having sworn privately to "outnigger" any political opponent. He stood in front of the school, as nationwide television cameras rolled, defiantly blocking the entrance of two black students into the all-white public institution until federal marshals finally intervened. The publicity allowed the one-time boxer to launch a brief bid for the 1964 Democratic presidential nomination, appealing to the prejudices of a nation. When Alabama law prevented him from running for another gubernatorial term, he prompted his wife, Lurleen, to succeed him but she died in 1968 of cancer while in office. That same year, Wallace ran for president as a "law and order" candidate on an independent-party ticket, winning five states and 14 percent of the total vote. By 1970, Wallace was preparing for another presidential run when he fell in love with Cornelia Ellis Snively, the niece of former Alabama Governor James E. "Big Jim" Folsom. Although aides warned him to keep the romance under wraps, Wallace married his Cornelia. At the time, a Gallup poll listed Wallace as one of America's most admired men, placing seventh, just ahead of the pope. "There was a lot of physical attraction, very passionate kind of love between us," Cornelia later explained.

In May 1972, a bullet cut down Wallace's presidential ambitions. As Wallace campaigned in the Maryland primary, a would-be assassin named Arthur Bremer pumped five .38-caliber slugs into his body. One shot severed Wallace's spinal cord, leaving him paralyzed. Some wondered whether his presidential quest could continue, just like Franklin D. Roosevelt after suffering a polio attack. Wallace had won both the Maryland and Michigan primaries, but he never fully recovered. His political dreams and personal life were left in tatters.

By the time he contacted Masters and Johnson, Wallace worried whether he would be able to perform sexually again. "Cornelia was trying so hard to do anything she could do to help him," Johnson recalled. "She had a hell of a time with him because he was not dealing terribly well with his condition." George Wallace's sad case was exactly the kind Bill Masters wanted to study for his next scientific mission—the neurophysiology of human sexual response. With the advent of computers and other high-tech medical equipment in the 1970s, Masters felt such medical research would be a worthy successor to their previously published work. Understanding the brain's role in sex—the symposia of nerve endings and synapses in reaching physical fulfillment and the accompanying mental functioning behind it—seemed a natural next step.

After Wallace's personal physician in Montgomery called, both Masters and Johnson agreed to visit the governor's mansion, offering their assistance. "Wallace sent a state plane for us and we went to Alabama—he wasn't traveling at the time," Johnson recalled. "We went down there twice and then Cornelia came up once by herself" to the St. Louis clinic. Masters later explained to Kolodny the severity of Wallace's spinal cord damage and concluded there was little he could do as a physician. Masters said the governor was impotent. "It was clear that there was no magic wand that was going to rescue the situation," Kolodny recalled. "It was a case of helping them cope, to do the best they could." Even Johnson's therapeutic touch didn't seem to help the governor and his First Lady. "He was willing to do anything," she recalled, having instructed them on the most basic sensate movements designed to stimulate. "There was just no possibility—it was physiologically impossible. But she [Cornelia] was willing to do anything for him. She was a superb human being and she was just lovely, one of the best."

Despite their braveness in seeking medical help, the Wallaces became increasingly frustrated with each other. "He began to accuse her of having affairs with state troopers," recalled Alabama journalist Wayne Greenhaw, in a PBS television documentary later made about the governor's life. "She accused him of talking to his old girlfriends on the phone all the time . . . then sooner or later, you know, it just turned so nasty." In 1978, the Wallaces filed for divorce. Cornelia moved out of the governor's mansion and told the press that she'd done everything she could to save her marriage.

In St. Louis, Masters and Johnson reminded their staff to keep quiet. While tape recordings and files about famed couples from Hollywood, television, or local politics were given discreetly to Kolodny to compile in the statistical profile of their patients, it wasn't so in this case. "Whatever was done with the Wallaces, a file was never compiled," Kolodny recalled. "It didn't fall into any of the ordinary categories."

CHAPTER THIRTY-TWO

Conversion and Reversion

Meet the Press host Bill Monroe stared somberly into the camera, introducing "the husband and wife research team" of Dr. William H. Masters and Virginia E. Johnson. Their long-awaited book, *Homosexuality in Perspective,* would be the main topic that Sunday, April 22, 1979, the first in the history of the NBC television program to carry a warning label. "Perhaps I should caution that we may get into some material which our audience—more accustomed to inflation, energy and politics—may find objectionable," Monroe advised.

Before millions of viewers, Masters and Johnson sat beside each other at a desk, ready to face their inquisitors together. Monroe quickly took aim at the most newsworthy aspect of the book. A transcript hints at the researchers' discomfort.

> MR. MONROE: I assume you consider it a key finding—which some people are surprised at and some people simply are disagreeing with, already—that you can convert people who wanted to be converted from homosexuality to heterosexuality; and in your findings, in your cases, you have had a failure rate of only one-third, which is a smaller failure rate than anybody has ever had before?
>
> DR. MASTERS: Actually, this is true, but one hastens to point out, as we make very clear in the publications, that there is a very high degree of selectivity in those individuals we would accept into treatment.

After a commercial break, *Washington Post* medical writer Victor Cohn inquired of Johnson whether "you feel that probably homosexuality is learned behavior, rather than something chemical or genetic, in most homosexuals." Should parents be worried, Cohn wondered, about "their children being exposed to a homosexual school teacher"?

Gini gave a rambling, somewhat disjointed answer, the same she resorted to whenever unsure.

"Truly learned—the fact that it is learned—and to date we know of no other conclusion to draw—I don't think is a source of fear or should be a source of fear," Johnson replied. "If things like this can be learned, then the things that parents want their children to learn or to know, to be, and to do, can also be learned."

When Cohn asked Gini to clarify her fuzzy statement, Bill jumped in. His answer was confident and unequivocal, his voice clear and direct.

"We are not genetically determined to be homosexual, and we are not genetically determined to be heterosexual," Masters lectured. "We are born man and woman and sexual beings. We learn our sexual preferences and our orientations, be it homosexual, heterosexual, bisexual, and, not infrequently, we change voluntarily our sexual preference."

Near the end of *Meet the Press,* Cohn pushed for more detail about Masters and Johnson's conversion therapy. He looked at Johnson again, perhaps knowing that therapy usually was her department, not her husband's.

"This very interesting group that you describe in your treatment—the changed homosexuals—those whom you have helped convert or revert to heterosexuality, you have had some of them for some years now," Cohn said. "Do they seem to be happy, content, relatively? Have some of them married? Have they had children?"

Johnson struggled again.

"These were highly motivated people," she said. "That was one of the criteria for accepting them in that particular phase of the therapy—"

"But these people—" Cohn interrupted.

"In many instances they have," Johnson said. "As a matter of fact, I think the failure rate of that particular population was, overall, 12 percent."

Bill burst in to correct.

"Actually, 35 percent in terms of failure to convert or revert," Masters said.

Now Johnson was flustered. "I am sorry; it was the other—" she started to amend.

With little patience, Masters interjected again.

"Actually, the answer to your question is, a number of them were married to start with when they came for help—about two-thirds of them," Masters explained. "A number of them have married since, those who were not failures in therapy. There have been children. Those who have not been listed as failures have responded to five years of follow-up with the statement that they are living effective, comfortable, involved heterosexual lives."

Aware the reporter might want more proof of their success among conversion patients, Masters added, "We have to go on their statement only." Similarly, America would have to rely on the word of Masters and Johnson on this matter, whether their claims about conversion and "learned behavior" could be proven or not.

"Thank you, Doctors Masters and Johnson," Monroe concluded, repeating the mistake commonly made about her credentials, "for being with us today on *Meet the Press*."

Television was hardly the place to judge *Homosexuality in Perspective*—touted as a landmark study of more than three hundred homosexual men and women over a fourteen-year period. When it finally appeared in spring 1979, their publisher claimed the new 450-page book would "revolutionize current thinking about homosexuality." Masters called it "the third leg in a stool"—the culmination of their trilogy built on sex research. Their previous textbooks had focused primarily on heterosexual coupling and mentioned homosexuality only fleetingly. With the same clinical eye, this new book would map out the physical and psychosexual behavior of male and female homosexuals.

When Masters and Johnson began in the mid-1960s, most Americans barely acknowledged homosexuality's existence. The term "gay" wasn't a part of everyday language, at most a code word in subterranean bars and social circles. Masters and Johnson had difficulty gaining the cooperation of homosexuals in surrounding St. Louis. As word got out in the press, however, some contacted the clinic, offering to be volunteers. "After reading the article in the December 1970 *Atlantic,* I am convinced that you are sincere in your professional goals and avoiding sensationalism," wrote one twenty-eight-year-old Indiana man, who signed his name but said he was still "in the closet" as a seeming heterosexual. "I believe I would be categorized as a homosexual although I have never been diagnosed professionally as such."

Once again, Masters and Johnson showed great empathy for those troubled by their sexuality. As a physician, Bill seemed particularly convinced of their therapy's effectiveness with the most challenging cases. "He would say, 'These are men and women who are unhappy—and sometimes deeply disturbed—by their homosexuality,'" recalled Dr. Robert Kolodny. "These are people who are highly motivated to try to change to something that will either reduce their stress, make their lives easier, or remove a burden."

In *Homosexuality in Perspective,* Masters and Johnson aptly put their findings in societal context. A foreword by Dr. H. Tristram Engelhardt Jr., a Georgetown University bioethicist, characterized their findings in almost noble terms, as "the physical framework within which one soul can touch another in pleasure and love." Engelhardt underlined Western culture's duplicity and asked why the ancient Greeks portrayed in Plato's *Phaedrus* and *Symposium* could "depict homosexuality as a paradigm of love and the erotic, [while] English law characterizes it as a sin one should not even name." He wondered why homosexuality, affecting such a sizable portion of the population, could be judged with such "scorn, condemnation and punishment."

Though some ancients viewed same-sex relations as benign, Christianity's spread throughout Europe brought little tolerance beyond procreative sex and the norms of marriage. To those in fear of their immortal soul, St. Augustine warned "that of all these—namely the sins belonging to lust—that which is against nature is the worst." Religions and societies around the globe prohibited sodomy, effeminate behavior, and other "unnatural" acts, calling for physical punishments, dismemberment, and even death. Nevertheless, civilization's honor roll featured several believed to be homosexual, including Socrates, Julius Caesar, Alexander the Great, Michelangelo, Leonardo da Vinci, and King James I of England. By the twentieth century, theorists debated whether genetics, family environment, hormones, birth order (or some combination) determined sexual orientation. Sigmund Freud's theory about "inversion" suggested all people are born bisexual, with biological and environmental factors in childhood development deciding an adult's persuasion. Psychiatrist Richard von Krafft-Ebing listed homosexuality among forms of sexuality he considered misdirected, including sadism, masochism, and other fetishes. Homosexuality was labeled a mental illness for years until the American Psychiatric Association in 1973 removed this sexual orientation from its handbook, the *Diagnostic and Statistical Manual of Mental Disorders,* lumped in with psychosis, delusional, and other abnormal behavior. Geneticists looking for a biological answer—a "gay gene" in the DNA code—never found one. Modernity certainly didn't end the brutality toward homosexuals in civil law or criminal violence, including their mass imprisonment in Nazi Germany. In America, gays and lesbians were suppressed by numerous laws against "degenerates" until the 1969 Stonewall riots in New York, prompted by police harassment. A howl of protest nationwide inspired a gay liberation movement in many cities. By the time *Homosexuality in Perspective* appeared, homosexuals were routinely called "gay," slowly but effectively gaining influence in society. Many once-closeted gays now lived openly at home and at work. Still, as with heterosexual sex, organized medicine had ignored basic biological questions surrounding homosexuality.

In their study, Masters and Johnson repeated Alfred Kinsey's earlier projections that up to 10 percent of American adults had some previous homosexual experience. (Critics later pointed out that U.S. Census and other studies estimated that figure as low as 2 percent of U.S. adults.) More significant, Masters and Johnson relied on Kinsey's rating system to calibrate sexual orientation. Based on patient interviews, a rating of "Kinsey 0" was given to a man or woman who claimed never to have had an "overt homosexual experience"; a "Kinsey 3" rating for those with an "equal homosexual and heterosexual experience"; and a rating of "Kinsey 6" for those with "no overt history of heterosexual experience." In applying for therapy, patients with a Kinsey rating of 5 or 6—considered "overt homosexual lives"—were candidates for "conversion" to heterosexuality. Candidates with a Kinsey rating between 2 and 4—who were either singles in the closet or married with covert homosexuality—were considered for "reversion" to heterosexuality. Of the sixty-seven total cases, they said, fifty-four were men and only thirteen were female.

To the authors' surprise, about 60 percent of both genders seeking changes were married (though many were estranged and rarely had intercourse with their spouses). With "reversal of a sex preference," success often depended on a patient's reasons for seeking treatment. Those who did poorly often feared public exposure or were pressured by their spouse. "When such self-incrimination phrases as 'of course I'll need an occasional chance to be with my friends' or 'I want to be 95 percent heterosexual' were used in private with a therapist, the couples were refused treatment," their book explained. Particularly with male patients, they didn't want treatment used "as a means of misleading their wives."

Conversion cases posed numerous challenges for therapists, by stretching the definitions of gender and what was best for their patients. In their book, Masters and Johnson described a married man who couldn't consummate his marriage, failed at having sex with other women, and then "turned to homosexual interaction as an ego-salvaging measure." Four years later, this same man and "his still-committed wife" arrived at the clinic, with the hope of "neutralizing" his gay tendencies and becoming a heterosexually functioning couple. In another seemingly impossible case, a woman with a Kinsey 6 rating who, "after living approximately 11 years as a sexually active but completely frustrated homosexual," had succeeded in finding a man with whom she wanted to live and "to function sexually at orgasmic levels with him." Without strong motivation by patients, Masters and Johnson admitted, their chances were "markedly reduced." Still, their "success rate"—actually defined in terms of failure—appeared stellar and gained headlines around the world. Of the sixty-seven male and female patients with "homosexual dissatisfaction," only fourteen failed in the initial two-week treatment. During a five-year follow-up, the overall failure rate of 28.4 percent—or better than a 70 percent success rate in altering sexual preference—was an unimaginable claim in the world of psychiatry and psychoanalysis. Some follow-up cases couldn't be tracked, they acknowledged in their book, making these final figures somewhat "misleading." Mindful of Freudian theory's grip on American society, Masters and Johnson knew their findings would be perceived as further repudiation of psychoanalysis. "The current concept that the sexually dysfunctional or dissatisfied homosexual male or female cannot be treated without an 80 to 90 percent overall failure rate is simple erroneous," their book declared. They blamed psychotherapists for accepting "failure" too readily and not keeping their own biases at bay. Too many assumed patients would eventually return to homosexuality—a view that "the homosexual community has also adopted and freely propagandized," they wrote.

Nothing in *Homosexuality In Perspective* was more controversial than conversion, with ramifications that lasted for decades. Activists in the gay liberation movement and social scientists who studied homosexuality sharply criticized this theory as dangerous or simple-minded. As writer Janice Irvine later observed, "Throughout the book, they insist that it's okay to be gay, but they know how to fix it just in case we think it's not." Almost immediately, religious conservatives and right-wing commentators seized on Masters and Johnson's research to contend a gay and lesbian lifestyle was a matter of personal choice and not by divine design. In the eternal "nature versus nurture" debate, they underlined a lack of genetic evidence and suggested improper behavior and environment as the main cause of homosexuality. Evangelicals offered to "heal" homosexuals through prayer, sending them back on the road to heterosexuality, just as the Bible and now secularists like Masters and Johnson proscribed. Their message was clear: gays and lesbians could change if they really wanted to.

But even Masters and Johnson's old friends and admirers expressed doubts. *The Journal of the American Medical Association,* whose praise of *Human Sexual Response* was once so vital, now expressed reservations. "The authors state that homosexuality is a learned pattern of behavior that can be unlearned—an arguable view," *JAMA* concluded. Dr. Lawrence J. Hatterer of what was then New York Hospital–Cornell Medical Center declared, "It's inconceivable to me that you could take a person with a long-standing involvement in homosexuality and in two weeks change him into a heterosexual." When *Playboy* magazine, another longtime ally, challenged their conversion theory, Johnson showed little patience. "We are not in the business of determining what is right or wrong in matters of individual choice," she snapped in an interview, invoking a constant refrain. "Incidentally, it's hardly news that there are homosexuals who do not want to be homosexual."

But behind the scenes, the only one who really believed the conversion theory was Bill Masters.

During *Meet the Press* and throughout the press tour, Johnson dutifully defended *Homosexuality in Perspective* as though it had been equally her work. But privately Gini was deeply upset with its methods and results, enough that she cried at one point and considered distancing herself from the project. Years later, she appeared far from certain about the book's claims in converting gays into straights. "We had a great number of gay couples come to us—a few women, and quite a large number of men," she said. "But we never said, 'We'll change you.'"

The turmoil surrounding this book began a decade earlier, when many believed Masters and Johnson could transform virtually anyone's sex life. Dr. Alex Levay, then a clinical professor of psychiatry at Columbia-Presbyterian Medical Center in New York, referred a young man in his twenties to them. The young man worked with his father, a prominent, affluent figure in New York's garment industry, and very much wanted to have a family. The conversion therapy succeeded for a time but didn't last. "He got married and had children. He became functional," Levay recalled. "But as happens with people who are predominantly gay, there was no interest in maintaining the gains. He could do it, but he went back to his gay life." Despite its initial success, the eventual outcome for this young man led Levay to a different conclusion. "It was silly [to think he could be converted] but at that time we were all silly," recalled Levay. "If you talk to anyone who works in the field you know that these orientations are very powerful, very fixed, and very hard to change."

Masters's cryptic reasons for pushing the conversion/reversion theories were hard to decipher for his friends, foes, and even Johnson herself. If Bill harbored a deep resentment or fear of homosexuality, he certainly didn't reveal it. Throughout his career, he displayed none of the crude biases of his post–World War II generation that vilified homosexuals in the same breath as Communists. During the landmark 1973 American Psychiatric Association debate about removing homosexuality from its list of mental disorders, the group's president, Judd Marmor, recruited Masters to lobby others for his reform. As a scientist, Masters produced work that suggested sexual orientation might have a hormonal or other biological cause. In 1971, he cowrote a limited study with Kolodny, published in *The New England Journal of Medicine,* that found depressed levels of testosterone in homosexuals compared to heterosexuals, and that the male hormone diminished as the patient became more committed to homosexuality. Nevertheless, Masters believed sexual orientation was decided by numerous factors that expressed themselves as a person developed into adulthood. He believed a patient's happiness with his or her sexual identity was paramount and based his actions accordingly, just as he once had fashioned artificial vaginas for female patients as a surgeon. The conversion therapy was a direct result of Masters's compassion for his patients, rather than some grand scheme to prove a point, Kolodny maintained. "People from all walks of life, and all sort of problems, contacted them in desperation because there really weren't any places to go," he recalled. "So they responded to these cries from the heart, by trying to figure out an approach that worked."

Homosexuality in Perspective contained far more speculation than science, violating one of Masters's cardinal rules. As in the past, some chapters, laden with statistics, compared physiological responses between gays, lesbians, and a comparative group of heterosexuals. They measured the size and color of engorged penises, clitoral responses, the sex flush, and physical characteristics during sex—all basically the same regardless of orientation.

But throughout the text, differences quickly turned into improvable generalizations. "Sexual fakery does not appear to be nearly as prevalent in the lesbian population as it is among heterosexual women," the book declared. "First, it is obviously far more difficult for a woman to deceive another woman in a continuum of sexual encounters than it is to practice fakery successfully with an unsuspecting man." Homosexuals were portrayed as better lovers than heterosexuals, at least when stimulating their partners through cunnilingus or fellatio, because they "*took their time* in sexual interaction in the laboratory," Masters and Johnson emphasized, this time without a stopwatch cited. "Fantasies patterns"—dreams or visions of forced sex, group sex, and anonymous encounters—were more prevalent with homosexuals, they determined, but without much quantifiable evidence. The lack of any proof particularly was evident in Masters and Johnson's declaration that men and women are not born homosexual, but rather "homosexually oriented by learned preference." To those therapists who believed in a genetic predisposition toward homosexuality, they scolded there "must no longer be blind support of cultural concepts that are obviously based on the vagaries of supposition, presumed potential, or scientifically unsupported contention." They offered no clear-cut reason why they believed homosexuality was a "learned preference" other than noting that "there currently is not any convincing evidence" of a genetic root.

Secrecy shrouded the conversion cases more than usual at the Masters and Johnson Institute. Most staffers never met any of the sex preference change cases during the study period of 1968 through 1977. Therapist Rose Boyarsky heard gay patients talking of a switch to heterosexuality, but she was told the tapes of these sessions were kept in a hidden vault at Masters and Johnson's home. Lynn Strenkofsky, who organized patient schedules during this period, said she never dealt with any conversion cases. Therapist Mary Erickson explained the few gay couples who enrolled at the clinic "were wanting relationship problems addressed, to solve the sexual problems between them—it wasn't about converting." Drs. Marshall and Peggy Shearer, perhaps the institute's most experienced therapy team in the early 1970s, said they never treated homosexuals and heard virtually nothing about conversion therapy. Among those who knew, it seemed Masters, usually more approachable than Johnson, didn't want to hear their concerns about conversion. "I certainly didn't agree—I told him frankly that it was totally, absolutely a wrong way to approach it," recalled Dr. Roger Crenshaw, a psychiatrist there in the early 1970s. Eventually staffers learned not to debate the topic with Masters, and his determination even became a source of humor among the staff. "Bill could look at somebody and say 'Have an erection!' and they would," said J. Robert Meyners with a laugh. Meyners eventually became an assistant director in the 1980s.

Initially, Kolodny didn't doubt the program's ability to treat any case. With a fine eye for detail, he had carefully reviewed the patient files from the two earlier books, listened to many tapes, and was convinced of their results. "I was prepared to believe that if Bill said they were doing successful conversion therapy, who was I to say it wasn't possible?" he recalled. Kolodny heard the same vague explanation about the Ladue residence as a site for special therapy. "From 1968, when I started working with them, I cannot remember a single instance of a gay couple or lesbian couple being treated at the clinic for conversion," he said. "When I asked Bill, 'Where are the conversion files?' he said, 'Oh, we don't keep those on the premises.' None of us on the professional staff heard or sat in on discussions of actual conversion therapy cases going on. And that troubled me when Bill announced he was writing his book."

As *HIP* neared publication, however, Kolodny was asked to help in its preparation. The book's acknowledgments later mentioned "the skills of Robert C. Kolodny, who carefully critiqued this text," listed first among the handful who had assisted Masters and Johnson. Aware of his own limitations as a writer, Masters wanted Kolodny to go over the vignette-like portraits of individual case studies spread throughout the text and to make them more readable. All of their previous books contained such patient profiles, without mentioning anyone by name. Homosexuality, given its complicated nature, would particularly require vivid renderings from real life. In this book, for example, "Case Report: Couple 10," devoted two pages to telling the story of "R," labeled as a "30-year-old Kinsey 6." In this tale, R was "a completely committed homosexual"—so much that "when in need, he cruised the local bars and public toilets wherever he was located." Then R met and "fell in love" with a twenty-three-year-old woman who shared many interests, including piano playing. He wound up living with this completely heterosexual woman (a "Kinsey 0" on the orientation meter) for ten months until they wed. But after eighteen months, they had yet to consummate their marriage. "Despite every sexual effort on his wife's part, R could not achieve or maintain an erection," the vignette stated. In their commentary, Masters and Johnson summarized their success with R and his wife:

> He did convert. He began functioning successfully in intercourse on the tenth day of therapy. The follow-up of this couple has been uneventful. The family has children, R is having a successful career as a clinical psychologist, and both partners describe an effective marriage. Obviously, this storybook type of history is the exception, not the rule, in any sexual relationship between a Kinsey 6 man and a Kinsey 0 woman. As emphasized before, the limitations in ability to convert or revert to homosexuality are dependent not only upon the degree to which the client is motivated to become subjectively involved in heterosexuality, but also upon the rewards potentially available from such a conversion.

When Kolodny asked to see the files, to hear the tape recordings of these "storybook" cases, he was refused. As both staffers and patients were fully aware, virtually everything said in therapy sessions was recorded on reel-to-reel machines, for everyone's protection. "If a patient couple ever made a claim that one of the therapists had seduced them or whatever, we had the tape, and they *knew* we had the tape," explained Kolodny. "Bill felt that was a helpful legal backup." Thus, it seemed strange that no tape recordings existed in this volatile circumstance.

As the work progressed, Kolodny began to suspect some, if not all, of the sixty-seven cases were not entirely true. Details were constructed from fragments of Masters's memory or completely fabricated. "My own opinion at the time—and it hasn't changed in the twenty-seven years since then—was that they had done some number of cases less than they indicated in the book," Kolodny said. "There was some element of either exaggeration or fabrication in the composition of the book, in wishing to present a more compelling case." Although Kolodny was Masters's top aide at the clinic and admired him greatly, he couldn't explain it any other way. Part of his job was reviewing patient applications and helping to assign couples to therapists, yet Kolodny had never seen any conversion cases himself.

Handed a draft of the manuscript, Kolodny tried to improve its prose and enhance the believability of the patient vignettes. "When I read through them, I told Bill they sounded like they weren't real, they all sounded the same—so we worked on how to add some color to them," Kolodny said. "We took things that had nothing to do with the case whatsoever. I might have added a sentence here or there based on stuff that wasn't factual. These were somewhat composite anyway. It was a question of trying to improve their readability."

Eventually, Kolodny realized the extent of the problem, and he approached Johnson privately to express his alarm. He approached this conversation very warily, unsure of what to expect. At that time, Kolodny was considered Masters's protégé, the young man who would someday take over. The relationship between Kolodny and Johnson had always been a tenuous one, dependent on Masters's confidence in him. Voicing such serious criticism about her husband, to appear to be going behind Bill's back, could prompt a defensive or even angry reaction from Gini. When Kolodny told her, however, Johnson immediately acknowledged their dilemma. She too held similar suspicions about Masters's conversion theory. "She understood exactly what I was saying," Kolodny recalled. "Gini really didn't like the book. It was like having been tied to a train track. I had told her, in no uncertain terms, what the reaction to this book was going to be—professional ridicule, public outrage, and accusations of hubris, nonobjectivity, attacks from the gay-lib movement, the psychiatric community, from every quarter, except maybe Bible-thumping conservatives who said, 'See, we always told you so—if these [homosexual] guys wanted to change, they could!'"

The prospect of public embarrassment, of being exposed as a fraud, greatly upset Johnson. She'd spent her whole adult life overcoming taunts about her credentials and credibility. She possessed a much better sense than Masters of the political and social world around them and recognized the inherent dangers in promoting an unproven theory. With tears in her eyes, Johnson told Kolodny she couldn't tolerate being listed as coauthor.

"I do not want to be judged or remembered for this idiocy," she moaned, almost operatically. "He has written junk! He has made it all up!"

For a time, she considered demanding that the book's cover list only Masters as author, with a tag line that read—"Based on research done in collaboration with Virginia E. Johnson." But such a proviso would only draw more skepticism. She asked Kolodny to try to delay its publication. Perhaps, with enough time, some of the basic flaws could be fixed or mitigated.

"I can't talk to him," Johnson confided to Kolodny, in a rare show of weakness. "We can't argue about this anymore because we've had big arguments, and I have to live with the man. You have to fight it out with him."

Kolodny put his concerns in writing, expressed as friendly but directly as he knew how. In August 1978, he sent a handwritten, two-page letter to Masters about the second draft of the manuscript, reiterating his earlier warnings that the chapters regarding sex preference changes needed to be reevaluated. "I am even more convinced that this is far from publishable and will only provide fodder to critics who would like to impugn your reputation and the validity of your work," wrote Kolodny to his longtime mentor, the man who had inspired his career. When Masters read Kolodny's letter, he refused to concede anything. Masters hadn't worked this hard, traveled so far, to be denied this prize—the finale of his long-term study of human sexuality. Their conversation turned into a heated argument and eventually spilled into Johnson's office. Neither she nor Kolodny could prevail with Masters. "This is very important material," Masters insisted repeatedly. "We need the world to know what we can do. It is the logical third leg of the triumvirate of books we first set out to do."

With Johnson's approval, Kolodny spoke to their publisher about a delay but it came too late in the process. "That was a bad book," Johnson recalled decades later. "Kolodny was beside himself too." She said she favored rewriting and revising the whole book "to fit within the existing [medical] literature" and feared that Masters simply didn't know what he was talking about. At worst, she said, "Bill was being creative in those days" in the compiling of the case studies.

With the publishing gears in motion, both Johnson and Kolodny decided the only option left—short of a public insurrection, one that neither was inclined to provoke against Masters—was to hope for the best with this latest creation. "Gini just washed her hands of the whole thing," said Kolodny. "So the book was published, just as Bill wanted it to be that April. And I was basically ignored."

Homosexuality in Perspective arrived with great expectations. Astutely, the book publisher revealed its contents in advance to *Time* magazine, which launched it with fanfare and favorable coverage based on the two researchers' vaunted reputation. "No doubt about it," the magazine proclaimed, Masters and Johnson "are a contemporary phenomenon."

Like many other respectful press accounts, *Time* began by quantifying Masters and Johnson's impact in the late 1970s—selling 750,000 hardcover copies of their books, observing more than 10,000 orgasms in their research, and treating 2,500 "sexually dysfunctional" couples with an 80 percent success rate. As with Masters and Johnson's earlier scientific books, *Time* noted the same tortured use of the English language, with phrases such as "stimulative approach opportunity" for foreplay and "vocalized performance concerns" for talking about sex. It also faulted the book for having "almost nothing to say about psychology, ethics or the origins of homosexuality." But these were mere quibbles compared to other, more scathing criticisms. The *Los Angeles Times* review, for example, said the book "abounds in fallacies" and directly questioned the truthfulness of the conversion statistics. Summing up the overall message of the book, it mocked, "'Conversion' to heterosexuality is possible more than half the time. You could change if you wanted to." The most painful reaction came from the scientific and medical community, which questioned the sampling methods and their validity. If a study relied on homosexuals willing to spend $2,500 over two weeks to "reverse" their homosexuality, "then you've got a hopelessly biased, self-selected sample skewed in favor of success," said John Money of Johns Hopkins University Medical School, an expert on sexual identity. Even Judd Marmor, the past president of the American Psychiatric Association who had asked for Masters's help in eliminating homosexuality from its list of mental illnesses a few years earlier, questioned their results. "I would doubt very much that you could reverse a group of [Kinsey] 6 persons in two weeks," said Marmor.

Controversy over conversion therapy continued for decades. Numerous charlatans and religious zealots, pointing to Masters and Johnson's claims of success, created "ex-gay" programs designed to "cure" homosexuals. Over the next three decades, Christian Coalition founder Pat Robertson and the Reverend Jerry Falwell, among many others, supported programs designed to convert homosexuals away from sin and into the arms of God-fearing heterosexuality. In 2006, the Catholic Medical Association declared that scientific research, including the Masters and Johnson study, "counters the myth that same-sex attraction is genetically predetermined and unchangeable and offers hope for prevention and treatment." During the 2008 presidential campaign, the Alaska church attended by Republican vice presidential candidate Sarah Palin promoted a local conference on gay conversion through prayer put on by Focus on the Family, the national Christian fundamentalist organization run by Dr. James Dobson. "Sex researchers Masters and Johnson (hardly a pair of standard-bearers for the traditional view!) said the 'homosexuality cannot be changed' concept was 'certainly open to question,'" claimed Dobson's group on its Web site, citing as a footnote *Homosexuality in Perspective,* nearly three decades after its publication. In the meantime, nearly every medical professional group eventually opposed this conversion therapy and said claims of success could not be replicated in other studies. Indeed by 2007 the American Medical Association said it officially "opposes the use of 'reparative' or 'conversion' therapy that is based on the assumption that homosexuality per se is a mental disorder or based upon the a priori assumption that the patient should change his/her homosexual orientation." Paul Gebhard of the Kinsey Institute wondered why no one ever stopped Masters from embarrassing himself in this case. "That's my one big disappointment with M&J," Gebhard said of this third book. "I have a high respect for Kolodny and I'm a little surprised that he went along with that 'curing' of the homosexuals."

Masters felt confident their book would be embraced eventually, just as the two earlier books had. He believed most criticism came from the Freudian analytic community, which complained the two-week treatment was too simplistic, far from sufficient in understanding the riddles of a patient's sex life. For all of its limitations in size and scope, many of which he acknowledged, Masters felt the prospect of conversion therapy offered more hope, more freedom to patients than psychoanalysis ever could. "The criticisms are based on old concepts," Masters replied dismissively to the press. "We're reporting on ten years of work with five years of follow-up—and it works."

Among the closest staffers, including Kolodny, there remained a sense of bewilderment about why Masters had pushed his theories on conversion and reversion so hard, so incessantly beyond the point of believability. In the past, Masters had been a visionary, a bit strident in his views, but always with ample documentation. How could he leave the institute so vulnerable this time? The media carried some criticisms but never attacked the book's fundamental integrity. No one had any idea of the worry inside the clinic itself. "At this point, I had basically come to the conclusion that Bill's theories about conversion therapy were more a figment of his imagination than a data-collected therapeutic study, so that really threw me for a loop," recalled Kolodny, about the possible ramifications. "Clearly, it was a change in the way their work was accepted or received by both the profession and by the public."

Embarrassed and upset by the whole experience, Johnson vowed never to let Masters put her in such a position again. By the early 1980s, she returned as more of a presence at the clinic. "Gini felt that he was beginning to become a little bit of a loose cannon, a little danger in being able to make decisions," Kolodny said. "And certainly she tried from that point on to grab much more control of the reins of the institute." That power shift was most evident by 1982, when the Masters and Johnson Institute moved from its offices at 4910 Forest Park Boulevard to a new, sleek location nearby. Johnson oversaw the entire production and approved the floor map. From then on, there would be no doubt where all the major decisions would be made. "Gini took the larger, fancier corner office and gave Bill a much smaller office," recalled Kolodny. "It was very symbolic."

When outsiders pointed out this reversal in roles, Masters tried to make light of it. "I hired her to work for me and now I work for her—but that's fine," Masters replied when a female St. Louis reporter inquired. "I was the world's worst administrator. I enjoy the research side, the clinical side."

CHAPTER THIRTY-THREE

The Promise of a Future

Regal in a black gown, Virginia Johnson strolled into the elegant hotel ballroom on Bill Masters's arm, basking like a matron queen in the admiring glow of nearly four hundred guests who stood and clapped loudly. Around the nation, Masters and Johnson had been celebrated and paid tribute, but they'd never experienced a reception like this in their hometown of St. Louis. Even Masters, with his stone-faced demeanor, couldn't resist a grin.

Inside the Park Terrace Hilton, the orchestra played a slight timpani as the night's master of ceremonies introduced them. A sense of overdue recognition by an entire city pervaded this evening in November 1984, including a proclamation from Missouri's Republican governor, Kit Bond. Prominent at this $250-per-person dinner dance were local Congressman George Hoblitzelle, whose daughter was delivered by Masters, and *Playboy's* new female president, Christie Hefner, a member of their board of trustees. "Two of our most distinguished St. Louisans have not been publicly honored here at all," declared Webster University president Leigh Gerdine, chairman of the dinner, to the crowd, "even while the rest of the world applauds."

The twenty-fifth anniversary celebration of Masters and Johnson's study of human sexuality was very much Virginia's night. She arranged every detail, from the burgundy-covered tables with oversized crystal rose bowls and white gardenias to the gaggle of press photographers snapping their picture. Along with the clinic's day-to-day operations, she now managed their public image. Onlookers were astounded at how she made sure the three important men from her life—Dr. Masters, Judge Noah Weinstein, and her former husband, George Johnson, whose orchestra provided the evening's music—got along so well at the event. "It was the only time I met Mr. Johnson—he was like one of those people on a ship who smiles all the time," recalled June Dobbs Butts. On this lovely night, bad memories from St. Louis dissolved. Forgotten were the harassing midnight phone calls, the professional snubs, Washington University's studied distance from their clinic, the snide insinuations and rumors of sordid activities behind closed doors. Even if the city's salute was tardy, Masters and Johnson expressed thanks. "We've always felt that the work was best originated and maintained here in the Midwest," she told the *St. Louis Post-Dispatch,* the city's biggest newspaper.

Masters's speech sounded like a valedictory. As he neared age seventy, his eyes appeared more hollow and distant, his shoulders stooped and hunched. His bow tie now hung from his collar like a wilted flower no longer in bloom. "The tincture of time has taken over," he said softly into the microphone. "I've lived long enough. My opposition has been somewhat neutralized—some even buried." The crowd rippled with gentle laughter at Masters's blunt but truthful assessment of his critics. He spoke like a man whose work was complete. "It's time to turn it over to younger people," he told the crowd. "I'll probably do this with relatively poor grace, but it's time."

Looking instead to the future, Johnson, at age fifty-nine, was enjoying the most glorious time of her life, reaping the sort of acclaim and personal fortune few professionals ever enjoy. Her husband might seem to be retiring, but Johnson, as lively and intense as ever, wasn't ready to fade away. "I don't think it would be incorrect to say Bill does long to live by a body of water in the sun and sand," she assured an interviewer, "but not enough to abandon something that works for us."

To the increasingly sex-obsessed American media, Virginia Johnson remained a figure of fascination, a mature and worldly woman who seemed to understand many of life's deepest mysteries. "At the time she was talking about sex, that was revolutionary," recalled Helen Gurley Brown, then editor of *Cosmopolitan,* who beseeched Virginia to discuss her personal life for the magazine.

"She was sound and wise and convincing. She had everything to do with what we were talking about with female sexuality."

Writer Gay Talese, in preparing his book *Thy Neighbor's Wife*, a firsthand account of America's sexual revolution, had attempted a few years earlier to get Masters and Johnson to unveil their lives together.

"How often do you make love?" Talese inquired after they finished a speech before the American Society of Newspaper Editors convention.

Johnson smiled at Talese as though he was a naughty boy. "Who keeps count?" she replied demurely. Several hundred delighted newspapermen burst into applause.

Masters and Johnson were both ubiquitous by name and yet personally hard to pin down. Their fame, a source of instant recognition, became fodder for cartoonists and late-night comedians. *"Look, friend, people go to St. Louis other than to see Drs. Masters and Johnson,"* read the caption on a *New Yorker* magazine cartoon, one of several framed and put on the clinic's interior walls. In another, a doctor in a white lab coat informed a skeptical young woman, *"Well, the machine says you had one!"* Still another showed two middle-aged women gazing in a bookstore window at a copy of *Human Sexual Response. "With my Harold,"* one lady told the other, *"I'd welcome a response of any kind!"*

Despite constant offers in the 1970s and 1980s, Masters and Johnson declined Johnny Carson's late-night variety show ("We don't want to be between Jackie Mason and a tap dancer," she explained) or to face a prime-time grilling by Mike Wallace on *60 Minutes.* Instead, they appeared on Phil Donahue's morning show from Chicago and on the syndicated Mike Douglas chatfest in Philadelphia, where they felt more relaxed. Sex in the midday carried a certain titillating appeal to the audience. Although daytime television was still sedate, certainly compared to the tabloid standards of later years, Donahue recognized Masters and Johnson as a ratings-grabber. "He would call us constantly," recalled Johnson about the genial host with a shock of white hair and wide, aviator-like eyeglasses. She felt Donahue acted smarmy, playing to an uptight American double standard. "He could embarrass easily," said Johnson. While Masters acted remote and persnickety with television interviewers, Johnson loved playing the diva, thriving on their massive public acclaim and its financial rewards. "I suppose my need to be a star—the love of being a star—was a little high, I'll have to admit to that," she said, recalling how eventually even cabbies in New York knew her by name.

Fame never translated to fortune, however. By the early 1980s, the Masters and Johnson Institute had dwindled into a money-loser, with its two partners unable to find an easy solution. In 1983, the institute posted a $226,000 deficit, and the following year, despite an increase in their patient fee structure, they collected barely enough to maintain their staff and facility. The steady proliferation of sex therapy clinics around the nation eroded the need for expensive treatment in St. Louis. Their waiting list, which once stretched months, dwindled to a few weeks. Nearly 85 percent of those at the institute first sought treatment somewhere else. Sufferers from such common "dysfunctions" as frigidity and premature ejaculation were now far more conversant about such matters than the previous generation. They learned to cure themselves by reading graphic how-to manuals purchased at the local bookstore or by seeing their neighborhood physician or therapist. In fact, while the twenty-fifth anniversary party reminded the world of Masters and Johnson's landmark contributions, the evening's main purpose was to raise $5 million through a series of events first in St. Louis, and later in New York, Los Angeles, and other cities. Government funding for sex-related studies at the institute remained virtually nonexistent, just as it had for decades. As Johnson informed the crowd that night, an endowment would allow them to continue "the work as we know it, risk-taking and daring work that others may not be able to do."

Money remained a constant worry, aggravated by Bill and Gini's lack of business savvy, recalled board member Donna Wilkinson. Both researchers "didn't like to ask for money, so that made it difficult to raise it if you don't want to ask for it." In 1983, the institute's board finally approved an organized effort to raise funds. "Should they retire, we want to make sure that the Institute and their work continues," said Daniel J. Sullivan, the clinic's first director of development at the time of the fund-raiser. But the clinic had trouble identifying large sources of reliable funding outside of a handful of grateful former patients. When business ventures related to their work were offered, Masters and Johnson often resisted, as they did when Kolodny suggested franchising their clinics. In the 1980s, with the advent of home video, Masters and Johnson were presented with a $1.5 million proposal by Time-Life for a series of tapes illustrating their celebrated methods. But the couple balked at the bid, convinced it wasn't enough money. Even though the clinic was running a deficit, they worried about selling themselves short. Masters listened to the cautious advice of the institute's lawyer, Walter Metcalfe, and didn't seem all that interested in the proposal, while Johnson seemed preoccupied by other matters.

Masters and Johnson remained wary of being exploited and of those who would make a buck off their name. While the level of chicanery in the sex therapy industry certainly invited caution and reasonable doubts, their apprehensiveness sometimes hurt valued colleagues who were legitimately trying to advance their careers. In the 1970s, for example, Marshall and Peggy Shearer informed Masters of their upcoming book called *Rapping About Sex,* based on their previously taped public discussions with college students on campus. On the back cover, they planned to mention their current affiliation with the Masters and Johnson clinic until Bill expressed his displeasure. "He thought we were using their name for our own gain," recalled Peggy. Marshall argued that every author cites his or her background on a dust jackets, yet Masters remained adamant. A few months later, the Shearers decided to return to Michigan, despite Masters and Johnson's urgings to stay in St. Louis.

Kolodny had nothing to gain directly from the Time-Life video proposal, other than ensuring the promise of a future for the institute, where he'd worked for more than a decade. He had become the clinic's associate director overseeing training. He also supervised Joan Bauman and others in the endocrine research section, studying the impact of illicit and prescription drugs on sexual function and how chronic illnesses such as diabetes, cancer, and hypertension affected sexual well-being. Aside from his considerable talents as a doctor, Kolodny possessed a certain knack for business and for being a writer. He put together the book resulting from Masters and Johnson's 1977 seminar on ethical issues in sex therapy, and would collaborate with them on several other professional books, including a 1982 college textbook called *Human Sexuality*. Years later in his unpublished autobiography, Masters called Kolodny a "uniquely talented individual" and conceded he did "most of the writing for a number of books we have published together."

For years, Masters indicated Kolodny would be his successor, the "heir apparent," as *Time* magazine designated him, though Johnson remained uneasy about this impending change. Without an advanced degree of her own, she needed to rely on a licensed physician—either Kolodny or someone with his credentials—to help supervise the clinic if her husband retired. She couldn't do it alone, even though Masters became increasingly detached from daily decisions and allowed her great latitude on medical-related matters. After years of accompanying Masters to scientific meetings, Kolodny had a standing among professionals in their field that almost rivaled hers, especially after he won a prestigious national professional service award. "There was tension," recalled Donna Wilkinson, who at first dismissed the friction between Johnson and Kolodny as the natural outcome among highly intelligent, motivated minds. "Bob started to receive a lot of recognition and deservedly so. While that wasn't so bothersome to Bill—because I think Bill felt 'This is my boy,' as a pupil I have nurtured—it was a little more threatening to Gini."

Kolodny, a tall, dark-haired man who grew a mustache to make himself appear a bit older, took personal pride in being trained by the best—both at Harvard and under the tutelage of Masters, whom he once idolized as a farsighted genius. He spoke and acted with deliberate precision and had trouble hiding his distaste for mediocrity in the staff or with Johnson's unprofessional indulgences. Of the several books that bore their names jointly, he later claimed, "I don't believe Gini ever read any of them." While a handful of staffers were talented, Kolodny couldn't understand why so many lacked the kind of solid medical training he thought necessary for the clinic's success. Some never had experience with therapy, some had little idea about human physiology or anatomy, and some had backgrounds in unrelated areas, such as theology. "For a certain level of expertise, it costs money, and I don't think they [Masters and Johnson] wanted anyone else to shine," said Wilkinson, who admired Kolodny's professionalism. But Kolodny soon had a rival when Mark Schwartz joined the staff in the mid-1970s. With his long, blond hair and cool, confident demeanor, Schwartz's excellent skills as a therapist and his doctorate in psychology from Johns Hopkins made him a genuine alternative to Kolodny's earnest but more stolid approach. "Everybody expected Kolodny to do that [become the heir apparent to Masters] because Kolodny made it known, and when Mark [Schwartz] came along, there was kind of a tension there because I think Mark thought that he was going to be," recalled Mae Biggs-Lonergan, who worked with both as a staff therapist.

As a trusted adviser, Kolodny once was directed by Masters to tell him if he had bent the rules too far or if time had sapped his mental or physical abilities. Soon after he returned from Harvard in 1972, Kolodny remembered, Masters talked metaphorically about aging football players who didn't know when to hang up their cleats. In a long stream of thought, Bill mentioned surgeons who kept the knife in their hands longer than they should. Then he grabbed Kolodny on the forearm and looked him straight in the eye. "I'm going to demand that you do this for me," he said quite solemnly. "We're going to work together for a long time. If you see me starting to lose it, I want you to sit me down and tell me that I have to be put out to pasture. It's going to be your responsibility to prevent me from embarrassing myself."

Although the soliloquy seemed melodramatic, Kolodny realized Masters's abiding sense of himself, that confident air of superiority he carried throughout his career, wouldn't allow for slippage, for anything less than what he'd always been. As Masters grew older, when he wasn't as sharp, especially in public, where he once dazzled, Kolodny didn't have the heart to tell his mentor. Certainly if Kolodny intended to become his successor, he couldn't insist that Masters slow down or quit seeing patients altogether, not without appearing self-serving. Besides, Kolodny felt his most important advice affecting the institute's future went virtually ignored. His frustration was never more evident than when he urged Masters and Johnson to move their institute to New York City. In America's media capital, he contended, their reputation would be enhanced, their innovative therapies further embraced by the medical community, and they would gain many more patients. In one memo marked *"Advantages of NYC Office,"* Kolodny contended the institute would be "more appealing to international clientele" and could "increase fundraising." Kolodny's family ties to New York undoubtedly made the idea appealing to him. Given Bill and Gini's propensity for moving—they sold their Ladue house to move to a succession of other homes in St. Louis—the idea of transferring made sense. But Johnson said she wouldn't dream of moving to New York—a wrenching dislocation from their longtime base to a place where they would likely face increased criticism, especially from the die-hard Freudians. Plenty of New York programs already used their techniques, including Helen Singer Kaplan at Cornell, Alex Levay at Columbia, and Sallie Schumacher on Long Island. Neither Johnson nor Masters wanted to start over again, not at this point in their lives. There also remained another unspoken concern. Though they both had come to rely heavily on Kolodny, Johnson still didn't trust him. "He's very clever and has a driving need to dominate the situation," she recalled years later. "He wanted to take the whole thing to New York and go back on his home ground. And curiously enough, we were happy for him to take it over." (But only, they insisted, if he agreed to stay in St. Louis.) Gini felt strongly their clinic benefited from its Midwest roots. "If we had gone back into the eastern, old-line medical world, we would have had to re-create ourselves and I'm not sure we would have been very well received," she said.

In the end, Kolodny decided to plan his own farewell. In a meticulous memo, he outlined all of the tasks he performed and supervised, and what the credentials of his successor should be. He moved to Connecticut with his then-wife, Nancy, and their young daughters, opening his own behavioral medicine clinic. Kolodny agreed to remain on the institute's board and to occasionally fly back to St. Louis for a meeting. He would also continue his writing collaboration with Masters and Johnson, including an upcoming book called *Masters and Johnson on Sex and Human Loving,* which proved quite successful.

But by the time of Bill and Gini's anniversary gala in 1984, when all of St. Louis seemed to recognize their success, Dr. Robert C. Kolodny—the would-be heir apparent and all that he represented for the clinic's future—was gone.

CHAPTER THIRTY-FOUR

Beauty and the Beast

"Every movement she made, every shuffle and ripple, helped me to conceal and improve the secret system of tactile correspondence between beast and beauty—between my gagged, bursting beast and the beauty of her dimpled body in its innocent cotton frock."

—VLADIMIR NABOKOV, *LOLITA*

Naked on the bed, Maureen Sullivan murmured to her client to move closer, enough so their skin could touch. Her words of instruction were as gentle and inviting as her caress.

Near the headboard, Sullivan sat up Indian-style, like some irresistible goddess of eros, looking face to face at this anxious young man. Inside their cozy room at the Chase Park Plaza Hotel, the lights remained on. The blankets were pushed down near the foot of the bed so there was nowhere to hide between the sheets. Then she placed her smooth, tanned legs over each of his knees so that their genitals nearly joined.

At age twenty-seven with curly, light brown hair, her breasts full and upright, Sullivan resembled an aerobics teacher, exuding infectious enthusiasm. With her athletic good looks, Sullivan smiled constantly like a trained professional, paid by her client under the direction of therapists at the world-renowned Masters and Johnson Institute.

When the moment appeared right, Sullivan grasped her client's limp penis, authoritatively and without hesitation, rubbing it against her vulva and labia. An air of anticipation existed between them, but she issued no demands. Only when she felt him ready—

what the Masters and Johnson textbook described as the flow of vasocongestion through his penile arteries, inflating and elevating his flaccid tissue—did Sullivan move to the next position on this guided tour.

"Now I will get on top and put your penis in my vagina—just for you to feel," she whispered to him. "Don't try to thrust. Don't try to do nothin'. *Just feel.*"

As a sex surrogate, Sullivan engaged in "genital pleasuring" near the end of her two-week employment with genuine sensitivity and impressive effectiveness. Leading up to this moment, she and her client had spent several days of "sensate focus" therapy as prescribed by Masters and Johnson's techniques.

Penetration was barely the point. During both morning and afternoon sessions, they rubbed, nuzzled, nibbled, fondled, and sometimes kissed virtually each area of their bodies, without the expectation of intercourse. They sometimes stood in front of full-length mirrors and examined each other. As Sullivan explained, the touching exercises removed the fear and ignorance of a woman's body for these worried men. "And you do it to them too," she recalled. "You show them how the testicles are like the ovaries, the scrotum is like the larger labia, and how the penis is like the clitoris. So they feel that it's not strange territory."

The men who relied on Sullivan's expertise generally suffered from "erectile dysfunction," the new jargon for impotence, or from premature ejaculation, or were virgins whose fear of performance kept them from being with a woman. For these men, Sullivan became a miracle worker. She didn't require any satisfaction on her part and appeared fully dedicated to achieving theirs. "I thought I was Wonder Woman," she said. By the time they arrived at the "genital pleasuring" stage, Sullivan focused on the client's erect member, stroking it like an artist's brush along her own genitalia. "It's called 'painting'—you take their penis and paint yourself," she explained. Her words of encouragement were meant to transform the futile into the fulsome. "And if it [the penis] starts to go down, you go back to hand caresses. If it stays hard, well, then you might just flip it in. You're in control but you don't kind of advertise that that's what you're going to do. You kind of surprise 'em, when they're not looking!" she explained wryly.

Sullivan's *joie de vivre* made her a favorite of Bill Masters for his most desperate cases. Along with the institute's usual $5,000 fee, patients paid nearly double to retain the services of this California-based woman or a handful of other surrogates Masters surreptitiously provided in the mid-1980s. These arrangements were far more secretive than in the early days, mainly because Masters and Johnson had publicly disavowed the practice. Painfully, they learned surrogate sex therapy, which they originally championed in the 1960s, could now lead to scorn and even mockery. "My method is basically the same principle as Masters and Johnson's," argued former New York City madam Xaviera Hollander in *The Happy Hooker,* her popular book from that era. "Only they charge thousands and it's called therapy. I charge fifty dollars and it's called prostitution." Since their ethics seminar in 1976, Masters and Johnson repeatedly indicated to the press and fellow professionals that they no longer relied on surrogates for their patients. Masters worried some might act as untrained therapists, unaware of how they could create emotional harm. "For legal and ethical reasons, Masters and Johnson have discontinued the surrogates program," reported the *New York Times'* Jane E. Brody in 1980. *Newsweek* said they had "abandoned the practice, and today most therapists think that surrogates aren't necessary—or even beneficial." Following Masters and Johnson's example, the American Psychological Association and the American Association of Marriage and Family Therapists said therapists who allowed their clients to use surrogates were breaking ethical rules, even though no formal policy condemned it. Most reputable professionals agreed with Masters and Johnson's stance. By the 1980s, mainstream therapists believed surrogates posed an unreasonable risk to their license and possible criminal prosecution. "I personally would never do it," explained Dr. Ruth Westheimer. "I can see a justification for that, but I would never be involved in that because it's not legal."

Very few knew Masters continued to rely on surrogates or that his belief in their effectiveness had never wavered. Despite the legal risk and personal duplicity, Masters wasn't going to forgo this treatment. "The physician always wants to improve the patient, regardless of the method used," explained his friend, Paul Gebhard of the Kinsey Institute.

Along with Maureen Sullivan, Masters and Johnson patients relied on other female surrogates who flew into St. Louis from around the country, paid to sexually resuscitate a man they'd never met before. Surrogates like Vena Blanchard, then a divorcée in her early twenties from the Los Angeles suburbs, knew Masters's clandestine actions contradicted his public position. "The truth is, after they officially stopped working with surrogates, they continued but they referred clients to [surrogate] people and the clients made their own contracts," explained Blanchard, who later became president of a surrogates support group. Although Masters often dealt directly with them, Blanchard said, the famous doctor kept an arm's-length from the exchange of money and other logistical matters between surrogates and his patients. "It was kept very hush-hush because they'd been advised that there was some risk," Blanchard remembered. "They had a legal contract with everyone to keep it secret."

While Blanchard said she received payment for only one case in St. Louis, Sullivan and another surrogate named "Ann from Florida" handled several more. Rather than looking askance at this doctor playing fast and loose with the law and professional guidelines, Blanchard admired Masters. "He actually said that at some point they were torn about it," said Blanchard, "but he couldn't in all good conscience deprive clients of a treatment that would work for them, the *only* thing that would work for them."

Maureen Sullivan claimed to be the highest paid surrogate in Southern California when she sent a "résumé" to the Masters and Johnson clinic, listing her previous experience and training with sex therapist William Hartman, a licensed marriage counselor. Though Hartman's approach could be controversial—he and his partner, Marilyn Fithian, sometimes coached partially dressed clients about their caressing techniques—he offered formal training for women like Sullivan who worked as surrogates. At Long Beach State University, Sullivan, then an anthropology major from Englewood, took a class in human sexuality taught by Hartman and soon enlisted in his efforts. "I had no career in mind, so I got some clients from Bill Hartman and I figured, 'What the hell, I'll give it a try!'" explained Sullivan. She quickly built up a list of sixteen clients a week, collecting a then-hefty sum of $300 a day as a sex surrogate.

In California, Sullivan heard so much about Masters and Johnson that she figured their wealthy clients would be willing to pay top dollar for her services. She received a prompt acceptance soon after mailing her credentials, but Masters also asked for a photo. Sullivan resisted. "Screw you, I'm not sending you no picture," Sullivan thought to herself at that time. "It doesn't matter what I look like—I'm a surrogate and that's all there is to it. Here's my training."

Masters told her "this client was champing on the bit to know what I was looking like, and he wouldn't sign up with them unless he saw me," she recalled. "He just wouldn't do it. So I finally sent him a picture."

Soon after, Masters called her from St. Louis to say the patient wanted to schedule a visit.

"I don't see why you didn't send us the photo in the first place," said Masters in his most charming voice. "You're very good-looking."

"Well, that's not why I was sending it," Sullivan said in her equally blunt, almost tomboy style.

The rest of their conversation revolved around money. "If you pay me $300 a day with my expenses, then I'm there," Sullivan said she told him. "I got paid three thousand dollars a client [for the ten-day period]. It was a price that I set because that's what I made at home." When she arrived in St. Louis, Dr. Robert Kolodny conducted a gynecological exam before allowing any therapy sessions with a patient. Kolodny, who would soon depart for the East Coast, remained ambivalent about the use of surrogates but deferred to Masters, who thought highly of Sullivan's abilities. "Bill clearly felt that, of the various surrogates that men had found on their own, she was probably the best one, the most qualified," Kolodny recalled.

In a career encompassing about three hundred cases, Sullivan said, she performed as a surrogate "at least a half dozen times" in St. Louis. She became so familiar that she stowed a bicycle next to the copying machine at the clinic, to relax and ride around the Forest Park lake when in town. "I was getting kind of adopted like a daughter in some ways," she recalled. Sullivan, who had taken psychology courses, realized that becoming a surrogate brought pleasure and happiness to others, in a way she hadn't always experienced in her own life. "I was still in my twenties, still finding out who I was," she reflected. "I wasn't a lost soul as a surrogate—I was a lost soul *before* I was a surrogate. My dad was a wife beater. I never saw my parents with much affection." Working as a surrogate, under the direction of older physicians who suggested what to do, somehow filled a psychological need in Sullivan. "I came from a dysfunctional family and when I took Bill Hartman's class and started learning about relationships and love—I needed a dad," she explained.

Surrogates, for all of their intimate moments with patients, were expected to be unemotional instruments of the supervising therapy team. They weren't supposed to make treatment decisions or psychological assessments. "I was kind of a meat-and-potatoes surrogate," she explained. "When they were having psychological problems, the therapist would generally try and deal with that, before they got to me." Surrogates were mindful of transference, the concern that a patient might become emotionally tied to them. In one case, however, Sullivan committed a fundamental mistake—she fell in love with her client.

A wealthy out-of-town lawyer about thirty years old hired Sullivan to help him with "ED," standard code for impotence. "Masters and Johnson told you very little about a client, because I was not the one calling the shots," Sullivan recounted. The young attorney generously paid for separate rooms at the Chase Park Plaza, which allowed her to sleep alone and have some privacy when they were not at the clinic or engaged in sensate exercises in his suite. Over two weeks, Sullivan spent more time than she ever anticipated just talking with this client, eating at restaurants and walking through the park. As one of two strangers wandering the city together, Sullivan felt herself falling in love with this nearly anonymous man, grateful to her for restoring his manhood. As a surrogate, she'd always kept physical relations distinct from her personal feelings, but this case seemed different. "That was a rarity—it was not professional at all," she recalled. "It was my neediness. A professional surrogate wouldn't do that. Those feelings shouldn't happen. I fell in love with this guy, just like anybody else does."

As her client's sessions ended, she confided her feelings to Mark Schwartz, the therapist in charge of their case, explaining how they had grown emotionally attached while having sex. Schwartz recognized the dilemma and gave her simple advice.

"Just think of this as a summer romance and go your separate ways," he suggested, as she recalled their conversation.

Sullivan said she had little choice. "What else were we going to do? I'm a surrogate. I can't break my ethics. Having the feelings is OK. You can't stop your feelings. It's unprofessional, though, to act on it."

Sullivan flew home to Southern California and the lawyer went back home, to a location she never learned.

"And now, here's Johnny!"

On September 9, 1982, the *Tonight Show Starring Johnny Carson* featured the comedian host with his sidekick announcer, Ed McMahon. Conductor Doc Severinsen led the NBC band and a guest, actor George Segal, played the banjo. During his opening monologue, Carson cracked several jokes about California, Doc's pants, President Ronald Reagan, Mount Rushmore, and the pro football strike. With his last humorous comment, Carson mentioned his show's other guest that night—Maureen Sullivan.

When she parked next to Carson for an interview, Sullivan discussed her life as a sex surrogate with remarkable candor. They chatted about how she found her job, the type of problems she faced, the age range of the men she worked with, and what it was like to become physically involved with a client. At one point, she demonstrated a hand caress as Carson mugged to the camera, amusing his nationwide audience. Sullivan told the TV host that sex surrogates were usually found on either America's West or East Coasts. She never mentioned her stops in the Midwest at the famed Masters and Johnson clinic. The Carson show became just one of several television appearances for Sullivan, as word spread of her media availability. She became the most prominent woman in this notorious area of sex therapy, building up a network of surrogates around the country. "I was on the fast track," she boasted.

Back in St. Louis, however, Sullivan caused considerable uneasiness. If she somehow slipped and mentioned their institute, a scandal would erupt. Despite their respect for Masters's past achievements, his closest associates now worried the surreptitious dealings with Sullivan and other women threatened the hard-earned reputation of the institute and everyone associated with it. Masters had spent his career pressing the outer limits, outsmarting his critics and the guardians of moral codes. But now he seemed oblivious to reality, that they could be rightly accused of the rankest hypocrisy and questionable ethical judgments. He believed no one would ever find out. His secret arrangements with Sullivan and other surrogates were "an example of his insanity," said Mark Schwartz. He recalled patients—such as "a thirty-year-old virgin with no social skills"—who had their lives transformed by surrogates, even though it was "pure prostitution by law" at the time. "It was a catch-22: They were never going to find a partner if they were impotent and they were never going to be able to reverse their impotence if they didn't have a partner," Schwartz explained. "It was the key to his success but he was so close to the edge all the time that he asked for trouble."

Perhaps most upset about the surrogacy scheme was Gini Johnson herself. Although she once had excelled at recruiting female volunteers for their program, she became convinced surrogates weren't worth the risk. The nasty lawsuit involving Barbara Calvert's husband had nearly destroyed them. "I thought it was fraught with liability and so forth," remembered Johnson, who was wary of being sued again. "But he still insisted on doing it every now and then, knowing how I felt about it." She warned him the institute must not become a clearinghouse for these possibly illegal liaisons.

Donna Martini, the clinic's bookkeeper, often dealt with surrogates. Shortly after being hired in 1982, Martini got wind of the public deception. "When people would ask if they had surrogates, they would always say no—but they did, at times," she said. "They were never real open about the surrogate program." With each patient, Martini accepted the clinic's standard fee and then she collected a second check, exchanging additional money with the surrogate. She remembers at least four women who were paid in this way. "I never got a receipt because they didn't want a paper trail," she explained. Wanda Bowen, Johnson's chief administrative aide, made sure Martini kept her mouth shut about the surrogate program and anything she might witness. "People were always interested in what was going on," Martini recalled. "Wanda used to say, 'Now, if anyone asks you where you work, you just say I work for a doctor in the Central West End.' I never could understand that, but she was sort of secretive."

Sexually transmitted diseases with surrogates carried as much concern as the transmission of money. In August 1982, *Time* heralded the spread of genital herpes—calling it "Today's Scarlet Letter," with a big red "H" on the magazine cover. Within a year, the emergence of the deadly AIDS virus posed an even greater threat, particularly because men with erectile difficulties rarely used condoms. On the job, Sullivan had never before relied on prophylactics. "I had birth control pills for my own personal life, but we didn't do a whole lot with rubbers back then," she recalled. "It wasn't until AIDS came out in the early 1980s that rubbers became a necessity." No longer did Sullivan, sobered by the threat of infection, giddily suggest successful patients slip one in unprotected. The fear of contracting a fatal disease soured the surrogate experience for patients expecting sex. "It was terrible and scary at the very beginning," Sullivan explained. "We tried to defocus on intercourse because the important part was not the penetration but everything leading up to it. A good client is going to quit before he gets to penetration. He's going to find a woman on his own."

Ultimately, neither disease nor money ended Sullivan's career. In 1984, at her height as a successful surrogate, she visited St. Louis for two separate cases, with a brief weekend stint in between. On a whim, she decided on a short vacation, traveling many miles to a health spa near Kansas City. Returning to St. Louis, she kept driving through a snowstorm, determined to keep her second appointment. On the slippery highway, her rental crashed with another car spinning out of control. In the head-on collision, Sullivan's face hit the steering wheel. She crushed the whole left side of her skull, along with other devastating injuries. "No eye socket, no nose, no cheekbone, too numerous punctures in my abdomen to count, collapsed lungs," she recounted, "and I was unconscious for seven weeks."

In St. Louis, news of Sullivan's near-fatal accident stirred recriminations once more. If the story of the California-based sex surrogate leaked out, the national media undoubtedly would discover her business plans in Missouri, placing the Masters and Johnson program in jeopardy. Gini again voiced her objections to Bill.

Eventually Sullivan's bicycle was shipped back to California while she endured months of surgery and rehab therapy on her broken bones. Sullivan tried to keep her surrogate career alive, without much luck. "I didn't have many [clients after the accident]—I didn't have sixteen clients a week, that's for sure," Sullivan said ruefully. "I had seventeen reconstructive surgeries on my face, every three months. So I really couldn't see a client on an ongoing basis, because I was going to therapy and having my face reconstructed. I was really smashed up after the surgery."

With her gorgeous face now disfigured, Sullivan realized the anonymous men looked at her much differently than before. No longer did she hold the same allure. She stared in the mirror and knew her life would never be the same. It was a cruel lesson on beauty's part in the equation between love and sex. "I didn't realize that was probably why I was getting so many clients," she observed. "I thought it was because I was going to conferences and because I'm sending out résumés. Nah, it was because I was young and good-looking. Who do you think you're kidding? They say men are more turned on visually."

Months later, Masters visited California for a lecture at the University of California–Los Angeles. When she heard about it, Sullivan made sure to attend. After the lecture, she walked up to Masters, not sure if he would recognize her. She hadn't been in contact with him since leaving the hospital. He politely asked about her recovery—and then asked if she was still willing to work as a surrogate. "When he saw me, he said, 'I got a case—can you come out?'" Sullivan recalled.

None of the Masters and Johnson cases were easy, and this new one posed a particular challenge for Sullivan. He was a wealthy young man who happened to be a pedophile. Like some real-life Humbert Humbert in *Lolita*, this client was obsessed with underage female children of prostitutes he met in his hometown. "He's out there picking up hookers and screwing their daughters and thinking he's their savior," Sullivan said. "In his mind, he would pretend that he was their daddy and buy them bicycles and nice presents and all that stuff. And he would diddle them on the side. He felt he was 'rescuing' these kids, these little girls, from their mothers who were selling them off for sex." As Sullivan recalled, this client landed in trouble, with an extended stay at Masters and Johnson as part of his court-ordered rehabilitation. "When I heard about the case, one side of me said, 'What a joke—this isn't going to work,'" she remembered. "But I said, 'Why not give it a try? What's there to lose?'"

Instead of the usual ten-day surrogate sessions, Masters wanted Sullivan to live with the client for three months. His socialite family compensated Sullivan $10,000 for her services. During his extended stay, this young, somewhat overweight man lived in a spacious condominium with little furniture. Masters wanted to realign this young man's pedophilia, turning his alleged taste for little girls into an attraction for more physically mature, heterosexual women, represented by Sullivan. "He really wanted this client to get a real sense of living with an adult woman," she said incredulously. "It takes a lot more than just an understanding woman like me to reverse somebody like that, that's for darn sure."

After days of therapy, Sullivan had gone through her whole repertoire of coaxing, coddling, and caressing—all to his supreme discomfort. "One time when we did a back caress, I could feel the sweat pouring off his forehead onto my back," she said. Despite her best efforts in bed, though, Sullivan wasn't able to raise an erection from her client. They spent every hour of every day together until they tired of each other's company. "I was like his roommate, his girlfriend. But he was just so nervous, like a cat. It didn't work. He really didn't have an interest in me. You can't expect every man and woman thrown in a room together to become lovers. I became like a piece of furniture to him."

This failed attempt by Masters turned out to be Sullivan's last gig in St. Louis. She went home with her money, underwent a series of facial reconstruction surgeries that restored her looks, and soon married. During her periodic visits to St. Louis, she'd never gotten to know Virginia Johnson. "I don't remember her being around much," said Sullivan. "She didn't really like it [using surrogates], so she stayed out of the way."

For all the legal and ethical questions surrounding surrogacy—including the emotional toll for a woman involved in such a task—Sullivan "never felt exploited at all" by Masters or anyone on their staff. In retrospect, Sullivan said surrogates performed a much-needed service, especially for lonely, frustrated, and sexually dysfunctional men. Those who condemned the practice often did so out of their own ignorance and fear of sex. "We surrogates are feminists," Sullivan insisted twenty years later. "We're not getting paid for sex. We're getting paid to teach sexuality—and sex is the least of it. But some people are never going to change their minds."

CHAPTER THIRTY-FIVE

Crisis

"The AIDS epidemic has rolled back a big rotting log and revealed all the squirming life underneath it, since it involves, all at once, the main themes of our existence: sex, death, power, money, love, hate, disease and panic."

—EDMUND WHITE

With a sheepish grin, U.S. Attorney General Edwin Meese III stood before the *Spirit of Justice*—a large Art Deco statue of a half-draped Lady Justice with one breast exposed—to announce his commission's 1986 report condemning pornographic images in America. In declaring war on smut, President Ronald Reagan's chief law-enforcement officer insisted the permissive days of the sexual revolution were over.

"Although there are many members of this society who can and have made affirmative cases for uncommitted sexuality, none of us believe it to be a good thing," declared Meese's report, released in a press conference in the Grand Hall of the Department of Justice. In the marketplace of ideas, a *laissez-faire* approach to sex would no longer be tolerated. "Although the evidence may be slim," insisted U.S. Surgeon General Dr. C. Everett Koop, who joined Meese's campaign, "we nevertheless know enough to conclude that pornography does present a clear and present danger to American public health."

To many conservatives, the frank dissemination of sexual information in society, personified by Masters and Johnson, had opened the gates to disease and moral corruption, turning America into a modern-day Sodom and Gomorrah. With avenging certainty, they believed the constant media talk of orgasms and ever-expanding license had resulted in a surge of premarital sex, adultery, abortion, homosexuality, and broken families. Their religious sensibilities were offended by movies and cable television featuring nudity, and talk shows discussing birth control pills, condoms, and vibrators. Some preachers viewed the deadly 1980s AIDS epidemic as a viral thunderbolt from on high, as retribution from God for the sexual insurrection started in the 1960s. "I see a definite spiritual revival that is touching the standards of conduct of the entire society, which has gone too far toward sexual freedom," proclaimed Pat Robertson, a televangelist for the Christian Broadcasting Network, then preparing a run for president in 1988 to succeed Reagan. As society's pendulum swung backward, those like Christie Hefner, chief of Playboy Enterprises and a board member for the Masters and Johnson Institute, publicly challenged the Meese report, only to discover the Justice Department had chilled 7-Eleven shops and other convenience stores from carrying copies of Hefner's magazine. It took a federal lawsuit to get *Playboy* back on the shelves next to the Slurpees.

Masters and Johnson knew better than to comment about the Meese commission. "So many individuals are unable to handle the subject of sex with any degree of objectivity," Masters explained. "I have always felt that the best way to handle any form of public criticism of our research program was to ignore it." By the mid-1980s, however, Masters and Johnson no longer seemed immune to public rebuke. For years, commentators had lavished praise on the two researchers, due to their impressive findings but also because the pair had handled their image skillfully. "Masters was the prototypical godlike figure that people hesitated to challenge," psychiatrist Raul Sciavi told *Time* in 1983. "And people were so taken by the initial optimism about sex therapy that they did not actually look at the long-term data as carefully as they should have." In their books, Masters and Johnson acknowledged several shortcomings, particularly in their sampling of research subjects. Nearly all volunteers were middle-class and college educated, with a "basic interest . . . in sexual performance," meaning that both men and women had generally masturbated to orgasm and experienced premarital sex. Few came from poor, black, or other minority backgrounds. A propensity for sex might not matter regarding anatomy and basic physiology, critics suggested, but it skewed expectations. "In short, Masters and Johnson studied middle-class orgasm enthusiasts (who could climax without a hitch even while being observed in a lab)," observed critic Debbie Nathan. "Hardly a typical group, but with the data they generated, Masters and Johnson elaborated a sexual response cycle that they claimed was gender neutral and applicable to all human beings." June Dobbs Butts, the staff's only African American, tried to broaden the mix but she said many minorities were reluctant to participate in Masters and Johnson's program. "Blacks were almost ashamed to admit they had a problem," Butts said.

As the decade progressed, Masters and Johnson faced increasing skepticism, starting with a 1980 *Psychology Today* attack on Masters and Johnson's purported 80 percent therapy success rate. A cover story by Bernie Zilbergeld and Michael Evans claimed *Human Sexual Inadequacy* relied on loose criteria for judging success and was never replicated by others. "Masters and Johnson's research is so flawed by methodological errors and slipshod reporting that it fails to meet customary standards—and their own—for evaluation research," the authors charged. Zilbergeld, a clinical psychologist in Berkeley, California, and Evans, also a psychologist, didn't fault the physiological findings of *Human Sexual Response.* Instead, they said, a reputation for rigorous scientific research from Masters and Johnson's first book "created a halo effect" that influenced reception to their later work. While they aimed mostly at *Human Sexual Inadequacy,* the two critics also questioned the claim of converting homosexuals to heterosexuality. "Many of their homosexuals weren't really homosexuals," they said of the volunteer sampling, suggesting many were bisexuals or "confused" heterosexuals. (Other critics of *Homosexuality in Perspective* pointed out that little mention was made of rectal intercourse—another sign of the misleading patient sample.) When *Psychology Today* editors asked for a response, Masters and Johnson declined. "It has always been our policy not to reply to criticism in any popular forum," Johnson insisted, a curious stance since so much of their own work appeared in popular books and journals that were not peer-reviewed.

Another dispute occurred in 1983 when editor Philip Nobile of *Forum* magazine, published by Bob Guccione's *Penthouse,* repeated similar allegations. As leaders of the new field of "sexology," Masters and Johnson realized they could no longer dismiss their critics quite so easily.

In *The Journal of Sex Research*, Robert Kolodny prepared a written defense "to clear up several misunderstandings." He emphasized that cases were defined in terms of failure, not success, with statistics compiled in the "*most conservative fashion possible.*" For instance, a dysfunctional man achieving "good, firm erections" on three occasions of intercourse during therapy might seem good news. But if this same man also suffered "three other episodes of erectile failure" during intercourse attempts, he was marked a "failure" in their ledger books. Similarly, a woman failed if she "did not reach orgasm in a consistent fashion during sexual opportunities." Even if a patient's sexual function revived shortly after he or she returned home, or if he or she returned again and became successful on the second try, the patient was still considered a "failure" for statistical purposes. Replicating Masters and Johnson's results was difficult, Kolodny said, because other therapists didn't disclose outcome statistics, didn't follow up thoroughly with patients, or were based on a part-time, once-a-week therapy model rather than their intensive two weeks. Nevertheless, among 1,872 primarily heterosexual cases handled by the team from 1959 to 1977, there was an 81.8 percent "success" rate—a remarkable claim by any standard. By comparison, 86 percent who sought treatment had been in psychotherapy elsewhere for at least six months before knocking on their door, he noted, and "fewer than five percent" improved while waiting to get in.

Before the World Congress of Sexology held in Washington, D.C., in 1983, Kolodny, Masters, and Johnson stressed that other peers had "listened to countless audio tapes of therapy sessions" in assessing the long-term outcome of their therapy and expressed confidence. "There are no so-called 'secrets,'" they insisted. Critics asking for more studies replicating their results didn't seem to understand that Masters and Johnson had accomplished their long-term sex study without any government grants, paying for it with their own private fees. At this convention, they admitted their work "has been less than perfect" but asked that it be "judged in the light of current knowledge, then and now." Most in this emerging field still viewed them as heroes, but even the reverential hoped for more scientific confirmation. "Until we can replicate their work," said psychologist F. Paul Pearsall of the Institute for Sex Research, "we will remain either awed, envious or suspicious of its validity."

After a tiring ride across the Atlantic in March 1988, C. Everett Koop received an urgent message from his wife, Betty, back home. Over the telephone, she warned him of a brewing controversy surrounding Masters and Johnson's latest book, an exposé about the AIDS crisis and its threat to the heterosexual population. "My wife heard on television how it showed that AIDS was transmitted by all these spurious methods," Koop recalled. "She knew very well what I had been telling the public and what my concerns were."

The seventy-one-year-old U.S. surgeon general had flown to London for a medical conference about the emerging AIDS epidemic. During his watch, the deadly virus, contracted mainly through bodily fluid transmission during sex or intravenous needle exchange, had claimed thousands of lives. The first fatalities affected mostly homosexual men—including actor Rock Hudson, a Hollywood friend of President Reagan's—and drug addicts spreading the blood virus through dirty needles. For nearly five years, the Reagan administration stalled in its response to the AIDS plague, which many blamed on the sexual revolution and decaying moral standards. Finally in 1986, Koop launched an AIDS task force and began busily warning the American people about the risks they faced. The bearded former pediatrician, who had once likened abortion to the Holocaust, now found himself on a perilous balancing act, teaching a nation about condoms for AIDS prevention while extolling the virtues of chastity outside of marriage. "During the early days of the AIDS crisis, I had spent a lot of my time telling people not only how you catch AIDS but also, more important for most people, how you *don't* catch it," recalled Koop. "Because there were all kinds of rumors around that mosquitoes did it. Drinking out of the same water glass. Using the same towel. Typewriter keyboards. Briefcase handles. Doorknobs. And all of that was making everybody in the country very jittery."

Their new book, *CRISIS: Heterosexual Behavior in the Age of AIDS,* had been written mainly by Kolodny, but coauthors Masters and Johnson were the familiar faces on television and in press conferences heralding its findings. With a photo of an empty, unmade bed on its cover, *Newsweek* touted excerpts from their "controversial new book." In effect, America's most trusted couple on intimacy was now claiming a government cover-up of a looming sexual problem that could kill anyone. They said at least three million Americans were infected with the virus—twice the official estimate—and that the risks were far greater than government scientists were admitting in a "benevolent deception." According to the book, people could contract the AIDS virus, at least theoretically, through such simple occurrences as mosquito bites, sitting on a toilet seat, French kissing, or any situation where a slight transferal of blood might take place. They warned that undetected AIDS virus infections were "now running rampant in the heterosexual community." Like some Paul Revere awakening a sleeping citizenry, Masters proclaimed, "We are sounding an important warning. A lot of people think we are not in a serious situation. We think we are."

Alerted by his wife, Koop quickly went into action to repudiate the Masters and Johnson book. "I called my good friend Timothy Johnson, who is the medical editor of ABC, and told him the situation and he got me on *Good Morning America,*" said Koop, referring to the network television program where he vilified Masters and Johnson's work. "I told people that everything that I had read in this book and heard about it was wrong. I couldn't believe anybody could be so far off base."

The public reception of the book soon jeopardized Masters and Johnson's reputation. For the second major book in a row, Johnson invested only a minimal amount of herself in coauthorship with Kolodny and Masters. She hadn't been involved in the research in any meaningful way. Instead she went along for the ride, lending her brand name to the venture. She could no longer rely on Masters, as she once did, to check all the assertions and to make sure they were on solid ground, medically and scientifically.

She looked to Kolodny for that task, more than willing to blame him if anything went awry. By then, the clinic's once–heir apparent had moved away and established his own new career. However, their book-writing partnership remained intact, with Masters nearly as dependent on Kolodny's writing skills as Virginia Johnson. In explaining her role in *Crisis,* Johnson portrayed herself as a captive to her collaborators, aware of the impending doom but unable to do anything about it. "That wasn't our production—I mean, Bob did it," recalled Virginia, distancing herself years later. "I got so tired of arguing points . . . I washed my hands of it and didn't read the last versions at all. What could I do?"

Ever aware of public appearances, Johnson blamed Kolodny for their disastrous press conference unveiling *Crisis*. She and Masters hoped to repeat their earlier media success, when science writers respectfully listened to their findings in seminar-like roundtables. Instead of a polite reception, Kolodny approved a full-scale press conference at a New York hotel ballroom, where they faced a swarm of media sharks in search of a sound bite. "We had the television people with their cameras blocking the print media and they got to fighting among themselves and crawling for space and so on," she recalled. Kolodny was horrified too. "Nobody could be heard because the three hundred reporters crammed into this room were shouting over one another and screaming," he recalled. "One guy was yelling, 'Bill, how much money were you paid to sell out for this?' It was unbelievable stuff."

With klieg lights glaring in her face, Johnson bristled at suggestions their book was written for only commercial reasons. She decried the government's slow response to the AIDS killer. "There has to be a strong stand taken to reverse these years of complacency," she implored. However, unlike other times when they spoke with precision and aplomb, the deficiencies in Masters and Johnson's reasoning, the gaping holes in their new book, were on display for all to see. "We were interested in rapidity, in getting this information to the public," Masters explained, without excuse for violating his long-held methods. Some of the data in the book, based on a study of eight hundred men and women in Atlanta, New York, Los Angeles, and St. Louis, had been obtained only months before its publication. Given the public health urgency of AIDS, Masters said he didn't want to wait "not one year" for their work to be evaluated in a peer-reviewed journal. With their biggest claim—that the AIDS virus was "running rampant" among heterosexuals—they appeared particularly naked. Pressed for proof by reporters, Masters offered none.

"I simply believe this," Masters declared, as if his mere words were enough.

When asked the same question at the press conference, Johnson gave an equally unsatisfactory reply.

"I'm not sure we chose the word 'rampant' ourselves," she dissembled, acting as though she didn't know how that provocative phrase on page seven landed there in the first place.

Immediately following the Masters and Johnson conflagration, another competing press conference in Manhattan organized by Mathilde Krim, chair of the American Foundation for AIDS Research, and other health experts, condemned this heretical new book. Krim, a research scientist and the wife of a wealthy New York movie executive, scolded Masters and Johnson like a schoolmarm. "For Masters and Johnson—household names in our nation—to revisit the theoretical 'parade of horribles' concerning AIDS transmission will serve no purpose except to fuel senseless hysteria," Krim said. Joining the chorus, Dr. Stephen Joseph, New York City's public health commissioner, also criticized their book. "I don't see anything in their own data that would lead one to make the sweeping statements about casual transmission and mandatory testing that I think they've made," Joseph said.

In their text, Masters, Johnson, and Kolodny called for routine AIDS testing of pregnant women, anyone admitted to a hospital between the ages of fifteen and sixty, convicted prostitutes, and all applicants for marriage licenses. They believed the tests were a sensible protective measure in preventing the spread of AIDS. However, Joseph and other government officials generally resisted mandatory testing. Unlike other communicable disease outbreaks where notification was routine, many in the gay community said widespread notification would violate the privacy of closeted homosexual AIDS victims and only frustrate efforts to contain the epidemic. Though Masters and Johnson's book echoed *And the Band Played On* by Randy Shilts and other published broadsides against

Reagan administration policy, AIDS experts sharply disagreed with their suggested remedies for dealing with the crisis. "The key to behavioral change is voluntary," Joseph insisted.

As architect of the book, Kolodny watched the reaction with dismay. "I was pretty stunned," he recalled. For two years, he listened to health experts mention heterosexual AIDS cases anecdotally, urging a more comprehensive look. The U.S. Centers for Disease Control and Prevention had yet to conduct a large-scale survey of heterosexual exposure to the virus. Unlike Americans before them, baby boomers had never faced the scarlet letter of venereal disease, certainly not with such deadly consequences. "For a generation raised with penicillin and antibiotics, the long historical association of sexual promiscuity with disease had faded as an inhibitor of behavior," observed historians John D'Emilio and Estelle B. Freedman. In the early days of the AIDS crisis, health experts objected to labeling the disease's threat only in homosexual terms. At the behest of other researchers, Kolodny convinced Masters and Johnson to wander outside their usual expertise, lending their prominent voices to help avoid a sexual catastrophe, especially if the government failed to perceive the warning signals of a much wider epidemic. Once again, Masters and Johnson would be at the vanguard of American sexual health. "They thought our names were so powerful then," Johnson said, "that if we produced a book that would outline the dire circumstances of AIDS" federal officials would be forced to do more.

When *Crisis* debuted, however, several gay leaders—who Kolodny thought would support the book's central message—instead became incensed. Not only did they object to calls for mandatory testing, but they didn't like the unflattering statistical portrait of young homosexual men who seemed oblivious to the AIDS hazard. "We were seeing signs of returning to riskier behaviors, like anonymous anal intercourse without the use of a condom," Kolodny said, "and the leadership was trying very hard to project this image that the entire gay male community was cooperating, in the effort to stop going to everybody's funerals."

Over time, the book's major findings proved largely accurate. The numbers of heterosexual-related AIDS infection soared in the 1990s, as the disease spread from Western nations to the Third

World. "The heterosexual epidemic is no myth—it is real," said Dr. Jerome Groopman, then head of the AIDS program at Harvard's New England Deaconess Hospital. In 1996, a joint UN panel reported that "AIDS cases related to heterosexual contact represent an increasing proportion of newly diagnosed cases in North America," with heterosexual transmission as the leading cause in Asia and Africa. Even once-ridiculed warnings—such as the link between prolonged "French kissing" and the spread of AIDS—were now taken seriously. Reflecting the book's initial reaction, a wiseacre columnist asked in 1988, "How could Masters and Johnson, the celebrated sex researchers, be so cruel as to put a hex on kissing, just as young people all over America are preparing to take off in search of fun and romance at the beaches during the spring vacation break?" But twenty years later, the CDC Web site reported "high-risk heterosexual contact" as the disease's second leading cause and echoed the old warnings from Masters and Johnson's book. "Prolonged open-mouth kissing could damage the mouth or lips and allow HIV to pass from an infected person to a partner and then enter the body through cuts or sores in the mouth," the federal agency cautioned. "Because of this possible risk, the CDC recommends against open-mouth kissing with an infected partner." In 2008, the CDC admitted significantly underreporting the national annual number of new HIV infections by as much as 40 percent than previously estimated.

In retrospect, Kolodny didn't fully appreciate the book's volatility, especially the term "rampant" in describing the disease's spread among heterosexuals. "Somehow it was a poor word choice that gave the impression that we were talking about entire high school classes being wiped out and every other house on the street being infected—that wasn't at all what we were saying," he said. Unyieldingly, critics charged Masters and Johnson and their coauthor with exploiting a public health crisis. "No matter what he [Kolodny] thought, what his intentions were, the result of what he wrote in the book upset the orthodox teaching about how you do and do not get AIDS, and really threw a tizzy into the whole educational project," remembered Koop, who claims he received an apology letter from Masters and Johnson soon after the book's appearance. Kolodny disputes such a letter was written because "Bill was never one to apologize." Michael Fumento called it "a classic of the terror genre" in a blistering attack in *The New Republic*. "Their primary aim is to sell themselves and their books," Fumento wrote. "One wonders if there isn't a possible connection beyond a measure of opportunism. Could it be that after years of at least being perceived as saying 'Have fun! Have guilt-free sex until you drop!' they are mortified to see people doing just that." Even their old patrons at *Playboy* were disappointed. "We have always counted Masters and Johnson among our friends: We have always respected the discipline that allowed them to produce landmark research," the magazine editorialized. "We have admired their courage in the face of controversy. But this time, they broke a number of their own rules and sacrificed objectivity in the name of compassion."

Friends from the old days were perplexed by Masters's involvement in such a fiasco. "The Bill Masters that I knew would not have done that book," said New York therapist Dagmar O'Connor, who trained at the St. Louis clinic in the early 1970s. "He was much more of an upstanding researcher. Something must have happened to him." Dr. Roger Crenshaw, a psychiatrist who worked on staff from 1973 to 1974, said Masters and Johnson's celebrity prompted too many compromises in their later work, too much delegating of responsibility. "Robert Kolodny had more undue influence on Bill and certainly on Virginia than he should have had," Crenshaw observed. "I think Bill and Virginia ran out of a lot of steam after writing their first two books, and Kolodny was there and he was prolific when it came to writing. The fact was that Bill was happy to have Bob Kolodny, who was an endocrinologist, cranking out some of the stuff that he may have never agreed with." Virginia Johnson pointed fingers without accepting any culpability herself. "He [Kolodny] got a little carried away," she explained. "I got really tired and Masters was monitoring the book more than I was. Bob's style at that time—he was, as I said, so very young—he'd pick up on, well, the *provocative* aspects. He loved that part of Masters and he tried to emulate it a lot. And so, he was pulling these things out that we knew to be ridiculous and they became tools against the work."

Despite her excuses, *Crisis* forced Virginia to face a predicament in her own life—the partnership was falling apart. For years, she'd endured this quandary by taking comfort in money and acclaim. But now, Johnson became convinced—both in their professional lives at the clinic and in their lackluster marriage at home—that she and Masters could no longer proceed as usual. Something soon would have to change.

CHAPTER THIRTY-SIX

Breakup

From behind a curtain in the examination room, Bill Masters beckoned his assistant director, J. Robert Meyners, to join him immediately. There was something he wanted Meyners to see. As he entered, Meyners noticed Masters performing a physical exam on a middle-aged woman, with her legs elevated in stirrups.

As newly arrived patients, the woman and her husband were going through the customary initial physical exams in separate rooms, having paid $5,000 for two weeks of treatment. Masters told Meyners to move closer for a better look. The woman's light cotton robe was open and Masters was manipulating her vagina. "Bill was trying to show me what vaginismus was like," he recalled. "And so, what he did was place his finger on the outside of the vagina. You could see the constriction of the woman's musculature and the whole pubic area and that's what he wanted me to see. It was very obvious and dramatic."

Meyners had never entered an exam room like this before. He had replaced Robert Kolodny as the clinic's top assistant, but unlike his predecessor, Meyners wasn't a medical doctor. Instead Meyners held a PhD in theology, hired by Masters as a therapist to deal with psychosexual problems caused by America's lingering puritanism. "I was there really not as a professional but as a theologian because Bill thought so much of male dysfunction was the product of narrow religious views," explained Meyners. "When people are very young and given a lot of negative judgments about sexuality, it influences them—especially the male erection." Meyners advised male patients feeling guilty about masturbation that touching themselves wouldn't impair sex with their wives. In treating patients, Meyners didn't rely much on the Bible or the godhead of Sigmund Freud. He just followed the "sensate focus" exercises until the therapy performed its magic. Without his medical degree, however, Meyners wasn't supposed to be standing before this naked woman. The recording devices throughout the clinic allowed the therapy team to listen to all ongoing conversations. And when Johnson heard Masters invite Meyners to view this woman's genitalia, she erupted.

In her white lab coat, Johnson rushed in, secured the curtain, and shooed away Meyners with utter exasperation.

"You stay out of the examining room," she rebuked. "You're *not* a physician!"

Meyners followed her command immediately. "Before I was even introduced to this woman, Gini came steaming into the room, grabbed and pulled me out," he remembered.

In retrospect, Meyners said he agreed with Virginia's sense of impropriety in witnessing the woman's vaginismus. Although he enjoyed Masters's relaxed manner, Meyners realized he shouldn't have been invited into the exam room in the first place. "She was just concerned to protect the reputation of the place as a professional scientific institute and she was quite right about that," Meyners recalled.

Incidents like this became part of an alarming reality with Masters, who had lost much of his skill as a doctor and much of his mental acuity. He no longer possessed the right answer to every question, as he once had in correcting the department elders at Washington University. More alarming, the daring ambitiousness of his early career, the impressive amount of effort poured into the decade-long study for *Human Sexual Response,* had devolved into a kind of sloppiness inviting disaster. Slowly, the strains of Parkinson's disease and encroaching age played tricks on him. By his late fifties, he had given up obstetrics, saying that getting up at three in the morning to deliver babies was a young man's game. He stopped doing gynecologic surgery, then resumed it so his fees could keep the institute solvent, only to give it up again when he couldn't handle a surgical knife. Bill sensed these changes, but as a proud man, he kept it to himself. "He never shared the fact that he was losing his faculties so much," recalled Gini.

One untold story of his decline involved Peggy Shepley, wife of the institute's board chairman, Ethan Shepley Jr. Before she married for a second time, to Ethan, Peggy switched to Masters's gynecological practice, mainly as a courtesy among friends. Around 1985, near her fiftieth birthday, Peggy scheduled her annual physical with Masters and brought up having a mammogram.

He reacted disagreeably. "I don't think that's necessary at all," he replied.

Masters performed a breast and pelvic exam and declared her fine.

Peggy, who had been married previously to a pathologist, wasn't satisfied. She called her ex-husband and asked whether he could find her another physician for a second opinion. She visited the chief of surgery at St. Luke's Hospital in the St. Louis suburbs, who conducted another exam, ordered a mammogram, and discovered Peggy had breast cancer. Equally shocking was Masters's reaction when she mentioned the outcome.

"When I told him what had happened—that I had had breast cancer, that I had a lumpectomy and had radiation—he patted me on the shoulder and he said, 'I'm glad you got over whatever you think it is that you had,'" Peggy recalled. "I said, 'Bill, I think it's very important for women, particularly women over fifty, even forty, to have a baseline mammogram. And he just shoved it off. Didn't even think it was true—that it was in my mind and not my right breast." When Peggy complained to Ethan, he was horrified but didn't confront Masters. Eventually, she chalked it up to Masters's ego. But others said incidents like these reflected Masters's steady mental erosion. "His mind was no longer what it was," Kolodny said. "He was crumbling under the effects of both the Parkinson's, the medicine he was having, and aging."

To Virginia Johnson, the changes in her seventy-five-year-old husband, the man who had given her so much, became painfully obvious. His authoritative voice was now strained and weak. During speeches or medical seminars, Bill suffered "little breakdowns"—lapses in thoughts, erratic comments—noticed by outsiders. At one professional gathering, friends expressed their concerns to Johnson. She told them frankly about his bout with Parkinson's. When Masters sensed they knew about his health problems, he became upset and confronted his wife.

"You're the only one who could have told them," he said, as if she'd betrayed his greatest secret.

"Bill, your hands are trembling. You're breaking down in presentations," she replied. "Better that they know, and that their sympathies are well placed, than wondering what in the world is going on."

By 1990, the patient caseload at the Masters and Johnson Institute had dropped by half, to about 125 cases a year. Inside the clinic, Masters became a secondary, almost shadowy figure, deferring to his wife's judgments. "Bill was pretty docile in those days," recalled Meyners. "He would do what Gini told him and Gini made the decisions." Masters continued training therapists, though he didn't see patients very much. "Bill never liked to argue with anybody," Meyners recalled. "Even if a student therapist would argue with him, he'd say, 'OK, you know better.'"

Staffers appreciated Masters's affability compared to Johnson's imperialness, and they were protective of the fading old man they admired. "You could tell that the disease was affecting him, but he was still a pretty sharp individual," said bookkeeper Donna Martini. Virginia's tolerance for her husband's decline had reached its limit, though. She often spoke with irritation about Bill and never showed any affection toward him. "I always got the impression that she wouldn't feel bad if they broke up," recalled Martini.

The steady loss of business revenue left Johnson with many hard decisions to make on her own. Masters seemed unwilling, or incapable, of facing their dim reality. Without any government research grants and a dwindling supply of private funding, the institute retrenched in a depressing march. Earlier, the clinic had been forced to close its endocrinology lab, the source of much research funded by pharmaceutical firms, and to say good-bye to talented researchers. The most experienced therapists departed or were let go. Mark Schwartz left to start his own practice in New Orleans. Once the enforcer of clinic rules, Wanda Bowen, Johnson's aide de camp, exited bitterly and considered breaking her vow of *omerta*. "I thought a couple of times of writing my own book," she said. "I got through half—but it will never see the light of day. You have to ask yourself, 'Why am I doing this? Is this nothing but revenge?'" Mae Biggs, perhaps the institute's most talented therapist, was asked to leave in 1988. For years, she had worked as Masters's partner in the dual-therapy teams but the decision to terminate her came from his wife. "Virginia told me that they could no longer afford me," recalled Biggs. "They gave the appearance that we were all very close, but in the long run we were not."

With Kolodny having relocated to the East Coast, Johnson needed someone she could trust at the clinic. She wanted to retire and hand off her duties to a replacement. William Young, her daughter's husband, became the natural candidate.

Virginia Johnson's son, Scott, and her daughter, Lisa, were now adults with lives of their own. Johnson often felt guilt for missing so many important moments during their childhood. Her relationship with Lisa could be fraught with difficulty. "My son is pretty much my pride and joy," she explained. "My daughter was a little bit of a wild child of sorts." Eventually, Lisa met and married William Young, a forty-year-old Southern Baptist minister, who didn't know much about sex therapy when he landed a job at his mother-in-law's clinic. "That is problematic for a lot of people that a Baptist, or anybody, would even consider sexuality as a career," Young told a reporter. "But I have always preached that sexuality is not only wholesome and natural, but also Godly. It's like fire; it's how we choose to use it that's the key." Not many at the clinic were impressed with his abilities, however. "He was ill-equipped as a therapist," recalled Meyners. Johnson didn't seem concerned when Meyners shared this critical assessment. "I don't think she was interested in his therapeutic capacity," Meyners recalled. "She was interested in him being a husband for her daughter. It's the type of thing that tends to happen in business more than therapy." Young didn't seem bothered by Meyners's judgment of him, either. "I remember us have a shouting match one time about what he'd been doing in therapy," said Meyners about losing his temper with Young. "He had the idea, 'Well, I'm going to own the place—I don't have to pay any attention to you.'" Young turned out to be correct regarding daily operations at the clinic. He eventually became the institute's director, replacing Meyners, who was offered a lesser position at reduced pay. "I think I was probably fired but didn't know it at the time," Meyners remembered with a laugh.

From a distance in New York, Howie Masters was saddened by the reversals at his father's institute. Though always emotionally distant, Howie still revered his father as someone who told him the unvarnished truth. Bill Masters later described his only son as "a great people person, an attribute he must have inherited from his mother, as he certainly didn't get it from me." Successful in his own life, Howie married Victoria Baker, a fellow producer-director at ABC News, where his credits included documentaries and working briefly for the nightly news with Peter Jennings. Howie wondered why his father allowed Johnson to select her son-in-law as the clinic's new leader. "Bill Young was someone who didn't have any real credentials for being in that place at all, whatsoever," said Howie. "This was one of the real measures of how the place was dying." Young wound up in that pivotal position, Howie said, because he was someone she could trust—"or probably someone she could control." Young declined comment for this book, and Lisa offered only opaque comments about her life as Johnson's daughter. (When asked whether her mother really loved Masters or married him mainly to provide a home for her children, Lisa replied, "It was just an unusual thing. I don't know about my mother. But I think he was [in love].") As Johnson disengaged herself from the institute, she left behind her strongest bond with Masters—their work. "I think Gini finally got tired of it and walked away," explained Howie. "Gini is restless and he's not. He could, honestly, get up every morning, put on the same bow tie, take the same route to work, and sit around to wrestle with the same problems for the next hundred years if he could live that long—and he would have been happy doing so. I don't think Gini would."

With Masters's illness, Johnson's detachment only widened. "Bill was not an easy man to live with, he was so different from her," explained Kolodny, often the intermediary between the couple. Bill preferred watching a football game at home or reading a detective novel, Kolodny explained, "whereas Gini was the most social of creatures. She would have been out at a black-tie gala every night if she could. She loved the name-dropping and the fact that once they were famous, everyone wanted to be around her. Bill found that all tedious. They would leave the hottest social event of the year at nine o'clock because Bill wanted to go to bed. I know she didn't like it, but she didn't say, 'Well, I'm staying' and stick it to him. She went home with him." In these years of his decline, Gini watched out for Bill, tending to his needs as a faithful, caring wife. Her devotion to him was something close friends and colleagues noticed and admired. She knew him better than anybody and understood how much the clinic meant to him. Whatever discomfort his actions might cause, Bill's behavior would have to be excused as the eccentricities of a medical genius. "I had had ten horrible years with him," she explained. "Masters, by then, was living in Never-never Land. I had a choice of either getting rid of him, which even I couldn't imagine. But by the same token, it was very hard to encounter, to accept in a way."

Friends in St. Louis said Gini felt like a trapped bird, encased by bonds that no longer involved love, if such a feeling had ever existed between them. They watched the affectionless interaction between the two partners and wondered why Gini, still a vibrant, engaging woman, stayed with this selfish, hard-hearted man. At times they sensed Johnson once and for all might have had enough of Masters's demands. "You could hear fatigue in her voice," recalled Peggy Shepley. "I don't remember when it came apart. I just know it suddenly wasn't wonderful." Donna Wilkinson, the football coach's wife and an institute board member, remembered a small dinner party of about twelve people that included Bill and Gini at the table. Throughout the night, Masters said virtually nothing, as if he were a child being dragged from home against his will. "He would shut down at various things," recalled Wilkinson. "I think those tendencies were always there but age exacerbates all the bad qualities that we have." After Bill and Gini left the party early, Wilkinson recalled the reaction of other guests. "To a person, everyone would say, 'Oh, we just love Gini, she's so wonderful! We never met her before. But, boy, is *he* strange!'"

In their talks, Wilkinson listened to Gini conspire about leaving him someday. Bitterly, she rued wasting her remaining life with a man who preferred sitting in the living room alone, gazing at TV sports in his underwear. She spoke of retiring from the clinic. Any day now, she promised, she was going to separate herself from Bill's world, the emotional orbit to which she had devoted nearly her entire adult life. Wilkinson wondered if her friend would ever make good on this vow. "You can love someone without being in love with them," explained Wilkinson, describing Johnson's dilemma. "You maybe love what he represents. You love the collaboration and the partnership in the work. You love the recognition. But do you love the person? That comes down to another issue." Without any resolution, Gini mulled this over as the year 1992 drew to an end.

On Christmas Eve, Johnson invited Lisa and William and their two young children, Anna and Lark, over to the house for their traditional feast. Everyone filled their plates from a groaning board filled with smoked salmon and turkey. Masters popped open a bottle of champagne and they offered toasts to each other. The house was aglow with candlelight, ribbons, and a large, decorated tree as they exchanged gifts.

As the family finished eating, Bill stood up and excused himself.

"I'm pretty tired," said the seventy-six-year-old doctor in a weary voice. Then, without further explanation, he marched upstairs to bed.

Left at the table, Gini continued to entertain her family until they decided to leave. She kissed her grandchildren good-bye, amid talk of what Santa might bring the next day. Then she cleared off the table, cleaned up the mess, and followed her husband to bed.

When she entered the master suite, Bill was waiting for her. As was his wont, he didn't mince words.

"I want a divorce," Masters declared.

His mind was made up, he told her. Nothing she said could dissuade him. In no uncertain terms, Bill declared their marriage of twenty-one years was over. For he had found, once more, the only true love of his life.

CHAPTER THIRTY-SEVEN

For the Roses

Geraldine Baker Becker Oliver reacquainted herself with long-lost friend William Masters and his wife, Virginia Johnson, when the famous sex researchers visited Arizona in the 1980s. From their Tucson home, Geraldine and her husband, Bill Hume Oliver, a retired engineer, drove up the highway to attend their lecture. Afterward, the two couples agreed to go out for a bite to eat.

Prior to this friendly get-together, Bill mentioned to Gini that he'd bumped into "Dody"—Geraldine's nickname as the sister of his medical school roommate, Francis Baker—quite by accident in a hotel elevator. They hadn't seen each other in decades, he avowed. While in Arizona, he suggested getting together with Dody and her husband. Usually, Bill didn't like to socialize on the road, but Gini knew how much he enjoyed reminiscing about the old days. She didn't give this unfamiliar woman too much mind. As Gini recalled, "She was nothing to rave about."

But in fact, Bill and Dody had been in contact for many years, without Gini knowing it. "We always kept in touch, no matter what our lives were like," Dody said about their long-distance telephone conversations. "We'd call two or three times a year and report in and see how each other were. *We cared.*"

Gini never realized that her husband still adored this elderly blond woman, whom he'd once hoisted on his shoulders while water-skiing on Rainbow Lake. Bill never confided how he'd fallen in love with Dody during that summer in upstate New York—perhaps the happiest time of his life—and how he'd hoped to marry her, the sweetheart of his youth. True to form, Bill didn't reveal his feelings of rejection at how Dody had ignored his marriage proposal, leaving his two dozen roses at the hospital. Bill never stopped wondering "what if" about Dody. "It's amazing how such a little thing can make a tremendous difference in one's life," he later commented in his memoir.

To skeptical friends and family, this tale of unrequited love after so many years sounded like another fantasy concocted by a man who was slowly losing his mind to Parkinson's disease and senility. But to Bill Masters, meeting Dody again—now a woman past seventy with streaks of gray throughout her hair—was a rare gift, a second chance in the name of love.

Bill and Dody chatted with keen interest about their lives and about the past. At one point when they were alone, Bill finally summoned the courage to pose the question that had nagged at him for years. "What was it that I did or didn't do that influenced your consideration of me as a potential husband?" he inquired.

Dody looked surprised. "It's not that I wasn't interested," she replied. "I thought *you* lost interest." She'd never learned that Bill flew his airplane hundreds of miles with the two dozen roses, in a grand gesture of his affection. Dody figured Bill didn't care when he failed to show up at the hospital, even though he lived only two blocks away. So she turned her attention to another suitor, a young physician named Charles Becker, who drove from Buffalo to Rochester to visit her that night. He later became Dody's first husband, with whom she raised four children.

Masters couldn't believe it. He'd spent his whole life convinced Dody had spurned him. Bill explained how he'd traveled so far for the flowers attached to his love note, which he'd left for her at the desk while she slept. Didn't she see his two dozen long-stemmed roses?

"What roses?" Dody asked incredulously. She had no idea what he was talking about.

As they pieced together the past, Bill realized that Dody had checked out of the hospital the next morning without ever seeing his roses. The young couple's silence the next morning—when Bill flew Dody home to Buffalo in his plane with barely a word spoken—was based on a mutual misunderstanding.

"I was heartbroken. Why? I never knew," Masters later explained. "I carried a torch for her for 55 years!" His "bittersweet end" to this misunderstanding occurred when he learned that Dody's second husband, Bill Oliver, had died of cancer. He wasn't about to let the chance to marry Dody pass through his hands again, no matter the consequences.

On Christmas Day 1992, the morning after Masters asked Johnson for a divorce, she called Lisa and William and asked them to return to her house. Still visibly stunned, Gini appeared at a loss to explain the reasons for their breakup. Her grandchildren, Anna and Lark, burst out crying. "Though I don't think it was a terrific surprise to her that it had finally come down to this, she was obviously shattered, if nothing else by the timing," William Young later said of his mother-in-law's reaction. "She wasn't crying. It wasn't even sadness or relief. Divorce wasn't her choice. It was his choice. And she seemed, if anything, just resigned to the fact that this was what he wanted." While Gini discussed the impending divorce with her family, Bill stayed upstairs and then slipped away to work, opening up the clinic on Christmas Day.

After twenty-one years of marriage, the task of announcing Masters and Johnson's split fell to William Young, the director of the institute bearing their names. Reporters from around the world rushed to St. Louis to find out why these two experts on sex and love were ending their longtime union. For years, Masters and Johnson had helped married couples understand intimacy, counseling them with practical advice that seemed borne of their own experience together. And now it was all ending. To the *New York Times* and countless others, Young articulated the question on everyone's mind: "I'm sure people will say, 'If these two people can't get along, who can?'" Perhaps mindful of his mother-in-law's feelings, Young hinted the separation was mutual and their marriage had petered out long ago. "They became so involved in keeping up appearances, and in helping other couples who had problems, that they simply chose to forget that there is another side to marriage besides work."

Bill indicated he wanted to marry Dody as soon as possible and that they'd contemplated this move for a long time. He moved out of his stucco house in the University City section of St. Louis and into a spartan apartment within walking distance of work. At the clinic, he carried on blithely, as though nothing had happened. Longtime friends, such as Peggy Shepley, thought it remarkable how the prospect of getting married again had enlivened him after so many years of decline. "This represented a chance to have a little bit of fun, as he perceived it," Peggy said. She comforted her friend Gini, who poured out her unhappiness with Bill over the years.

Gini recalled her own opportunities for marriage with such men as Noah Weinberg and Hank Walter, and how she had declined them out of loyalty to Bill, their partnership, and their family. No matter how she mitigated it, Gini couldn't hide the surprise at her predicament. "The fact that he dumped her had a terribly hurtful reaction," Peggy recalled. "She was staying with him because she thought it was good for business, and off he goes with a woman who thought he was something special. And I think everything is colored by that. She said to me, 'If I had known, I would have been long gone.'" After hearing Gini's complaints for years, her friend Donna Wilkinson had expected something to happen, but not in this way. "Bill just forged ahead and made the decision for everyone."

When Bill announced his wedding plans—eight months after his divorce from Virginia Johnson—his grown children worried about his actions. A story of long-lost love sounded too contrived to Howie, who knew his father was losing his grip on reality. "He was caught up in the fantasy that this was a woman who he'd courted as a young girl," Howie said. "I'm amazed that she married him, given that he was so far along in his Parkinson's at that stage. I worried about him being able to walk to the altar." Gini suggested a less charitable motive. "She married him this time because she needed the money," she said.

To Dody, though, Bill was simply misunderstood. "He was very quiet, a wonderful man with a delicious sense of humor," she said. "He was very kind and warm, very caring. He was quite a marvelous person." Bill never disclosed what went wrong with his marriage to Virginia, nor did she ever ask. Dody pleased Bill with her immaculately prepared outfits, her swept-back bouffant, and her cheery Junior League demeanor. She considered it bad form to ask men too much about their personal affairs. From her perspective, Bill seemed stuck in a marriage of convenience with Virginia. "I don't think either one of them loved each other, but they wanted to keep the team together and to carry on from there," Dody explained. "All things are not ever talked about, but you know how they are. I think hers was more or less a business deal. She was part of a team. They did a lot of good and contributed a lot to society. It took a lot of courage to do that."

During that summer of 1993, Bill rediscovered the warm pleasures of Rainbow Lake. The old rustic cabin once owned by Dody's mother was different than when Bill last stepped into it more than a half century earlier. The cabin was renovated and expanded, with the old sleeping porch converted into two guest rooms with double beds. After their mother's death, the lakefront summer home had been bequeathed to Dody and her brother, Dr. Francis Baker, an orthopedic surgeon who spent much of his career in the Adirondacks. The crisp mountain air, the strong rays of sunshine beaming through the trees, were reminders of the halcyon days of their youth. Bill talked eagerly about old times, but his sudden reintroduction into their family life surprised Fran. After graduating from the University of Rochester medical school, the two former roommates had lost touch with each other. When Bill became famous, Fran followed his achievements but never called to say hello. While staying that summer in the old family cabin, Fran remembered all that he liked and disliked about Bill Masters. Late one night, after Dody had gone to bed, Bill relaxed in the cabin's main room, wearing a bathrobe over his pajamas. Fran asked about Virginia and why they had married. Bill intimated that he never loved his ex-wife. Fran heard a familiar emotional detachment in his voice, one that he remembered from his experience as Bill's roommate. "It was very consistent with Bill because he was so analytical and really a cold personality," he described. That night, Bill talked with similar detachment about his first wife, Libby, and his two children, Howie and Sali, and how he never saw them much because of his endless work schedule. "I don't think it concerned him," Fran said about Bill's indifference. "I think it's fair to say Dody was the only real love of his life."

In a church near Lake Placid, William Masters, at age seventy-nine, married his seventy-six-year-old bride, Dody. A few friends and colleagues from St. Louis flew in for the August 14, 1993, ceremony. After an exchange of vows, Bill gave a slight peck on his bride's lips. "C'mon, Bill, you can do better than that," the minister clucked. *People* later profiled the two septuagenarian lovebirds among its celebrity married couples of the year. To an inquiring press, Bill reaffirmed his earlier findings about the viability of sex among the elderly. "It goes on until we die," he said. "But what's romantic to me is to sit across the breakfast table and look at her—she's a beautiful woman."

Howie and Sali—protective of their mother, Libby, who was still alive—frowned on Bill's fanciful tale of forgotten roses recounted to the national media. Yet from the dreamy look on his usually stern face, there was no denying Bill's pleasure at the wedding. "He was the real romantic and he had known her a long time," said Martin Paul, a science writer then married to Sali. "It made all the sense in the world." Judith Seifer, a therapist who worked with Bill in the last stages of his career, said those who knew Bill only as Virginia's famous bookend partner, as a driven scientist chained to his lab, never believed his claims about Dody even though they were genuine. "Doc's work, as far as most people were concerned, was the passion of his life—and that's not really true," Seifer explained. "Dody was the passion of his life, his last wife."

When the newlyweds vacationed soon afterward in Orlando, they went to dinner with Bill's old friends, Max and Della Fitz-Gerald, a couple trained at the institute during its 1970s heyday. Max couldn't get over the change from Bill's usually constrained personality.

"It was beautiful," Max recalled. "Hell, he was like a schoolboy."

CHAPTER THIRTY-EIGHT

Couples

"Coming up next, the latest word in sex from the king and queen of sex research—the new Masters and Johnson study, when *Larry King Live* continues," the CNN announcer trumpeted, as the show on March 29, 1994, cut away for a commercial break.

Virginia Johnson, her hair coiffed and tinted nearly blond, moved herself toward the interview desk and smiled genially at the cable television talk-show host. She was now a sizable woman, prone to weight gains that could be amplified on-screen. Ever the trouper, Johnson wanted very much to project an image of dignity and grace, though these were not the best of times for her. After three decades in the limelight, this tour marked the last go-round for the team of Masters and Johnson.

For two days in Washington, D.C., Johnson appeared dutifully with her ex-husband as part of the promotion for *Heterosexuality*—a popularized version of twenty years of sexual research by them and others. Earlier they had discussed their new book on National Public Radio's *Diane Rehm Show.* But that night, Masters couldn't appear on television. His Parkinson's disease and early stages of dementia made public speaking difficult, and he tired quickly from the publicity rounds. By showtime, it was decided that Dr. Robert Kolodny—who, after all, had written the book with little input from his coauthors—would sit next to Johnson.

"'Tis spring, and the birds and the bees top a lot of people's headlines," King began, staring into the camera when his show returned from commercial. "Sex is biology, psychology, love, lust, and more, including the focus of another major book from the folks whose very names are synonymous with sex, Masters and Johnson. With co-author Dr. Robert Kolodny, they have compiled a comprehensive study of male-female love, *Heterosexuality*."

King immediately focused on Johnson.

"You're based in St. Louis, right?" he asked.

"St. Louis, yes," she repeated.

"And even though you and Dr. Masters are no longer Dr. and Mrs. Masters . . ."

"That's right," she said with a nod.

". . . you continue to work together?" King asked.

Johnson was prepared with her stock reply.

"Oh my, yes," she said, her voice as smooth and harmonious as ever. "Thirty-four years, you don't write it off with a divorce."

Although Kolodny chimed in with other answers, King kept turning his attention to Johnson, as if she might share some lessons about human desire from her own life.

"Love is still love, though, right?" asked the host, himself no stranger to the vagaries of marriage.

"Oh, yes," she said.

King arched his eyebrow and continued gesturing. "You meet, and whatever that is. Have you ever figured out what *that* is?"

Johnson shook her head gently, with her paradoxical grin.

"No," she said. "People refer to the chemistry. They refer to finding things in another person that you like and you feel good about and they make you feel good about yourself. But no, I don't think there's a good scientific definition of love. It's as many things as many people think."

Johnson hoped her partnership with Masters wouldn't end because their marriage had failed. After four decades together, they couldn't sever their business ties as easily as the emotional ones, especially with her son-in-law, William Young, as the institute's director. Johnson had invested too much of herself to see the clinic collapse. It was her main source of income, along with their writing partnership with Kolodny. In her discussions with Masters about divorce, they agreed amicably to keep the institute's doors open. "I'll do cases when I'm asked by my son-in-law or by Bill Masters when they feel the client, who is very often a VIP, wants the team or me specifically," Johnson said two months after their Christmas disintegration.

Divorce for Masters and Johnson would be the same as their marriage—a respectful accommodation of each other's needs, devoid of any obvious passion. Their concerns centered mainly on the institute, the most visible by-product of their union. "We continue to have a comfortable working relationship," Masters explained. "We separated because of different lifestyles and goals, and will be divorced shortly." No longer would they have to portray themselves as a loving couple. With their divorce, an old fiction was replaced with a new—that their separation carried no pain or strife. To their public, both acted as though they just awoke one day, declared a divorce, and went off to work merrily. "If you're going to get divorced, this is the way to do it: without rancor, bitterness, hatred or public displays of foolishness," said Young, intending to keep the institute intact. Scores of cards, letters, and telephone calls poured in after the world's press carried stories of their dissolution. "It's like my mother and father are getting a divorce," one letter said. Another less sympathetic writer wondered, "How can you help others if you can't help yourselves?" Some letter writers assumed they had a sexual problem and offered guidance. "We would tell them we did help ourselves," Johnson told *The New York Times.* "We did exactly what we wanted to do, in accord with our clear and considered requirements." Her initial bonhomie in divorce seemed too perfect, almost utopian. She even told a journalist that she remained friends with Masters's first wife, Libby, who had called the previous night looking for a recipe. Libby stayed on the phone for an hour, talking about her new grandson. "My friends are friends for life," Johnson avowed. She suggested she'd grown away from her reliance on Masters as his acolyte. "He was a natural teacher and I was a classic student—subliminally, it was always an uneven relationship," she reflected. "The nicest thing since the divorce from my standpoint is that I'm treated more as a person, as an entity. When we were together, we were always thought of as Masters and Johnson."

Still, the press and public remained bewildered.

"Now, I have to ask you something personal for just a moment," insisted a National Pubic Radio interviewer, not long after the announcement. "A lot of our listeners will remember that a little over a year ago, William Masters and Virginia Johnson, you got a divorce."

"Yes, we did," Johnson replied, almost cheerily.

"People were stunned," said the NPR host. "You said at the time that you would continue working together. I think a lot of people, including me, did not believe it. But here you are."

"Here we are, and we've been, many times together," she replied. "Our relationship had such a high percentage of professional involvement. If you're working seven days a week, year after year after year, then that's your world, that's who you are, and when we finally got to a point where we could look to our own selves as individuals, and the kinds of life we wanted to lead, we happily had enough energy and interest—and I want to call it courage, encouragement if you will—to go our separate ways."

"So you can tell couples who are getting divorced now, or thinking about it, that you can enjoy each other, you can have fun together after divorce?" the NPR host asked, with incredulity thick in his voice.

"Certainly," Masters replied.

In keeping up appearances after their divorce, Masters and Johnson flew to Denver for the twenty-fifth anniversary celebration of the American Association of Sex Educators, Counselors and Therapists, an organization inspired by Masters and Johnson's pioneering research. Therapist Judith Seifer volunteered to pick them up at the airport and dreaded the possibility that Masters and Johnson might trade angry barbs in the car. Instead, they arrived like an old contented couple, with Johnson caring for a visibly weakened Masters. Throughout the day, she helped him get dressed and made sure he didn't stumble and enjoyed himself at the formal dinner. "It was like nothing had changed for Gini—like 'This is my job and I'll take care of him, and get him settled and everything is fine,'" recalled Seifer. "In her mind, they may no longer be married but they were still colleagues and he was her charge."

If Johnson's initial reaction to divorce appeared saccharine, her mood soon soured. As the final decree and its fine-print codicils became glaringly apparent, she realized the spoils went largely to Masters. For that inequity, she blamed Walter Metcalfe, the institute's lawyer. When Masters commenced divorce proceedings, he had retained Metcalfe's law firm to represent him, even though Metcalfe had been linked closely with the clinic run by Johnson. She felt Metcalfe's knowledge of the institute's inner workings and finances gave her ex-husband an unfair advantage. But Metcalfe said he'd always been loyal first to Masters, a friend with whom he would watch football games on Sunday afternoon. "I represented Bill in all of his divorces," explained Metcalfe. In tallying the divorce outcome, however, Johnson's friends, such as Peggy Shepley and even Robert Kolodny, who generally sided with Masters, agreed she fared poorly. "Obviously everything changed between Bill and Gini after the divorce," said Kolodny.

With Masters's exit, Gini looked for a new man in her life. She accepted invitations to gala affairs and dinner parties among the city's tightly knit social elite—all that a lively, convivial woman like her enjoyed. No longer would she sit home alone with a husband refusing to go out. Her circle included such recently widowed friends as Peggy Shepley, whose husband, Ethan Shepley Jr., had died in 1991, and Donna Wilkinson, wife of coach Bud Wilkinson, who passed away in February 1994. At her lowest points, Johnson relied on these two friends for comfort and advice, as she cursed her misfortune. Though nearly seventy years old, Gini wasn't retiring and wasn't going to relinquish her self-image of being desirous to the opposite sex. As she mentioned to one reporter, her social life consisted of "going out with various men, some older and some younger—I won't tell who. As for dating younger men, well I put in my younger years with older men." At some future point, she told the *Times,* "I probably will remarry."

Through her coterie, she met Lee Zingale, whom she spotted one night at a banquet. Delightful and charming, Zingale possessed the good looks of an aging matinee idol. He seemed everything Masters wasn't. His blue eyes danced around the room, and his finely chiseled cheeks and jawline highlighted a bright smile with gleaming white teeth. His white shock of hair remained intact and wavy. "He was *beautiful,* with dimples and so forth," Johnson remembered. Zingale agreed to escort her to a St. Louis benefit, and the two were seen around town together at various functions. "She became a lot more social than she had been for a long time and I think she enjoyed that," recalled Zingale, about eight years younger than her.

He soon joined business ventures designed to capitalize on Johnson's fame. With his contacts and the backing of another investor, Johnson recorded radio spots called "Relationship Minute," presenting advice on matters of sex and love. However, they weren't able to land a syndication deal. Talk of a possible television project on her life also went nowhere. Although Zingale's background was in advertising, Johnson hired him to assist with her autobiography. He sifted through photos and scrapbooks, stuffed with newspapers articles about her career. "We never really got very far on it," he recalled. "I'm not a writer but she felt that I could help her do it." In conversations, Zingale gained a sense of her history with men. She spoke of her early marriages and her romance with Hank Walter. It wasn't difficult to see why she drew so much male attention. "I'm sure men were attracted to her," Zingale said. "She had that personality and the great voice." However, he never understood why Johnson had married Masters, a partnership with more layers than he could unravel. Zingale had yet to meet Masters, but he formed an opinion about her ex-husband from Johnson's reaction every time Masters's name came up. "I think he was a very powerful man, very strong, and I think he just took over," said Zingale. "I think she's a woman who liked to please men. I call them men's women. I know a lot of gals who really enjoy being around men, and not just for sex. They are really good with men and men like them for that."

As their projects fell by the wayside, Zingale said, Johnson continued to pay him. Companionship seemed more her concern than entrepreneurship. Zingale accepted payments from her until he began to feel uncomfortable about it. "I can't—this isn't working and I'm not doing anything for you," he finally told her when she offered more money. "Nothing's happening."

The lack of results didn't matter to Gini. "No, no, no . . . I *want* you around," she told him. By that point, Zingale said, "I began to think she needed me around more for the social side of it than for the part that I was supposedly being paid."

The gossip columns soon identified Zingale as the new man in Johnson's life to replace Bill Masters. "I think there was something that appeared in some national newspaper about her getting a new friend and my name was put in it. Old friends called me and said, '*What??*' and I said, '*No!*'" he recalled with a laugh. "My friends all looked at me questioningly. They didn't understand."

Although they might appear to be a handsome couple on the social circuit or when Johnson conducted press interviews in New York, the improbability of an intimate affair was well understood between them. In her eyes, Zingale "was not marriage material in any way, shape, or form," she recalled. "Lee is gay. I used to take him with me when I traveled a lot because I hated it so. He loved going, so I paid his way. He fit in everywhere. He was delighted to meet Leontyne Pryce and to meet Barbara Walters—I was moving in such circles—and he was enthralled and he was wonderful."

Zingale deliberately left things ambiguous. Years earlier, he had been married and he became a father and a grandfather, establishing his heterosexual bona fides among those inclined to conjecture. But in recent years, without expressly identifying his sexual orientation, he shared a long-term partnership with another man in the St. Louis community. Gini was well aware of his other life. There were never any false pretensions, only nights filled with laughs and pleasantries before saying goodnight at the door. Zingale figured Johnson wanted his company as a "good PR thing," so people would assume she'd found someone new after Masters. "I think she was lonely, she wanted to do things, and so we did," he explained. "I still kept my life. I had my other friends and my regular friends whom she really didn't know. We were not intimate. I don't know if she wanted to be or not. It didn't make any difference to her what it [his sexual orientation] was because we weren't having a sexual affair."

At the time, mutual friends like Donna Wilkinson were mystified by Gini's behavior. In St. Louis, women of a certain age knew Zingale as an affable "walker"—men who act as perfectly lovely escorts but aren't interested in a heterosexual relationship. "Gini was pretending this was the love of her life," said Wilkinson, who knew better. "Lee was married but it doesn't mean anything. He was living in this double world." She didn't know whether to discuss

Zingale's background with Johnson or to just play along when her friend pretended over lunch that their relationship was something more. Wilkinson liked Zingale as a friend as well, but she didn't want to see Gini's feelings hurt again. She felt compelled to say something. "If you care about your friends, you say, 'If this is making you happy—fine,'" explained Wilkinson. "Gini can be naive, that it is true. But you have to be blind not to see this."

Virginia Johnson's amiable charade with Lee Zingale extended to the last public appearance for Masters and Johnson as a team. When she learned Masters planned to bring Dody to the Larry King interview and other book-tour events around the country, Johnson begged Zingale to accompany her as well. "[Virginia] just didn't want to do this alone with him and her [Bill and Dody] and Kolodny—and I was company," recalled Zingale, who tagged along. At the Smithsonian Institution, Johnson and Kolodny gave a short lecture that was well received by a crowd of some three hundred people. Masters felt so weak from his illness and looked so haggard that his speaking part was kept to a minimum. To prep for television, Kolodny prepared a "cheat sheet" of questions and answers for Johnson because, he said, "I knew she hadn't read the book."

In front of the lights and camera, Kolodny marveled at her performance. "She was extremely adept at speaking beautifully and saying nothing," he said. "She would take a question that she knew nothing about and segue beautifully with 'That reminds me' and she would go back to something that she had learned from Bill and could talk about in her sleep. She handled interviews like that for many, many years. She looked terrific that night on the Larry King show. She really had a presence about her." The next day, Masters and Johnson granted a joint interview for *The Washington Post*'s "Style" section and seemed tense with each other. "Bill and Gini were none too happy," recalled Kolodny. "Gini really wanted to strangle Bill." No longer did the sex-drenched American media fawn over the researchers from St. Louis. By the 1990s, there was no vicarious thrill to mentioning sex in clinical detail. Rather snarkily, the *Post* complained that "no two people have ever talked so candidly about sex as much as Masters & Johnson and continued to be so hopelessly unsexy." The reporter didn't take note of Zingale but observed that Masters's new wife looked "a little like Lovey

Howell from 'Gilligan's Island,' all meringued blond hair and perfect Chanelish suit."

Several months after the book tour, Johnson and Zingale stopped seeing each other. Their biggest project together—her autobiography—was never completed because "her heart wasn't in it," he recalled. Once again, Virginia's complex personal and business relationship with the man in her life had come to an end. "She seemed to be blissfully happy, but then it all fell apart," recalled Donna Wilkinson. "Being her age and where she was in her life, it just seemed sad."

For reasons of her own, Johnson soon agreed to go out to dinner in St. Louis with Masters, who brought along his new wife.

"Did I ever tell you how Dody and I met?" asked Bill, sitting next to her.

"No, tell me," Gini replied reflexively, in the same voice she'd once used to compile case histories from patients.

Johnson had heard his rather contrived "story of the roses" enough to make her stomach rot. Since discovering the lost woman in his life, he mentioned it in every press interview. Still, Gini's own innate curiosity kept her seated for one more rendition. "We were eating in a seafood restaurant and drinking margaritas, which made it tolerable to listen to," she remembered. With his croaking voice, Bill relived the romance of his young life in upstate New York. In this new version, though, he somehow triumphed over love's adversities and the men who had married his beloved Dody until he found her once again. He finished with a defiant, boastful assessment of Dody's second husband, whom they'd first met in Arizona.

"You know, when I met him, I always knew I was the better man," he crowed.

Johnson didn't reply, except to titter and move on to the next topic. His assessment could be easily dismissed as the ramblings of a sick and weakened man tottering on senility. His words stayed in her mind for years afterward, though, as perhaps the truest distillation of Bill Masters, with all his cruel bombast and deep-seated insecurities. "Here's the clue to where he was, to his whole motivating baseline," she said, still mulling it over in her memory a decade later. "But that—'I always knew I was a better man'—*that* is the driving force. To always be the best."

CHAPTER THIRTY-NINE

In Memoriam

The lifelong habit of going to work every day died slowly for Bill Masters. As he approached age eighty, neither his mind nor body could sustain him. With Virginia's departure, the Masters and Johnson Institute seemed oddly misnamed. The number of patients seeking treatment slowed to a trickle. "His schedule was minimal," said Frederick Peterson, who in 1994 was the last clinical fellow trained by Masters.

Under his guidance, Peterson compiled a case study about a married couple, unconsummated after seven years, who achieved intercourse following one week of treatment. Although the institute was falling apart, Masters's "magic in working with these people," as Peterson described it, provided a glimpse into the therapy's healing powers. With so few left on staff, Peterson's duties extended to retrieving documents and tapes collected over forty years. One day, Masters asked him to hunt down an old film called *The Female Orgasm,* which he and Johnson had made at Washington University in 1959. A television crew producing a historical documentary about Masters and Johnson asked him whether they could see this film taken in their lab. Masters had no idea where it might be.

When the young man finally found it, Masters rejoiced. He set up a projector and showed the old film to Peterson, just as he'd done many years ago with training fellows at the medical school. As the moving pictures flickered before them, he made no mention of who the naked woman rubbing herself might be.

"Doc was in his glory," Peterson recalled. "He sat in the front of the conference room, giving commentary that was very difficult to hear. He pointed to images of the woman on the screen with his cane, which he was using to walk." This relic from an older, more daring time was perhaps the high point of his career, when Bill Masters and Virginia Johnson were determined to achieve medical history.

Finally, as the reel unwound, Peterson asked, "Who's the narrator of this film?"

"That's me!" Masters exclaimed, surprised his charge didn't know.

Peterson didn't reply, but it became for him another reminder of how things had changed at the Masters and Johnson Institute. "I didn't recognize him because his voice was so dramatically different than the one I knew," Peterson said.

Masters tried to keep his beloved clinic running with an assortment of new projects, none of which repeated his past successes. The institute opened a center to treat sexually abused children and moved to a state office building in St. Louis. As Masters knew from previous research, many abused children grew up to become adults with a history of sexual dysfunction, serious depression, painful flashbacks, and destructive relationships. With referrals from around the country, patients received treatments for a month, living in apartments arranged by the center. Masters teamed up with Mark Schwartz, who became codirector, though this partnership didn't last very long. "It was a way of generating some income," recalled Judith Seifer, a friend and former institute trainee. "Doc was terribly worried that the institute wouldn't continue." Bill also tried to launch the Masters and Johnson Sex Information Help Line—where customers could call a toll-free number and talk to a qualified sex expert about any issue—but that enterprise failed to take off as well. By December 1994, Bill acceded to Dody's wishes to retire. He would shut down the clinic and move away from St. Louis, where he had spent nearly his entire adult life. "At my age it's time to smell the roses a little bit," he said in retiring. "I'll be doing some writing and lecturing but no more therapy, no more research." He soon settled in Arizona, enjoying the weather and spending time with Dody in her old home.

To help his ailing father, Howie Masters oversaw the closing of the clinic. He agreed to be listed as a vice president of the institute, making sure paperwork was in order as the nonprofit research foundation filed its last tax forms with the government. "There was nothing big going on—no therapy going on, no research, which had been stopped a long, long time," he said. "It just gave him a place to go every day." Howie had been a good and loving son to both his parents. With his sister, he remained particularly supportive of their mother, Libby, in the years after her divorce from their father. Libby met and married Rear Admiral William F. Royall in March 1982 and moved from St. Louis to Maine, where she spent her final days gardening, doing needlework, and enjoying friends at the Episcopal Church in Boothbay, just as she had done in Ladue.

Howie's relationship with his father, however, remained strained. "It's very sad but Bill remarked several times that Howie knew so little about him—who he was and what his work was," Robert Kolodny recalled. "Bill lamented the fact that he had been somewhat unavailable to him." Gini never understood Bill's attitude toward Howie, as though Masters, for all of his psychotherapy training, had not learned any lessons from the torturous relationship with his own father. "[Bill] was really mean and cruel to him in many ways," she reflected. "Howie had no reason to like him at all. He's the man who made lemonade out of the lemon. He's a lot more like his mother."

In shuttering the institute, William Masters left many aspects of human sexuality unstudied, hoping the clinic would pursue them after his retirement. He attempted, without success, to secure federal grants for a rape crisis center, intending to research the underlying causes and symptoms of sexual violence. The neurophysiology of sex remained the biggest puzzle. Scientifically, he never answered the fundamental mystery underlined in *Human Sexual Response,* when he admitted "the question of why men and women respond as they do is not answered in this text." Other researchers in Europe repeated and confirmed the essential four phases of sexual response first mapped out by Masters and Johnson, but little beyond that. By the 1990s, medical equipment like CAT scans and MRIs, which allowed doctors to peer into the inner workings of the brain and other organs, were vastly more sophisticated than the devices Masters and Johnson had used in their lab. If only the government shed its moral restrictions and provided funding, if only an academic institution like Washington University had re-embraced his work to allow sufficient staffing and support, Masters believed they would have unlocked more intangibles. Perhaps they could have provided more comfort and relief to victims of stroke, neurological disease, and spinal cord injury, trying to reclaim some semblance of their sexuality.

By the time its doors closed, the Masters and Johnson matrix had been adopted around the nation. Just as their bodily findings had dispelled Sigmund Freud's views about female sexuality, their therapy directly challenged and radically altered traditional psychoanalytic methods of treating people with sexual problems. Although their fees for treatment had climbed significantly, they remained far cheaper than the Freudian couch. "Take two or three years of psychotherapy and see how much that costs you!" Masters insisted. Yet by 1994, the mainstay of Masters and Johnson's approach—the dual therapeutic team, where couples were treated by both a male and female therapist working together—fell victim to the overall cost controls in medicine brought by managed care and clinical reappraisals by others. "With two therapists, the cost is twice as high," recalled Dr. Alex Levay, whose life and career had been transformed by Masters and Johnson, in an interview several months before he died. "Now people are much more comfortable with sex. So a couple who comes in with a specific sexual problem, they don't care if it's a man or a woman [therapist]."

The medicalization of sex, introduced by Masters and Johnson with their anatomical discoveries and clinical descriptions, soon entered a new realm of drug-induced orgasms fostered by America's pharmaceutical industry. Big Pharma, previously on the fringes of psychosexual research, reaped a fortune from Viagra and other highly marketed methods for solving erectile dysfunction. Pfizer, the company that put Viagra on the market in 1998, was earning $1.3 billion annually by decade's end from the little blue pills. "If performance anxiety is the problem, a Masters-and-Johnson approach to treatment can be effective, risk-free and, in the long run, less expensive," advised the *New York Times* in 1998.

Within five years of its introduction, however, more than sixteen million men tried the drug. Suddenly, in this "age of Viagra," the patina of serious medical purpose alleviated the old puritanism and moral taboos about such discussions. After being mentioned enough on TV, even the specter of four-hour erections as a possible painful side effect of these drugs didn't seem unusual. If Bill Clinton's randy affair with a White House intern personified one end of America's sexual spectrum in the 1990s—symbolic of the aging baby boomers' libertine ethos from the sexual revolution—then his Republican opponent, Bob Dole, who grumbled on television about the Viagra elixir in solving "ED," personified the future. "Every pharmaceutical company that pursues a quality-of-life drug like Viagra does so because William Masters and Virginia Johnson made sexual health a legitimate endeavor," declared *Playboy,* with its own sense of perspective as a patron of their work. Sex was now physically possible in a way most elderly Americans never imagined. As Masters once implored, "As we age, you can't run around the block like when you were 18, but you can still enjoy walking." But could the keys to love be found in a lab? Viagra and other pills, patches, and lotions, pushed by a sexually motivated Big Pharma, offered miracle cures by appointment only. "*Go ask your doctor for help,*" advised the ads. The Masters and Johnson methods were reflected in the American Psychiatric Association's *Diagnostic and Statistical Manual of Mental Disorders* (DSM), the so-called bible of the mental health and health insurance industries. But their medical-oriented approach—with its remarkably effective cure rates—was now supplanted by more surefire solutions in a bottle. Scientists rushed back to the lab to find a similar pill for women in need of a boost to their sex lives. *The Journal of the American Medical Association* (*JAMA*) reported 43 percent of women and 31 percent of men suffered from some form of sexual dysfunction. Half of women reported regularly having orgasm during intercourse but 10 percent had never experienced one at all.

By the twenty-first century, however, many difficult cases still couldn't be solved with a prescription. As Masters and Johnson underlined late in their career, knowledge of carnal functions couldn't replace wisdom of the heart. Trained therapists blamed pervasive sexual imagery in marketing and widespread online pornography—

an estimated $1 billion business within five years of its appearance—for exacerbating this disconnect between mutual love and sexual urges. "In some ways there are more problems today than in the 1970s," said Joyce Penner, a California therapist who once trained at the Masters and Johnson Institute with her husband, Cliff. Like their famous mentors, the Penners have written books and worked together as a married team. They advise conservative Christians about sex in married life, speaking candidly with the blessings of pastors such as Rick Warren. Couples are quite conversant in the how-to details of sex, they report, but often unable to articulate their sexual feelings toward each other in a meaningful way. "There's a false expectation, based on what we see on television, that married life should be this hypersexed experience," she explained. "The attraction to pornography is very addictive and then you want that in a relationship."

For all the societal excesses, however, few would choose to return to the days of ignorance in the bedroom and unconsummated marriages. Sex in America, in nearly all its forms, had changed dramatically in less than a half century. The lasting contributions of Masters and Johnson helped to ensure there would be no going back. As their clinic closed, some timeless issues lingered—the elusiveness of true love, the failure of partners to connect emotionally, the inequality of sex roles and expectations, and the narcissism of adults unable to commit or express themselves—beyond the grasp of an easy biological fix. "On one hand, Viagra is a fantastic pharmacological breakthrough," explained Dr. Ruth Westheimer, the most visible successor to Masters and Johnson as America's expert on sex and love. "But the point is that the other partner has to be involved, it cannot be just that you give somebody a pill and say 'Go.'"

Bill Masters's days in Arizona brought him a sense of happiness as his health further deteriorated. Without complaint, Dody tended to his needs as a faithful caretaker, an amiable companion for his remaining years. In style and demeanor, Dody seemed a throwback to another age, the kind of smiling and unquestioning doctor's wife he'd had in Libby during the 1950s. Certainly, Dody was no Virginia Johnson, with her restless ambitions and acute intellect. In retirement, without ambitious research studies or a waiting list of patients, Masters had no need for further challenges. All that had transpired in St. Louis now rested behind him. For years, Masters discouraged staffers from discussing events inside the clinic. A decade earlier, he had dismissed the idea of a memoir, telling a reporter in 1984, "I can't imagine anything that would make for more dull reading." But after a few idle years in Arizona, he was ready for one last project. By 1999, Bill had collected some vignettes from his career and declared himself ready to publish an autobiography. He called Judy Seifer—who'd become a prominent sex therapist with her own line of published advice, including instructional videos—for some help in possibly ghostwriting his book. With sentimental regard for her old mentor, Seifer flew to Tucson. In the study of his home, she listened to Masters read the terse, guarded language of his recollections. She advised him that it was unsellable without more candor and self-reflection.

"You know, Doc, this isn't what people are going to want to read," Seifer said.

He seemed mystified. "What do you mean?" he asked.

"This has to be woven around who you are as a person," Seifer said with her rapid-fire West Virginia twang. "People want to know things like, 'Why did you and Virginia ever marry and why did you divorce?'"

He frowned immediately. "I'm not going to go into character assassination," he growled.

Masters and Johnson had been international best-selling authors despite the turgid prose in their textbooks, but America's appetite for the tell-all demanded more, she explained. If Seifer were to be his ghost, she needed more glimpses of his soul. "If you trust me enough to tell the human side of your story, people want to see how they can relate to you. Not that you're just a trailblazer but how they can relate to you as a man, as a father. And they want to hear about your foibles and your mistakes—and we both know there have been a lot of them," she added with a knowing smile.

Masters didn't budge.

"This is what I'm willing to talk about," he repeated, clutching his manuscript, unmoved by her advice.

Seifer left Tucson promising to pitch the idea to some New York publishers despite her doubts. She contacted Howie to make sure he was comfortable with the idea and to ask for his aid in overcoming the obstacles ahead. "I don't know that I can get Gini's cooperation," Seifer confided, "and somebody needs to help Doc see that we have got to show the human side of him."

"I'd like a glimpse of that myself," Howie said, laughing at this insurmountable task.

Ultimately, none of the publishers was interested in Masters's last project. Nevertheless, he kept dictating his thoughts until his manuscript grew to a hundred pages. Rejection had never stopped him before. Most pages contained recollections of his early victories in sexual research, how he overcame detractors and apocryphal tales he had repeated dozens of times to audiences. He recalled his early romance and later marriage to Dody, but he evaded the two women with whom he'd shared most of his adult life. In a single page devoted to his marriage to Libby, he admitted being "something less than a good father" to their children and, like everything in his life, placed their divorce in the overall context of his career. ("Either I had to retreat from the overwhelming time demand of the sex research program, or we could no longer continue as a married couple," he summarized.) With Virginia Johnson, there wasn't much more reflection. He gave her credit for explaining the "psychosexual orientation of the human female" to him and for coming up with their medical-based therapy "although not having a college degree." But he left no insights about their relationship as a man and a woman—first as unmarried colleagues, then as a married couple reigning as America's premier experts on human intimacy. Perhaps aware of Johnson's own thoughts of writing a memoir, he wouldn't reveal anything between them. "I would not dream of writing in regard to our personal relationship," he wrote. "It is my hope that she will reach the same conclusion."

Johnson never read his admonition in print. She didn't even know his memoir existed. Howie reviewed the manuscript and decided his father's advancing dementia made the whole work suspect. "In later years, he began to write some material because he had nothing else to do," Howie said. "But frankly, the authenticity of what he was writing was less than credible. As a son, I made sure that the book got buried."

The inescapable, terminal decline of William Howell Masters ended on February 16, 2001. Inside a Tucson hospice, he died of Parkinson's disease complications at the age of eighty-five. Until his health gave out, he and Dody spent their winters in Arizona and summers in the Baker cabin along Rainbow Lake. His last months passed by in an assisted-living facility in the Catalina foothills. And in one of his final lucid moments, he told Dody that he'd always loved her.

Around the world and in his own backyard, obituary writers assessed Dr. William H. Masters's importance. Glibly, the *Washington Post* said Masters "monitored the tender act of lovemaking with science-lab instruments." *Newsweek* said "Masters and Johnson—who analyzed more than 14,000 orgasms in the course of their research—became the country's most famous voyeurs." More respectfully, his hometown newspaper, the *St. Louis Post-Dispatch*, called him "a pioneer in studying problems and devising solutions in the previously neglected and controversial area of human sexuality." In a lengthy obituary of a size usually reserved for presidents or potentates, the *New York Times* declared that Masters had "revolutionized the way sex is studied, taught and enjoyed in America." Building on the findings of both Alfred Kinsey and Sigmund Freud, the *Times* said, Masters and Johnson "devoted more than half a century to observing, measuring, pondering and demystifying the mechanics of sexual intercourse and determining how to make the sexual experience better for couples who found its pleasures elusive if not unattainable." With an eye toward history, the newspaper properly noted that Masters and Johnson had debunked "the 1758 assertion of Simon Andre, a Swiss researcher, that masturbation caused blindness; the research of Elizabeth Osgood Willard in the 19th century, who argued that the orgasm was more debilitating than a day's work in the fields and that sex for pleasure would ruin the body; and Sigmund Freud's belief in the 20th century that clitorally induced pleasure probably revealed unresolved psychological problems."

Despite his celebrity, best-selling books, and remarkably successful therapy clinic, Masters left little behind. Going through the institute's books, Howie discovered missed opportunity. "They could have made tens of millions of dollars if they had heeded the call of Wall Street and franchised [their therapy] out and owned this larger corporation, but it never got any larger than a room and a desk and my father and Gini," his son explained. "The money that was made was poured right back into the business. My father walked away in the end as a pauper." Despite the passing headlines, many felt Masters had been cheated in lasting recognition as well. Washington University—the site of Masters and Johnson's most important work—chose to ignore his contributions to medicine. Unlike Indiana University, where an institute was established in Kinsey's name, there are no plaques, no scholarships, and hardly a mention of Masters and Johnson on the school's Web site. It's as if nothing ever happened on the third floor of Maternity Hospital. Friends and admirers noted the snub with irony, saying Masters help put Washington University on the map. "Washington University, for years and years, was recognized through Bill Masters," recalled Dr. Ernst Freidrich, who retired in 1998 after forty years at the medical school. "When I went to international meetings, everyone knew Bill Masters. When I said 'Washington University,' they would say, 'Oh, that's Masters and Johnson!' They knew Bill Masters better than anyone else."

While producing a television documentary in Australia, Howie received a call about his father's passing. In fact, he'd been preparing to leave because of the death of his mother a few days earlier. Elizabeth Ellis Royall died at age eighty-six in a nursing home in Wilton, Connecticut, not far from where her grown children lived. She had moved from Maine after the 2000 death of her second husband, Rear Admiral William Royall. Now Howie would be attending two funerals. He stopped first in Tucson for a private service, the only one from his family who could attend. "I didn't know a soul there," he recalled. "It was basically all of the Tucson folks" who had known his father in his last years. According to Fran Baker, Masters's remains were cremated and his ashes dropped by plane over Arizona and over the Rainbow Lake section of the Adirondacks, little pieces of himself embedded in the places where he'd known Dody.

The main tribute to Bill Masters was organized by Robert Kolodny and other friends and family several weeks later, a memorial service at the Graham Chapel on the grounds of Washington University. Although he'd left the clinic long ago, Kolodny never lost his idealistic admiration for Masters. He wrote a long tribute in the *Journal of Sex Research* and called his friend "one of the giants of the field of sexology in the twentieth century." He viewed Masters as a courageous, disciplined professional who championed this volatile study of human behavior with an unerring eye. But Masters also seemed blind at times to his personal life, about the risks that courted disaster, and about the darker, colder sides of his nature that invited profound disappointments and even tragedy. "He habitually kept his emotions and feelings pretty well-hidden, at least during the thirty-three years I knew him," Kolodny reflected. "Bill's life was steeped in lots of fantasies about who he wanted to be and how things ought to go. Reality proved much more cumbersome." For a time, Kolodny considered writing a book about his friend but ultimately couldn't bring himself to do it.

Johnson initially offered to attend the memorial service on Sunday, May 20, 2001, as well as a small private dinner held the evening before at the Chase Park Plaza Hotel. Eight years had passed since their divorce. Friends and colleagues who were part of their lives together, such as Peggy Shepley, Dr. Mike Freiman and his wife, Mark Schwartz, and former *Playboy* editor Nat Lehrman, said they would gladly remember Masters at this private affair.

Shortly before the memorial service, Johnson's only brother, Larry, died of lung cancer. The bereavement of her beloved younger sibling—coupled undoubtedly with her regrets about Masters's passing—sent her into an emotional tailspin. "That was the only loss of my life that was, still is, terrible because he was my baby brother," she explained. A successful insurance salesman, Larry enjoyed a happy marriage with several remarkable children, one smarter than the next. He'd been a father figure at times to Scott and Lisa when their own dad, George Johnson, was out of the picture or Bill Masters seemed too busy to care. "His death was just brutal for her," recalled Peggy Shepley. "She was devastated by his death." Initially, Johnson indicated she'd be there for Masters's memorial service but didn't want to be one of the speakers. After Larry's death, she decided not to go at all.

When he heard of Johnson's refusal, Kolodny tried to change her mind. Her absence might be misinterpreted as some lingering animus toward Bill. "I said to her, 'Gini, that's just not going to reflect well on you or on the legacy and there may well be some reporters in the room,'" he said, appealing to her sense of public appearances. She steadfastly declined. Other friends, such as Donna Wilkinson, offered to escort her to the chapel. Wilkinson tried to convince Johnson to show up one last time for Masters and to "not let go of the legacy that was hers." Johnson cut her off, indicating she was already in enough grief.

Johnson's curiosity about the tributes to Masters couldn't be contained, though. At the dinner before the service, her granddaughter, Lark, showed up unexpectedly at the Chase Park Plaza, after the guests had finished and were sipping coffee. "Gini sent one of her granddaughters by, as she told me later, to give her a report on who had come," recalled Kolodny, who was frustrated by Johnson's behavior. Donna Wilkinson called Johnson immediately after the memorial service to fill her in. "So much of the eulogies were about the tremendous work that Bill had accomplished and it was too bad that she didn't go," said Wilkinson. "I have the feeling that she felt uncomfortable."

After the service, former colleagues mingled about, conversing with old friends about the fate of the institute. Marshall Shearer remembered Bill's ambitious plans in the early 1970s when Masters and Johnson were on the cover of *Time,* touted as therapy geniuses. "When Bill retired, the foundation ceased to exist," recalled Marshall, chagrined by its collapse. Like so many others, he had been out of touch with Masters and Johnson for too long to know the reasons why.

As the crowd exited the chapel, the rain fell hard on the ground but a lively conversation continued among those still fascinated by Masters and Johnson.

"Let's run over to the Ritz and I'll buy you a drink," offered Freiman, one of the oldest and most gregarious of Masters's friends, to Nat Lehrman and another psychiatrist from New York who had spoken of Masters's professional legacy at the service.

Inside the Cigar Club, the plush bar at the Ritz-Carlton in St. Louis, the men relaxed in brown leather chairs and sipped martinis. Each had seen the close interaction between Masters and Johnson for years, and they'd been involved in dispensing sexual information to the public. Yet the secrets of desire—the attraction between men and women and their endless quest for love—remained unfathomable, they agreed. "It was so interesting because the conclusion was that nobody knows what this sex thing is all about anyway," Freiman recalled with a chuckle. "These guys who knew Bill had been around the research and we all admitted that we didn't know much. It's still a mystery that women protect very well."

CHAPTER FORTY

Forget-Me-Nots

"We forget all too soon the things we thought we could never forget. We forget the loves and the betrayals alike, forget what we whispered and what we screamed, forget who we were."

—Joan Didion

With the men in her life gone, Virginia felt lonely and betrayed. Once again, she knew she must rely on her own wits to find a way with love and her depleted finances.

During the late 1990s, she opened the Virginia Johnson Masters Learning Center, designed to battle "dysfunction, disorder and dissatisfaction" without any face-to-face therapy. As part of its mission, the center planned to sell tapes over the Internet and mail order on such topics as "Couples and the Power of Intimacy" and, for the over-fifty set, "Intimacy for a Lifetime (It's Not Over 'Til It's Over)." To a curious reporter wondering why she came out of apparent retirement to start all over again, Gini replied, "A lot of people still haven't gotten it right." The venture failed to take off, even though she used the name Masters to remind people who she was.

Without a degree of her own and no longer associated with Bill, Gini found it hard to pursue sexual therapy in a field whose standards she'd helped raise and regulate. "Her credibility came from being at his side," explained Judy Seifer, a former colleague and friend of Bill's. "She didn't have licensure. She had honorary degrees but there was not a whole lot you can do if you don't have some substance behind you other than under somebody's wing."

For years, Gini had paid for a newspaper clipping service to keep track of "Masters and Johnson" mentions in the papers, but she no longer professed an interest in fame. "If there was anything going on, we'd always be called for a quote," she remembered. "Masters was good at one-liners but I was not. I always wanted to give a lecture every time I'm asked a question. It's only in the last ten years that we're not quoted every time anybody raises the issue [of sex]. I'm kind of grateful for that."

With Bill's death and Lee Zingale's departure, Gini depended more than ever on her grown children, Lisa and Scott. She recognized the emotional toll her nonstop career had on them. "I will always regret the fact that I missed a lot of mothers' meetings at school, and that there were very sad little children—and a sad mother—when I traveled a lot, when we were lecturing constantly in those early years," she admitted in the press. To another interviewer, Lisa's husband explained what it was like growing up in Virginia Johnson's home. "Her daughter Lisa was raised by housekeepers and she was teased by other children," said William Young. "They thought her mother must be a whore because of her work. They couldn't miss it—Masters and Johnson were on the cover of *Time*."

A year after Bill's death, Gini suffered a mild heart attack, enough to leave her helpless on the floor until help arrived. She also suffered from diabetes, a bout with cancer, knee replacement surgery, and other maladies that eroded her vitality. She relied on her son to advise her on where to live and how to manage her remaining assets. "Scott has been masterminding my life right now and it's a sadness that he's here, but he's so afraid that I'm going to die," she explained. "He wanted me somewhere I would be monitored carefully." Never one to stay in a place for long, Gini sold her house in University City and eventually moved into an upscale assisted-living facility with a restaurant, entertainment, and limousine service. Among the widows and other gray-haired ladies at this retirement compound, Gini spotted Sylvia—the woman Judge Noah Weinstein had married after their affair—but she didn't say hello.

Virginia at times seemed eager to forget the past. Her old scrapbooks fell into disarray, packed off into boxes. She destroyed the sex therapy recordings and documents from the institute. "I kept all of the tapes of the clinical work—hundreds of them—and stored them until the last time I moved," she recalled. "I was paying about $300 a month just to store the tapes, and had been for years at that point. My son said, 'What do you plan to do with these?' He destroyed them all. He did with my permission." When he heard about this destruction, Dr. Robert Kolodny was horrified. Lost were all the tapes of the sessions that supplanted Freudian analysis, the case histories of hundreds of patients whose dysfunctions could undoubtedly be studied in the future by medical schools, aspiring therapists, and chroniclers of America's cultural mores in the twentieth century. "Gini had all the records and tapes—all those tapes were a treasure trove and the letters which were unbelievable—and had it hauled off to the dump," Kolodny said with disgust. "I think it was out of abject anger at Bill, for deserting her and blowing things up. I told her if she let me broker a deal with a university library that I could have gotten them a very large financial package."

Though Gini tried to forget him, her anger at Bill boiled to the surface at the slightest provocation. Her private recriminations turned increasingly at odds with how she presented their story publicly. In a television interview for *Biography* in the mid-1990s, Gini seemed humble and grateful to Masters for giving her the opportunity of a lifetime. "He wanted someone whose mind was a fresh page which he could write on, draw on," she explained, reprising the Pygmalion aspects of their collaboration. "It was a gift that he gave me, but I think it served him quite well." Yet in private, she cast him as a toxic Machiavellian, tricking and cajoling her into whatever he wanted. "He was a completely self-centered person—he invented himself," she claimed. "He knew what he wanted to be and—whether he achieved it or not—*he lived it.*" Not only did Bill forge his own persona, but she resented him for creating her image, for controlling her actions, her emotions, more than she had realized at the time. She blamed him for blocking her attempts at getting a degree, for stealing time from her children while she and he toiled in the lab, for using her as a wedge between his first wife, Libby, and their children, and for preventing her from ever finding lasting happiness with another man. Only one other person in her life had ever wielded such power over her, she said. "He manipulated me just like Mother did—praise and punishment, punishment and praise," she said, peeling back layers of her own history. "He loved to make me cry so he could comfort me." The pain of divorce sometimes compelled her to rewrite how their relationship had ended. "Dody was so jealous of me," she insisted. "He dug her up when I divorced him. It was so pathetic. He so loved to relive any part of the past." Gini scoffed at any suggestion that she may have still loved him.

Bill's death only intensified Gini's feelings of loss, anger, and regret. Her social isolation worsened as longtime friends in St. Louis, such as Mike Freiman, could no longer stand her bile against Masters, still so alive posthumously in her mind. "The last time I saw Gini she was in a mode that made me uncomfortable because she had unkind things to say about Bill," said Freiman, who had admired Masters since their days at Washington University's medical school. "She would like to think she did it more on her own than with Bill's help. She would like to tell the story that she dismissed him. She implied that he was impotent [as a symptom of his Parkinson's illness]. She was getting back at him. And I didn't feel it was my business to try and find out." Several months later, Freiman spotted Gini while passing through the renovated Chase Park Plaza, where she lived in one of the cooperative apartments. At age eighty-one, Virginia looked far different from the vivacious woman he'd known. "I almost did not recognize her," said Freiman. "She'd turned into an old lady. She's wearing her bathrobe sitting in the lobby of this hotel, looking disheveled." A robust man nearly the same age, Freiman waved to her. Gini smiled in recognition. "Her voice sounded good and we chatted and she said, 'Yes, we'll get together some time,' and that was the end of it," he recalled.

During long-distance telephone conversations, Kolodny also tired of Gini's complaints but he, too, felt sorry for her. Unlike outsiders who never worked in the clinic, Kolodny knew how much Gini truly meant to the success of it all. Though he sometimes railed at her shortcomings, Kolodny agreed she'd been shortchanged in the way Bill treated her. (Gini's disagreements with Bill extended past his death. In November 2008, a Delaware-based mental health care provider—associated with Masters after the famous team's breakup—was ordered to pay $2.4 million to Johnson for trademark infringement. A federal jury found the company, Universal Health Services, had misused the Masters and Johnson name by marketing their trademark therapy beyond sexual problems to include eating disorders.)

The physiological findings engineered by William Masters were a medical triumph, a long-awaited scientific understanding of the human body during the central act of procreation. But Virginia Johnson's native genius was putting this storehouse of knowledge to good use with every patient. Kolodny was astounded at her originality, drawing upon threads from Freudian analysts, social hygienists, behaviorists, cognitive therapists, urologists, neurologists, marriage counselors, pharmacologists, nature enthusiasts, and feminists to form a whole fabric. Her intuitive wisdom about human nature, her willingness to experiment and constantly adapt to find what worked, virtually willed their therapy into a success, improving countless lives around the world. "In the developing of the couples' therapy and the very sophisticated psychotherapy program, Gini was at least a full partner," Kolodny said. "She made Bill look at a lot of things that he would have just been oblivious to."

For those who knew her well, there was something disturbing about Virginia Johnson's ignominious fate. How could one of the most remarkable American women of the twentieth century—who had witnessed more about human sexuality than anyone in the world, who had explored its multitude of physical wonders and emotional expressions—be relegated to such obscurity? How could an independent-minded woman who embodied so many cultural changes in the world's view about female sexuality be so underappreciated? Where were the 1970s feminists and the sexually confident professional women of Generation X, those who emulated *Sex and the City* and text-messaged men proposing a weekend getaway? These urbane sophisticates—as much as any conservative suburban wife who might sneak a peek at Masters and Johnson's books—owed a debt to her more than they knew. As much as any in the past half century, Johnson advocated effectively for a woman's right to be treated equally in the most intimate, often most personally satisfying area of life. Yet somehow her own fate made it seem as if she'd suffered one more indignity in a man's world.

Despite her many ailments, Virginia didn't feel sorry for herself. The unsinkable spirit of a Missouri farm girl inside wouldn't allow it. "This neuropathy is stupid," she said one afternoon slouched in a chair, her legs too weak to stand for very long. "Normally it leads to amputation and I'm not going to go that way." Instead she dreamed of seeing her own memoir finished or perhaps a movie that might tell her story. When asked by a St. Louis gossip columnist if she planned to write an autobiography, she replied, "Yes, because I am afraid someone else will do it." Years earlier, ABC had tried to make a television film about the famous sex researchers, reportedly with Shirley MacLaine portraying her, but production collapsed because Gini wouldn't cooperate with the scriptwriter's demands. In recollections of her glorious past, she dropped enough names to hint at the breadth of her fame, sometimes with an air of unreality. She wanted Mike Nichols to produce the movie of her life and for Gore Vidal to write its screenplay. Maybe someone like Joanne Woodward could play her, and perhaps Robert Duvall as Bill Masters. The memories and reveries were still vivid enough to fill an empty afternoon.

If television producers didn't call anymore for bookings, if publishers didn't offer large sums for her advice, it didn't matter to her, Virginia claimed. "I don't want any more credit," she insisted. "I don't give a damn. Every talk show immediately knows what my role was. The fact that I didn't have an MD, half the people don't even know it."

The only thing about sex and love that still mattered to her remained the most unattainable, the most elusive part of her own life.

One afternoon, eighty-three-old Isabel Smith received a telephone call that surprised her—a familiar voice from her youth, inquiring about her brother, Gordon Garrett. Long ago, Isabel had married and moved miles from Golden City, Missouri, the tiny farm town that now seemed a lifetime away. Nearly all of her friends from Golden City High in the late 1930s had passed away. Yet here on the other end of the receiver was the voice of someone she once knew, the sweet wisp of a girl named Mary Virginia Eshelman, who had seemed so in love with her younger brother, Gordon, the one with fiery red hair.

"Mary Virginia called me to see about Gordon, what happened to him," Isabel remembered. "And I told her that he had died."

From the initial hush on the phone, Isabel said, Virginia sounded crushed. She'd had no idea Gordon had passed away only a few months earlier.

"I don't know why she called," said Isabel Smith, recalling the disappointment in Virginia's voice. "I guess she just wondered about him. She was very sorry about it." Afterward, Isabel theorized Virginia had called to possibly rekindle a relationship with her brother.

Virginia often thought of the men she'd never married and wondered whether things would have turned out differently—the Army captain who broke her heart, Judge Noah Weinstein, business tycoon Hank Walter, and, on this particular day, Gordon Garrett, the boy with whom she shared her first love. Rediscovering a lost romance sounded preposterous to her, like one of those Hollywood melodramas she would watch as a teenager in Golden City's only movie theater. Real life was much more complicated, she found, than the novels she once read in a pear tree. But in his own life, Bill Masters had done just that by reclaiming the past. He upset everything between them by declaring his undying affection for Dody, whom he declared his first and only true love. In the months after Bill's death, as she reflected on her life, often alone in her apartment, Virginia remembered her happy days with Gordon and decided to find his whereabouts. If Bill had found such bliss later in life, why couldn't she?

With news of Gordon's passing, the phone conversation with Isabel ended quickly. That same day, Virginia called Gordon's other sister, Carolyn Evans, to learn more of his life after they had left Golden City High School. Carolyn, at age seventy-six, politely engaged in conversation with her about old times. In the back of Carolyn's mind, however, she remembered how Virginia had once broken her brother's heart. "I think he liked her a lot," she recalled. "But as I say, her mother's attitude was 'the best you can get.' Mary Virginia was like that too. She wouldn't marry him because he lived on a farm."

Virginia's assumptions about Gordon Garrett's future proved mistaken. World War II pulled Garrett, like so many midwestern farm boys, into a wider world. Soon after Virginia left for college, Gordon joined the U.S. Army Signal Corps. He commenced a long career over the next three decades in government intelligence, deciphering secret messages around the globe. He became a spy during World War II and worked as a cryptographer for the CIA. After he retired from the government, Gordon moved to the Chicago suburbs, employed by a computer firm. In the last years of his life, he settled down in Richland, Missouri, about 150 miles from Golden City, to live closer to his younger sister, Carolyn. "He came back here and he never did marry," Carolyn recalled later. "When his cleaning lady asked why he never got married, he said he didn't have time."

Virginia's prognosis for the "boy with fiery red hair," as she later admitted, proved one of many miscalculations about the men in her life. Gordon's enlistment as a spy, an international man of mystery, came as a complete surprise to her. "That's about as far from farm work as you could get," Virginia reflected with a rueful laugh. "I guess I was wrong."

On a cold, overcast day in October, Virginia stopped reminiscing about her life for a moment so she could rise from her living room chair, stretch her aching body, and gaze out the window. From several floors above, she watched the people walking along the street near Washington University, where she and Bill once made medical history.

Unopened boxes and storage crates filled the room. On the floor rested a framed eight-by-ten publicity photograph of herself from a decade earlier, when men, she said, still found her attractive. Now at age eighty-three, she cared little about her appearance. "I like being married—I *hate* not being married now," she confided.

This apartment in St. Louis was her third residence in two years, each move to a place slightly less grand. The doorman and apartment manager were instructed to keep any visitors from her, even deny she lived there if asked. The aura of secrecy from her work as a famous sex researcher still enveloped her existence. She had lived in so many different places, adopting numerous name variations as her own. Forgotten were the names Gini and Mary Virginia. Even the name by which she'd been known to the world, Virginia E. Johnson, appeared abandoned. In the telephone book, she was now listed as "Mary Masters"—still identified with the man who had been her partner, if not her love.

For a woman of such independence, who had proven sexual equality in the lab, she found it inexplicable why men had defined her life so often. Was this yearning her own fault, the result of society's conditioning, or simply the nature of things between men and women? She still wasn't sure. "I was raised to be one of the greatest support systems to great men," she explained in a moment of revelation. "I can remember saying out loud—and I'm appalled as I remember it—being very pleased that I could be anything any man wanted me to be." She shook her head slowly, her thick eyeglasses balanced on her nose.

Twilight now turned the street scene below into shadows. Winter was coming to St. Louis and a chill could be felt against the windowpane. She turned and stared at the old publicity photograph of herself on the rug. "In retrospect, I ask myself, 'Geez, did I lose myself that *totally*?'" she wondered. "But I was very much a product of my time, of the era. In my mind, that was the ultimate as a woman. And I lost myself in there for quite a while."

Afterword

Once published, books take on a life of their own, often in surprising ways that the author never anticipated. Certainly, *Masters of Sex*—now a Showtime television series based on this biography of William Masters and Virginia Johnson—is a good example. For millions, Showtime's new dramatic interpretation will bring the pair's remarkable story to life. Together with this new edition of my book, it also provides a second chance to consider their lasting significance.

Invited to the set of the Showtime series, I watched as this tale—full of love, jealousy, ambition, hypocrisy, pride, betrayal, courage, and of course, sex in all of its expressions—was translated from words into high-definition images. Even as the book's author, I felt a sense of newness to the Showtime production. The written scenes that sprang to life ranged from the human comedy of sexual experiments by Masters and Johnson under the nose of a puritanical society, to the tragedy of this couple who "taught America how to love" but remained both fascinated and repelled by each other in private. Television is our most personal medium. It seemed the perfect canvas to capture both the audacity and nobility of Bill and Gini's work. In this series, there are indeed scenes of naked volunteers testing the boundaries of orgasm in the name of science. But there are also many moments of yearning and even desperation among sexually dysfunctional couples, most of them married, seeking Masters and Johnson's help in order to express themselves intimately, in communion with each other.

Particularly for today's young people unaware of Masters and Johnson, it's difficult to realize how so much has changed between then and now. In the 1960s, their graphs, charts, and photographs of human sexual response—learning how the body worked so they could "fix" sexual problems with their therapy—seemed revolutionary. To their contemporary chroniclers, Masters and Johnson symbolized the triumph of modernity and medicine over the religious taboos and cultural ignorance of the past. Their facts of life seemed much more definitive than ancient biblical screeds or even Freud's twentieth-century theories. Sex had suddenly left the church and entered the clinic. Instead of consulting black-robed ministers, Americans could now rely on doctors in white. With the Pill's advent, America's belief in "better living through chemistry" was brought into the bedroom. The brave research of Masters and Johnson provided men and particularly women with the freedom and fundamental knowledge to make vital personal choices in their relationships. And at great risk to their lives and reputations, the two underlined medicine's responsibility to remain at the forefront of society's debate about human sexuality.

Yet, at its heart, you might say that *Masters of Sex* is a postmodernist parable about the limits of science, how modern medicine can never truly understand our deepest, most intimate feelings. Between machines and animal instinct, Masters and Johnson sought a humanity. Their study of hormones, electrocardiogram impulses, and sensate therapy grounded in behaviorism could arouse our skin and corpuscles. But alone it could not touch the soul, the essence of the bond between two people. By the 1970s, they realized this limitation of science themselves. Ironically, the newly liberated Id of America's sexual revolution seemed as clueless about love as ever, perhaps more so.

Masters and Johnson's own relationship embodied much of this postmodern dilemma, harkening back to eternal questions between men and women throughout the ages. After all, was Bill's willingness to place Gini on an equal plane—creating the world-famous Masters and Johnson partnership—the necessary act of a subtle manipulator willing to exploit anyone in search of a Nobel Prize? Or was giving Gini a chance to share the limelight, to encourage her extraordinary abilities and insights, an act of true love by Bill in a way that even Aristotle or Thomas Aquinas might have defined it? Years after I first spoke with both of them, I still wonder. And apparently so does Virginia Johnson in her own way.

Several months after publication, I called Gini for her eighty-fifth birthday and we got to talking about the book. She said there were plenty of parts about her personal life where she flinched, parts about the sex experiments where she laughed remembering their boldness, and other parts, like Bill's later theories on gay conversion based on her therapy, where she had genuine remorse. She said she still hoped to write a memoir herself someday. Then the conversation turned to Bill and whether she ever really loved him. During my research, Gini insisted she never did, though her actions seemed to belie that claim. Perhaps their relationship was too complex for such a simple term.

Even now, more than a decade after their divorce and Bill's death, she seemed obsessed, infuriated, thrilled, and immensely proud of their time together.

I suggested she was still in love. For the first time, her tone sounded different.

"I guess so," she said, wistfully.

When this book appeared in 2009, the reception was almost unflaggingly gracious among reviewers and the public, although the still-controversial nature of the subject gave me a slight idea of what Masters and Johnson had faced in the 1960s.

After another venue bumped us because of the topic, the New York Academy of Medicine and the Playboy Foundation jointly hosted an opening event to launch the book. Gay Talese, who makes a cameo and rather humorous appearance in this book, joined me on a discussion panel remembering the Masters and Johnson legacy along with Pulitzer Prize–winning medical writer Laurie Garrett and Dr. Robert Kolodny, whose generous insights are found throughout this book. One of America's best writers, Talese recalled his worry when Virginia Johnson reviewed *Thy Neighbor's Wife,* his 1981 landmark book about sex in America. Talese feared he might have offended her earlier when, at a newspaper editors' convention, he asked how often Masters and Johnson made love. "Who keeps count?" Gini replied, to the roar of the crowd. Yet, on this panel, Talese remembered with delight that Johnson gave his book one of its few good reviews.

Of all the reactions to *Masters of Sex*, the most remarkable came from Sarah Timberman, executive producer of the new Showtime series. Shortly after a review appeared in the *New York Times,* Sarah contacted my Hollywood agent, Scott E. Schwimer, and myself. She wanted to turn the story of Bill and Gini into a narrative television drama capturing their life and times more than a movie could ever do. She convinced two terrifically talented people to join her—writer Michelle Ashford and director John Madden. A pilot for the Sony Pictures Television–produced project was filmed in New York City and Long Island in March 2012. My wife, Joyce, and our sons and I visited the set and met the cast in costume, including Lizzy Caplan as Virginia Johnson and Michael Sheen as Bill Masters. Both asked me about the enigmatic characters they were playing. In my role as a consulting producer, I did my best to share my insights. But I couldn't help thinking of Johnson's words from one of our first conversations. "We were absolutely the two most secretive people on the face of the earth," Gini said, an admonition I mentioned in this book's preface. "There's simply no one who knew us well. People have a lot of speculation, but they don't know."

It'll be fascinating to watch as Michael and Lizzy introduce the world to Masters and Johnson once again. I'd hoped with this book to prevent the memory of this amazing couple from slipping into historical obscurity. And with this new television series perhaps we can offer even more insights about love, sex, and the interaction between men and women.

Let the show begin.

—Thomas Maier
Long Island, New York
APRIL 2013

A Note on Sources

This book relies upon on-the-record interviews with family, friends, and former colleagues of William H. Masters (WHM) and Virginia E. Johnson (VEJ), access to many of their clinic's internal documents, and an unpublished memoir by Dr. Masters finished shortly before his death in 2001. In particular, much of this narrative was informed by extensive tape-recorded interviews conducted from 2005 through 2008 with Virginia Johnson and Dr. Robert C. Kolodny, a physician who was associate director, director of training, and a board member of the Masters and Johnson Institute and a coauthor with them on several works. The interviews included visits to VEJ's residence in St. Louis and Kolodny's home in New Hampshire. Further research assistance was provided by the Washington University School of Medicine, the Kinsey Institute at Indiana University, and by researchers Fred Winston and Suzanne McGuire of the Commack, New York, Public Library.

In preparing this book, I would like to thank my wife, Joyce, who edited the original drafts and provided many insights, and my three sons, Andrew, Taylor, and Reade, who offered their encouragement and support. I also appreciate the help of many at Basic Books, particularly Amanda Moon, Whitney Casser, Chris Greenburg, and the late Elizabeth Maguire.

Notes

CHAPTER 1—GOLDEN GIRL

Opening quote by WHM in Mary Harrington Hall, "A Conversation with Masters and Johnson," *Medical Aspects of Human Sexuality,* no. 12, December 1969. The opening scene in Gordon Garrett's car described in VEJ interviews, with further details of Golden City and VEJ as a young girl supplemented by interviews with Vaughn Nichols, Phil Lollar, Carolyn Evans, Isabel Smith, and Lowell Pugh. Documents from Springfield Library Historical Collection in Missouri, including obituary of Harry H. Eshelman, *Springfield News Leader,* October 4, 1964. Mention of the pear tree at the Eshelman farm in Jerome P. Curry, "The Life of a Sex Researcher," *New York Post,* May 2, 1970; nineteenth-century sexual behavior in the Ozarks mentioned in John D'Emilio and Estelle B. Freedman, *Intimate Matters: A History of Sexuality in America,* (New York: Harper and Row, 1988); details of VEJ and Gordon Garrett from 1941 Golden City High School yearbook, provided by Lowell Pugh. Also, "Golden City, Mo.—Our History—Our Heritage, 1866–1966," a privately published pamphlet.

CHAPTER 2—HEARTLAND

Opening quote from "Don't Let the Stars Get in Your Eyes," written by Slim Willet, which was recorded by Red Foley on Decca Records, October 7, 1952. Details of VEJ's early marriages come from Myra MacPherson, "Masters and Johnson at Home," *Washington Post,* July 22, 1973, as well as documents in Springfield Library Historical Collection, including local newspaper clippings. Missouri for women during World War II described in Katharine T. Corbett, "In Her Place—A Guide to St. Louis Women's History."

CHAPTER 3—MRS. JOHNSON

Opening quote from Gustave Flaubert, *Madame Bovary* (New York: Bantam Classic, 2005 (originally published 1857; trans. Lowell Bair), p. 43. Details of VEJ's June 1947 wedding to Ivan Rinehart from local clippings in Springfield Library Historical Collection. VEJ's early studies and musical career discussed in Steve Friedman, "Everything You Always Wanted to Know About Masters & Johnson," *St. Louis Magazine,* June 1988. VEJ's marriage to George Johnson discussed in Paul Wilkes, "Sex and the Married Couple," *The Atlantic,* December 1970; Myra MacPherson, "Masters and Johnson at Home," *Washington Post,* July 22, 1973; and Jerome P. Curry, "The Life of a Sex Researcher," *New York Post,* May 2, 1970. Author's interviews with VEJ, Ira Gall, Robert C. Kolodny, and Alfred Sherman.

CHAPTER 4—NEVER GOING HOME

WHM's remembrances of his childhood were from his unpublished memoir unless otherwise noted. Description of WHM's college and medical school studies, as well as his romance at Rainbow Lake, were supplemented by author's interviews with VEJ, Geraldine Baker Masters, Francis Baker, Addison Wardwell, Pam Appenfeller, Paul R. Schloerb, Townsend Foster Jr., and Howie Masters. Further details about Francis Baker in *Rochester Medicine,* University of Rochester School of Medicine and Dentistry alumni magazine, Fall/Winter 2004.

CHAPTER 5—A WONDER TO BEHOLD

Opening quote comes from George W. Corner, *Anatomist at Large: An Autobiography and Selected Essays* (New York: Basic Books, 1958). WHM's medical studies at University of Rochester and relationship with Elisabeth Ellis were described in memoir and supplemented with interviews with Francis Baker, Marshall Shearer, Martin Paul, Townsend Foster Jr., Addison Wardwell, and VEJ. Further information about Corner's influence on WHM also comes from Jane Maienschein, Marie Glitz, and Garland E. Allen, *Centennial History of the Carnegie Institution of Washington, Volume V—The Department of Embryology* (Cambridge, UK: Cambridge University Press, 2004); "The Personal Perils of Sex Researchers: Vern Bullough and William Masters," *SIECUS Reports,* March 1984; Harry Henderson, "Exploring the Human Sexual Response," *Sexual Medicine Today,* April 1981; WHM and VEJ, "How Our Sex Research Program Began," *Redbook,* October 1974; "Biographical Memoirs," vol. 65, National Academy of Sciences, 1994; Adele Clarke, *Disciplining Reproduction: Modernity, American Life Sciences and the Problem of Sex* (Berkeley: University of California Press, 1998). Description of Willard Allen's relationship with WHM from interviews with Francis Baker, John Barlow Martin, Mike Freiman, Ira Gall.

CHAPTER 6—THE FERTILITY EXPERT

WHM's career as medical professor, ob-gyn surgeon, and fertility expert at Washington University Medical School based on interviews with Mike Freiman, Marvin Rennard, Frances Riley, John Barlow Martin, Eugene Renzi, Robert Goell, H. Marvin Camel, Ira Gall, Elfred Lampe, Ernest Friedrich, Marvin Grody, Addison Wardwell, Dodie Joseph Brodhead, Robert C. Kolodny, VEJ, as well as unpublished WHM memoir.

CHAPTER 7—THE GOOD WIFE

Opening quote by Theodore Roosevelt in *History as Literature and Other Essays* (New York: Charles Scribner's Sons, 1913). Details of WHM's marriage described in interviews with Marge Sheldon, Marvin Grody, Elfred Lampe, Howie Masters, Mike Freiman, Rita Levis, Dodie Joseph Brodhead, John Brodhead, John Barlow Martin, Phyllis Schlafly, Townsend Foster Jr., Torrey Foster, and VEJ. In addition, Marvin H. Grody, MD, Donald W. Robinson, MD, and William H. Masters, MD, "The Cervical Cap—An Adjunct in the Treatment of Male Infertility," *Journal of the Amer-*

ican Medical Association, May 31, 1952. In interviews and correspondence with the author, Dr. Grody confirmed that the two successful pregnancies of a woman identified only as "E.M." in the *JAMA* article were actually those of Elisabeth Masters; other details of their case match the Masterses as well, including their ages as parents at the time of pregnancy.

CHAPTER 8—ACADEMIC FREEDOM

Opening quote by Shepley from address to Newcomen Society, October 14, 1958. WHM's relationship with Shepley, Willard Allen, and medical school colleagues described in interview with Peggy Shepley, Walter L. Metcalfe, Marvin Rennard, William H. Danforth, Thomas Gilpatrick, Sandra Sherman, Ernst R. Friedrich, VEJ, and WHM memoir. Further details from "The Personal Perils of Sex Researchers: Vern Bullough and William Masters," *SIECUS Reports,* March 1984, and Marion K. Sanders, "The Sex Crusaders from Missouri," *Harper's,* May 1968. Historical references to sex in society found in Plato, *The Republic* (New York: Penguin Classics, 2003); Hippocrates mentioned in Angus McLaren, *Impotence: A Cultural History* (Chicago; University of Chicago Press, 2007); Arthur William Meyer, Aristotle in *The Rise of Embryology* (Oxford, UK: Oxford University Press, 1939); St. Augustine mention in Matthew Levering, ed., *On Marriage and Family: Classic and Contemporary Texts* (Lanham, Md.: Rowman & Littlefield, 2005); Martin Luther mention in Theodore G. Tappert, *Luther: Letters of Spiritual Counsel* (Vancouver, B.C.: Regent College Publishing, 2003); John Hunter mention in Robert Darby, *A Surgical Temptation: The Demonization of the Foreskin and the Rise of Circumcision in Britain* (Chicago: University of Chicago Press, 2005); James Graham mention in Amanda Foreman, *Georgiana, Duchess of Devonshire* (New York: Random House, 1999); Cotton Mather mention in Tracy Fessenden, Nicholas F. Radel, and Magdalena J. Zaborowska, eds., *The Puritan Origins of American Sex: Religion, Sexuality, and National Identity in American Literature* (New York: Routledge, 2000); Benjamin Franklin mention in Walter Isaacson, ed., *A Benjamin Franklin Reader* (New York: Simon & Schuster, 2003); John Humphrey Noyes mention in Lawrence Foster, *Religion and Sexuality: The Shakers, the Mormons, and the Oneida Community* (New York: Oxford University Press, 1981); H. G. Wells mention in Ellen Goodman, *At Large* (New York: Summit Books, 1981); Havelock Ellis, *Studies in the Psychology of Sex—Vol. VI* (Philadelphia: F. A. Davis Company, 1913); and Robert L. Dickinson, "Tampons as Menstrual Guards," *Journal of the American Medical Association,* June 16, 1945.

CHAPTER 9—THROUGH THE PEEPHOLE

Details about Sam Priest from interviews with Margaret Priest, Torrey Foster, VEJ and WHM memoir. Details of prostitution in St. Louis from Ruth Rosen, *The Lost Sisterhood: Prostitution in America, 1900–1918* (Baltimore: Johns Hopkins University Press, 1982); "Fifth Annual Report of the Board of Health of the City of Saint Louis," June 27, 1872. WHM's handling of prostitutes in study detailed in interviews with Ira Gall, Elfred Lampe, Walter Metcalfe, H. Marvin Camel, Francis Riley, as well as Steve Friedman, "Everything you always wanted to know about Masters & Johnson," *St. Louis Magazine,* June 1988; Earl Ubell, "Science," *New York Herald Tribune*, November 21, 1965; and John Corry, "Research Into Sexual Physiology

Disclosed After 11-Year Inquiry," *New York Times*, April 18, 1966. Archbishop Ritter's meeting with Masters was recounted in WHM memoir and confirmed with VEJ interview.

CHAPTER 10—THE MATRIX

Opening quote from George Bernard Shaw, *Pygmalion* (Whitefish, MT: Kessinger Publishing Company, 2004). Details of VEJ's original employment with WHM described in interviews with Mike Freiman, Alfred Sherman, H. Marvin Camel, Sandra Sherman, John Barlow Martin, Ira Gall, and VEJ. In addition, "The Personal Perils of Sex Researchers: Vern Bullough and William Masters," *SIECUS Reports,* March 1984.

CHAPTER 11—THE EXPERIMENT

Details of the clinic's physiological study of sex from interviews with Paul Gebhard, Alfred Sherman, Robert Burstein, Cramer Lewis, and VEJ. Additional details from "*Playboy* Interview: Masters and Johnson," *Playboy,* November 1979; *Time Magazine,* May 25, 1970; "Sex Under Scrutiny," *Newsweek,* April 25, 1966; Marion K. Sanders, "The Sex Crusaders from Missouri," *Harper's,* May 1968; Paul Robinson, *The Modernization of Sex* (New York: Harper & Row, 1976); WHM and VEJ, *Human Sexual Response* (Boston: Little, Brown & Co., 1966); and Mead comment about Kinsey found in "Behavior, After Kinsey," Time, April 12, 1948.

CHAPTER 12—VOLUNTEERS

Details of sex study volunteers provided in interviews with VEJ, Mike Freiman, Robert Goell, Ira Gall, Torrey Foster, Marvin Rennard, John Barlow Martin, Cramer Lewis, Eugene Renzi, Alfred Sherman, Thomas Gilpatrick, and WHM memoir. VEJ confirmed much of Gilpatrick's personal account. Additional information from WHM and VEJ, "How Our Sex Research Program Began," *Redbook,* October 1974; Albert Rosenfeld, "Inside the Sex Lab," *Science Digest,* November–December 1980; WHM and VEJ, "Intravaginal Contraceptive Study: Phase I. Anatomy," *Western Journal of Surgery, Obstetrics and Gynecology,* July–August 1962; Tom Buckley, "All They Talk About Is Sex, Sex, Sex," *New York Times Magazine,* April 20, 1969; and "Sex Under Scrutiny," *Newsweek,* April 25, 1966.

CHAPTER 13—NOAH

Details about VEJ's relationship with Noah Weinstein from interviews with Harry Froede, Joan Froede, Sylvia Weinstein, H. Marvin Camel, Dodie Josephine Brodhead, Peggy Shepley, Mike Freiman, and VEJ. In addition, physical description of Weinstein from Missouri Historical Society, Photographs and Prints Collection; William C. Lhotka, "Retired Judge Noah Weinstein Dies," *St. Louis Post-Dispatch,* July 16, 1991; and "A Judge for the Young—Editorial," *St. Louis Post-Dispatch,* July 19, 1991.

CHAPTER 14—MASKS

Estabrooks Masters described in interviews with VEJ, Cramer Lewis, and WHM memoir. WHM's marriage to Libby/Betty Masters detailed in interviews with Mike

Freiman, Sandra Sherman, H. Marvin Camel. WHM's early sexual relationship with VEJ discussed in interviews with Robert C. Kolodny, Roger Crenshaw, and VEJ. End of relationship between VEJ and Weinstein described in interviews with Sylvia Weinstein, Harry Froede, Joan Froede, and VEJ.

CHAPTER 15—LEAVING SCHOOL

Opening quote from Jonathan Swift, *Gulliver's Travels* (New York: Pocket Books, 2005). Medical school reaction to sex study described in interviews with Ernst R. Friedrich, Michael Freiman, H. Marvin Camel, Alfred Sherman, Robert Goell, Cramer Lewis, Eugene Renzi, Marvin Grody, John Barlow Martin, and Robert Burstein. Willard Allen quoted in WHM memoir.

CHAPTER 16—A MATTER OF TRUST

WHM's relationship at home and at work discussed in interviews with Torrey Foster, Marge Foster Sheldon, Peggy Shepley, John Brodhead, Dodie Brodhead, Sandra Sherman, Alfred Sherman, H. Marvin Camel, Ira Gall, Howie Masters, Mike Freiman, Joyce Renzi, and VEJ. WHM's physical description in Paul Wilkes, "Sex and the Married Couple," *The Atlantic,* December 1970.

CHAPTER 17—REVEALING SECRETS

Opening quote from Alexis de Tocqueville, *Democracy in America* (New York: Penguin, 2004). Mention of *Globe-Democrat's* Richard Amberg's cooperation in Steve Friedman, "Everything You Always Wanted to Know About Masters & Johnson," *St. Louis Magazine,* June 1988, and also VEJ interview and Masters memoir. WHM's "dynamite" comment in Earl Ubell, "Science," *New York Herald Tribune,* November 21, 1965. Reaction to study in Leslie H. Farber, "I'm Sorry, Dear," *Commentary,* November 1964; Marion K. Sanders, "The Sex Crusaders from Missouri," *Harper's,* May 1968. Greenson's comments in "Trouble Between the Sexes," *Time,* December 9, 1966.

CHAPTER 18—THE HUMAN RESPONSE

Details of analysis from WHM and VEJ, *Human Sexual Response* (Boston: Little, Brown & Co., 1966). Additional comment from John Corry, "Research into Sexual Physiology Disclosed After 11-Year Inquiry," *New York Times,* April 18, 1966; Tom Buckley, "All They Talk About Is Sex, Sex, Sex," *New York Times Magazine,* April 20, 1969; and Paul Robinson, *The Modernization of Sex* (New York: Harper & Row, 1976).

CHAPTER 19—THE EXCITEMENT OF RELEASE

Reaction to *HSR* book in Marion K. Sanders, "The Sex Crusaders from Missouri," *Harper's,* May 1968; John Corry, "Research into Sexual Physiology Disclosed After 11-Year Inquiry," *New York Times,* April 18, 1966; Harry Henderson, "Exploring the Human Sexual Response," *Sexual Medicine Today,* April 1981. Gagnon's comment in Albert Rosenfeld, "Inside the Sex Lab," *Science Digest,* November–December 1980. VEJ's "public opinion" comment in "Sex Under Scrutiny," *Newsweek,* April 25, 1966. Also interviews with Mary Erickson and VEJ.

CHAPTER 20—FOCUSING FEELINGS

Opening quote from Leo Tolstoy in Fred R. Shapiro, ed., *The Yale Book of Quotations* (New Haven, CT: Yale University Press, 2006). Questions used in therapy from author's interviews with VEJ and Alexander Levay, and from WHM and VEJ, *Human Sexual Inadequacy* (Boston: Little, Brown & Co., 1970), as well as Robert C. Kolodny, "Evaluating Sex Therapy," *Journal of Sex Research,* November 1981, and Myra MacPherson, "Masters and Johnson at Home," *Washington Post,* July 22, 1973.

CHAPTER 21—SEXUAL HEALING

Details of Kolodny's background and relationship with WHM and VEJ from interviews with Robert C. Kolodny, Rose Boyarsky, Della Fitz-Gerald, Roger Crenshaw, and VEJ. Further details of the clinic operations from interviews with Wanda Bowen and Mae Biggs. Details of Semans's influence from interviews with Mary Semans and VEJ. Additional information from J. H. Semans, "Premature Ejaculation: A New Approach," *Southern Medical Journal* 49, 1956.

CHAPTER 22—SURROGATES

Opening quote from Geoffrey Chaucer, *The Canterbury Tales* (Boston: Houghton Mifflin, 2000). Details of the Calvert case from interviews with Ernst R. Friedrich, Michael Freiman, Alfred Sherman, Robert Hoemche, Dagmar O'Connor, Torrey Foster, Robert C. Kolodny, and VEJ. Additional details found in "Sex Suit Secrecy Studied," December 5, 1970, *St. Louis Post-Dispatch*; "2 Sex Researchers Sued for $750,000," *St. Louis Post-Dispatch,* Aug 25, 1970; A. J. Vogl, "Are Masters and Johnson Really Infallible?" *Hospital Physician,* November 1970; and Myra MacPherson, "Masters and Johnson at Home," *Washington Post,* July 22, 1973.

CHAPTER 23—PLAYBOYS AND PATRONS

WHM and VEJ dealings with *Playboy* and other attempts at financial support from interviews with Hugh M. Hefner, Nat Lehrman, J. Robert Meyners, Marshall Shearer, Peggy Shearer, Thomas Lowry, Paul Gebhard, Robert C. Kolodny, and VEJ, and WHM memoir. *Playboy's* contributions are tallied in clinic's financial records. Additional details found in Marion K. Sanders, "The Sex Crusaders from Missouri," *Harper's,* May 1968; and "*Playboy* Interview: Masters and Johnson," *Playboy,* November 1979.

CHAPTER 24—REPAIRING THE CONJUGAL BED

Opening quote from Sigmund Freud, *An Outline of Psycho-Analysis* (New York: W. W. Norton & Co., 1949). Cover story about WHM and VEJ in "Repairing the Conjugal Bed," *Time,* May 25, 1970. Details of therapy described in "The $2,500 Understanding," *Newsweek,* June 10, 1968; WHM and VEJ, *Human Sexual Inadequacy* (Boston: Little, Brown & Co., 1970); review by Alan F. Guttmacher, "Human Sexual Inadequacy for the Non-Layman," *New York Times Book Review,* July 12, 1970. Gallant and Gadpaille comments in A. J. Vogl, "Are Masters and Johnson Really Infallible?" *Hospital Physician,* November 1970. Additional comment from Mike Freiman and VEJ.

CHAPTER 25—THE SCENT OF LOVE

Opening quote from Charles Darwin, *The Descent of Man and Selection in Relation to Sex* (Princeton, NJ: Princeton University Press, 1981). The working and personal relationship between Masters and Johnson and Hank Walter described in interviews with Gail Tullman, Joan Bauman, Torrey Foster, Rosalind P. Walter, Wanda Bowen, Marshall Shearer, Robert C. Kolodny, and VEJ. Theories about olfaction and sexual behavior expressed in WHM and VEJ's *Human Sexual Inadequacy* and further detailed in private correspondence between Hank Walter, WHM, and Robert C. Kolodny, who allowed author to review these papers. Additional information from Melva Weber, "New Cures for Sex Problems," *Ladies' Home Journal,* July 1970, and Lee Smith, "Adventures in the Sex and Hunger Trade," *Fortune,* August 9, 1982.

CHAPTER 26—BETRAYALS

Details about Masters marriage and family life from Howie Masters, Dodie Josephine Brodhead, John Brodhead, Judith Seifer, Peggy Shepley, Marge Foster Sheldon, Martin Paul, Robert C. Kolodny, and VEJ. Additional details from WHM memoir and Paul Wilkes, "Sex and the Married Couple," *The Atlantic,* December 1970; Myra MacPherson, "Masters and Johnson at Home," *Washington Post,* July 22, 1973; and Judy J. Newmark, "Conversation with Masters and Johnson," *St. Louis Post-Dispatch,* September 16, 1984.

CHAPTER 27—THE MARRIAGE COMPACT

Marriage of WHM and VEJ described in interviews with Paul Gebhard, Robert C. Kolodny, Alfred Sherman, Dodie Josephine Brodhead, Peggy Shepley, June Dobbs Butts, Torrey Foster, Michael Freiman, Lynn Strenkofsky, Sally Bartok Taylor, and VEJ. Additional information from Steve Friedman, "Everything You Always Wanted to Know About Masters & Johnson," *St. Louis Magazine,* June 1988, and Myra MacPherson, "Masters and Johnson at Home," *Washington Post,* July 22, 1973.

CHAPTER 28—FEMINIST MOVEMENT

Opening quote from Betty Friedan, *The Feminine Mystique* (New York: W. W. Norton, 1963). Relationship of Masters and Johnson to their clinic staff described in interviews with Rose Boyarsky, Doris McKee, Howard McKee, Della Fitz-Gerald, Max Fitz-Gerald, Thomas P. Lowery, Sally Bartok Taylor, Walter Metcalfe, Wanda Bowen, Peggy Shearer, Dagmar O'Connor, and VEJ. Additional information in Jane Gerhard, "Revisiting 'The Myth of the Vaginal Orgasm': The Female Orgasm in American Sexual Thought and Second Wave Feminism," *Feminist Studies* 26, no. 2 (Summer 2000), Women and Health. Additional information from John D'Emilio and Estelle B. Freedman, *Intimate Matters: A History of Sexuality in America* (New York: Harper and Row, 1988); Paul Robinson, *The Modernization of Sex* (New York: Harper & Row, 1976); Myra MacPherson, "Masters and Johnson at Home," *Washington Post,* July 22, 1973; Elaine Sciolino, "Sex Talk," *Newsweek,* March 17, 1975; Anne Koedt, "The Myth of the Vaginal Orgasm," 1970 essay contained in Jeffrey Escoffier, *Sexual Revolution* (New York: Thunder's Mouth Press, 2003); Norman Mailer, *The Prisoner of Sex* (Boston: Little, Brown & Co., 1971); Germaine Greer, *The Female Eunuch*

(New York: McGraw-Hill, 1970); and Barbara Ehrenreich, Elizabeth Hess, and Gloria Jacobs, *Re-Making Love: The Feminization of Sex* (New York: Doubleday, 1986).

CHAPTER 29—THE BUSINESS OF SEX

Masters and Johnson's involvement in sex therapy centers and field of sexology discussed in interviews with Sallie Schumacher, Rhea Dornbush, Robert C. Kolodny, Torrey Foster, Shirley Zussman, June Dobbs Butts, Peggy Shearer, and VEJ. Additional details from Tom Buckley, "All They Talk About Is Sex, Sex, Sex," *New York Times Magazine,* April 20, 1969; Albert Rosenfeld, "Inside the Sex Lab," *Science Digest,* November–December 1980; Joanne Koch and Lew Koch, "A Consumer's Guide to Therapy for Couples," *Psychology Today,* March 1976; "Playboy Interview: Masters and Johnson," *Playboy,* November 1979; Ruth Macklin, "Ethics, Sex Research and Sex Therapy," *Hastings Center Report,* April 1976; Joan Dames, "A Celebration of the Pioneering Work of Masters and Johnson," *St. Louis Post-Dispatch,* November 11, 1984; "Adelbert Schumacher—Obituary," *Union Leader* (Manchester, NH), September 8, 2004; "Arthur N. Levien—Obituary," *New York Times,* August 24, 1987; and Helen Singer Kaplan, *The New Sex Therapy: Active Treatment of Sexual Dysfunctions* (New York: Brunner-Routledge, 1974).

CHAPTER 30—THE PLEASURE BOND

Opening quote from Virginia Woolf, *A Room of One's Own* (New York: Harcourt, Brace and Jovanovich, 1957). WHM and VEJ as a married couple recalled in interviews with June Dobbs Butts, Peggy Shepley, Paul Gebhard, Marshall Shearer, Donna Wilkinson, Robert C. Kolodny, Howie Masters, Max Fitz-Gerald, and VEJ; WHM memoir; and WHM and VEJ, *The Pleasure Bond* (Boston: Little, Brown & Co., 1976). Additional detail in Shana Alexander, "Coming Out of the Closet," *Newsweek,* February 3, 1975; Harry Henderson, "Exploring the Human Sexual Response," *Sexual Medicine Today,* April 1981; "Out of the Lab," *Time,* February 3, 1975; "Sex and Sexuality: The Crucial Difference," from *McCall's,* reprinted in *Reader's Digest,* November 1966; and Lois Timnick, "Sex Researchers' Book Stresses Commitment," *St. Louis Globe-Democrat,* January 17, 1975.

CHAPTER 31—GUIDE TO THE STARS

Masters and Johnson's relationship with well-known clients and use of their Ladue house was described in interviews with Doris McKee, Lynn Strenkofsky, Marshall Shearer, Peggy Shearer, Judith Seifer, William J. Seifer, Cindy Todorovich, Mae Biggs-Lonergan, Mary Erickson, Sally Bartok Taylor, Peggy Shepley, Roger Crenshaw, Rose Boyarsky, Robert C. Kolodny, and VEJ. Barbara Eden, through her spokesman, Michael Casey, declined an interview. Additional information in "I'm Marion, Fly Me," *Newsweek,* January 26, 1976; John J. Miller, "Geraldo's Jive," *National Review,* September 1, 1998. Details about George Wallace marriage after assassination attempt detailed in "George Wallace: Settin' the Woods on Fire," produced by Paul Stekler and Dan McCabe and written by Steve Fayer, shown on PBS's *The American Experience,* 2000.

CHAPTER 32—CONVERSION AND REVERSION

Meet the Press opening scene from NBC transcript of April 22, 1979. Analysis of homosexuality in WHM and VEJ, *Homosexuality in Perspective* (Boston: Little, Brown

& Co., 1979). Many internal institute documents provided by Kolodny, including signed letter from Indiana man and August 8, 1978, memo from Kolodny to WHM regarding problems with *HIP* book. Discussion of conversion/reversion theories from interviews with Robert C. Kolodny, J. Robert Meyners, June Dobbs Butts, Marshall Shearer, Alex Levay, Lynn Strenkosky, Rose Boyarsky, Thomas P. Lowry, Roger Crenshaw, Mary Erickson, Nancy Mund, Paul Gebhard, and VEJ. Additional details from Paul Wilkes, "Sex and the Married Couple," *The Atlantic,* December 1970; "The Personal Perils of Sex Researchers: Vern Bullough and William Masters," *SIECUS Reports,* March 1984; "Playboy Interview: Masters and Johnson," *Playboy,* November 1979; "Homosexuality: Help for Those Who Want It," *Science News,* April 28, 1979, "Target: Masters and Johnson," *Time,* August 11, 1980; Matt Clark, "Sex and the Homosexual," *Newsweek,* April 30, 1979; Bernie Zilbergeld and Michael Evans, "The Inadequacy of Masters and Johnson," *Psychology Today,* August 1980; Lawrence J. Hatterer review of *Homosexuality in Perspective* in *Journal of the American Medical Association,* December 28, 1979; and Joan Kuda, "Gerdine Hosts Dinner Honoring Sex Therapist," *Webster University Journal,* November 1984.

CHAPTER 33—THE PROMISE OF A FUTURE

Anniversary celebration for Masters and Johnson and their impact described in Joan Kuda, "Gerdine Hosts Dinner Honoring Sex Therapist," *Webster University Journal,* November 1984; Judy J. Newmark, "Conversation with Masters and Johnson," *St. Louis Post-Dispatch,* September 16, 1984; and Steve Friedman, "Everything You Always Wanted to Know About Masters & Johnson," *St. Louis Magazine,* June 1988. Talese recalled in Myra MacPherson, "Masters and Johnson at Home," *Washington Post,* July 22, 1973, and his book *Thy Neighbor's Wife* (New York: Doubleday, 1980). Additional details from interviews with June Dobbs Butts, Donna Wilkinson, Helen Gurley Brown, Marshall Shearer, Robert C. Kolodny, Mark Schwartz, and VEJ.

CHAPTER 34—BEAUTY AND THE BEAST

Opening quote from Vladimir Nabokov, *Lolita* (New York: Vintage, 1991). Surrogate use during the 1980s discussed in interviews with Maureen Sullivan Ward, Paul Gebhard, Vena Blanchard, Alex Levay, Mark Schwartz, Max Fitz-Gerald, Ruth Westheimer, Donna Martini, Robert C. Kolodny, and VEJ. Additional information from Xaviera Hollander, *The Happy Hooker: My Own Story* (New York: Dell, 1972); Jenifer Hanrahan, "Time Has Overcome Surrogate Partners: Sexual Healer Is One of the State's Last in Practice," *San Diego Union-Tribune,* October 14, 2001. Details of Maureen Sullivan's appearance on the *Tonight Show with Johnny Carson* from NBC transcript of the September 9, 1982, program. Discussion of surrogates and ethics and the IPSA in Robert T. Francoeur, ed., *Sexuality in America: Understanding Our Sexual Values and Behavior* (New York: Continuum Publishing, 1999).

CHAPTER 35—CRISIS

Opening quote from Edmund White, *States of Desire: Travels in Gay America* (New York: Plume, 1991). Meese scene reported in Ronald J. Ostrow, "Meese Panel Asks Porn Crackdown," *Los Angeles Times,* July 10, 1986, and Richard Stengel, "Sex Busters," *Time,* July 21, 1986. Further comment on Masters and Johnson in Guy D. Garcia, "Sexology on the Defensive," *Time,* June 13, 1983; A. J. Vogl, "Are Masters and Johnson Really Infallible?" *Hospital Physician,* November 1970; Bernie Zilbergeld and Michael Evans, "The Inadequacy of Masters and Johnson," *Psychology Today,* August 1980; Robert C. Kolodny, "Evaluating Sex Therapy," *Journal of Sex Research,* November 1981; Michael Fumento, "What the Press Release Left Out," *New Republic,* April 4, 1988; Michael Fumento, "The AIDS Cookbook," *New Republic,* April 4, 1988; David M. Alpern, "It Scares the Hell out of Me," *Newsweek,* March 14, 1988; Jean Seligman, "The Storm over Masters and Johnson," *Newsweek,* March 21, 1988; John D'Emilio and Estelle B. Freedman, *Intimate Matters: A History of Sexuality in America* (New York: Harper and Row, 1988); Lawrence K. Altman, "H.I.V. Study Finds Rate 40% Higher than Estimated," *New York Times,* August 3, 2008; and WHM, VEJ, and Robert C. Kolodny, *CRISIS: Heterosexual Behavior in the Age of AIDS* (New York: Grove Press, 1988). Additional information from interviews with C. Everett Koop, June Dobbs Butts, Robert C. Kolodny, Howie Masters, Roger Crenshaw, Dagmar O'Connor, J. Robert Meyners, Rose Boyarsky, and VEJ.

CHAPTER 36—BREAKUP

Deterioration of Masters and Johnson partnership discussed in interviews with J. Robert Meyners, Peggy Shepley, Donna Martini, Robert C. Kolodny, Howie Masters, Martin Paul, Lisa Young, Donna Wilkinson, and VEJ. Additional details from Robert Kerr, "Sex Therapist Does Battle with Myths," *Commercial Appeal* (Memphis), February 25, 1993; "A Life in the Day of Virginia Johnson," *Seen,* February 1993; and Sharon Churcher, "They Told the World All About Sex . . . ," *The Mail on Sunday* (London), April 18, 1993.

CHAPTER 37—FOR THE ROSES

Discussion of WHM's personal relationships from interviews with Geraldine "Dody" Baker Masters, Francis Baker, Howie Masters, Peggy Shepley, Max Fitz-Gerald, and VEJ. Additional description of relationship with Dody from WHM unpublished memoir; "Love Styles of the Love Advisers—Special Issue—Celebrity Romance 1995," *People,* February 13, 1995; Sharon Churcher, "They Told the World All About Sex . . .," *The Mail on Sunday* (London), April 18, 1993; Gail Sheehy, "Men Grieve More When Spouse Dies," *Dallas Morning News,* July 3, 1996; and Nadine Brozan, "Chronicle," *New York Times,* March 31, 1993.

CHAPTER 38—COUPLES

Opening scene from Larry King show, CNN transcript of March 29, 1994. VEJ's breakup with WHM discussed in interviews with Donna Wilkinson, Peggy Shepley, Lee Zingale, Walter Metcalfe, and VEJ. Additional information from Enid Nemy, "Masters and Johnson; Divorced, Yes, But Not Split," *New York Times,* March 24, 1994; Nadine Brozan, "Chronicle," *New York Times,* March 31, 1993; and Martha Sherrill, "What's Love Got to Do With It?: From Masters & Johnson, Another Passionless Look at Sex," *Washington Post,* March 29, 1994.

CHAPTER 39—IN MEMORIUM

WHM's final days and lasting impact described in interviews with Frederick Peterson, Mark Schwartz, Howie Masters, Michael Freiman, Geraldine Baker Masters,

Judith Seifer, Alex Levay, Joyce Penner, Cliff Penner, Francis Baker, Michael Perelman, Ernst R. Friedrich, Nat Lehrman, Donna Wilkinson, Robert C. Kolodny, and VEJ. Further details of institute's closure from its tax forms, including Howie Masters's involvement on his father's behalf. Cynthia Gorney, "Designing Women: Scientists and Capitalists Dream of Finding a Drug That Could Boost Female Sexuality. There's One Little Problem . . . ," *Washington Post,* June 30, 2002; "Transition: What Lives They Lived—William Masters," *Newsweek,* December 31, 2001; Robert C. Kolodny, "In Memory of William H. Masters," *Journal of Sex Research,* August 1, 2001; Suzie Hayman, "William Masters," *Manchester Guardian,* February 21, 2001; and Richard Severo, "William H. Masters, a Pioneer in Studying and Demystifying Sex, Dies at 85," *New York Times,* February 19, 2001.

CHAPTER 40—FORGET-ME-NOTS

Opening quote by Joan Didion, *Slouching Toward Bethlehem* (New York: Farrar, Straus and Giroux, 1968), p. 139. VEJ's life in recent years discussed in interviews with Isabel Smith, Carolyn Evans, Judith Seifer, Michael Freiman, Lisa Young, Robert C. Kolodny, and VEJ. Additional information from Stephen Farber, "Masters and Johnson TV Film is Set," *New York Times,* February 6, 1985; and Harry Levins, "Sex and the Single Expert: Virginia Johnson of 'Masters And' Will Be Working Solo on Her Next Book," *St. Louis Post-Dispatch,* May 18, 1994.

Selected Bibliography

BYLINED ARTICLES IN NEWSPAPERS, PERIODICALS, AND JOURNALS

Alexander, Shana. "Coming Out of the Closet." *Newsweek,* February 3, 1975.

Alpern, David M. "It Scares the Hell Out of Me." *Newsweek,* March 14, 1988.

Altman, Lawrence K. "H.I.V. Study Finds Rate 40% Higher Than Estimated." *New York Times,* August 3, 2008.

Brody, Jane E. "30 Years of Pioneering in Sex Therapy." *New York Times,* October 29, 1984.

Brozan, Nadine. "Chronicle." *New York Times,* March 31, 1993.

Buckley, Tom. "All They Talk About Is Sex, Sex, Sex." *New York Times Magazine,* April 20, 1969.

Churcher, Sharon. "They Told the World All About Sex . . ." *The Mail on Sunday* (London), April 18, 1993.

Clark, Matt. "Sex and the Homosexual." *Newsweek,* April 30, 1979.

Corry, John. "Research into Sexual Physiology Disclosed After 11-Year Inquiry." *New York Times,* April 18, 1966.

Curry, Jerome P. "The Life of a Sex Researcher." *New York Post,* May 2, 1970.

Dames, Joan. "Masters and Johnson Launch $5 Million Endowment Campaign." *St. Louis Post-Dispatch,* October 7, 1984.

Dickinson, Robert L. "Tampons as Menstrual Guards." *Journal of the American Medical Association,* June 16, 1945.

Fadem, Susan Sherman. "Masters and Johnson: Institute Celebrates 25 Years of Research." *St. Louis Globe-Democrat,* August 3, 1984.

Farber, Leslie H. "I'm Sorry, Dear." *Commentary,* November 1964.

Farber, Stephen. "Masters and Johnson TV Film is Set." *New York Times,* February 6, 1985.

Friedman, Steve. "Everything You Always Wanted to Know About Masters & Johnson." *St. Louis Magazine,* June 1988.

Fumento, Michael. "The AIDS Cookbook." *New Republic,* April 4, 1988.

Garcia, Guy D. "Sexology on the Defensive." *Time,* June 13, 1983.

Gerhard, Jane. "Revisiting 'The Myth of the Vaginal Orgasm': The Female Orgasm in American Sexual Thought and Second Wave Feminism." *Feminist Studies* 26, no. 2 (Summer 2000), Women and Health.

Gorney, Cynthia. "Designing Women: Scientists and Capitalists Dream of Finding a Drug that Could Boost Female Sexuality. There's One Little Problem . . ." *Washington Post,* June 30, 2002.

Grody, Marvin H., MD, and Donald W. Robinson, MD, and William H. Masters, MD. "The Cervical Cap—An Adjunct in the Treatment of Male Infertility." *Journal of the American Medical Association,* May 31, 1952.

Guttmacher, Alan F. "Human Sexual Inadequacy for the Non-Layman." *New York Times Book Review,* July 12, 1970.

Hayman, Suzie. "William Masters." *Manchester Guardian,* February 21, 2001.

Henderson, Harry. "Exploring the Human Sexual Response." *Sexual Medicine Today,* April 1981.

Kerr, Robert. "Sex Therapist Does Battle with Myths." *Commercial Appeal* (Memphis), February 25, 1993.

Koch, Joanne, and Lew Koch. "A Consumer's Guide to Therapy for Couples." *Psychology Today,* March 1976.

Kolodny, Robert C. "Evaluating Sex Therapy." *Journal of Sex Research,* November 1981.

———. "In Memory of William H. Masters." *Journal of Sex Research,* August 1, 2001.

Kuda, Joan. "Gerdine Hosts Dinner Honoring Sex Therapist." *Webster University Journal,* November 1984.

Levins, Harry. "Sex and the Single Expert: Virginia Johnson of 'Masters And' Will Be Working Solo on Her Next Book." *St. Louis Post-Dispatch,* May 18, 1994.

MacPherson, Myra. "Masters and Johnson at Home." *Washington Post,* July 22, 1973.

Masters, William H., and Virginia E. Johnson, "How Our Sex Research Program Began." *Redbook,* October 1974.

———. "Intravaginal Contraceptive Study: Phase I. Anatomy." *Western Journal of Surgery, Obstetrics and Gynecology,* July–August 1962.

———. "A Team Approach to the Rapid Diagnosis and Treatment of Sexual Incompatibility." *Pacific Medicine and Surgery* (formerly *Western Journal of Surgery, Obstetrics and Gynecology*), November–December 1964.

Nathan, Debbie. "The Battles Over Sex Education in the United States: A New View of Women's Sexual Problems—Book Review." *The Nation,* November 18, 2002.

Nemy, Enid. "Masters and Johnson; Divorced, Yes, But Not Split." *New York Times*, March 24, 1994.

Newmark, Judy J. "Conversation with Masters and Johnson." *St. Louis Post-Dispatch*, September 16, 1984.

Ostrow, Ronald J. "Meese Panel Asks Porn Crackdown." *Los Angeles Times*, July 10, 1986.

Rosenfeld, Albert. "Inside the Sex Lab." *Science Digest*, November–December 1980.

Sanders, Marion K. "The Sex Crusaders from Missouri." *Harper's*, May 1968.

Sciolino, Elaine. "Sex Talk." *Newsweek*, March 17, 1975.

Seligman, Jean. "The Storm over Masters and Johnson." *Newsweek*, March 21, 1988.

Semans, J. H. "Premature Ejaculation: A New Approach." *Southern Medical Journal* 49, April 1956.

Severo, Richard. "William H. Masters, a Pioneer in Studying and Demystifying Sex, Dies at 85." *New York Times*, February 19, 2001.

Sheehy, Gail. "Men Grieve More When Spouse Dies." *Dallas Morning News*, July 3, 1996.

Sherrill, Martha. "What's Love Got to Do With It?: From Masters & Johnson, Another Passionless Look at Sex." *Washington Post*, March 29, 1994.

Smith, Lee. "Adventures in the Sex and Hunger Trade." *Fortune*, August 9, 1982.

Stengel, Richard. "Sex Busters." *Time*, July 21, 1986.

Timnick, Lois. "Sex Researchers' Book Stresses Commitment." *St. Louis Globe-Democrat*, January 17, 1975.

Ubell, Earl. "Science." *New York Herald Tribune*, November 21, 1965.

Vogl, A. J. "Are Masters and Johnson Really Infallible?" *Hospital Physician*, November 1970.

Weber, Melva. "New Cures for Sex Problems." *Ladies' Home Journal*, July 1970.

Wilkes, Paul. "Sex and the Married Couple." *The Atlantic*, December 1970.

Zilbergeld, Bernie, and Michael Evans. "The Inadequacy of Masters and Johnson." *Psychology Today*, August 1980.

BOOKS

Chaucer, Geoffrey. *The Canterbury Tales*. Boston: Houghton Mifflin, 2000.

Clarke, Adele. *Disciplining Reproduction: Modernity, American Life Sciences and the Problem of Sex*. Berkeley: University of California Press, 1998.

Corbett, Katharine T. *In Her Place—A Guide to St. Louis Women's History*. St. Louis: Missouri Historical Society Press, 1999.

Corner, George W. *Anatomist at Large: An Autobiography and Selected Essays*. New York: Basic Books, 1958.

Darby, Robert. *A Surgical Temptation: The Demonization of the Foreskin and the Rise of Circumcision in Britain.* Chicago: University of Chicago Press, 2005.

Darwin, Charles. *The Descent of Man and Selection in Relation to Sex.* Princeton, NJ: Princeton University Press, 1981.

D'Emilio, John, and Estelle B. Freedman. *Intimate Matters: A History of Sexuality in America.* New York: Harper and Row, 1988.

Ehrenreich, Barbara, Elizabeth Hess, and Gloria Jacobs. *Re-Making Love: The Feminization of Sex.* New York: Doubleday, 1986.

Ellis, Havelock. *Studies in the Psychology of Sex—Vol. VI.* Philadelphia: F. A. Davis Company, 1913.

Escoffier, Jeffrey. *Sexual Revolution.* New York: Thunder's Mouth Press, 2003.

Fessenden, Tracy, Nicholas F. Radel, and Magdalena J. Zaborowska, eds. *The Puritan Origins of American Sex: Religion, Sexuality, and National Identity in American Literature.* New York: Routledge, 2000.

Flaubert, Gustave. *Madame Bovary.* New York: W. W. Norton, 2005.

Foster, Lawrence. *Religion and Sexuality: The Shakers, the Mormons, and the Oneida Community.* New York: Oxford University Press, 1981.

Francoeur, Robert T., ed. *Sexuality in America: Understanding Our Sexual Values and Behavior.* New York: Continuum Publishing, 1999.

Freud, Sigmund. *An Outline of Psycho-Analysis.* New York: W. W. Norton & Co., 1949.

Friedan, Betty. *The Feminine Mystique.* New York: W. W. Norton, 1963.

Goodman, Ellen. *At Large.* New York: Summit Books, 1981.

Greer, Germaine. *The Female Eunuch.* New York: McGraw-Hill, 1970.

Hollander, Xaviera. *The Happy Hooker: My Own Story.* New York: Dell, 1972.

Irvine, Janice M. *Disorders of Desire: Sexuality and Gender in Modern American Sexology.* Philadelphia: Temple University Press, 2005.

Isaacson, Walter, ed. *A Benjamin Franklin Reader.* New York: Simon & Schuster, 2003.

Kaplan, Helen Singer. *The New Sex Therapy: Active Treatment of Sexual Dysfunctions.* New York: Brunner-Routledge, 1974.

Lawrence, D. H. *The Complete Poems of D. H. Lawrence.* New York: Penguin Books USA, 1993.

Levering, Matthew, ed. *On Marriage and Family: Classic and Contemporary Texts.* Rowman & Littlefield, 2005.

Maienschein, Jane, Marie Glitz, and Garland E. Allen, eds. *Centennial History of the Carnegie Institution of Washington, Volume V—The Department of Embryology.* Cambridge: Cambridge University Press, 2004.

Mailer, Norman. *The Prisoner of Sex.* Boston: Little, Brown and Co., 1971.

Masters, William H., and Virginia E. Johnson. *Human Sexual Response.* Boston: Little, Brown and Co., 1966.

———. *Human Sexual Inadequacy.* Boston: Little, Brown and Co., 1970.

———. *The Pleasure Bond.* Boston: Little, Brown and Co., 1976.

Masters, William H., Virginia E. Johnson, and Robert C. Kolodny. *CRISIS: Heterosexual Behavior in the Age of AIDS.* New York: Grove Press, 1988.

———, eds. *Ethical Issues in Sex Therapy and Research.* Boston: Little, Brown, 1977.

Masters, William H., Virginia E. Johnson, and Robert C. Kolodny. *Masters and Johnson on Sex and Human Loving.* Boston: Little, Brown and Co., 1986.

McLaren, Angus. *Impotence: A Cultural History.* Chicago: University of Chicago Press, 2007.

Meyer, Arthur William. *The Rise of Embryology.* Oxford, U.K.: Oxford University Press, 1939.

Roach, Mary. *Bonk: The Curious Coupling of Science and Sex.* New York: W. W. Norton, 2008.

Robinson, Paul. *The Modernization of Sex.* New York: Harper & Row, 1976.

Roosevelt, Theodore. *History as Literature and Other Essays.* New York: Charles Scribner's Sons, 1913.

Talese, Gay. *Thy Neighbor's Wife.* New York: Doubleday, 1980.

Tappert, Theodore G. *Luther: Letters of Spiritual Counsel.* Vancouver, BC: Regent College Publishing, 2003.

White, Edmund. *States of Desire: Travels in Gay America.* New York: Plume, 1991.

About the Author

Thomas Maier is an award-winning author, documentary-maker, and investigative journalist. He is also a producer for the Showtimes series "Master of Sex" based upon this biography. His previous work, *The Kennedys: America's Emerald Kings,* was one of the top annual holiday books chosen by *USA Today* in 2003, and was reissued in 2008 in conjunction with a two-hour documentary by Warner Brothers Home Video based on the book. Maier's biography *Dr. Spock: An American Life* was selected as one of the top ten nonfiction books of 1998 by the *Boston Globe* and as a Notable Book of the Year by the *New York Times*. Excerpts from *Dr. Spock* appeared in *Newsweek,* and it was condensed as a *Reader's Digest* version. Maier also served as a consultant and on-air commentator for a documentary about Spock, jointly produced by the BBC and A&E's *Biography.* His 1994 book, *Newhouse: All the Glitter, Power, and Glory of America's Richest Media Empire and the Secretive Man Behind It,* won the Frank Luther Mott Award as best media book of the year, given by the National Honor Society in Journalism and Mass Communication. As an investigative reporter for *Newsday* since 1984, Maier has won several honors, including the national Society of Professional Journalists' top reporting prize for a series on police misconduct. In 2002, Maier received the first-place prize from the International Consortium of Investigative Journalists for his reporting from El Salvador on immigrant workers. In 2010, Maier won the National Headliners Award for a Newsday documentary/print project investigating the actions of

Brookhaven National Lab with nuclear bomb test victims in the Pacific. At Columbia University Graduate School of Journalism, Maier won the John M. Patterson Prize for television documentaries. He later received the John McCloy Journalism Fellowship to Europe, awarded by Columbia's Journalism School and the American Council on Germany. He has a bachelor's degree in political science from Fordham University and lives on Long Island with his wife, Joyce McGurrin. They have three adult sons, Andrew, Taylor, and Reade.

Index

WITHDRAWN